SOLUTIONS MANUAL

LASER ELECTRONICS

Third Edition

Joseph T. Verdeyen

Department of Electrical and Computer Engineering
University of Illinois at Urbana-Champaign
Urbana, Illinois

Prentice Hall Series in Solid State Physical Electronics
Nick Holonyak, Jr., Series Editor

Prentice Hall
Englewood Cliffs, New Jersey 07632

A Paramount Communications Company
Englewood Cliffs, N.J. 07632

10 9 8 7 6 5 4 3 2

ISBN 0-13-706831-X
Printed in the United States of America

Contents

Chapter 1

1.1

Field quantities are usually specified in terms of peak values, rather than rms ones. Hence, the factor of 2 appears because of the average over an optical cycle.

1.2

The various operations $\nabla, \nabla\cdot$, and $\nabla\times$ become: $\nabla \rightarrow = j\mathbf{k}; \nabla\cdot \rightarrow -j\mathbf{k}\cdot; \nabla\times \rightarrow -j\mathbf{k}\times$ as can be verified by direct expansion.

1.3

$\mathbf{k} \times \mathbf{H} = -\omega\mathbf{D}$; $\mathbf{k}\cdot(\mathbf{k} \times \mathbf{H}) \equiv 0$; (a) $\therefore$ $\mathbf{k} \cdot \mathbf{D} \equiv 0$; (b) $\mathbf{D} = (1/\omega)\mathbf{k} \times \mathbf{H}$;

$\mathbf{B} = (1/\omega)\, \mathbf{k} \times \mathbf{E}$, use $(\mathbf{A} \times \mathbf{B}) \times (\mathbf{C} \times \mathbf{D}) = \mathbf{C}[\mathbf{A}\cdot(\mathbf{B} \times \mathbf{D})] - \mathbf{D}[\mathbf{A}\cdot(\mathbf{B} \times \mathbf{C})]$

$\therefore$ $\mathbf{D} \times \mathbf{B} = -\,(1/\omega^2)\,\{\mathbf{k}(\mathbf{k}\cdot(\mathbf{H} \times \mathbf{E})) - \mathbf{E}(\mathbf{k} \cdot (\mathbf{H} \times \mathbf{k})\}$;

Now $\mathbf{H} \times \mathbf{E} = -\,\mathbf{E} \times \mathbf{H}$ and $\mathbf{H} \times \mathbf{k} = \omega\mathbf{D}$ $\therefore$ $\mathbf{D} \times \mathbf{B} = (1/\omega^2)\, \mathbf{k}[\mathbf{k} \cdot (\mathbf{E} \times \mathbf{H})]$;

$\mathbf{k} \times (\mathbf{k} \times \mathbf{E}) = \omega\mu_0(\mathbf{k} \times \mathbf{H}) = -\omega^2\mu_0\mathbf{D}$;

Now $\mathbf{D}\cdot[\mathbf{k}(\mathbf{k}\cdot\mathbf{E}) - k^2\mathbf{E}] = -\omega^2\mu_0\mathbf{D}\cdot\mathbf{D}$, but $\mathbf{D}\cdot\mathbf{k} = 0$;

$$\therefore \boxed{k^2 = \omega^2\mu_0 \frac{\mathbf{D} \cdot \mathbf{D}}{\mathbf{E} \cdot \mathbf{D}}}$$

1.4

Consider the sampled by the beam shown in the diagram at the right.

The radius is given by:

$$R = \frac{D}{2} + \frac{L\theta}{2}; \quad \frac{\theta}{2} = \frac{2\lambda}{\pi D}; \quad \therefore \; R = \left[\frac{D}{2} + \frac{2L\lambda}{\pi D}\right]$$

Volume of frustrated cone:

$$V = \frac{1}{3}\pi L\left\{\left[\frac{D}{2}\right]^2 + \left[\frac{RD}{2}\right] + R^2\right\}:$$

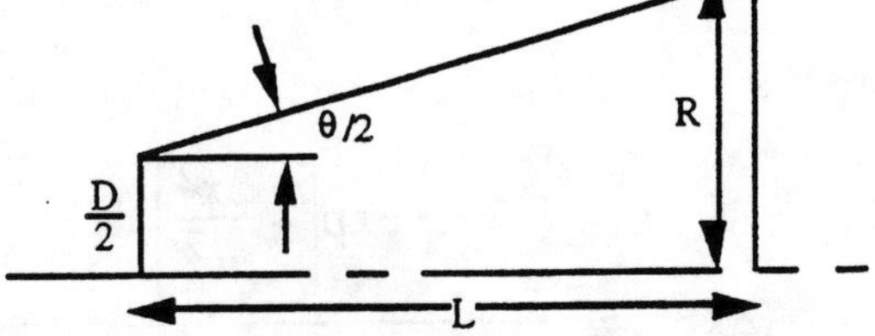

Minimize V(D/L); $\left[\frac{D}{L}\right]^4 = \frac{4}{3}\left[\frac{2\lambda}{\pi L}\right]^2$

or $D^4 = \frac{4}{3}\left[\frac{2L\lambda}{\pi}\right]^2$ $\therefore$ $D = 0.216$ cm;

$\frac{\theta}{2} = \frac{2\lambda}{\pi D} = 1.87\times10^{-4}$ rad; $2R = 0.589$

cm

1.5

	eV	Å	nm	Hz	cm^{-1}
GaAs	1.47	8434	843.4	3.56+14	11,857
Ar^+	2.41	5145	514.5	5.83+14	19,436
He:Ne	1.96	6328	632.8	4.74+14	15,803
CO_2	0.117	$\lambda = 10.6\ \mu m$		2.83+13	943
ISM(rf)	5.6−8	λ = 22.1 meters		13.56+6	4.5−4
KrF	4.98	2490	249	1.2+15	40,161

1.6

Covered in the text, sec. 1.11

1.7

$$E(y) = E_0 \exp[-(y/w_0)^2];\ \therefore\ E(k_y) = E_0 \int_{-\infty}^{-\infty} \exp[-(y/w)^2]\, e^{-jk_y y}\, dy;$$

$$\text{Complete square in exponent: } E(k_y) = w_0 E_0 \exp -(k_y w_0/2)^2 \left\{ \int_{-\infty}^{+\infty} \exp[-u^2]\, du = \sqrt{\pi} \right\}$$

$$E(k_y) = \sqrt{\pi}\, w_0\, E_0 \exp\left[-\left(\frac{k_y w_0}{2}\right)^2\right]$$

1.8

$$(\Delta x)^2 = \frac{\int_{-\infty}^{\infty} \frac{2x^2}{w^2} \exp\left[-\frac{2x^2}{w_0^2}\right] d\left(\frac{2^{1/2}x}{w_0}\right) \cdot \frac{w_0^3}{2^{3/2}}}{\int_{-\infty}^{\infty} \exp\left[\frac{-2x^2}{w_0^2}\right] d\left(\frac{2^{1/2}x}{w_0}\right) \cdot \frac{w_0}{\sqrt{2}}} = \frac{w_0^2}{2} \frac{\int_{-\infty}^{\infty} u^2 \exp[-u^2]\, du}{\int_{-\infty}^{\infty} \exp[-u^2]}$$

$$\text{Now } \int_0^{\infty} x^m \exp[-ax^2 dx] = \frac{\Gamma[(m+1)/2]}{2a^{(m+1)/2}}$$

with $\Gamma(1/2) = \sqrt{\pi}$; $\Gamma(3/2)) = \sqrt{\pi}/2$; $\Gamma(5/2) = 3\sqrt{\pi}/4$; Thus

$$\Delta x^2 = \frac{w_0^2}{2} \cdot \frac{\Gamma(3/2)}{\Gamma(1/2)} = \frac{w_0^2}{4}, \text{or} \qquad \boxed{\Delta x = \frac{w_0}{2}}$$

$$(\Delta k_x)^2 = \frac{\left\{\frac{w_0k_x}{2}\right\}^2 \int_{-\infty}^{\infty} \exp - \left[\frac{w_0^2k_x^2}{2}\right] d\left[\frac{w_0k_x}{\sqrt{2}}\right]\cdot\frac{2^{3/2}}{w_0^3}}{\int_{-\infty}^{\infty}\exp - \left[\frac{w_0^2k_x^2}{2}\right] d\left[\frac{w_0k_x}{\sqrt{2}}\right]\cdot\frac{2^{1/2}}{w_0}} = \frac{2}{w_0^2}\,\frac{\int_{-\infty}^{\infty} u^2\exp[-u^2]\,du}{\int_{-\infty}^{\infty} \exp[-u^2]\,du}$$

The product leads to an equality in the uncertainty relations

$$(\Delta k_x)^2 = \frac{2}{w_0^2}\,\frac{\Gamma(3/2)}{\Gamma(1/2)} = \frac{1}{w_0^2} \qquad \boxed{\Delta k_x \cdot \Delta x \;=\; \frac{1}{2}};$$

The same procedure is used for the $TEM_{1,0}$ field distribution.

(b) For $TEM_{1,0}$ $$(\Delta x)^2 = \frac{w_0^2}{2}\,\frac{\int_{-\infty}^{\infty} u^4\exp[-u^2]\,du}{\int_{-\infty}^{\infty} u^2\exp[-u^2]\,du} = \frac{w_0^2}{2}\,\frac{\Gamma(5/2)}{\Gamma(3/2)} = \frac{3}{2}\,\frac{w_0^2}{2}$$

$$E(k_x) = E_0 \int_{-\infty}^{\infty} \frac{\sqrt{2}x}{w_0}\exp\left\{-\left[\frac{x}{w}\right]^2\right\}\exp[-jk_xx]\,dx; \text{ Let } u = \left[\frac{x}{w_0} + j\,\frac{k_xw_0}{z}\right]$$

and thus $\dfrac{\sqrt{2}x}{w_0} = \sqrt{2}u - j\,\dfrac{k_xw_0}{\sqrt{2}}$

$$E(k_x) = w_0 \exp-\left[\frac{k_xw_0}{2}\right]^2\left\{\int_{-\infty}^{\infty}\sqrt{2}u\exp[-u^2]du - j\,\frac{k_xw_0}{\sqrt{2}}\int_{-\infty}^{\infty}\exp[-u^2]du\right\}$$

$$E(k_x) = \left[\frac{jk_xw_0}{\sqrt{2}}\right]\exp-\left[\frac{k_xw_0}{2}\right]^2\sqrt{\pi}$$

$$(\Delta k_x)^2 = \frac{2}{w_0^2}\,\frac{\int u^4\exp[-u^2]\,du}{\int u^2\exp[-u^2]\,du} = \frac{2}{w_0^2}\,\frac{\Gamma(5/2)}{\Gamma(3/2)}$$

Hence $\boxed{\Delta k_x \cdot \Delta x \cdot = 3/2}$ Part (b)

(c)

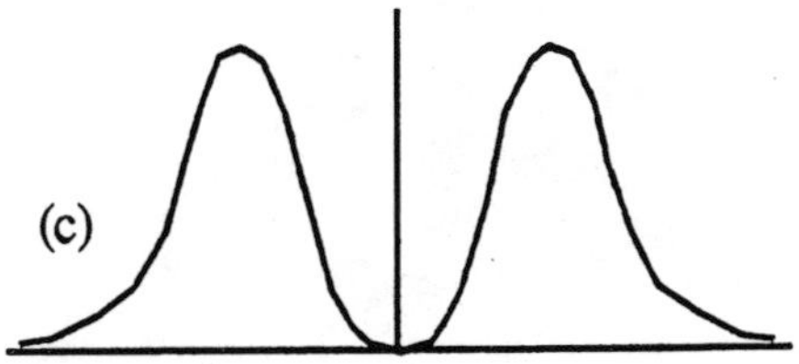

1.9

$E_T = E_0\{e^{-j[kz+\phi]}\} + e^{+j[kz]}\}$; The first term is the incidentwave, second is the reflected.

$$E_T = 2j\,E_0\,e^{+j(\phi/2)}\left\{\frac{\exp\{+j[kz+(\phi/2)]\} - \exp\{-j[kz+(\phi/2)]\}}{2j}\right\};$$

$$\therefore\; E_T \cdot E_T^* = 4E_0^2\sin^2\left[kz + \frac{\phi}{2}\right]$$

1.10

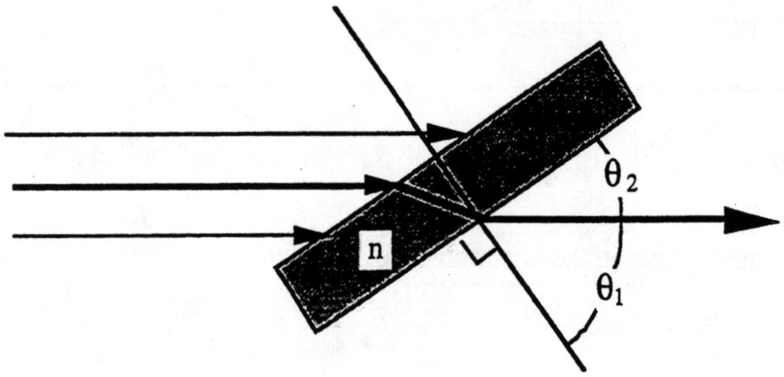

$\tan\theta_1 = n = 1.43$

$\therefore \theta_1 = 55°;\ \theta_2 = 35°$

2.1

Consider the geometry shown below: $r_2 = r_1$ ∴ A = 1 and B = 0 since the planes 1 and 2 are spaced an infinitesimal distance apart. Now use Snell's Law:

$$\frac{\omega}{c} n_1 \sin\phi_1 = \frac{\omega}{c} n_2 \sin\phi_2; \text{ For small angles: } n_1\phi_1 = n_2\phi_2$$

and $r_2' = (\theta + \phi_1) - \phi_2 = \theta + \phi_1\,[1 - (n_1/n_2)]$;

Since $r_1/R = \sin(\theta + \phi_1) \approx \theta + \phi_1$

$$\therefore \phi_1 = r_1/R - r_1'; \text{ Hence, } r_2' = r_1' + [1 - \frac{n_1}{n_2}]\,[r_1/R - r_1'] = \left\{\left[1 - \frac{n_1}{n_2}\right]\frac{1}{R}\right\} r_1 + \frac{n_1}{n_2} r_1';$$

Thus, the ray matrix is as shown on the side of the diagram.

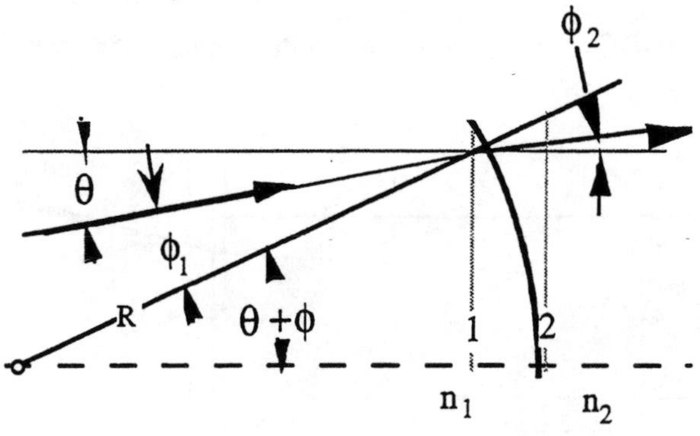

$$\begin{bmatrix} 1 & 0 \\ [1 - n_1/n_2]\frac{1}{R} & \frac{n_2}{n_1} \end{bmatrix}$$

2.2

Consider the geometry shown below:

Since the distance between the two planes → 0, then $r_2 = r_1$ and A = 1,B = 0

Use Snell's law for the interface: $\frac{\omega}{c} n_1 \sin\theta_1 = \frac{\omega}{c} \sin\theta_2$ and now use the small angle approximation:

$\therefore \theta_2 = r_2' = \frac{n_1}{n_2}\theta_1 = \frac{n_1}{n_2} r_1'$ or:

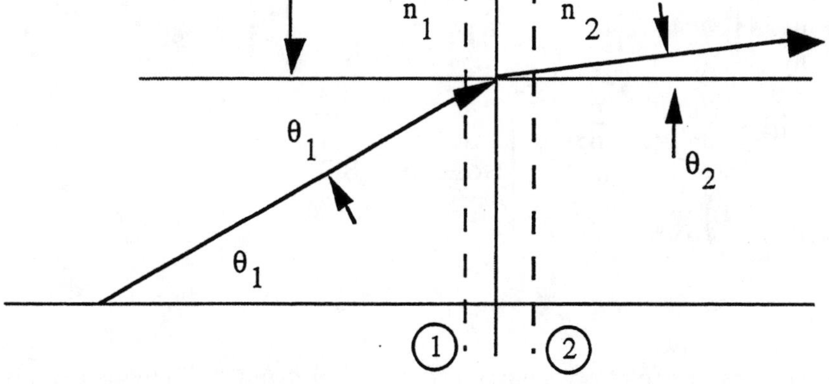

$$T = \begin{bmatrix} 1 & 0 \\ 0 & \frac{n1}{n2} \end{bmatrix}$$

Notice that AD–BC ≠1 because of the different indices of refraction.

2.3

Consider the diagram shown below and apply the results of problem 2.2 to reduce the number of matrices to be derived. The matrix for the last interface comes first with the interchange of n_1 and n_2, followed by the matrix for the length d, and finally by the matrix for the first interface.

$$\begin{bmatrix} r_2 \\ r_2' \end{bmatrix} = \begin{bmatrix} 1 & 0 \\ 0 & \frac{n_2}{n_1} \end{bmatrix} \cdot \begin{bmatrix} 1 & d \\ 0 & 1 \end{bmatrix} \cdot \begin{bmatrix} 1 & 0 \\ 0 & \frac{n_1}{n_2} \end{bmatrix} = \begin{bmatrix} 1 & 0 \\ 0 & \frac{n_2}{n_1} \end{bmatrix} \begin{bmatrix} 1 & \frac{n_1}{n_2} d \\ 0 & \frac{n_1}{n_2} \end{bmatrix} = \begin{bmatrix} 1 & \frac{n_1}{n_2} d \\ 0 & 1 \end{bmatrix}$$

Notice that the determinant, AD –BC=1 even though the optical path does include a different index.

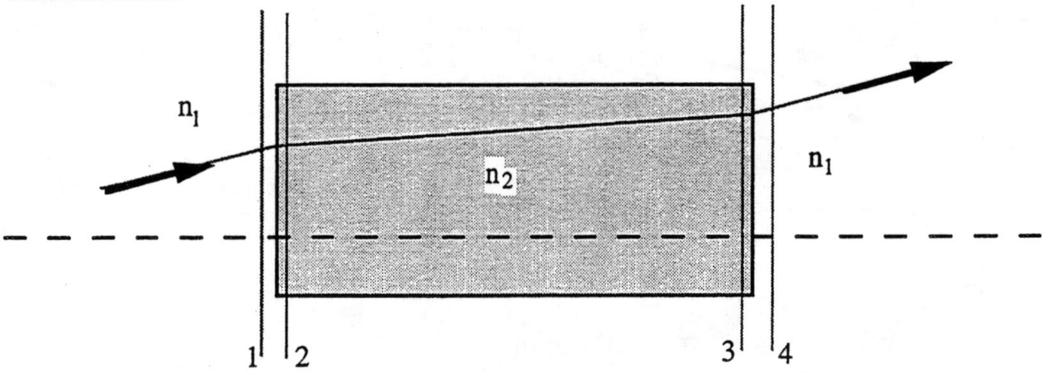

Figure for problem 2.3

2.4

Combine problems 2.1 and 2.3

$$T = \begin{bmatrix} 1 & 0 \\ 0 & \frac{n_2}{n_1} \end{bmatrix} \cdot \begin{bmatrix} 1 & d \\ 0 & 1 \end{bmatrix} \cdot \begin{bmatrix} 1 & 0 \\ \left(1 - \frac{n_1}{n_2}\right)\frac{1}{R} & \frac{n_1}{n_2} \end{bmatrix} = \begin{bmatrix} 1 & d \\ 0 & \frac{n_2}{n_1} \end{bmatrix} \cdot \begin{bmatrix} 1 & 0 \\ \left(1 - \frac{n_1}{n_2}\right)\frac{1}{R} & \frac{n_1}{n_2} \end{bmatrix}$$

$$T = \begin{bmatrix} 1 + \left(1 - \frac{n_1}{n_2}\right)\frac{d}{R} & \frac{n_1}{n_2} d \\ \left(\frac{n_2}{n_1} - 1\right)\frac{1}{R} & 1 \end{bmatrix}$$ Note: AD – BC = 1

2.5

For the purpose of this solution, we will use "t" rather than l ("el") to avoid confusing it with one (1). We include the GRIN-to-air exit interface as the first matrix, then

Eq.2.12.11 for the GRIN lens, and the last matrix represent the air-to-entrance interface where the results of Prob. 2.2 has been used.

$$T = \begin{bmatrix} 1 & 0 \\ 0 & n_0 \end{bmatrix} \cdot \begin{bmatrix} \cos(d/t) & t \sin(d/t) \\ -\frac{1}{t}\sin(d/t) & \cos(d/t) \end{bmatrix} \begin{bmatrix} 1 & 0 \\ 0 & \frac{1}{n_0} \end{bmatrix}$$

$$T = \begin{bmatrix} \cos(d/t) & \frac{t}{n_0}\sin(d/t) \\ -\frac{n_0}{t}\sin(d/t) & \cos(d/t) \end{bmatrix} \Rightarrow \begin{bmatrix} 0 & \frac{t}{n_0} \\ -\frac{n_0}{t} & 0 \end{bmatrix} \text{for } d = \pi t/2$$

Now consider the following simple lens centered between the input and output planes with d=f and use Eq. 2.3.2 to represent the two components so as to minimize the chore of matrix multiplication.

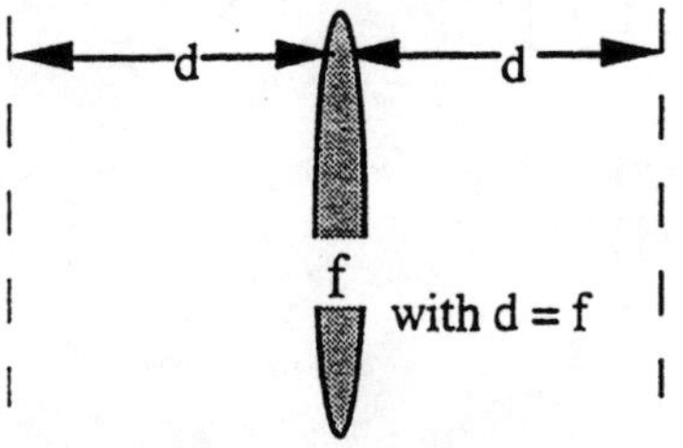

$$T = \begin{vmatrix} 1 & d \\ 0 & 1 \end{vmatrix} \cdot \begin{vmatrix} 1 & d \\ -\frac{1}{f} & \left(1 - \frac{d}{f}\right) \end{vmatrix}_{d=f} = \begin{vmatrix} 0 & f \\ -\frac{1}{f} & 0 \end{vmatrix}$$

Thus the focal length is $f = t/n_0$

2.6

The only way to have difficulties with this problem is to arrange the matrices in wrong order. Let's evaluate Eq. 2.3.2 for the negative lens + distance d combination (i.e. change the sign on f), multiply by the matrix for the postive lens, and evaluate for d=f.

$$T = \begin{bmatrix} 1 & d \\ +\frac{1}{f} & \left(1 + \frac{d}{f}\right) \end{bmatrix} \begin{bmatrix} 1 & 0 \\ -\frac{1}{f} & 1 \end{bmatrix}_{d=f} = \begin{bmatrix} 0 & f \\ -\frac{1}{f} & 2 \end{bmatrix}$$

2.7

The ray matrix for a flat mirror is A=D=1 and B=C=0 which is the limit for that of a curved mirror with R→∞. Hence one could insert three extra matrices in the unit cell and go through the excercise of matrix multiplication to prove the altermative of ignoring the flat mirrors, as being just re-directors of the optic axis, and measuring distances along that line. This viewpoint leads to the following:

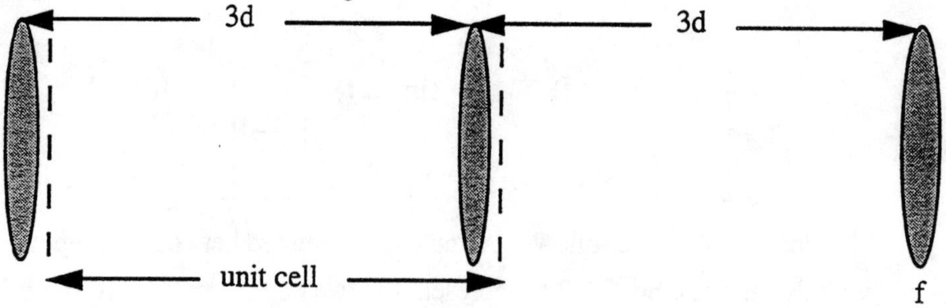

$$T = \begin{bmatrix} 1 & 0 \\ -\frac{1}{f} & 1 \end{bmatrix} \cdot \begin{bmatrix} 1 & 3d \\ 0 & 1 \end{bmatrix} = \begin{bmatrix} 1 & 3d \\ -\frac{1}{f} & \left(1-\frac{3d}{f}\right) \end{bmatrix};$$

$$S = \frac{A+D+2}{4} = 1 - \frac{3d}{4f} \qquad \therefore \boxed{0 \le 1 - \frac{3\,d}{4f} \le 1}$$

2.8

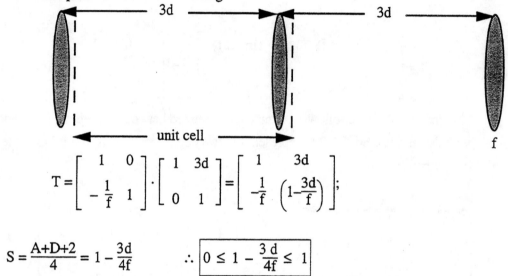

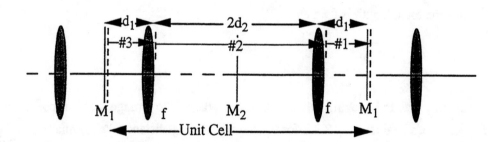

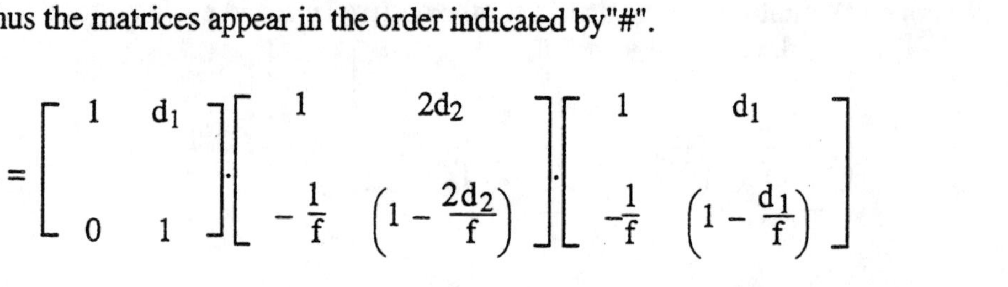

Thus the matrices appear in the order indicated by"#".

$$T. = \begin{bmatrix} 1 & d_1 \\ 0 & 1 \end{bmatrix} \cdot \begin{bmatrix} 1 & 2d_2 \\ -\frac{1}{f} & \left(1-\frac{2d_2}{f}\right) \end{bmatrix} \cdot \begin{bmatrix} 1 & d_1 \\ -\frac{1}{f} & \left(1-\frac{d_1}{f}\right) \end{bmatrix}$$

$$T = \begin{bmatrix} 1 - \frac{2d_1}{f} - \frac{2d_2}{f} + \frac{2d_1d_2}{f^2} & \left(1 - \frac{d_1}{f}\right)\left(2d_1 + 2d_2 - \frac{2d_1d_2}{f}\right) \\ -\frac{2}{f}\left(1 - \frac{d_2}{f}\right) & 1 - \frac{2d_1}{f} - \frac{2d_2}{f} + \frac{2d_1d_2}{f^2} \end{bmatrix}$$

Note: $A = D$ as it should since there is a plane of symmetry (M_2).

Stability: $0 \le 1 - \frac{d_1}{f} - \frac{d_2}{f} + \frac{d_1d_2}{f^2} < 1$ or: $0 \le \left(1 - \frac{d_1}{f}\right)\left(1 - \frac{d_2}{f}\right) \le 1$

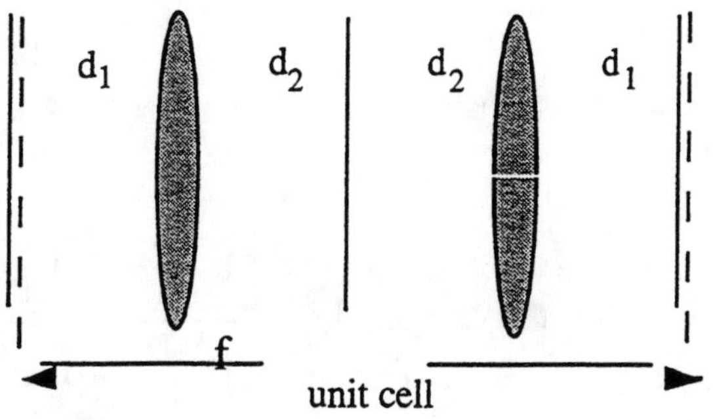

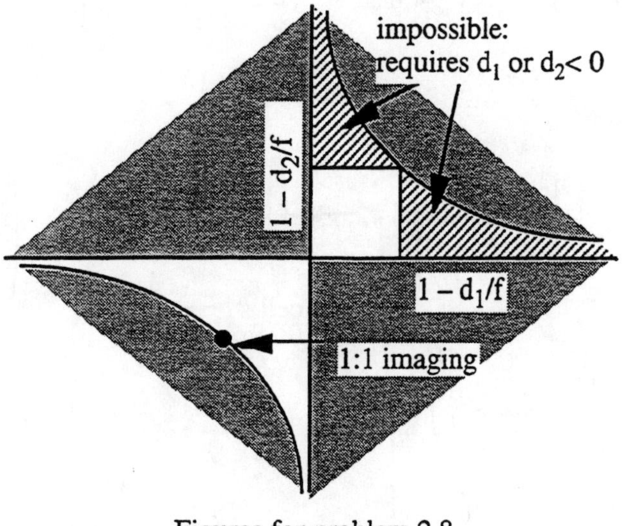

Figures for problem 2.8

2.9

$(d/R) = (1/2)$; $\therefore$ $d = f$; 4–Round trips as the figure below indicates

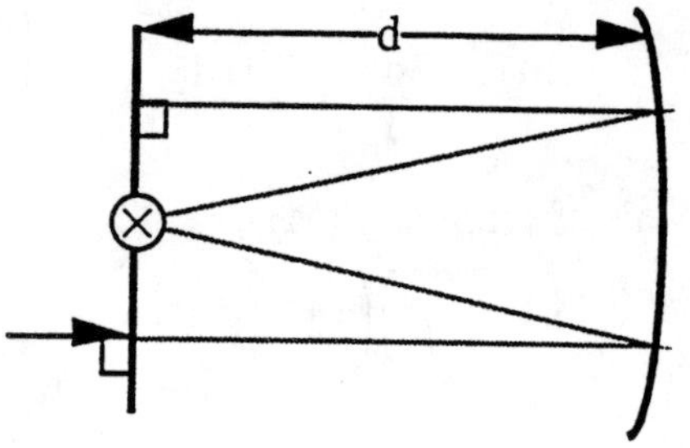

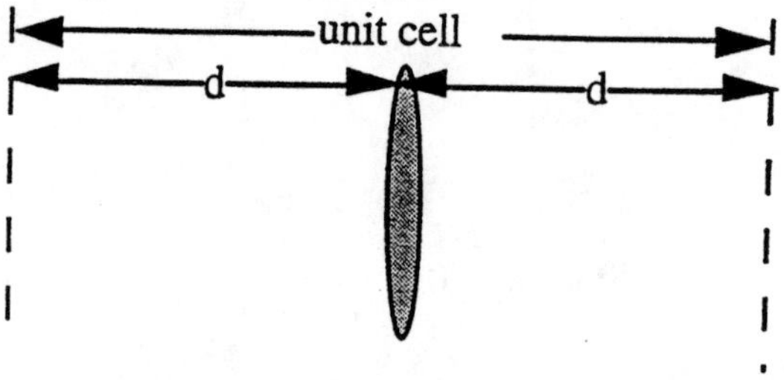

One can do this the hard way using the figure at the right: $T = \begin{bmatrix} 1 & 2d \\ \frac{1}{f} & \left(1 - \frac{2d}{f}\right) \end{bmatrix}$

$$\cos\theta = \frac{A+D}{2} = 0; \ \therefore \theta = \pi/2; \ \alpha = \tan^{-1}\left\{\frac{a\left[1 - \left(\frac{A+D}{2}\right)^2\right]^{1/2}}{a\left(\frac{A-D}{2}\right) + Bm}\right\}$$

For an input slope $m = 0$; $\frac{A+D}{2} = 0$; $\frac{A-D}{2} = \frac{d}{f} = 1$; $\alpha = \tan^{-1}(1) = \pi/4$;

$r_{initial} = r_{max} \sin\alpha = r_{max}/\sqrt{2}$; $r_{max} = -\sqrt{2}\, r_0 \sin\left[s\frac{\pi}{2} + \frac{\pi}{4}\right]$

2.10

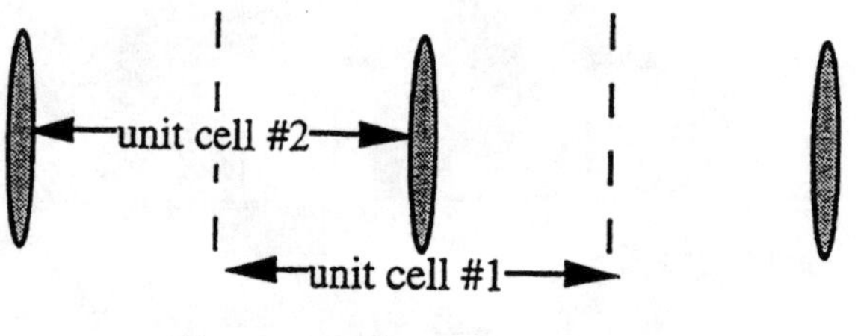

$$T_1 = \begin{bmatrix} 1 - \frac{d}{f} & d\left(2 - \frac{d}{f}\right) \\ -\frac{1}{f} & \left(1 - \frac{d}{f}\right) \end{bmatrix} \qquad T_2 = \begin{bmatrix} 1 - \frac{2d}{f} & 2d \\ -\frac{1}{f} & 1 \end{bmatrix}$$

$$F_{1,2} = \left[\frac{A + D}{2}\right] \pm \left\{\left[\frac{A + D}{2}\right]^2 - 1\right\}^{1/2};$$

$$\left[\frac{A + D}{2}\right] = 1 - \frac{d}{f} \text{ for both cases;}$$

Now $d/R = 1.01$; $d/f = 2.02$ $\therefore$ $\left[\frac{A + D}{2}\right] = -1.02$;

$F_1 = -0.8190$; $F_2 = -1.2210$;

Let $r = r_a(F_1)^s + r_b(F_2)^s$;

Unit Cell #1: $r_b = \dfrac{1}{F_1 - F_2}\{a(F_1 - A)\} = 0.5\times10^{-2}$;

$r_a = \dfrac{1}{F_1 - F_2}\{a(F_2 - A)\} = 0.5\times10^{-2}$;

Thus the position of the ray after s round-trips is:

$r_s = 0.5\times10^{-2}\{(0.819)^s + (-1.221)^s\}$; $r_s > 1$ cm after $s = 15$.

Unit Cell #2: $r_b = 0.5525$; $r_a = -0.4525$;

$r_s = -0.4525\,(0.819)^s + 0.5525(-1.221)^s$

at $s = 6$; $r = 1.694$ cm $\leftarrow$ misses spherical mirror after 12 round-trips plus 1 more pass to the spherical mirror; $\therefore$ $P_{out} = 1\ \mu W \times G^{13} = 1220$ watts!

2.11

The effective focal lengths are:

$f_x = \dfrac{R}{2}\cos\theta = \dfrac{\sqrt{3}}{4}R\ (\theta = 30°)$; $f_y = \dfrac{R}{2\cos\theta} = \dfrac{R}{\sqrt{3}}$;

Stability: $0 < 1 - 4d/3f_{x,y} < 1$;

$d < \dfrac{R}{\sqrt{3}}$ or $\dfrac{4}{3}\dfrac{R}{\sqrt{3}} = 0.577\ R$ or $0.7698\ R$;

$\therefore\ d < 0.577\ R$

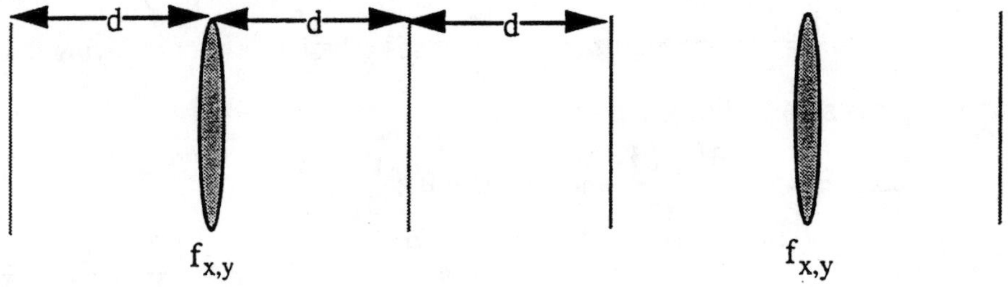

2.12

This is a situation that can and has happened in a gas discharge excited laser with the current heating the gas on the axis to a higher temperature than at the walls which are cooled by convection or by an intentional water jacket. In order for the pressure to be a constant across the radius, there is a greater density of atoms near the wall than on the axis and hence one has a negative gas lens. At first glance, one would guess that this would push the system towards instability away from the borderline situation as specified. Not so!

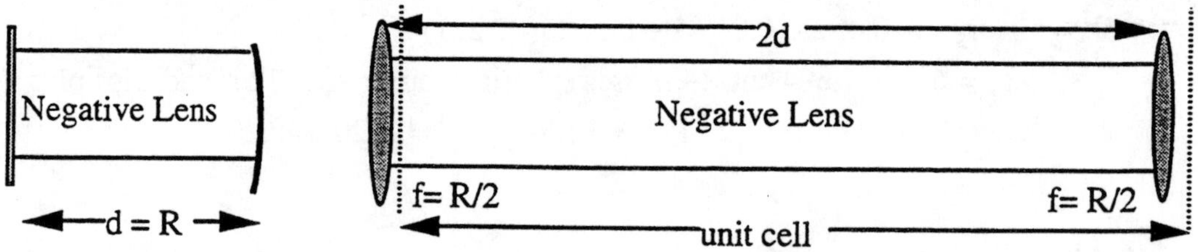

$$T = \begin{bmatrix} 1 & 0 \\ \frac{1}{f} & 1 \end{bmatrix} \begin{bmatrix} \cosh\frac{2d}{L} & L\sinh\frac{2d}{L} \\ \frac{1}{L}\sinh\frac{2d}{L} & \cosh\frac{2d}{L} \end{bmatrix} = \begin{bmatrix} \cosh\frac{2d}{L} & \text{(not needed)} \\ \text{(not needed)} & \cosh\frac{2d}{L} - \frac{L}{f}\sinh\frac{2d}{L} \end{bmatrix}$$

$$\frac{A+D+2}{4} = S = \frac{1}{2}\left\{1 + \cosh\frac{2d}{L} - 2\left(\frac{L}{2d}\right)\sinh\frac{2d}{L}\right\}$$

Let $\frac{2d}{L} = \theta$ and recognize that the lens is a "small" effect implying that L is large and that θ is small. For small θ:

$$\cosh\theta = 1 + \frac{\theta^2}{2} + \frac{\theta^4}{4!} \text{ and } \sinh\theta = \theta + \frac{\theta^3}{3!} + \frac{\theta^5}{5!}$$

$$S = \frac{1}{2}\left\{1 + 1 + \frac{\theta^2}{2!} + \frac{\theta^4}{4!} - \frac{2}{\theta}\left[\theta + \frac{\theta^3}{3!} + \frac{\theta^5}{5}\right]\right\} = \frac{1}{2}\left[\frac{\theta^2}{2} - \frac{\theta^2}{3}\right] = \frac{\theta^2}{12} = \frac{1}{3}\left(\frac{d}{L}\right)^2$$

Stability becomes positive, i.e. the cavity is **more stable** by virtue of the de-focusing element.

2.13

Temperature distribution: $T(r) = T_w + (T_c - T_w)\left[1 - (r/a)^2\right]$;

Density of [He] at 1 Torr,23°C $= \frac{2.69\times10^{+19}}{760} \cdot \frac{273}{296} = 3.26\times10^{+16}\ \text{cm}^{-3}$

Specific refractivity of a Helium atom $= \frac{n-1}{2.69^{+19}\text{cm}^{-3}} = 1.338\times10^{-24}\ \text{cm}^3$

Atoms must be conserved:

$$\therefore \quad N(r) = \frac{N_1}{1 - \left[\frac{T_c - T_w}{T_c}\right]\left(\frac{r}{a}\right)^2}; \text{ and } 2\pi\int N(r)rdr = \pi a^2 N_0 \text{ in all cases}$$

$$\therefore N_1 = \frac{T_c - T_w}{T_c}\,\frac{1}{\ln(T_c/T_w)}\,N_0 = 0.834\,N_0 = 0.834 \times 3.26\times10^{+16} = 2.7\times10^{+16}\ \text{cm}^{-3}$$

For helium: $n(r) - 1 = N_1\left\{1 + \frac{(T_c - T_w)}{T_c}\left(\frac{r}{a}\right)^2\right\}\times1.338\times10^{-24}$

$n(r) = 1 + 1.58\times10^{-8}\left(\frac{r}{a}\right)^2 \triangleq 1 + \frac{r^2}{2L^2}$; $\therefore L^2 = \frac{a^2}{2}\,\frac{1}{1.58\times10^{-8}} = 7.88\times10^{+6}$; $L = 2.81\times10^{+3}$ cm

For CO_2, the specific refractivity $= 1.67\times10^{-23}\text{cm}^3$; $N_1 = 2.7\times10^{+18}\ \text{cm}^{-3}$ (100 Torr)

$n(r) = 1 + 1.96\times10^{-5}\,(r/a)^2 \triangleq 1 + \frac{r^2}{2L^2}$; $L = 79.7$ cm; gas heating is more pronounced.

2.14

$$n(r) = n_0 - \Delta n\left(\frac{r}{a}\right)^2 \triangleq n_0\left[1 - \frac{r^2}{2l_f^2}\right]; \quad \frac{n_0}{2l_f^2}r^2 = \Delta n\frac{r^2}{a^2};$$

$l_f^2 = \frac{n_0}{2\Delta n}a^2$; $l_f = 9.68a = 1.94\times10^{-2}$ cm

$r(z) = r_1 \cos\frac{z}{l_f} + r'l_f \sin\frac{z}{l_f}$; Thus, when $z \sim \pi\, l_f$, the ray crosses axis or $z \sim 6.08\times10^{-2}$ cm.

Thus, in 1 km = 10^5 cm, the ray would cross ~ $1.64\times10^{+6}$ times (more–or–less).

2.15

One always starts and stops at the same point. Hence, $AD - BC \equiv 1$

2.16

Excellent paper and is highly recommended in order to introduce the students to the literature.

2.17

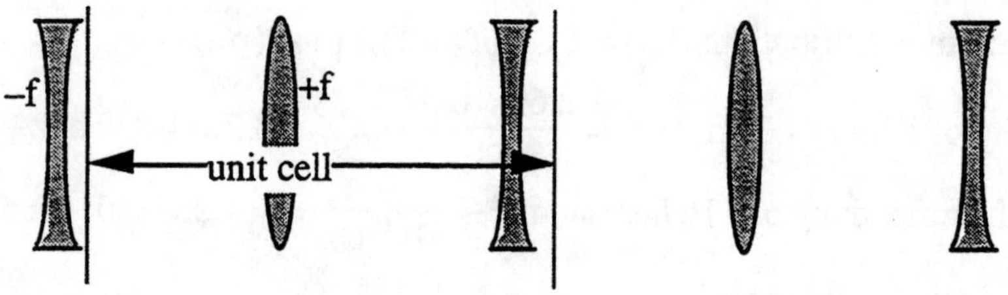

One can use the arithmetic in Sec. 2.4 by substituting $f_1 = -f$, and $f_2 = +f$.

Eq. 2.5.3 becomes: $0 < S = 1 - \left[\frac{d}{|R|}\right]^2 < 1$

2.18

A simple sketch of a general optical system points out that $r_a'(b\rightarrow a) = -\,r_a'(a\rightarrow b)$ and likewise for $r_b'(b\rightarrow a) = -\,r_b'(a\rightarrow b)$. Use that fact and solve for the matrix for the reverse direction to obtain the desired result.

2.19

For a system with a plane of symmetry, one can use the result of problem 2.18.

$$T = T_{12}\,T_{21} = \begin{bmatrix} A_1 & B_1 \\ C_1 & D_1 \end{bmatrix} \cdot \begin{bmatrix} D_1 & B_1 \\ C_1 & A_1 \end{bmatrix} = \begin{bmatrix} A_1D_1+B_1C_1 & 2A_1B_1 \\ 2C_1D_1 & A_1D_1+B_1C_1 \end{bmatrix}$$

2.20

$$T = \begin{bmatrix} 1 & 0 \\ -1/f & 1 \end{bmatrix} \cdot \begin{bmatrix} 1 & \delta d \\ 0 & 1 \end{bmatrix} \cdot \begin{bmatrix} 1 & 0 \\ -1/f & 1 \end{bmatrix} = \begin{bmatrix} 1-\delta d/f & \delta d \\ (-1/f)(1-\delta d/f) - 1/f & 1-\delta d/f \end{bmatrix}$$

Take the limit as $\delta d/f \rightarrow 0$ yields: $T = \begin{bmatrix} 1 & 0 \\ -2/f & 1 \end{bmatrix}$

2.21

Consider the diagram shown below. If we consider a positive r_2 as being measured counter-clockwise with respect to the chief ray as in (a), then A = D = –1 is the choice. If we consider a positive r_2 to be above the incident chief ray as in (b), then A = D = 1 is the choice. Both have selling points. For instance, using the A = D = –1 is most logical for grazing incidence on a mirror because it indicates an output position on the "other side" of the chief ray. Choice (b) is more intuitive for mirrors excited at near normal incidence since the ray stays on the same side of the axis. In any case, stability always involves the product of AD and is not affect by which option is chosen, except to require that the choice be maintained throughout.

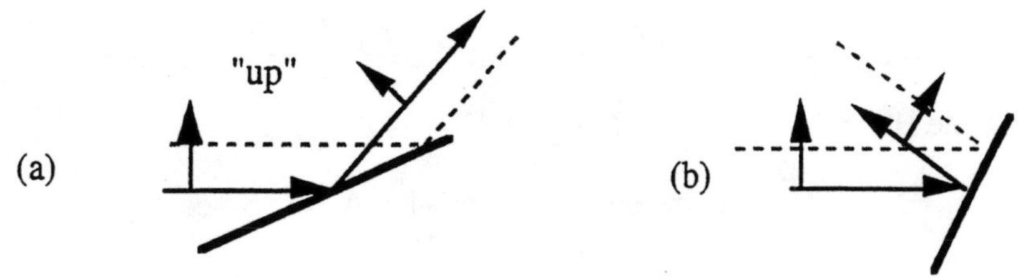

2.22

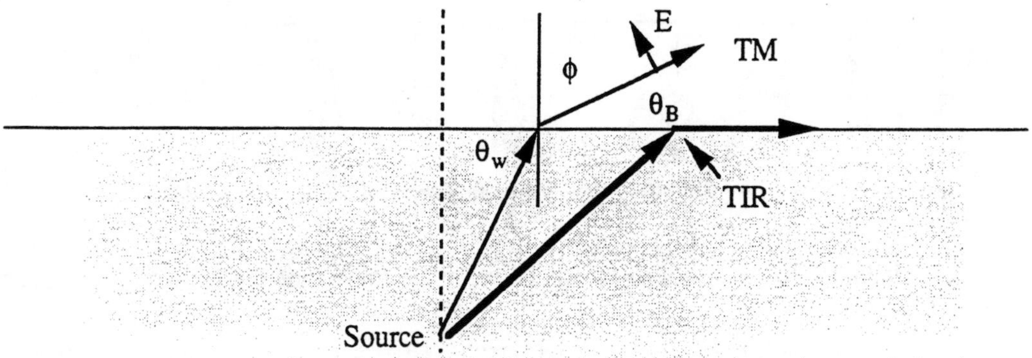

At TIR: $\frac{\omega}{c} n_w \cos\theta = \frac{\omega}{c} (n_a{=}1) \cos(\theta{=}0)$ $\therefore$ $\cos\theta = 1/n$. $\theta = 41.2°$.

(a) $(10/a) = \tan\theta$; $a = (10/\tan\theta) = a = 11.4$ cm. (b) The Fresnel reflectivity depends on polarization but at the Brewster's angle, there is no reflection. Thus the transmission for TM waves is a maximum. (c) $\tan\theta = n$ for Brewster's angle. $\phi = 53.1°$, $\theta_a = 36.9°$.

2.23

$$T_{\text{unit cell}} = \begin{bmatrix} D_a & B_a \\ C_a & A_a \end{bmatrix} \cdot \begin{bmatrix} A_a & B_a \\ C_a & D_a \end{bmatrix} = \begin{bmatrix} A_aD_a{+}B_aC_a & 2B_aD_a \\ 2A_aC_a & A_aD_a{+}B_aC_a \end{bmatrix}$$

$$0 < \frac{A_T+D_T+2}{4} < 1 \quad \Rightarrow \quad 0 < \frac{A_aD_a+B_aC_a+1}{2} < 1$$

$A_aD_a - B_aC_a = 1 \quad \therefore B_aC_a = A_aD_a - 1;$ $\boxed{\text{Stability} \rightarrow 0 < A_aD_a < 1}$

2.24

We use the results of the last problem and abbreviate:

$$T = \left\{ \begin{bmatrix} A_1D_1+B_1C_1 & 2B_1D_1 \\ 2A_1C_1 & A_1D_1+B_1C_1 \end{bmatrix} \triangleq \begin{bmatrix} A_a & B_a \\ C_a & D_a \end{bmatrix} \right\}^2 = \begin{bmatrix} A_a^2+B_aC_a & A_aB_a+B_aD_a \\ A_aC_a+D_aC_a & D_a^2+B_aC_a \end{bmatrix}$$

where $A_a = D_a$; Now stability require that: $0 \leq \frac{A_T+D_T+2}{4} < 1$; $0 \leq \frac{A_a^2+D_a^2+2B_aC_a+2}{4} < 1$;

Substitute $BC = AD - 1$; $A_a^2 + D_a^2 + 2(A_aD_a-1) + 2 = (A_a + D_a)^2$

(b) $0 \leq \left[\frac{A_a + D_a}{2}\right]^2 < 1 \Rightarrow 0 < A_a^2 < 1$ or $-1 < A_a < 1$; Since $A_a = D_a$

Now $A_a = A_1D_1+B_1C_1 = 2A_1D_1-1$; $\therefore -1 < 2A_1D_1-1 < 1$; or $0 < 2A_1D_1-1 < 2$;

$$\boxed{0 < A_1D_1 < 1}$$

(c) Unfold the cavity around the mid-plane:

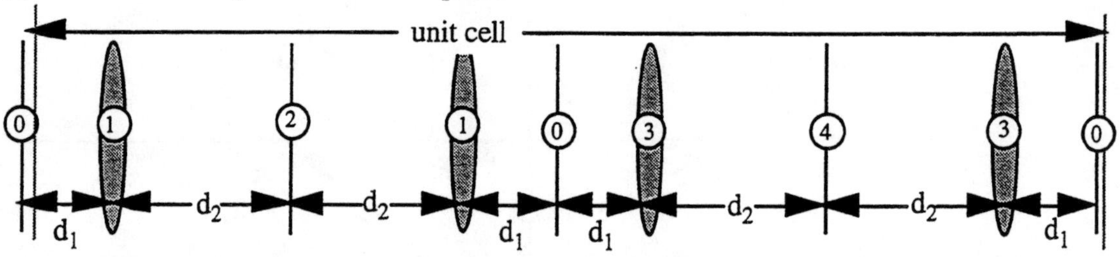

(d) Evaluate the transmission matrix between the mid-plane 0 and 2 and apply the above results:

$$T_1 = \begin{bmatrix} 1 & d_2 \\ 0 & 1 \end{bmatrix} \begin{bmatrix} 1 & 0 \\ -\frac{1}{f} & 1 \end{bmatrix} \begin{bmatrix} 1 & d_1 \\ 0 & 1 \end{bmatrix} = \begin{bmatrix} 1 & d_2 \\ 0 & 1 \end{bmatrix} \begin{bmatrix} 1 & d_1 \\ -\frac{1}{f} & \left(1 - \frac{d_1}{f}\right) \end{bmatrix}$$

$$T_1 = \begin{bmatrix} 1-d_2/f & d_1+d_2(1-d_1/f) \\ -\frac{1}{f} & (1-d_1,f) \end{bmatrix} \quad \text{or} \quad \boxed{0 < \left(1 - \frac{d_1}{f}\right)\left(1 - \frac{d_2}{f}\right) < 1}$$

3.1

Just a review is needed.

3.2

There are only two unknowns about a Gaussian beam: Where is the wave front planar $R = \infty$ and what is the minimum spot size w_0?

(a) Given information; $\theta = \frac{2\lambda_0}{\pi w_0} = 1\times10^{-3}$ rad; $\lambda_0 = 0.6328\ \mu m$

$$\therefore \qquad w_0 = 4.03\times10^{-2}\ \text{cm}$$

(b) $P = \frac{1}{2}\frac{E_0^2}{\eta_0}\left(\frac{\pi w_0^2}{2}\right) = 5\times10^{-3}$ watts; Solving for the electric field yields:

$$E_0 = 38.5\ \text{V/cm}$$

(c) The number of photons emitted per second in the beam is the power divided by the photon energy: $\bar{n} = P/h\nu$; $h\nu = 3.14^{-19}$ joules/photon (or $\frac{h\nu}{e} = 1.96$ eV/photon);

$$\bar{n} = 1.59^{+16}\ \text{photons/sec}$$

(d) There is absolutely no reason to worry about ± 1 more photon out of 10^{16}/s.

3.3

It is worthwhile making a sketch of the spot-size and the radius of curvature as a function of z in the manner shown in Fig. 3.2

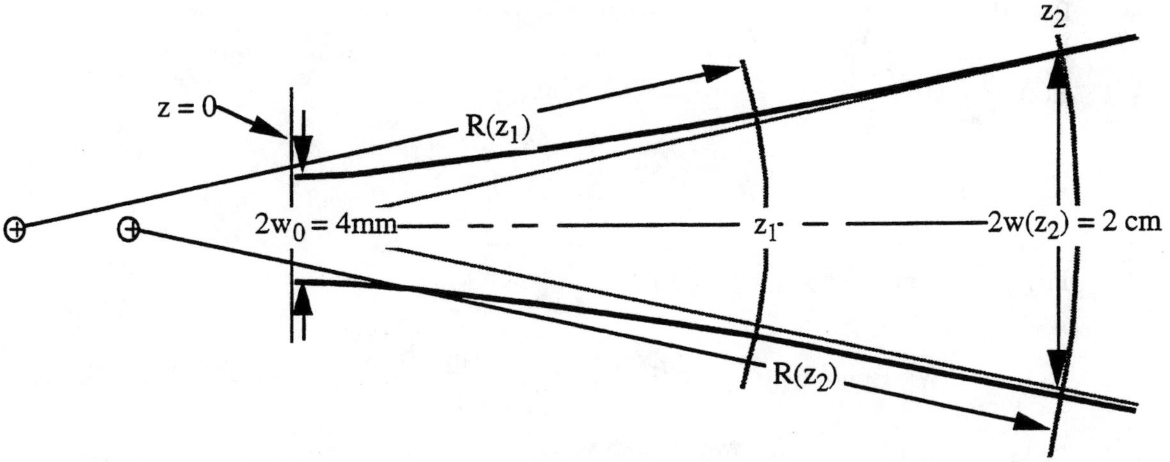

$w_0 = 0.2$ cm @ $z = 0$; $\lambda_0 = 5145\text{Å}$; $z_0 = \frac{\pi w_0^2}{\lambda_0} = 2.44\times10^{+3}$ cm = 24.4 meters

(a) $w^2(z_2) = w_0^2(1 + (z_2/z_0)^2)$ $\therefore \left(\frac{z_2}{z_0}\right)^2 = \frac{w^2}{w_0^2} - 1$; $\therefore z_2 = \sqrt{24}\, z_0 = 119.7$ m.

(b) $R(z_2) = z_2\left\{1 + \left[\frac{z_0}{z_2}\right]^2\right\} = 124.7$ m. This is almost z_2, implying that the center of curvature is just 5 cm to the left of the plane z = 0.

(c) at r = z = 0; $P = \frac{E_0^2}{2\eta_0}\left(\frac{\pi w_0^2}{2}\right)$ ∴ E = 109.5 V/cm.

At r = 0; z = z_2; $E(z_2, r=0) = E(z=0)\cdot\frac{w_0}{w(z_2)} = \frac{1}{5}E(z=0) = 21.9$ V/cm.

Note that the axial field has decreased in response to the beam area getting larger.

3.4

$P_0 = 10$ watt; $\lambda_0 = 4880$Å; $w_0 = 2$mm.

$z_0 = \pi w_0^2/\lambda_0 = 2.57\times10^{+3}$ cm; a)

$w^2 = w_0^2[1 + (z/z_0)^2]$ Thus $z = \sqrt{3}\, z_0 = 4.45^{+3}$ cm for the spot size to double and

$[z/z_0]^2 = [w/w_0]^2 - 1 = 24$ for w = 1 cm.;

$z = 4.9z_0 = 1.26\times10^{+4}$ cm = 126m

$$\text{Fraction of power in } r < a = \frac{\int_0^w \exp[-(2r^2/w^2)]\, rdr}{\int_0^\infty \exp[-(2r^2/w^2)]\, rdr} = \frac{\int_0^2 e^{-u}\, du}{\int_0^\infty e^{-u}\, du} = \frac{1 - e^{-2}}{1} = 0.865$$ b)

$\lambda_0 = 0.488$ μm; $\bar{\nu} = 20{,}492$ cm^{-1}; ν = 614 THz; hν/e = 2.54 eV

$P = 10 \text{ watts} = \frac{1}{2}\frac{E_0^2}{\eta_0}\left(\frac{\pi w_0^2}{2}\right)$; ∴ E(z=0) = 346 V/cm;

$E(z) = E(z=0)\cdot\left(\frac{w_0}{w(z)}\right) = \frac{1}{5}E(z=0) = 69.3$ V/cm

3.5

$P_{0,0} = 1$ W; $E_{0,0} = E_{00}\, e^{-(r/w)^2}$; $P_{1,0} = \frac{E_{00}^2}{2\eta_0}\left(\frac{\pi w_0^2}{2}\right)$

$P_{1,0} = 0.5$ W; $E_{1,0} = E_{10}\left\{\frac{\sqrt{2}x}{w}\, e^{-(r/w)^2}\right\}$; $P_{1,0} = \frac{E_{10}^2}{2\eta_0}\left(\frac{\pi w_0^2}{2}\right)$ ($\sqrt{2}$ not absorbed into E_{10})

∴ $E_{00}w_0 = 21.9$ volts; $(E_{10}w_0) = 15.5$ volts;

$E_T w_0 = (E_{00}w_0)[1 + (x/w)]\, e^{-(r/w)^2} = 21.9\,[1 + (x/w)]\, e^{-(x/w)^2}$ where we assume both have the same frequency, phase, and polarization, so as to add the fields. The intensity is given by:

$I \propto (E_T w_0)^2 \propto [1 + (x/w)]^2\, e^{-(2x^2/w^2)}$ as shown in (a)

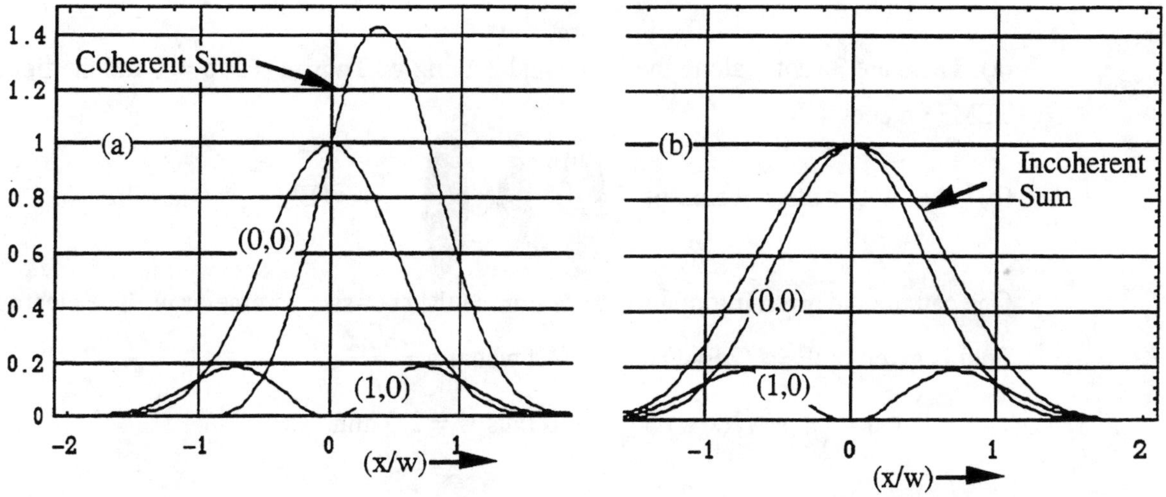

If the frequencies of the two modes were not the same, then one would add the intensities rather than fields. $I \propto (1 + (x/w)^2)\, e^{-(2x^2/w^2)}$ as shown in (b). If the phase between the two modes changed slowly with time, the intensity pattern would slowly "wobble" back and forth between the solution shown in (a) and it image. Coherence makes a significant difference in visual appearance.

3.6

$$E_T = E_0\left\{\hat{\mathbf{a}}_y\left(\frac{\sqrt{2}x}{w}\right)\exp[-r^2/w^2] \pm j\hat{\mathbf{a}}_x\left(\frac{\sqrt{2}y}{w}\right)\exp[-(r/w)^2]\right\};$$

$$I = \frac{E\cdot E^*}{2\eta_0} = \frac{1}{2}\frac{E_0^2}{\eta_0}\left(\frac{2r^2}{w^2}\right)\exp[-2r^2/w^2]$$

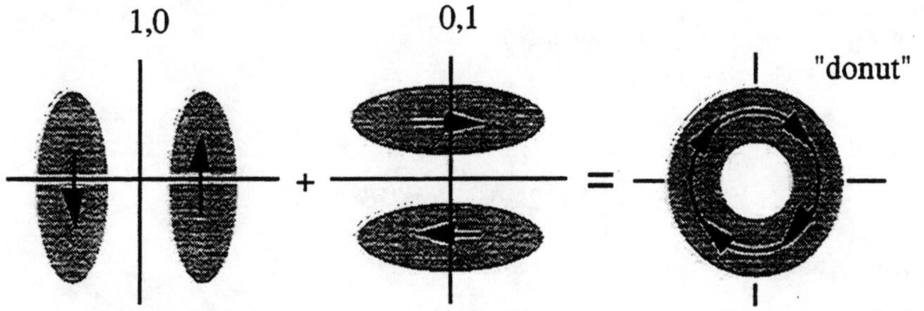

$$\frac{dI}{dr} = 0 = \frac{d}{du}(u^2\exp[-u^2]) = (-2u^3+2u)\exp[-u^2] = 0; \;\therefore\; u = 1 = \frac{2r^2}{w^2};$$

$$\therefore \quad \text{max at } r = \frac{w}{\sqrt{2}}$$

3.7

(a) There are 3 "dots" along the x axis and 2 along y. Thus m = 2, p = 1 and the field is a $TEM_{2,1}$ mode

(b) The "dot" pattern would be 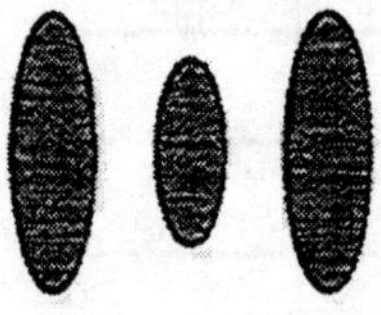 ∴ $TEM_{2,0}$ mode

One can use the given information to determine the spot-size parameter w. The electric field is given by: $E \Rightarrow (2u^2-1)\exp[-u^2/2]$ where $u = \frac{\sqrt{2}x}{w}$;

∴ $E = 0$ at $u = \frac{1}{\sqrt{2}}$ or $\sqrt{2}(x/w) = \frac{1}{\sqrt{2}}$ and thus w = 2.0 mm.

3.8

A first order theory is found by following ones intuition - the transmision is how much gets through the hole divided by the amount incident on it. This leads to:

$$T = \frac{\text{Power transmitted through the hole}}{\text{Total power incident on it}} = \frac{\frac{E_0^2}{2\eta_0}\int_0^{2\pi}\int_0^{a}\left(\frac{w_0}{w}\right)H_m H_p \exp[-2r^2/w^2]\,r\,dr\,d\phi}{\frac{E_0^2}{2\eta_0}\int_0^{2\pi}\int_0^{\infty}\left(\frac{w_0}{w}\right)H_m H_p \exp[-2r^2/w^2]\,r\,dr\,d\phi}$$

Let $x = r\cos\phi$, $y = r\sin\phi$, $u = (\sqrt{2}r/w)\cos\phi$ or $u = (\sqrt{2}r/w)\sin\phi$ in the above.

$$T_{00} = \int_0^{2(a/w)^2} e^{-u}\,du \qquad = 1 - e^{-2(a/w)^2}$$

$$T_{10} = \frac{\int_0^{2(a/w)^2} u\,e^{-u}\,du}{\int_0^{\infty} u\,e^{-u}\,du} \qquad = 1 - \left[1 + 2\left(\frac{a}{w}\right)^2\right]e^{-2(a/w)^2}$$

$$T_{11} = \frac{\int_0^{2\pi}\int_0^{a} 2\left(\frac{r}{w}\right)^2\cos^2\phi\left[2\left(\frac{r}{w}\right)^2\sin^2\phi\; e^{-2(r/w)^2}\,r\,dr\,d\phi\right]}{\int_0^{2\pi}\int_0^{\infty} 2\left(\frac{r}{w}\right)^2\cos^2\phi\left[2\left(\frac{r}{w}\right)^2\sin^2\phi\; e^{-2(r/w)^2}\,r\,dr\,d\phi\right]}$$

$$= 1 - \frac{1}{2}\left[4\left(\frac{a}{w}\right)^4 + 4\left(\frac{a}{w}\right)^2 + 2\right]e^{-2(a/w)^2}$$

These functions are plotted on the graph below. Diffraction effects have been neglected and thus the results have error but the above theory is a reasonable one.

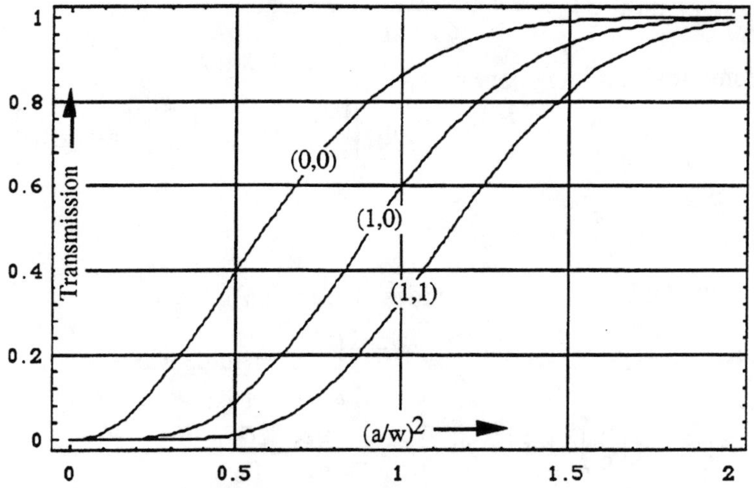

3.9

The Hermite–Gaussian beam modes are the Hermite polynomials times the (weighting function $= e^{-u^2})^{1/2}$ where $u = \sqrt{2}x/w$. For the proof of orthogonality, see Schaum Outline Series "Mathematical Handbook" McGraw–Hill (1968); Chapter 27.

3.10

For $\varepsilon(r) = n^2(r)$, the wave equation becomes:

$$\nabla_t^2 E + \frac{\partial^2 E}{\partial z^2} + k^2[1 - (r/l_f)^2]\, E = 0.$$

(Note that l_f is used rather than l to avoid confusing it with 1)
Assume $E = E_0 \psi\, e^{-jkz}$; neglect$(\partial^2\psi/\partial z^2)$;

$$\nabla_\tau^2 \psi - j2k\frac{\partial \psi}{\partial z} - \left[\frac{kr}{l_f}\right]^2 \psi = 0.$$

Don't assume field varying as: $e^{(-jk)[1-(r/l_f)^2]\, z}$. That would be ridiculous from a physical standpoint since it would mean that the field at r does not "keep up" with that at r=0. Assume $\psi = \exp[-j[P(z)+(kr^2/2q(z)]$ as before to obtain: $P'(z) = -j/q(z)$ and:

(a) $$\frac{q'(z) - 1}{q^2(z)} = +\frac{1}{l_f^2} \text{ which is different.}$$

(b) Integrate this last equation:

$$\tan^{-1}\frac{q(z)}{f} - \tan^{-1}\frac{q_0}{l_f} = \frac{z}{l_f};$$

Use the expansion of $\tan(\theta - \phi)$ to obtain:

$$q(z) = \frac{q_0 \cos(z/l_f) + l_f \sin(z/l_f)}{q_0[-(1/l_f)\sin(z/l_f)] + \cos(z/l_f)}$$

which is identical to ABCD law. Now $q_0 = jz_0$ (for same reasons as given in text.)

$$\therefore \qquad jP(z) = \ln\left\{\frac{q_0 \cos(z/l_f) + 1 \sin(z/l_f)}{q_0}\right\}$$

Separate into real and imaginary parts:

$$jP(z) = \ln\left\{\left[\cos^2(z/l_f) + \left[\frac{l_f}{z_0}\right]^2 \sin^2(z/l_f)\right]^{1/2}\right\} - j\tan^{-1}\left\{\left[\frac{l_f}{z_0}\right]\tan(z/l_f)\right\}$$

3.11

From any standard texts on waveguides (see Jordan)

$H_z = A\cos\frac{\pi x}{a}$, $H_x = \frac{j\beta a}{\pi} A \sin\frac{\pi x}{a}$; $\beta \triangleq \frac{2\pi}{\lambda_g}$; λ_g = guide wavelength;

$$\beta^2 = \frac{\omega^2}{c^2} - \left(\frac{\pi}{a}\right)^2 \approx \left(\frac{\omega}{c}\right)^2 \text{ for } \frac{\omega}{c} >> \frac{\pi}{a}, \therefore \frac{H_{zmax}}{H_{xmax}} = \frac{\pi}{\beta a} = \frac{\pi\lambda a}{2\pi a} = \frac{\lambda a}{2a}$$

3.12

Assume λ_0 = 6943Å (ruby), w_0= 1 cm, mean distance to the moon = 238,857 miles or $3.85\times10^{+5}$ km (according to Webster's dictionary)

(a) $z_0 = \frac{\pi w_0^2}{\lambda_0} = 4.52\times10^{+4}$ cm; thus $z >> z_0$; $w(z) \sim w_0(z/z_0) = 8.51\times10^{+5}$ cm; thus

$I = P/(\pi w^2/2) = 10^7$watts$\div$ $1.14\times10^{+12}$ cm^2 = 8.78 μW/cm^2 (safe!)

(b) If w_0 = 1 meter, $z_0 = 4{,}52\times10^{+8}$ cm; I = 87.8 mW/cm^2 (not safe!)

3.13

See solution to Problem 3.10

3.14

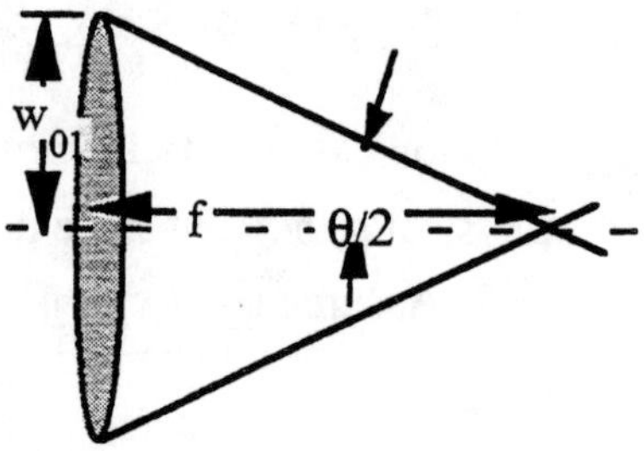

Assume that the beam is focussed to a point with the angle being correct and solve for the focal spot. $\tan\frac{\theta}{2} = \frac{w_{01}}{f} \triangleq \frac{\lambda_0}{\pi w_{02}}$ according to the Gaussian beam formula. Solve for w_{02}

$\therefore w_{02} = \frac{f\lambda}{\pi w_{01}}$ which is identical to that found via ABCD law.

3.15

$$z_m = \frac{f}{1 + [(f/z_{01})]^2}; \quad z_{01} = \frac{\pi w_{01}^2}{\lambda} = 1.257\times10^{+5}\ \text{cm}; \quad \text{or } \frac{f}{z_{01}} = 3.18\times10^{-5}\ \text{(small)};$$

$$\therefore\ z_m = f(1 - 3.18\times10^{-5});\ \tan\frac{\theta}{2} = \frac{w_{01}}{f} = \frac{2}{4};\ \frac{\theta}{2} = 0.464\ \text{rad. or } \theta = 0.927\ \text{radians}$$

3.16

Use l_g rather than l to distinguish it from 1.

$$\nabla^2 E - \frac{\omega^2}{c^2}\{\varepsilon' - j\varepsilon''[1 - (r/l_g)^2]\}E = 0.$$

Ignore $(r/l)^2$ for a moment and assume propagation as $\exp\{(+[(\gamma_0/2) - j\beta]z\}$ as you would for a uniform plane wave.

$$\frac{\partial^2 E}{\partial z^2} + \frac{\omega^2}{c^2}[\varepsilon' - j\varepsilon'']E = 0 \Rightarrow [(\gamma_0/2) - j\beta]^2 = -(\omega/c)^2[\varepsilon' - j\varepsilon''];$$

$$\text{or } (\gamma_0/2)^2 - \beta^2 = -(\omega/c)^2\varepsilon';\ \beta \approx (\omega/c)\sqrt{\varepsilon'})$$

since $(\gamma_0/2) << \beta$ for anything reasonable;

$$-j\gamma_0\beta = +j\,(\omega/c)^2\varepsilon'';\ \text{or} \qquad \gamma_0 = (\omega/c)\cdot(-\varepsilon'')/\sqrt{\varepsilon'});$$

If $\varepsilon'' < 0$, then $\gamma_0 > 0$, i.e. there is amplification.

Now return to the original equation and assume:

$$E = E_0\psi(x,y,z)\exp\{[(\gamma_0/2) - j\beta]z\}.$$

Substituteinto the wave equation, neglect $d^2\psi/dz^2$; assume $(\gamma_0/2)^2 << \beta^2$ and group terms:

$$\left\{\frac{\gamma_0}{2}^2 - \beta^2 + \left[\frac{\omega}{c}\right]^2\varepsilon'\right\}\psi - j\left\{\frac{\omega^2}{c}\varepsilon'' + \gamma_0\beta\right\}\psi$$
$$+\left[\nabla_t^2\psi + (\gamma_0 - j2\beta)\frac{\partial\psi}{\partial z} + j\,\frac{\omega}{c}^2\varepsilon''\frac{r^2}{l}\psi\right] = 0;$$

Set first two braces { } =0, let $\beta = (\omega/c)\sqrt{\varepsilon'} = k$ and $\gamma k = (\omega/c)^2(-\varepsilon'')$. The last [ ] determines the correction. Proceeding in the same manner as for Gaussian beams in free space. Assume:

$$\psi = \exp\left\{-j\left[P(z) + \frac{kr^2}{2q(z)}\right]\right\};$$

Substitute and equate powers of r^0, r^2 as before to obtain:

$$q' = 1 + j\frac{\gamma_0}{kl^2}q^2 \text{ and } P' = \frac{-j}{q(z)};$$

Let $a^2 = j\frac{\gamma_0}{kl^2}$ and integrate: $\frac{1}{a}\int_{q_0}^{q}\frac{aq'}{a^2q^2 + 1} = \int_0^z dz = z$ or:

$$az = \{\tan^{-1}[aq(z)] - \tan^{-1}[aq_0]\} = \{\tan^{-1}\theta - \tan^{-1}\phi\}$$

Use the trig identity:

$$\tan(\theta - \phi) = \tan(az) = \frac{\tan\theta - \tan\phi}{1 + \tan\theta\tan\phi} = \frac{a(q(z) - q_0)}{1 + a^2 q(z) q_0} = \frac{\sin(az)}{\cos(az)}.$$

Solve for q(z): $q(z) = \frac{[\cos(az)]q_0 + [(1/a)\sin(az)]}{[-a\sin(az)]q_0 + [\cos(az)]}$

which has the form of the ABCD law

If $q(z) = q_0$ (a constant), the beam parameter would not change with z.

$\therefore \quad q_0^2 = -\frac{1}{a^2}; \qquad \frac{1}{q_0} = \left[\frac{\gamma}{2kl^2}\right]^{1/2}(1 - j1);$

The last equation implies a beam with a curved phase front, whose parameters do not depend upon z. See also the discussion on gain guiding in chapter 12.

3.17

$\left[\frac{w_3}{w_0}\right]^2 = 1 + \left[\frac{\lambda d_3}{\pi w_0^2}\right] = 1.649; \therefore\ w_3 = 0.0642$ cm; $R = z\left[1 + \left(\frac{z_0}{z}\right)^2\right] = 2.54$ m

$\frac{1}{R_{out}} = \frac{1}{R_{in}} - \frac{1}{f} = \frac{1}{2.54} - 4 = -3.61\ \text{m}^{-1};$

$\therefore \quad R_{out} = -0.277$ m (i.e., converging)

3.18

The equivalent transmission system is shown below:

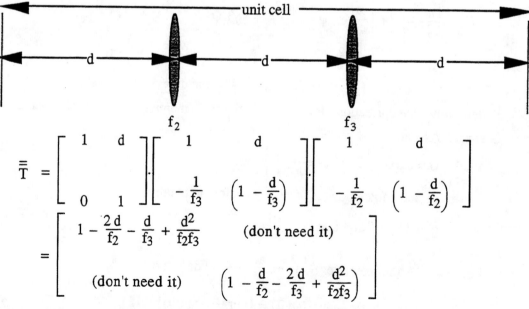

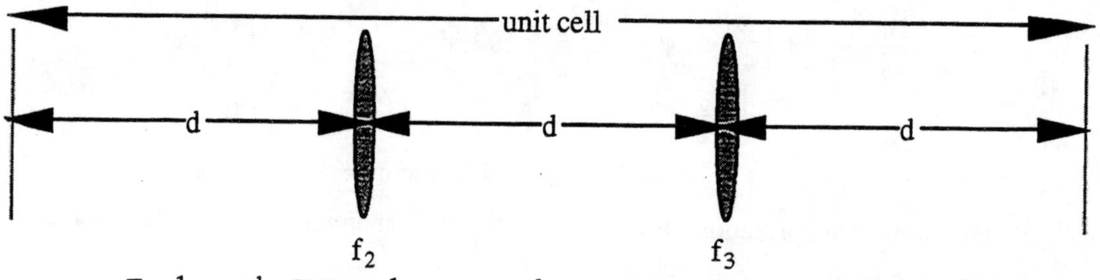

$$\bar{\bar{T}} = \begin{bmatrix} 1 & d \\ 0 & 1 \end{bmatrix} \cdot \begin{bmatrix} 1 & d \\ -\frac{1}{f_3} & \left(1 - \frac{d}{f_3}\right) \end{bmatrix} \cdot \begin{bmatrix} 1 & d \\ -\frac{1}{f_2} & \left(1 - \frac{d}{f_2}\right) \end{bmatrix}$$

$$= \begin{bmatrix} 1 - \frac{2d}{f_2} - \frac{d}{f_3} + \frac{d^2}{f_2 f_3} & \text{(don't need it)} \\ \text{(don't need it)} & \left(1 - \frac{d}{f_2} - \frac{2d}{f_3} + \frac{d^2}{f_2 f_3}\right) \end{bmatrix}$$

For d = 100 cm, $f_2 = 50$ cm and $f_3 = 25$ cm; A = +1, D = −1,

and $S = \frac{A+D+2}{4} = \frac{1}{2};$ $\quad\therefore$ Stable

If the entrance and exit planes have different indices of refraction, $AD - BC \neq 1$. This is impossible for a cavity since the start and stop planes are located at same place.

3.19

$\Gamma^2 = e^{-(tr)^2}$ and the field reflection coefficient is: $\Gamma = e^{-(tr)^2/2}$.

If $E_{inc} = E_0\, e^{-(r^2/w^2)}$, then $E_{ref} = E_0 \exp\left[-\frac{1}{w^2} + \frac{t^2}{2}\right] r^2$.

Now any wave front curvature will remain the same if the mirror surface is planar.

$$\therefore \quad \frac{1}{q_2} = \frac{1}{R_1} - j\frac{\lambda}{\pi}\left(\frac{1}{w_1^2} + \frac{t^2}{2}\right) = \frac{1}{q_1} - j\frac{\lambda}{\pi}\frac{t^2}{2}.$$

Now the ADCD law states that:

$$\frac{1}{q_2} = \frac{Cq_1+D}{Aq_1+B} = \frac{C+D(1/q_1)}{A+B(1/q_1)}.$$

Thus $A = 1$; $B = 0$; $D = 1$; $C = -j\frac{\lambda t^2}{2\pi}$;

Hence the ray matrix becomes:

$$T = \begin{bmatrix} 1 & 0 \\ -j\frac{\lambda t^2}{2\pi} & 1 \end{bmatrix}$$

3.20

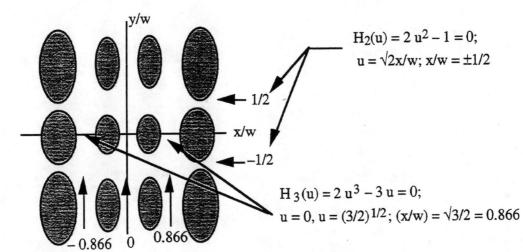

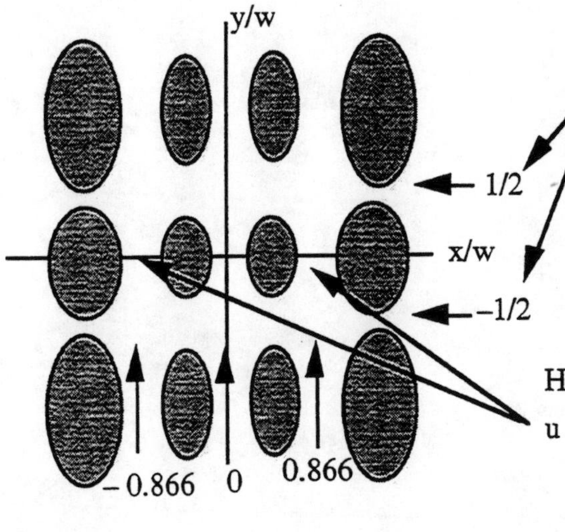

$H_2(u) = 2u^2 - 1 = 0$;
$u = \sqrt{2}x/w$; $x/w = \pm 1/2$

$H_3(u) = 2u^3 - 3u = 0$;
$u = 0$, $u = (3/2)^{1/2}$; $(x/w) = \sqrt{3}/2 = 0.866$

3.21

At the first minimum, $z_0 = \pi w_0^2/\lambda$; thus at z = d, $R_1(d) = [d^2 + z_0^2]/d$ by Eq. 3.3.11;
Use the ABCD law for the thin lens: $\frac{1}{R_2} = \frac{1}{R_1} - \frac{1}{f}$; thus $R_1 = f$ so that $R_2 = \infty$;
$d^2 + z_0^2 = df$; $z_0^2 = d^2 - df$; $\pi w_0^2/\lambda = [d^2 - df]^{1/2}$

Chapter 4

4.1

$$n(r) = n_0 - \Delta n\left(\frac{r}{a}\right)^2;\ a = 20\times10^{-4}\ \text{cm};\ n_0 = 1.5;\ \Delta n = 8\times10^{-3} = n_0\left[1 - \frac{1}{2}\left(\frac{r}{l}\right)^2\right]$$

$$\therefore\ l^2 = \frac{n_0 a^2}{2\Delta n}\ \text{or}\ l = 93.6\times10^{-4}\ \text{cm};\ \phi_{m,p} = k\left[1 - \frac{2}{kl}(1+m+p)\right]^{1/2} z;\ z = 10^5\ \text{cm};$$

$k = 2\pi n_0/\lambda_0 = 7.46\times10^{+4}\ \text{cm}^{-1}$; $2/kl = 2.86\times10^{-3}$ (dimensionless) and $2(m+p)/kl =$ 0.115, hence a Taylor series approximation is valid. To a good approximation, then $\phi_{m,p} - \phi_{0,0} = (kz)\,(1/kl)\,(m + p) = (z/l)\,(m+p) = 1.07\times10^{+7}$ radians. Thus any small perturbation can cause major deviations in the phase of one mode with respect to another.

4.2

$$n(r) = n_0\left[1 - \frac{r^2}{2l_f^2}\right] = n_0 - \Delta n(r{=}a);\ l_f^2 = \frac{n_0}{\Delta n}\,\frac{a^2}{2};\ l_f = 225.1\ \mu\text{m};$$

$$w^2 = \frac{\lambda_0 l_f}{n\pi} = 6.199\times10^{-7}\ \text{cm}^2;\ w = 7.87\ \mu\text{m};$$

$\beta_{0,0}/k = [1 - (2/kl_f)]^{1/2} = 0.999388$; $\beta_{1,0}/k = [1 - (4/kl)]^{1/2} = 0.998776$;
$(\beta_{0,0} - \beta_{1,0}) = 44.46\ \text{cm}^{-1}$; $(\beta_{0,0} - \beta_{1,0}) = z_1 = \pi$; $\therefore\ z_1 = 0.706$ mm;
At $z = 0$, the intensity is skewed to the right where the fields add; at $z = z_1$ the field is skewed to the left.

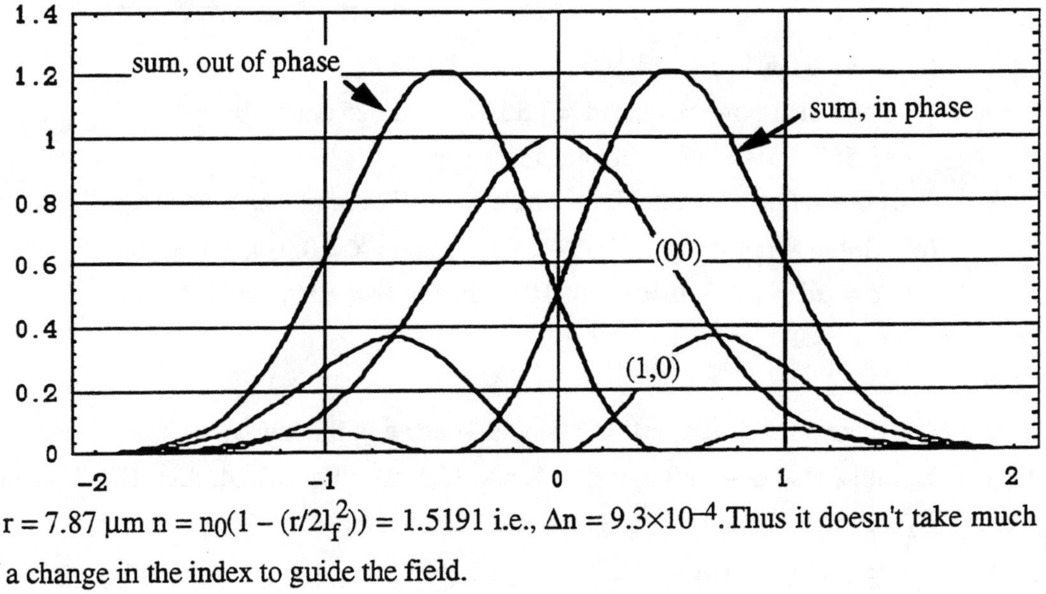

at $r = 7.87\ \mu\text{m}$ $n = n_0(1 - (r/2l_f^2)) = 1.5191$ i.e., $\Delta n = 9.3\times10^{-4}$. Thus it doesn't take much of a change in the index to guide the field.

4.3

$$E = E_0 \frac{w_0}{w}\left(\frac{\sqrt{2}x}{w}\right)\exp\left[-\left(\frac{x^2+y^2}{w^2}\right)\right]; \; y = 0 \text{ is a max;}$$

$$\frac{dE}{dx} = E_0 \frac{\sqrt{2}w_0}{w}\left[\frac{x}{w}\cdot\frac{2x}{w^2} + \frac{1}{w}\right]\exp\left[-\frac{r^2}{w^2}\right] = 0; \therefore 2\left(\frac{x}{w}\right)^2 = 1 \text{ or } \frac{x}{w} = \frac{1}{\sqrt{2}}$$

4.4

ψ was assumed to vary as $\exp[-j\,(kr^2/2q)]$. If $(1/q)$ had a positive imaginary part, then $E \propto \exp\left[\frac{+kr^2}{2}\left(\text{Im}\,\frac{1}{q}\right)\right]$ and E would grow without limit along r. That is not a beam.

4.5

$NA = \sqrt{n_1^2 - n_2^2} = 0.2983$

Only angles $\theta \leq \sin^{-1}(\text{N.A.})$ are captured;

$\theta \leq 17.35°$

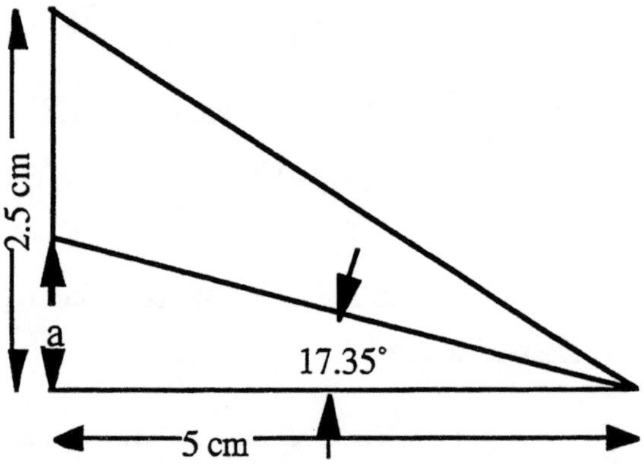

(a) $a = 5.0 \tan 17.35° = 1.563$ cm; $2a = 3.12$ cm;

Fractional power captured = 1.563/2.5 = 0.625 (slab fiber);

$(1.563/2.5)^2 = 0.392$ (round fiber)

(b,c) $R\# = (kd)\,NA < \pi/2$ for a single TE or TM mode; $\lambda_0 > 4d{\cdot}NA = 1.193\ \mu m$

(d) Solve $X \tan X = Y$; $X^2 + Y^2 = R$; to obtain $X = 0.934$, $Y = 1.263$;

(e) $Y = \alpha d = 1.263$; $\alpha = 1.263{\times}10^{+4}\ cm^{-1}$; $e^{-\alpha t} = 10^{-6}$; $t = 10.94\ \mu m$

4.6

(a) $\mathbf{E}(x,y,z) \perp$ to $\mathbf{R}(z) = |R(z)|\,(\sin\theta\,\mathbf{a}_t + \cos\theta\,\mathbf{a}_z)$; Since $\mathbf{E}\cdot\mathbf{a}_R = 0$;

$\mathbf{E} = |E|\,\{\cos\theta\,\mathbf{a}_t - \sin\theta\,\mathbf{a}_z\}$; $E_t = \mathbf{E}\cdot\mathbf{a}_t = |E|\cos\theta$ = Eq. 3.3.14; $|E|$ = (Eq.3.3.14)/$\cos\theta$

$E_z = \mathbf{E}\cdot\mathbf{a}_z = |E|\sin\theta$ = (Eq. 3.3.14)$\tan\theta$ where $\tan\theta = x/R(z)$

(b) $|E_z| = \frac{x}{R(z)}\,e^{-x^2/w^2(z)}$ $\frac{d|E_z|}{dx} = 0 = \left[\frac{-2x^2}{w^2R(z)} + \frac{1}{R}\right]|E_z|$; $\therefore\ x^2 = w^2/2$ and

$E_z = (\text{Eq. 3.3.13}) \cdot \frac{w(z)}{2R(z)}$ since $w^2(z) = w_0^2[1 + (z/z_0)^2]$

$|E_z|_{MAX} = (\text{Eq. 3.3.14})\Big|_{x=w/\sqrt{2}} \cdot \left(\frac{w_0}{2z_0}\right)\frac{(z/z_0)}{[1 + (z/z_0)^2]^{1/2}}$

$\therefore \frac{|E_z|}{E_0} = \frac{w_0}{R(z)} e^{-r^2/w^2(z)}$ with $x^2 = w^2/2$ for a max from part b.

The maximum along the z axis comes from the variation in 1/R(z):

$$\frac{1}{R(z)} = \frac{z/z_0}{1 + (z/z_0)^2} = \frac{u}{1+u^2};\ u = z/z_0;\ u^2 = 1 \text{ for a max. } \therefore \boxed{z = z_0 \text{ for a max}}$$

$$R(z_0) = 2z_0 \ \therefore \frac{w_0}{R(z_0)} = \frac{w_0}{2z_0} = \frac{w_0\lambda_0}{2\pi n w_0^2} = \frac{\lambda_0}{2\pi n w_0}$$

$$\therefore \frac{|E_z|}{E_0} = \left[\frac{\lambda_0}{2\pi n w_0}\right] \exp[-(r/w)^2|_{r=w/\sqrt{2}} = 9.65\times10^{-6}$$

4.7

$$\beta = k\left[1 - \frac{2}{kl_g}\right]^{1/2} = \frac{1}{l_g}\theta(1-2/\theta)^{1/2} = \frac{1}{l_g}[\theta^{1/2}(\theta-2)^{1/2}];\ \text{where } \theta = kl_g;$$

$$\beta_1 = \frac{\partial\beta}{\partial\omega} = \frac{\partial\beta}{\partial\theta}\frac{\partial\theta}{\partial\omega}; \qquad \beta_2 = \frac{\partial^2\beta}{\partial\omega^2} = \frac{\partial\beta}{\partial\theta}\frac{\partial^2\theta}{\partial\omega^2} + \frac{\partial\theta}{\partial\omega}\frac{\partial^2\beta}{\partial\theta^2};$$

$$\frac{\partial\theta}{\partial\omega} = \left[\frac{n}{c} + \frac{\omega}{c}\frac{\partial n}{\partial\omega}\right]l_g; \qquad \frac{\partial^2\theta}{\partial\omega^2} = \left[\frac{\omega}{c}\frac{\partial^2 n}{\partial\omega^2} + \frac{2}{c}\frac{\partial n}{\partial\omega}\right]l_g; \qquad (\beta l_g)^2 = \theta(\theta\text{-}2);$$

$$\frac{\partial[\beta l_g]^2}{\partial\omega} = 2\theta = 2(\beta l_g)\frac{\partial\beta l_g}{\partial\omega};\ \therefore \beta_1 l_g = \frac{\theta}{\theta^{1/2}(\theta\text{-}2)^{1/2}} = \frac{\theta^{1/2}}{(\theta\text{-}2)^{1/2}};\ [\beta_1 l_g]^2 = \frac{\theta}{(\theta\text{-}2)};$$

$$\frac{\partial(\beta_1 l_g)^2}{\partial\omega} = 2(\beta_1 l_g)(\beta_2 l_g) = \frac{\theta - 2 - \theta}{(\theta - 2)^2} = -\frac{2}{(\theta - 2)^2};\ \therefore \beta_2 l_g = -\frac{1}{\theta^{1/2}(\theta\text{-}2)^{3/2}};$$

$$\therefore \quad \beta_1 = \frac{\theta^{1/2}}{(\theta\text{-}2)^{1/2}}\left[\frac{n}{c} + \frac{\omega}{c}\frac{\partial n}{\partial\omega}\right]; \qquad \beta_2 = -\frac{1}{\theta^{1/2}(\theta\text{-}2)^{3/2}}\left[\frac{\omega}{c}\frac{\partial^2 n}{\partial\omega^2} + \frac{2}{c}\frac{\partial n}{\partial\omega}\right]$$

4.8

The ray matrix assumes a very simple form when $z = \pi l_g/2$;

$$T = \begin{bmatrix} 0 & l_g/n_0 \\ -\frac{n_0}{l_g} & 0 \end{bmatrix};\ \text{thus the output beam parameter } q_2 = \frac{Aq_1+B}{Cq_1+D} = \frac{B}{Cq_1};$$

$$\frac{1}{q_2} = \frac{Cq_1}{B} = -\left[\frac{n_0}{l_g}\right]^2 \frac{\pi w_{01}^2}{\lambda};\quad \therefore \frac{\pi w_2^2}{\lambda} = \left[\frac{l_g}{n_0}\right]^2 \frac{\lambda}{\pi w_1^2}; \qquad R_2 = \infty$$

4.9

(a) Start with the wave equation: $\nabla^2 E + (\omega n/c)^2 E = 0$ with $n = n_0 + n_2|E|^2$

thus $n^2 = n_0^2 + 2n_0 n_2|E|^2$.

Assume $E = E_0\psi \exp[-j\beta z]$ and follow procedure used for 3.2.6→3.2.7.

$$\nabla_t^2\psi - j2\beta\frac{\partial\psi}{\partial z} + \frac{\partial^2\psi}{\partial z^2} + \left\{\left(\frac{\omega n_0}{c}\right)^2\left[1 + \frac{2n_2}{n_0}E_0^2\,|\psi|^2\right] - \beta^2\right\}\psi = 0 \qquad (1)$$

(b) Neglect $\partial^2\psi/\partial z^2$ in comparison to $2\beta\partial\psi/dz$ per usual; let $\beta^2 = (\omega n_0/c)^2 = k^2$

$$\nabla_t^2\psi - j2k\frac{\partial\psi}{\partial z} + \left[2k^2\frac{n_2}{n_0}E_0^2\,|\psi|^2\right]\psi = 0 \qquad (2)$$

(c) For a one dimensional beam, $\nabla_t^2\psi \to \partial^2\psi/\partial x^2$, and (2) becomes:

$$\frac{\partial^2\psi}{\partial x^2} - j2k\frac{\partial\psi}{\partial z} + [2k^2(n_2/n_0)E_0^2|\psi|^2]\psi = 0;$$

$$\left[\frac{\partial^2\psi}{\partial(x/\omega)}\right] - j2\left[\frac{\partial\psi}{\partial(z/kw^2)}\right] + 2(kw)^2[(n_2E_0^2/n_0]\cdot|\psi|^2\psi = 0.$$

Let $F = E_0kw(n_2/n_0)^{1/2}\psi$ and $u = x/w$; $z' = z/kw^2$, the equation for the 1-D beam becomes:

$$\boxed{\frac{1}{2}\frac{\partial^2F}{\partial u^2} - j\frac{\partial F}{\partial z'} + |F|^2F = 0} \qquad \text{(See Eq. 4.6.6).}$$

If one makes the following identification: $u \leftrightarrow T$; $z' \leftrightarrow z'$ then 4.8.14(c) is the solution.

(d) If we choose a Gaussian as being a representative "beam" and expand $|\psi|^2 = \exp[-2r^2/w^2] \simeq (1 - 2r^2/w^2)$ in the index term, Eq. 1 becomes:

$$\nabla_t^2\psi - j2\beta\frac{\partial\psi}{\partial z} + k^2\{1 + (2n_2E_0^2/n_0)\,[1 - (2r^2/w^2)] - \beta^2\}\,\psi = 0.$$

With $\beta^2 = k^2[1 + (2n_2^2E_0^2/n_0)] \simeq k^2$; $\nabla_t^2\psi - j2k\frac{2\psi}{\partial z} - \left[4\,\frac{k^2}{w^2}\frac{n_2E_0^2}{n_0}r^2\right]\psi = 0 \qquad (3)$

(e) Compare this equation to a GRIN medium with $n^2(r) = n_0^2(1 - r^2/l_G^2)$ where the paraxial wave equation is:

$$\nabla_t^2\psi - j2\beta\frac{\partial\psi}{\partial z} + \{k^2[1 - (r/l_G)^2] - \beta^2\}\psi = 0.$$

If we let $\beta^2 = k^2$, the paraxial wave equation becomes:

$$\nabla_t^2\psi - j2k\frac{\partial\psi}{\partial z} - [(kr/l_G)^2]\psi = 0.$$

After comparison with Eq. 3, we find $(kr/l_G)^2 = \frac{4k^2}{w^2}\frac{n_2E_0^2}{n_0}r^2$;

$\therefore \quad 1/l_G^2 = \frac{4}{w^2}(n_2E_0^2n_0)$ and the transmission ABCD matrix is:

$$\text{(f)}\;\; T = \begin{bmatrix} \cos(d/l_G) & l_g\sin(d/l_G) \\ -(1/l_G)\sin(d/l_G) & \cos(d/l_G) \end{bmatrix} \simeq \begin{bmatrix} 1 - (1/2)(d/l_G)^2 & d \\ -d/l_G^2 & 1 - (1/2)(d/l_G)^2 \end{bmatrix}$$

$\therefore$ The focal length is: $\quad f = \frac{l_G^2}{d} = \frac{n_0w^2}{4n_2E_0^2d} = \frac{n_0w^2}{4n_2'I(0)d'}$

Now $P_T = (\pi w^2/2)I(0)$. The intensity on axis is: $I(0) = 2P_T/\pi w^2$; thus the power induced focal length is:

$$\boxed{f = \frac{\pi}{8}\frac{n_0 w^4}{n_2' P_T d}}$$

(g) Assume $\psi = \exp\left\{-j\left[P(z) + \frac{kr^2}{2q(z)}\right]\right\}$ and use the expansions 3.3.2 → 3.3.3:

$$\nabla_t^2\psi = \left\{\left[-\frac{k^2r^2}{q^2(z)}\right] - j\left[\frac{k}{q(z)}\right]\right\}\psi;$$

$$-j\,2k\frac{\partial\psi}{\partial z} = \left\{-2kP'(z) + \left[k^2 r^2 \frac{q'(z)}{q^2(z)}\right]\right\}\psi;$$

$$[-----]r^2\psi = \left[-\frac{4k^2}{w^2(z)}\right]\left[\frac{n_2E_0^2}{n_0}\right] r^2\,\psi_0.$$

Equating factors of r^0 and r^2:

$$k^2\left\{\frac{(q'(z)-1)}{q^2} - \left[\frac{4}{w^2(z)}\right]\frac{n_2E_0^2}{n_0}\right\} r^2 = 0.$$

If $q'(z) = 0$, the beam parameter does not change with z implying that self focusing is compensating for the natural tendency to spread. This represents the onset of self-focusing with $w^2(z) \neq f(z)$. A solution for $1/q$ follows:

$$-\frac{1}{q^2} = \frac{4n_2E_0^2}{w^2n_0};\ \frac{1}{q} = -j\frac{2}{w}\left[\frac{n_2E^2}{n_0}\right]^{1/2} = -j\frac{\lambda}{\pi n_0 w^2};\ \frac{n_2E^2}{n_0} = \frac{\lambda^2}{4\pi^2 n_0^2 w^2} = \frac{n_2' I(0)}{n_0}.$$

Thus the critical intensity is:

$$I(0) = \frac{\lambda^2}{4\pi^2 n_0 w^2}\frac{1}{n_2'}$$ Watts/m^2 if a Gaussian beam is assumed for the input.

4.10

$NA = [n_2^2 - n_1^2]^{1/2} = 0.242$; $\theta = 14.0°$

4.11

Dispersion ~ 10^3 ps/nm from figure 4.8;

(a) Bandwidth is $\Delta\nu = 2 \times 250 \times 10^9$ Hz = 500 GHz;

In terms of λ: $\frac{\Delta\lambda}{\lambda_0} = \frac{\Delta\nu = 500^{+9}}{\nu = 3^{+10}\text{cm/s} \div 0.8^{-4}\text{ cm}}$; $\Delta\lambda = 1.07$ nm;

$\Delta t = (10^3\text{ps/nm})(1.07)\text{nm} = 1.07$ ns

(b) At $\lambda_0 = 0.8\ \mu$m; $\alpha = 3$dB/km; $T = -33$ dB $= 0.5 \times 10^{-3}$

4.12

(a) Let $\tau = (t - z/v_g)$; $z = z'$ and follow the procedures of 4.7.8 → 4.7.10.

$$\frac{\partial E}{\partial z'} = j\,a\,|E|^2 E = j\,a\,E_0^2 \left\{ \exp{-(\tau/\tau_p)^2} \right\} E$$

(b) Substitute $E = A(\tau)\exp[j\phi(z')]$;

$$j\phi'(z')\,A(\tau)\,\exp[j\phi(z')] = j\,a\,E_0^2 \exp\left[-\frac{\tau}{\tau_p}\right]^2 A(\tau)\exp[j\phi(z')];$$

The factor $A(\tau)$ appears on both sides and cancels and thus does not change with z . The phase does, however. The integration is trivial:

$$\phi(z') = a|E_0|^2\{\exp[-(\tau/\tau_p)^2]\}z' = \phi(\tau,z')$$

(c) Thus, $e(t,z) = E_0\{\text{original envelope}\}\, e^{j[\omega_0 t+\phi(\tau,z)]}$;

$$\omega(t) = \frac{d[\omega_0 t+\phi(\tau,z)]}{dt} = \omega_0 + \frac{\partial\phi(\tau,z')}{\partial\tau} \quad \text{since } \frac{\partial}{\partial t} = \frac{\partial}{\partial\tau};$$

$$\text{"chirp"} = \frac{\partial\phi}{\partial\tau} = -2\,a\,|E_0|^2 \frac{t-(z/v_g)}{\tau_p^2}\left\{\exp-\left[\frac{t-(z/v_g)}{\tau_p}\right]^2\right\} z.$$

Thus, the Gaussian beam attains a frequency "chirp" as it propagates.

5.1(a), (b1)

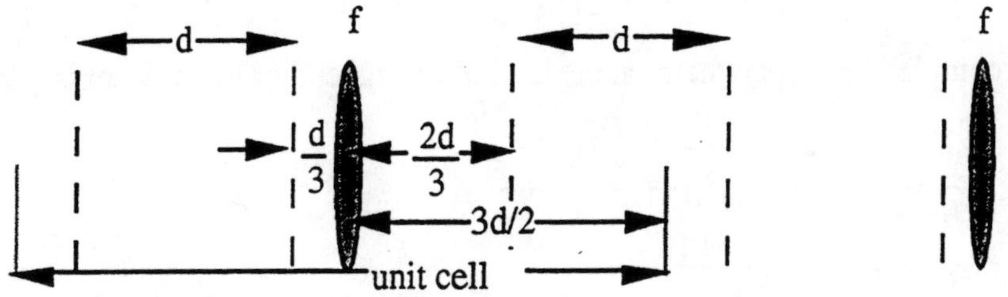

b(2) The unit cell is symmetric and thus z = 0 at (3d/2) from lens.

$$T = \begin{bmatrix} 1 & \frac{3d}{2} \\ 0 & 1 \end{bmatrix} \begin{bmatrix} 1 & 0 \\ -\frac{1}{f} & 1 \end{bmatrix} \begin{bmatrix} 1 & \frac{3d}{2} \\ 0 & 1 \end{bmatrix} = \begin{bmatrix} 1 - \frac{3d}{2f} & \frac{3d}{2}\left(1 - \frac{3d}{2f}\right) \\ -\frac{1}{f} & 1 - \frac{3d}{2f} \end{bmatrix}$$

$$\frac{1}{q} = -\frac{A-D}{2B} - j\frac{1}{B}\left\{1 - \left(\frac{A+D}{2}\right)^2\right\}^{1/2} = 0 - j\frac{\left[1 - A^2\right]^{1/2}}{B}$$ thus $R = \infty$ because $A = D$;

Formula only makes sense i.a.o.i. $\left[\frac{A+D}{2}\right]^2 < 1$ i.e., stable:

$$\frac{\lambda}{\pi w_0^2} = \frac{[1-A^2]^{1/2}}{B} \quad \text{or} \quad \frac{\pi w_0^2}{\lambda} = \frac{B}{\sqrt{1-A^2}} = -\frac{1}{C}\sqrt{1-A^2}$$

Now $BC = -(1-AD) = -(1-A^2)$; $\therefore$ $z_{02} = \frac{\pi w_0^2}{\lambda} = \sqrt{3df}\sqrt{1 - \frac{3d}{4f}}$

5.2

The first step is to construct an equivalent lens waveguide which is shown below with the flat mirrors ignored.

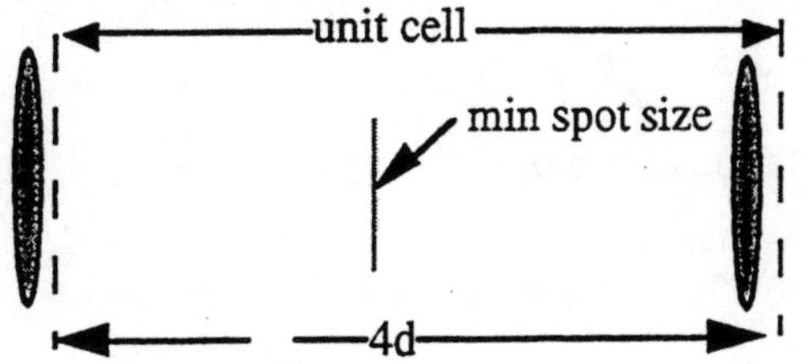

$$T = \begin{bmatrix} 1 & 0 \\ -\frac{1}{f} & 1 \end{bmatrix} \begin{bmatrix} 1 & 4d \\ 0 & 1 \end{bmatrix} = \begin{bmatrix} 1 & 4d \\ -\frac{1}{f} & 1 - \frac{4d}{f} \end{bmatrix}$$

Stability: $0 \le \left\{\frac{A+D+2}{4} = 1 - \frac{d}{f}\right\} < 1$ i.e., $0 < \frac{d}{f} < 1$;

The complex beam parameter at the beginning and end of the unit cel is given by:

$$\frac{1}{q} = -\frac{(A-D)}{2B} - j\frac{\left[1 - \left(\frac{A+D}{2}\right)^2\right]^{1/2}}{B}$$

$$\therefore \quad \frac{1}{R} = -\frac{(1 - 2 + 4d/f)}{8d} = -\frac{1}{2f}; \qquad \therefore \qquad R = -80 \text{ cm}$$

with the negative sign indicating a converging beam.

$$\frac{\pi w^2}{\lambda} = \frac{B}{\left[1 - \left(\frac{A+D}{2}\right)^2\right]^{1/2}} = \frac{4d}{\left\{1 - \left(1 - \frac{2d}{f}\right)^2\right\}^{1/2}} = 4d = 80 \text{ cm}$$

For $d/f = 1/2$; $\therefore$ $\qquad w = 0.391$ mm

5.3

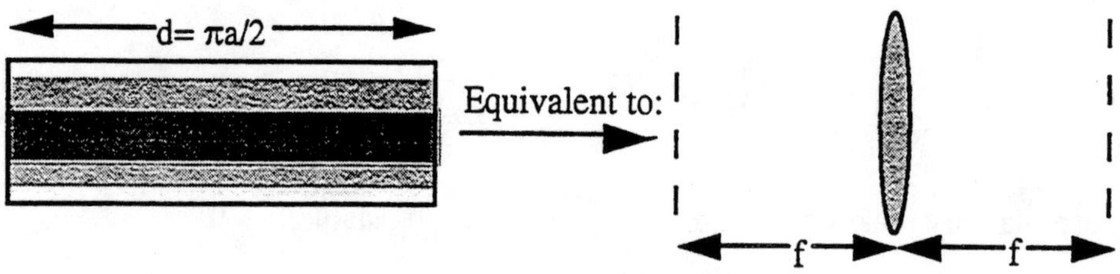

$$T = \begin{bmatrix} 1 & 0 \\ 0 & n_0 \end{bmatrix} \cdot \begin{bmatrix} \cos d/a & a \sin d/a \\ -\frac{1}{a}\sin d/a & \cos d/a \end{bmatrix} \cdot \begin{bmatrix} 1 & 0 \\ 0 & \frac{1}{n_0} \end{bmatrix}$$

$$= \begin{bmatrix} \cos d/a & \frac{a}{n_0}\sin d/a \\ -\frac{n_0}{a}\sin d/a & \cos d/a \end{bmatrix} (\text{for } d = \pi a/2) = \begin{bmatrix} 0 & \frac{a}{n_0} \\ -\frac{n_0}{a} & 0 \end{bmatrix}$$

(b) The matrix for a round-trip is:

$$T_{cavity} = \begin{bmatrix} \cos 2d/a & a \sin 2d/a \\ -\frac{1}{a}\sin 2d/a & \cos 2d/a \end{bmatrix}$$

$$\frac{\pi w^2}{\lambda} = \frac{B}{[1 - (A + B)^2/4]^{1/2}} = \frac{a \sin 2d/a}{[1 - \cos^2 2d/a]^{1/2}} = a$$

5.4

$$z_0^2 = \left[\frac{\pi w_0^2}{\lambda}\right]^2 = \frac{d(R_1 - d)(R_2 - d)(R_1 + R_2 - d)}{(R_1 + R_2 - 2d)^2} = \frac{dR}{2}\left[1 - \frac{d}{2R}\right] = \left[\frac{\pi w_0^2}{\lambda}\right]^2;$$

and z = 0 at mid-plane

$$\frac{\pi w_s^2}{\lambda_0} = \frac{\pi w_0^2}{\lambda_0}\left[1 + \left(\frac{d}{2z_0}\right)^2\right] = z_0\left[\frac{z_0^2 + \left(\frac{d}{2}\right)^2}{z_0^2}\right] = \frac{\frac{dR}{2}\left(1 - \frac{d}{2R}\right) + \left(\frac{d}{2}\right)^2}{\left(\frac{dR}{2}\right)^{1/2}\left(1 - \frac{d}{2R}\right)^{1/2}} = \left[\frac{dR/2}{1 - \frac{d}{2R}}\right]^{1/2}$$

$$V_{0,0} = \left[\frac{\pi w_0^2}{2}\left(\frac{d}{2} \times 2\right)\right] \qquad \text{(see sec. 5.3);}$$

$$V_{0,0} = \lambda R^2 \left(\frac{d}{2R}\right)^{3/2}\left(1 - \frac{d}{2R}\right)^{1/2} = \lambda R^2 x^{3/2}(1-x)^{1/2} \text{ where } x = d/R;$$

$$x = \frac{3}{4} \text{ for a max; i.e., } x = \frac{d}{2R} = \frac{3}{4} \text{ or } \frac{d}{R} = \frac{3}{2}$$

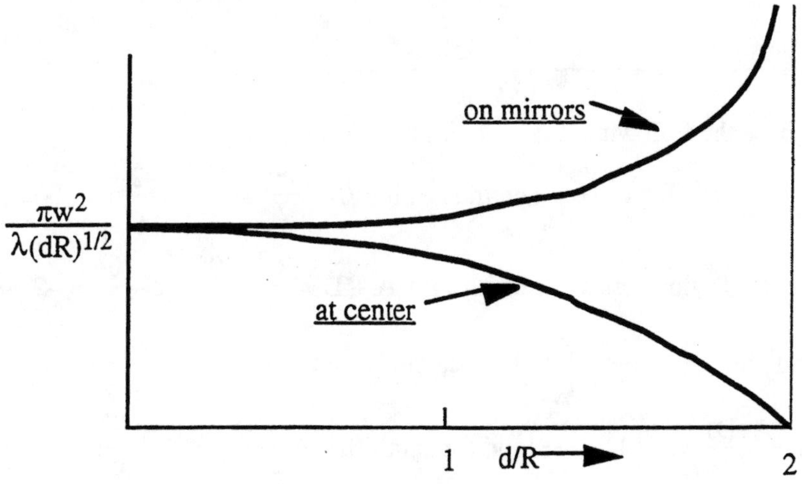

5.5

See the solution for problem 2.12, it is modified to address the problem below:

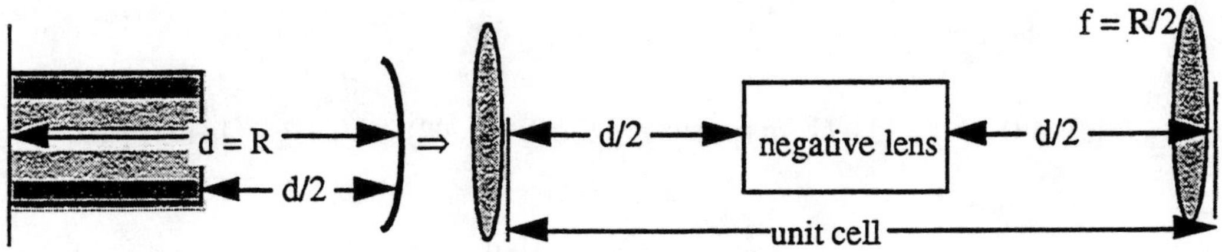

$$T = \begin{bmatrix} 1 & 0 \\ -\frac{1}{f} & 1 \end{bmatrix} \cdot \begin{bmatrix} 1 & \frac{d}{2} \\ 0 & 1 \end{bmatrix} \cdot \begin{bmatrix} \cosh\frac{d}{L} & L\sinh\frac{d}{L} \\ \frac{1}{L}\sinh\frac{d}{L} & \cosh\frac{d}{L} \end{bmatrix} \cdot \begin{bmatrix} 1 & \frac{d}{2} \\ 0 & 1 \end{bmatrix}$$

$$= \begin{bmatrix} \cosh\theta + (\theta/2)\sinh\theta & (d/L)[\cosh\theta + (\theta/2)\sinh\theta] + L\sinh\theta \\ -(2/d)\cosh\theta & -\cosh\theta - (2/\theta)\sinh\theta \end{bmatrix}$$

where $\theta = d/L$

$$A = \cosh\frac{d}{L} + \frac{d}{2L}\sinh\frac{d}{L};$$

$$D = -\frac{d}{2f}\cosh\frac{d}{L} - \frac{L}{f}\sinh\frac{d}{L} + \left(1 - \frac{d}{2f}\right)\left[\sinh\frac{d}{L} + \cosh\frac{d}{L}\right]$$

$$= -\frac{d}{2f}\cosh\frac{d}{L} - \frac{L}{f}\sinh\frac{d}{L} \qquad \text{since } d = 2f$$

$$S = \frac{A+D+2}{4} = \frac{(\theta/2 - 2/\theta)\sinh\theta + 2}{4}$$

Use the following Taylor series expansions:

$$\sinh\theta = \theta + \frac{\theta^3}{3!} \text{ and thus } \frac{\theta}{2}\sinh\theta = \frac{\theta^2}{2} + \frac{\theta^3}{12} \text{ and } \frac{2}{\theta}\sinh\theta = 2 + \frac{\theta^2}{3}$$

Use the Taylor Series expansions for $A + D = \frac{\theta^2}{2} + \frac{\theta^3}{12} - 2 - \frac{\theta^2}{3} = -2 + \frac{\theta^2}{6}$

Thus $S = \frac{\theta^2}{24} = \frac{1}{24}\left(\frac{d}{L}\right)^2 > 0$; $\therefore$ stable

(b) $\frac{(A+D)}{2} = -\left(1 - \frac{\theta^2}{12}\right)$ and for small θ; $\left[\frac{A+D}{2}\right]^2 = 1 - \frac{\theta^2}{6}$;

$\left\{1 - \left[\frac{A+D}{2}\right]^2\right\}^{1/2} = \theta/\sqrt{6}$; $B = d/2 + L\theta = 3d/2$

$$\frac{\pi w^2}{\lambda} = \frac{2d}{\sqrt{2/3}\,\theta} = \frac{3L}{2\sqrt{6}}$$

5.6

(a) $\phi(0 \rightarrow l) = kl - (1+m+p)\tan^{-1}\frac{l}{z_0}$; $\phi(0 - d + l) = k(d+l) - (1+m+p)\tan^{-1}\frac{(l+d)}{z_0}$

$$\therefore \phi(l \rightarrow d + l) = kd - (1+m+p)\left[\tan^{-1}\frac{l+d}{z_0} - \tan^{-1}\frac{l}{z_0}\right] = q\pi$$

$$\therefore \nu = \frac{c}{2d}\left\{q + \frac{(1+m+p)}{\pi}\left[\tan^{-1}\frac{l+d}{z_0} - \tan^{-1}\frac{l}{z_0}\right]\right\}$$

(b) $\nu_{m,p,q} - \nu_{0,0,q} = \frac{c}{2d}\cdot\frac{3}{\pi}\left[\tan^{-1}\frac{100}{125} - \tan^{-1}\frac{25}{125}\right] = 91.16 \text{ MHz}\left(\frac{c}{2d} = 200 \text{ MHz}\right)$

(c) $-R_1 = \frac{z^2 + z_0^2}{z}\Big|_{z=l} = \frac{l^2 + z_0^2}{l} = 650 \text{ cm}; \; R_2 = \frac{z^2 + z_0^2}{z}\Big|_{z=l+d} = 205 \text{ cm}$

5.7

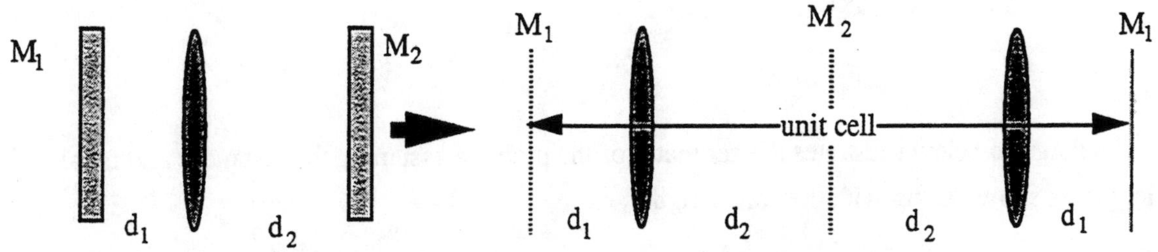

$$T = \begin{bmatrix} 1 & d_1 \\ 0 & 1 \end{bmatrix}\begin{bmatrix} 1 & 0 \\ -\frac{1}{f} & 0 \end{bmatrix}\begin{bmatrix} 1 & 2d_2 \\ 0 & 1 \end{bmatrix}\begin{bmatrix} 1 & 0 \\ -\frac{1}{f} & 1 \end{bmatrix}\begin{bmatrix} 1 & d_2 \\ 0 & 1 \end{bmatrix}$$

$$= \begin{bmatrix} \left(1 - \frac{d_1}{f}\right)\left(1 - \frac{2d_2}{f}\right) - \frac{d_1}{f} & \left(1 - \frac{d_1}{f}\right)\left[2d_1 + 2d_2 - \frac{2d_1d_2}{f}\right] \\ -\frac{1}{f}\left(2 - \frac{2d_2}{f}\right) & \frac{-d_1}{f} - \frac{2d_2}{f}\left(1 - \frac{d_1}{f}\right) + \left(1 - \frac{d_1}{f}\right) \end{bmatrix}$$

$S = [1 - d_1/f]\,[1 - d_2/f]$

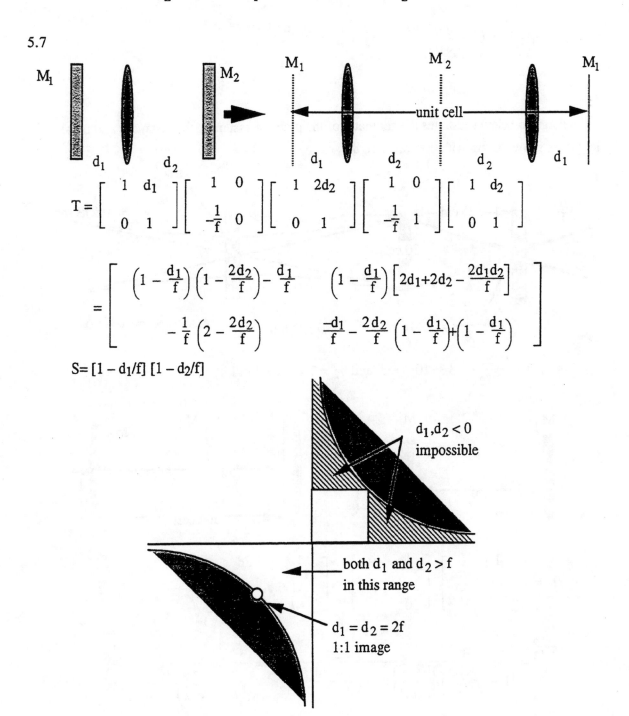

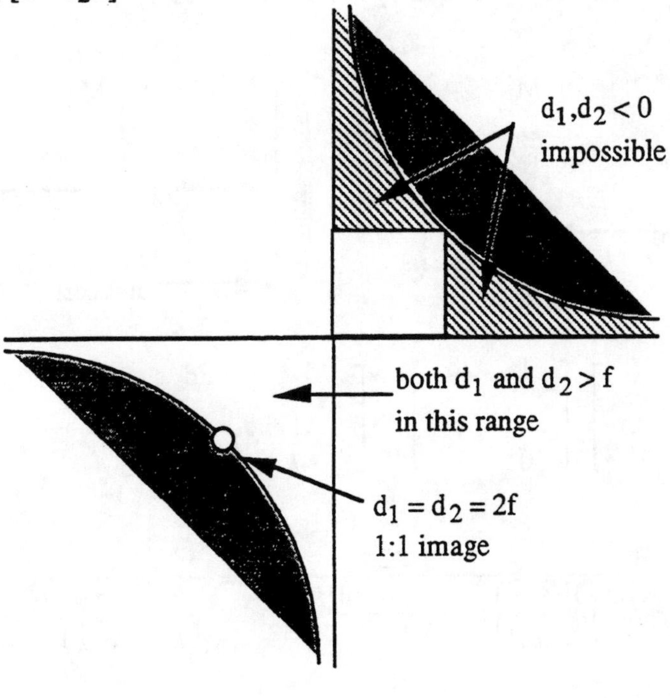

5.8

$$\frac{\pi w_{01}^2}{\lambda} = \frac{B}{\left[1 - \left(\frac{A+D}{2}\right)^2\right]^{1/2}} = \frac{B}{(1-A^2)^{1/2}} \text{ since } A = D;\ A = 1 - \frac{2d_1}{f} - \frac{2d_2}{f} + \frac{2d_1d_2}{f^2}$$

and $1-A^2 = (1-A)(1+A)$; $\frac{\pi w_{01}^2}{\lambda} = \left(\frac{1 - d_1/f}{1 - d_2/f}\right)^{1/2} \sqrt{f}\left(d_1 + d_2 - \frac{d_1d_2}{f}\right)^{1/2}$

$$\therefore \quad \frac{\pi w_{02}^2}{\lambda} = \left(\frac{1 - d_2/f}{1 - d_1/f}\right)^{1/2} \sqrt{f}\left(d_1 + d_2 - \frac{d_1d_2}{f}\right)^{1/2}$$

5.9

The diagram below illustrates the geometry of the problem assuming the distances and focal length as shown along with the wavelength.

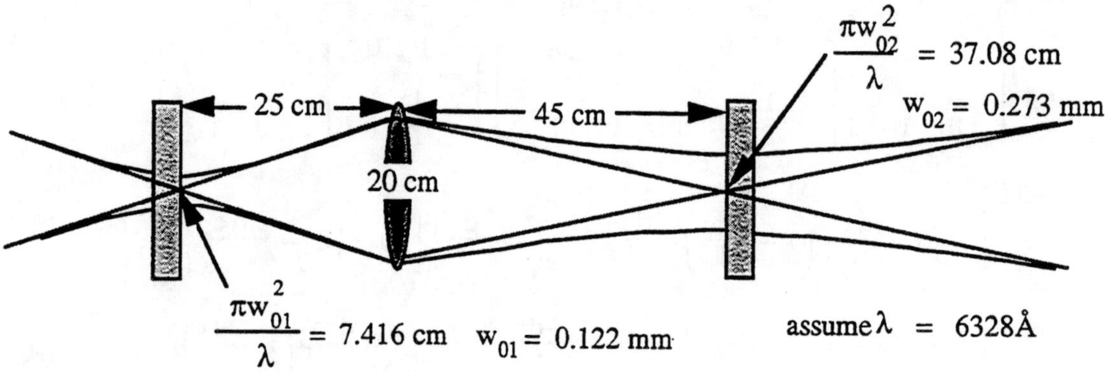

$$\theta_1 = \frac{2\lambda}{\pi w_{01}} = 3.3\times10^{-3} \text{ rad. and } \theta_2 = 1.48\times10^{-3} \text{ rad}$$

5.10

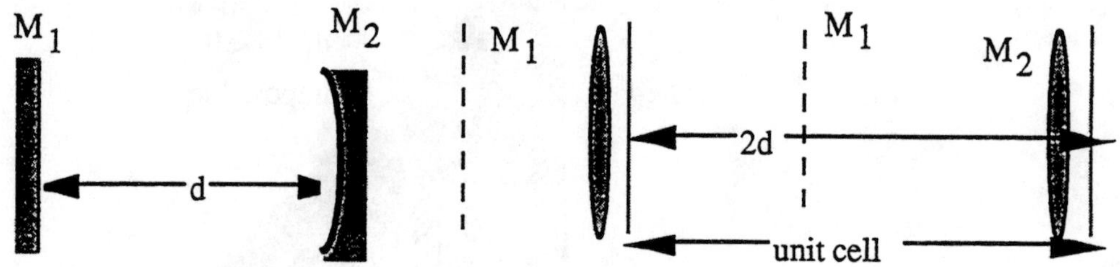

$$T = \begin{bmatrix} 1 & 0 \\ -\frac{1}{f} & 1 \end{bmatrix} \cdot \begin{bmatrix} 1 & 2d \\ 0 & 1 \end{bmatrix} = \begin{bmatrix} 1 & 2d \\ -\frac{1}{f} & 1 - \frac{2d}{f} \end{bmatrix}$$

$$\frac{\pi w_3^2}{\lambda} = \frac{B}{\left\{1 - \left(\frac{A+D}{2}\right)^2\right\}^{1/2}} = \frac{2d}{\left\{1 - \left(\frac{2 - 2d/f}{2}\right)^2\right\}^{1/2}} = \frac{2d}{\left\{\frac{2d}{f} - \left(\frac{d}{f}\right)^2\right\}^{1/2}}$$

5.11

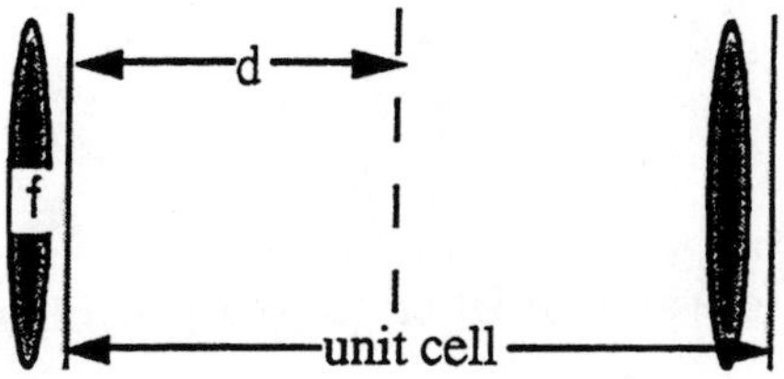

$$T = \begin{bmatrix} 1 & 2d \\ -\frac{1}{f} & 1 - \frac{2d}{f} \end{bmatrix}$$

(a) $\frac{A+D}{2} = 1 - \frac{d}{f};\ 1 - \left[\frac{A+D}{2}\right]^2 = 1 - \frac{1+2d}{f} - \left[\frac{d}{f}\right]^2 = \frac{d}{f}\left(2 - \frac{d}{f}\right);\ f = R/2;$

$$1 - \left[\frac{A+D}{2}\right]^2 = 2\frac{d}{R}\left(1 - \frac{d}{R}\right);\ \frac{\pi w_s^2}{\lambda^2} = \frac{B}{\left[1 - \frac{(A+D)^2}{4}\right]^{1/2}} = \frac{\sqrt{dR}}{\left[1 - \frac{d}{R}\right]^{1/2}};$$

$$\therefore\ w_s^2 = \frac{\lambda_0}{\pi}\frac{\sqrt{dR}}{\left[1 - \frac{d}{R}\right]^{1/2}};\quad w_s = 0.266\ \text{cm}.$$

(b) $\tau_p = \frac{(2d/c)}{[1 - (\Gamma_1\Gamma_2)^2]} = [150\ \text{cm}/3\text{x}10^{10}\text{cm/sec}] \div (1 - 0.98\text{x}0.8) = 23.1\ \text{ns}$

(c) $\nu = c/\lambda_0 = 2.98^{+13}$ Hz; $\omega = 1.778\times10^{+14}$ r/s; $Q = \omega\tau_p = 4.12\times10^{+6}$.

5.12

$$T_{2RT} = \begin{bmatrix} A & B \\ C & D \end{bmatrix}\begin{bmatrix} A & B \\ C & D \end{bmatrix} = \begin{bmatrix} A^2+BC=A_T & AB+BD=B_T \\ AC+DC=C_T & D^2+BC=D_T \end{bmatrix};$$

$B_T(1/q)^2 + 2(A_T - D_T/2)(1/q) - C_T = 0$; see Eq. 5.3.3.

Now $A_T - D_T = A^2 - D^2 = (A-D)(A+D)$; $B_T = B(A+D)$; $C_T = C(A+D)$; substitute and cancel common factors of A+D to obtain the same equation as for one round–trip.

5.13

The output plane of the laser is characterized by: $R_1 = \infty$ and z_{01}, and the input plane of the semi-confocal cavity is characterized by $R = \infty$ and z_{02}. For the mode–matching lens system:

$$T = \begin{bmatrix} 1 & d_2 \\ 0 & 1 \end{bmatrix}\begin{bmatrix} 1 & 0 \\ -(1/f) & 1 \end{bmatrix}\begin{bmatrix} 1 & d_1 \\ 0 & 1 \end{bmatrix} = \begin{bmatrix} 1 - (d_2/f) & d_1 + d_2(1 - d_1/f) \\ -(1/f) & 1 - (d_1/f) \end{bmatrix}$$

$$q_2 = \frac{(Aq_1+B)}{(Cq_1+D)};\ \frac{1}{q_2} = \frac{[C+D(1/q_1)]}{[A+B(1/q_1)]} = -j(1/z_{02}) = \frac{[C-jD(1/z_{01})]}{[A-jB(1/z_{01})]};$$

since $R_{1or2} = \infty$, and thus $\frac{1}{q_{1or2}} = -j\frac{1}{z_{01or02}}$; $-j\frac{A}{z_{02}} - B\frac{1}{z_{01}z_{02}} = C - jD\frac{1}{z_{01}}$.

Equate real and imaginary parts:

Real Part: $\frac{B}{C} = -z_{01}z_{02} = \frac{d_1+d_2(1-d_1/f)}{(-1/f)} = -[(d_1+d_2)f - d_1d_2]$ or: $(d_1+d_2)f - d_1d_2 = z_{01}z_{02}$;

Imag. Part: $\frac{A}{D} = \frac{z_{02}}{z_{01}} = \frac{(1-d_2/f)}{(1-d_1/f)}$;

Define $z_{01}/f = a$; $z_{02}/f = b$; $x = d_1/f$; $y = d_2/f$ transforms the above equations into:

$\frac{b}{a} = \frac{y-1}{x-1}$ and $x + y - xy = ab$; eliminate y:

$x^2 - 2x - [a/b - 1 - a^2] = 0$; $x = 1 \pm \sqrt{a/b - a^2}$; $y = 2 \pm (b/a)\sqrt{a/b - a^2}$;

The quantity inside the square root must be positive: $ab<1$ or $\boxed{f^2 > z_{01}z_{02}}$;

Solve for d_1 and d_2:

$d_1 = f \pm \sqrt{z_{01}/z_{02}} \cdot \sqrt{f^2 - z_{01}z_{02}}$;

$d_2 = 2f \pm \sqrt{z_{02}/z_{01}} \cdot \sqrt{f^2 - z_{01}z_{02}}$

6.1

For R = 200 cm, d/R = 3/4; d = 150 cm

(a) $\nu_{0,0,q} = \frac{c}{2d}\left\{q + \frac{1}{\pi}\left[\cos^{-1}\left(1 - \frac{3}{4}\right)^{1/2} = \pi/6\right]\right\} = \frac{c}{2d}\left\{q + \frac{1}{6}\right\}$

(b) FSR = c/2d = 100 MHz ; $\nu = 6^{+14}$ Hz; $\frac{d\nu}{\nu} = \frac{d\lambda}{\lambda}$; $\therefore\ d\lambda = \lambda\frac{d\nu}{\nu} = 8.3^{-4}$ Å

$\tau_p = \frac{2d/c}{1 - R_1R_2} = 251.9$ nsec; $\Delta\nu_{1/2} = \frac{1}{2\pi\tau_p} = 631.8$ kHz; $Q = \frac{\nu_0}{\Delta\nu_{1/2}} = 9.5^{+8}$

$F = \frac{c/2d}{\Delta\nu_{1/2}} = \frac{100^{+6}}{0.632^{+3}} = 158.2$

6.2

$\tau_p = \frac{\text{Round–trip time}}{\text{fraction lost}} = \frac{2(d_1+d_2)/c}{1 - R_1R_2R_3R_4} = 78.9$ nsec

6.3

$\lambda_0 = 5000$ Å; $\therefore\ \nu_0 = 6^{+14}$ Hz = 600 THz; $\Delta\nu_{1/2} = \frac{1}{2\pi\tau_p} = 2.02$ MHz;

$Q = \frac{\nu_0}{\Delta\nu_{1/2}} = 2.98\times10^{+8}$

6.4

(a) If path 1 had a power gain of G; $\tau_p = \frac{2(d_1 + d_2)/c}{1 - GR_1R_2R_3R_4} = 38.8$ ns if G = 0.85;

(b) If G = 1.1, $\tau_p = 253.8$ ns; (c)If τ_p is positive, dN_p/dt is negative, and N_p decreases (passive cavity). If τ_p is negative, dN_p/dt is positive, and N_p increases. Something has to give: N_p cannot increase indefinitely.

6.5

$\lambda_0 = c/\nu_0 = 0.6\ \mu m$

6.6

FSR = $\Delta\nu = \frac{c}{2d} = 125$ MHz; $\therefore$ d = 120 cm

6.7

$F = \frac{125\ \text{MHz}}{2.5\ \text{MHz}} = 50$

6.8

$$Q = \frac{\nu_0}{\Delta\nu_{1/2}} = 2\times10^{+8}$$

6.9

$$\tau_p = \frac{1}{2\pi\Delta\nu_{1/2}} = 63.6 \text{ ns}$$

6.10

$$\tau_p = \frac{2d/c}{1-R_1R_2} = 63.6 \text{ ns}; \ \therefore \ R_1R_2 = 0.8743;$$

For Oscillation:. $\tau_p \rightarrow$ (negative number)

$$\therefore \ 1 - G^2R_1R_2 < 0; \ \text{or } G > \frac{1}{\sqrt{R_1R_2}} = 1.069$$

6.11

$$\tau_p = \frac{3/c}{1-T_2R_1R_2R_3} = 78.7 \text{ ns};$$

$\therefore \Delta\omega_{1/2} = 1/\tau_p = 12.7\times10^{+6}$ r/s; $\omega_0 = 2.98^{+15}$ r/sec; Q= $2.43\times10^{+8}$

6.12

$\delta d = \lambda_0/2 = 0.3164\mu m$; $\nu_0 = c/\lambda_0 = 4.74\times10^{+14}$ Hz;

On a frequency scale: FSR = c/2d =15GHz;

peak = 4.5 cm in height ; 0.4 cm FWHM; spacing 3 cm; $\therefore$ $F = \frac{3}{0.4} = 7.4 = (c/2d)\div\Delta\nu_{1/2}$;

$\therefore$ $\Delta\nu_{1/2} = 2$ GHz; $Q = \nu/\Delta\nu_{1/2} = 2.37\times10^{+5}$

6.13

The distance 0.4 μ corresponds to 7.5 cm with the peaks spaced 5.9 cm ⇒ 0.3147 μm;

$\therefore$ $\lambda_0 = 0.6293$ μm;

$\nu_0 = 4.76\times10^{+14}$ Hz; peak height = 4.5 cm; FWHM = 0.9 cm;

$F = 5.9/0.9 = (c/2d)\div\Delta\nu_{1/2} = 6.56$;

c/2d = 7.5 GHz; $\therefore$ $\Delta\nu_{1/2} = 1.14$ GHz; $Q = (4.76\times10^{+14}\text{Hz}\div1.14\times10^{+9}\text{Hz}) = 4.17\times10^{+5}$;

$\tau_p = 1/(2\pi\Delta\nu_{1/2}) = 0.1396$ nsec

6.14

$$\Gamma_1 = \frac{(1/j\omega C) - Z_0}{(1/j\omega C) + Z_0} = \frac{1 - j\omega CZ_0}{1 + j\omega CZ_0} = 1\angle{-2}\tan^{-1}(\omega CZ_0);$$

$$\Gamma_2 = \frac{1 + j\,(Z_0/\omega L)}{1 - j\,(Z_0/\omega L)} = 1 \angle +2\tan^{-1}(Z_0/\omega L)$$

Condition for resonance: R.T.P.S. = $q \cdot 2\pi = \frac{\omega}{c} \cdot 2d + 2\tan^{-1}(Z_0/\omega L) - 2\tan^{-1}(\omega C Z_0)$

If $\frac{\omega}{c} \cdot 2d$ is small, then: $2\pi = [\tan^{-1}(\omega C Z_0) = A] - [\tan^{-1}(Z_0/\omega L) = B]$;

$$\tan 2\pi = 0 = \frac{\tan A - \tan B}{1 + \tan A \tan B}$$

$$0 = \frac{\omega C Z_0 - (Z_0/\omega L)}{1 + (C/L) Z_0^2} \quad \text{or} \quad \omega^2 = \frac{1}{LC} \text{ as one would expect.}$$

6.15

$R = d\left(1 + \frac{z_0^2}{d^2}\right)$ or $z_0^2 = \left(\frac{R}{d} - 1\right) d^2$; $\qquad R = 2d\left(1 + \frac{z_0^2}{4d^2}\right)$ or $z_0^2 = \left(\frac{R}{2d} - 1\right) 4d^2$

$\therefore \quad Rd - d^2 = 2Rd - 4d^2 \quad Rd = 3d^2;\ R = 3d;\ \therefore\ z_0^2 = 2d_0^2$;

Check stability: $\qquad S = \left(1 + \frac{1}{3}\right)\left(1 - \frac{1}{3}\right) = \frac{8}{9}$ O.K., it is stable.

$k \cdot 2d - (1+m+p)\tan^{-1}\frac{2d}{z_0} = \phi_2\ (0 \rightarrow M_2)$; $\quad k \cdot d - (1+m+p)\tan^{-1}\frac{d}{z_0} = \phi_1\ (0 \rightarrow M_1)$

$$\phi_2 - \phi_1 = q\pi = kd - (1+m+p)\left[\tan^{-1}\frac{2d}{z_0} - \tan^{-1}\frac{d}{z_0}\right]$$

$$\nu = \frac{c}{2d}\left\{1 + \frac{(1+m+p)}{\pi}\left[[\tan^{-1}\frac{2d}{z_0} - \tan^{-1}\frac{d}{z_0} = 0.108]\right]\right\};$$

Now $c/2d = 150$ MHz; $\therefore \quad \nu_{1,0,q} - \nu_{0,0,q} = 16.2$ MHz

6.16

$R_1R_2 = 0.876$; $[kd_1 + (1+m+p)\tan^{-1}\frac{d_1}{z_{01}}] + [kd_2 - (1+m+p)\tan^{-1}\frac{dz}{z_{02}}] = q\pi$

$$\nu_{m,p,q} = \frac{c}{2(d_1+d_2)}\left\{q + \frac{(1+m+p)}{\pi}\left[\tan^{-1}\frac{d_1}{z_{01}} + \tan^{-1}\frac{d_2}{z_{02}}\right]\right\}$$

$\tau_p = \frac{2d/c}{1 - T^4 R_1 R_2}$ (2 surfaces and 2 passes) = 8.9 nsec; $\Delta\nu_{1/2} = \frac{1}{2\pi\tau_p} = 17.9$ MHz

$\nu_0 = 6^{+14}$ Hz; $Q = 3.36^{+7}$

6.17

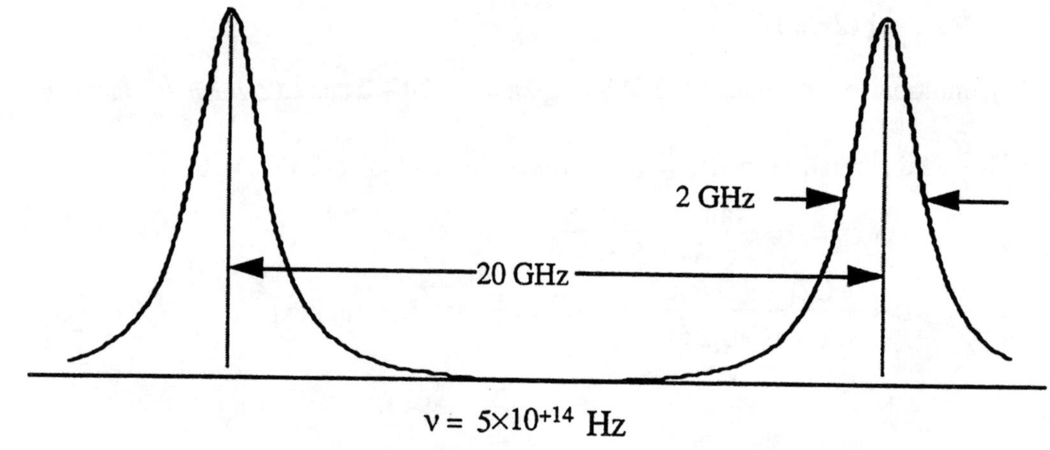

$$\text{FWHM} = 2\text{ GHz} = 0.067\text{ cm}^{-1}\ ;\ \frac{\Delta\lambda}{\lambda} = \frac{\Delta\nu}{\nu};\ \therefore\ \Delta\lambda = 6000\cdot\frac{2\times10^{+9}}{5\times10^{+14}} = 0.024\text{ Å}$$

$$Q = \frac{\nu_0}{\Delta\nu_{1/2}}\ \frac{5\times10^{+14}}{2\times10^{+9}} = 2.5\times10^{+5}$$

6.18

(a) Radius of curvature at R_2 matches that of M_2; $\therefore$ R = 100 cm

(b) $\tau_p = \dfrac{2(d_1+d_2+d_3)/c}{1 - T^2R_1R_2} = 47.01$ nsec

(c) RTPS = $q\cdot 2\pi$; $k(d_1+d_2+d_3) - (1+m+p)\left\{\tan^{-1}\frac{d_1}{z_{01}} + \tan^{-1}\frac{d_2}{z_{02}} + \tan^{-1}\frac{d_3}{z_{03}}\right\} = q\pi$

$$\nu = \frac{c}{2(d_1+d_2+d_3)}\left\{q + \frac{(1+m+p)}{\pi}\left[\tan^{-1}\frac{d_1}{z_{01}} + \tan^{-1}\frac{d_2}{z_{02}} + \tan^{-1}\frac{d_3}{z_{03}}\right]\right\}$$

6.19

$g_1 = 1 - \frac{d}{R_1} = \frac{3}{4}$; (a) $\therefore$ S < 1 i.e. stable ;

(b) $\nu = \frac{c}{2d}\left\{q + \frac{(1+m+p)}{\pi}\cos^{-1}\left(1 - \frac{d}{R}\right)^{1/2}\right\}$ and $\cos\frac{\sqrt{3}}{2} = \frac{\pi}{6}$

$\therefore\quad \nu = \frac{c}{2d}\left(q + \frac{(1+m+p)}{6}\right)$; $\frac{c}{2d} = 200$ MHz; $\nu_{1,0,q} - \nu_{0,0,q} = 33.3$ MHz

(c) Greatest loss near spherical mirror $T = 1 - \exp[-2a^2/w_s^2] = 0.999$

$\therefore$ a = 1.858 w_s; Now $\pi w_s^2/\lambda$ = $(dR_2)^{1/2}/(1 - d/R_2)^{1/2}$ from Chapter 5;

$w_s^2 = 3.31\times10^{-3}$ cm^2; $w_s = 5.75\times10^{-2}$ cm $\therefore$ a = 1.069 mm; 2a = diameter = 2.14 mm

(d) $R_1R_2 \exp[\gamma_0 \cdot 2l_g] = 1$ for an oscillator; $\gamma_0 = \frac{1}{2l_g}\ln\frac{1}{R_1R_2} = 5.13\times10^{-4}$ cm^{-1}

6.20

Round–trip time = 5 nsec = $\frac{2d}{c}$; $\therefore$d = 75 cm; $\nu_0 = 5.37\times10^{+14}$ Hz

Using the slope at t = 0, τ_p = 75 nsec (by extrapolating) = $\frac{2d/c}{1 - R_1R_2}$;$\therefore$ $R_1R_2 = 0.933$

$\Delta\nu_{1/2} = \frac{1}{2\pi\tau_p} = 2.12\times10^{+6}$ Hz; $\therefore$ $Q_0 = 2.53\times10^{+8}$ and $F = \frac{c/2d}{\Delta\nu_{1/2}} = \frac{200\times10^{+6}}{2.12\times10^{+6}} = 94.2$

With pumping, the photon lifetime increases to:τ_p = 125 nsec = $\frac{2d/c}{1 - G^2R_1R_2}$

$\therefore$ $G^2R_1R_2 = 0.960$;Using the value of R_1R_2 found above leads to: $G^2 = 1.0286$ or G = 1.0142 = $\exp[\gamma_0 l_g]$; $\therefore$ $\gamma_0 = 1.878\times10^{-4}$ cm^{-1}

6.21

$g_1g_2 < 1$ and thus stable;$z_0 = \frac{\pi w_0^2}{\lambda_0} = (dR_2)^{1/2}\left(1 - \frac{d}{R_2}\right)^{1/2} = 43.2$ cm;$w_0 = 2.95\times10^{-2}$ cm;

$\frac{\pi w_s^2}{\lambda} = \frac{(dR_2)^{1/2}}{\left(1 - \frac{d}{R_2}\right)^{1/2}} = 173.2$ cm; $w_s = 5.91\times10^{-2}$ cm;

tan θ_B = n for Brewster's Angle = 1.45; θ_B = 55.41°;θ (on diagram) = 34.59°

Fractional loss = $\exp[-2a^2/w_s^2]$ $a/w_s = 3.38 = 1.12^{-10}$ (a rather small value!)

$\nu = \frac{c}{2d}\left\{q + \frac{(1+m+p)}{\pi}\tan^{-1}\frac{d}{z_0}\right\}$

6.22

$\nu = q\frac{c}{2d}$; $\delta\nu = q\frac{c}{2d^2}\delta d$ or $\frac{\delta d}{d} = \frac{\delta\nu}{\nu} = \frac{10^3}{4.74^{+14}} = 2.1\times10^{-12}$;

$\therefore$ $\boxed{\delta d = 1.58^{-10} \text{ cm} = 0.0158 \text{ Å!}}$

This is less than 1/100 of the mean spacing between the atomic spacing of the atoms on the mirror. One would guess that it is impossible to hold the spacing to this accuracy, but it has been done!

6.23

(a) $M = R+T$; (See Eq. 6.7.1 & 6.7.2); evaluated at $\theta = 0$ and $R_1 = R_2$; $M = \dfrac{G_0\,(1-R)^2}{(1-G_0R)^2}$

(b) This is done in Fig. 6.8;

(c) $\text{FWHM} = \dfrac{2\pi\Delta\nu_{1/2}d}{c} = \dfrac{1-G_0R}{G_0^{1/2}\sqrt{R}}$ Osc.: $G_0R = 1$ or $G_0 = 1.11$

6.24

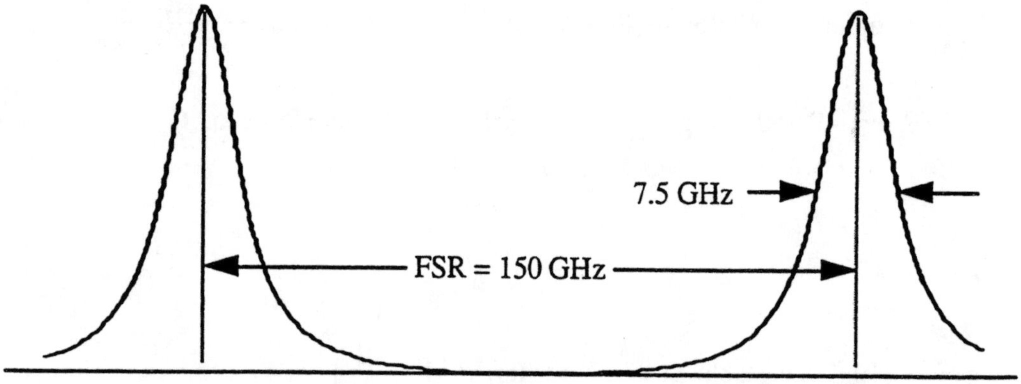

$\dfrac{\omega}{c} n_1 \cdot 2d = q \cdot 2\pi$ at the first peak; $\dfrac{\omega}{c} n_2 \cdot 2d = (q+1) \cdot 2\pi$ for the next.;

Subtract: $\dfrac{2\pi}{\lambda}(n_2 - n_1) \cdot d = \pi$ or $(n_2 - n_1) = \dfrac{\lambda_0}{2d} = 1.58\times10^{-4}$;

$\therefore n_2 - n_1 = 8\times10^{-4}\,(p_2 - p_1) = 1.58\times10^{-4}$

$p_2 - p_1 = 0.198$ atmospheres $= 2.91$ psi; $Q = 6.32\times10^{+4}$

6.25

Resonance: $\{(kd_1 - (1 + m + p)\tan^{-1}\frac{d_1}{z_{01}} + kd_2 - (1 + m + p)\tan^{-1}\frac{d_2}{z_{02}}) = q\pi$; or

$$\nu_{m,p,q} = \frac{c}{2(d_1 + d_2)}\left\{q + \frac{(1 + m + p)}{\pi}\left[\tan^{-1}\frac{d_1}{z_{01}} + \tan^{-1}\frac{d_2}{z_{02}}\right]\right\}$$

$\tau_p = \dfrac{2(d_1 + d_2)/c}{1 - T^2R_1R_2}$; For $T= 0.95, R_1= 0.98$ and $R_2= 0.93$, $\tau_p=28.1$ nsec

$\Delta\nu_{1/2} = 5.65$ MHz; $\nu = 5.83\times10^{+14}$; $Q = 1.03\times10^{+8}$; $\tau_p' = \dfrac{(2(d_1+d_2)/c)}{1 - G^2R_1R_2} = -99$ ns.

This means that the photons are **growing** in number with time i.e., beginning or build-up of oscillation.

6.26

$$\frac{1}{q} = -\left(\frac{A-D}{2B}\right) - j\frac{\left[1-\left(\frac{A+D}{2}\right)^2\right]^{1/2}}{2B};\ a = 1\ \text{(i.e."el")(see part d)}$$

$$T = \begin{bmatrix} \cos z/a & a \sin z/a \\ -\frac{\sin z/a}{a} & \cos (z/a) \end{bmatrix} \therefore \frac{1}{q} = -j\frac{1}{a};\ \therefore \frac{\pi w^2}{\lambda} = a;\ \therefore w = \left(\frac{\lambda_0 a}{\pi n}\right)^{1/2} = 6.52\ \mu m$$

$$\beta \cdot 2d = q \cdot 2\pi \text{ or } \left(\frac{\omega}{c} n_0 - \frac{1}{a}\right) d = q\pi;\ \text{or } \nu_q = \frac{c}{2n_0 d}\left(q + \frac{d}{\pi a}\right)$$

$$\Gamma = \frac{\eta_0 - \eta}{\eta_0 + \eta}$$ found from matching E and H at interface for uniform plane wave.

"Spot–size should be small compared to a for it to be valid.

$$\tau_p = \frac{(2nd/c)}{1-R_1R_2} = 1.66\times10^{-9}\ \text{sec};\ \Delta\nu_{1/2} = 95.75\ \text{MHz};\ F = \frac{c/2n_0 d}{\Delta\nu_{1/2}} = 8.38$$

6.27

(a) $\lambda_0/2$ between peaks; $\therefore$ $\Delta d_1 = 0.44\ \mu m$;

(b) At 1st peak, $d_0 = q\frac{\lambda_1}{2}$; At 2nd peak, $d_0 + \delta = q\frac{\lambda_2}{2}$

where $\delta = 1/4$ of $\Delta d_1 = 0.11\ \mu m$; Subtracting $\delta = q\left(\frac{\lambda_2-\lambda_1}{2}\right)$; $\therefore\ \lambda_2-\lambda_1 = \frac{2\delta}{q}$

But $q = \frac{2d_0}{\lambda_1}$; $\lambda_2-\lambda_1 = \lambda_1\left(\frac{\delta}{d_0+\delta}\right) \approx \lambda_1\left(\frac{\delta}{d_0}\right)$; $\delta = \frac{1}{4}\Delta d_1 = 0.11\mu m = 1.1\times10^{-5}$ cm

$\therefore\ \lambda_2-\lambda_1 = 8800\cdot\frac{1.1\times10^{-5}}{4} = 1.1\times 0.022$ or $\lambda_2 - \lambda_1 = 0.0242$Å;

(c) $F = \frac{FSR}{FWHM} = \frac{40\ \text{units}}{4\ \text{units}} = 10$

6.28

(a) TEM $_{0,1}$ mode; (b) Find $\tau_p = \frac{2d/c}{1 - T^4R_1R_2}$ where $T = 0.97$; $\tau_p = 4.14$ns;

Thus $Q = \omega\tau_p = 8.8\times10^6$ since $\omega = 2\pi\times(c/\lambda_0)$

(c) Since $z = 0$ is at the center, double the phase shift going from that plane to the curved mirror and set it equal to π:

$$\phi(\text{single pass}) = 2\{k(d/2) + [1 + (m{=}0) + (p{=}1)]\frac{\tan^{-1}(d/2z_0)}{\pi}\} = \pi$$

6.29

(a) At A, $(\omega/c)n_1d = q\pi$; at B $(\omega/c)n_2d = (q+1)\pi$; subtract: $n_2 - n_1 = \lambda_0/2d = 3.16\times10^{-5}$.

(b) The FSR = c/2d = 30 GHz which corresponds to the spacing between the peaks of 32divisions; The FWHM is ~2.2 divisions;

Thus F = 32/2.2 = 14.5. $\Delta\nu_{1/2}$ = 30 GHz÷F = 2.06 GHz; $\nu = 4.74\times10^{14}$ Hz;

$Q = \nu/\Delta\nu_{1/2} = 2.3\times10^5$.

6.30

(a) The distance between the peaks is $\lambda_0/2 = 3.75$ divisions with 1 division corresponding to 0.1 μm. Thus $\lambda_0 = 0.75$ μm

(b) The FWHM ~ 0.45 units = 0.045 μm. F= 3.75/0.45 = 8.33; FSR = c/2d = 30 GHz; $\Delta\nu_{1/2}$ = 3.6 GHz; $\nu = c/\lambda_0 = 4\times10^{14}$ Hz, $Q = \nu/\Delta\nu_{1/2} = 1.11\times10^5$; $\tau_p = 1/2\pi\Delta\nu_{1/2}$ = 44.2ps

6.31

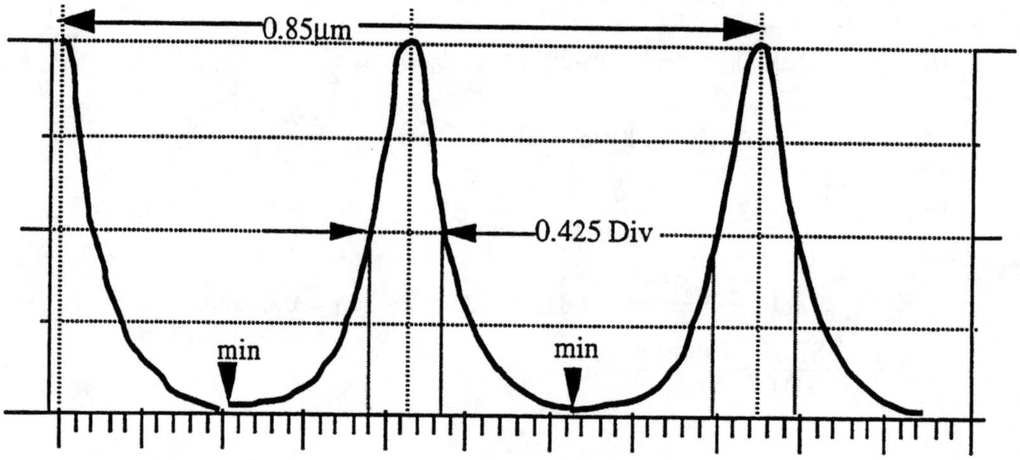

λ_0 =0.85 μm; c/2d = 15 GHz; FWHM = 1.5 GHz; $\Delta\bar{\nu}_{1/2} = 0.05$ cm^{-1}

7.1 $$\nu = \frac{c}{2}\left\{\left(\frac{m}{a}\right)^2 + \left(\frac{p}{b}\right)^2 + \left(\frac{q}{d}\right)^2\right\}^{1/2}$$

m	p	q	ν (GHz)	mode	Σ
1	0	1	3.91	TE_{101}	1
1	0	2	5.83	TE_{102}	2
2	0	1	6.50	TE_{201}	3
2	0	2	7.81	TE_{202}	4
0	1	1	7.96	TE_{011}	5
1	0	3	8.08	TE_{013}	6
1	1	0	8.08	TM_{110}	7
1	1	1	8.46	TE,TM_{111}	9
0	1	2	9.01	TE_{012}	10
3	0	1	9.34	TE_{301}	11
1	1	2	9.5	TE,TM_{112}	13
2	0	3	9.61	TE	14
2	1	0	9.61	TM	15
2	1	1	9.93	TE,TM	17

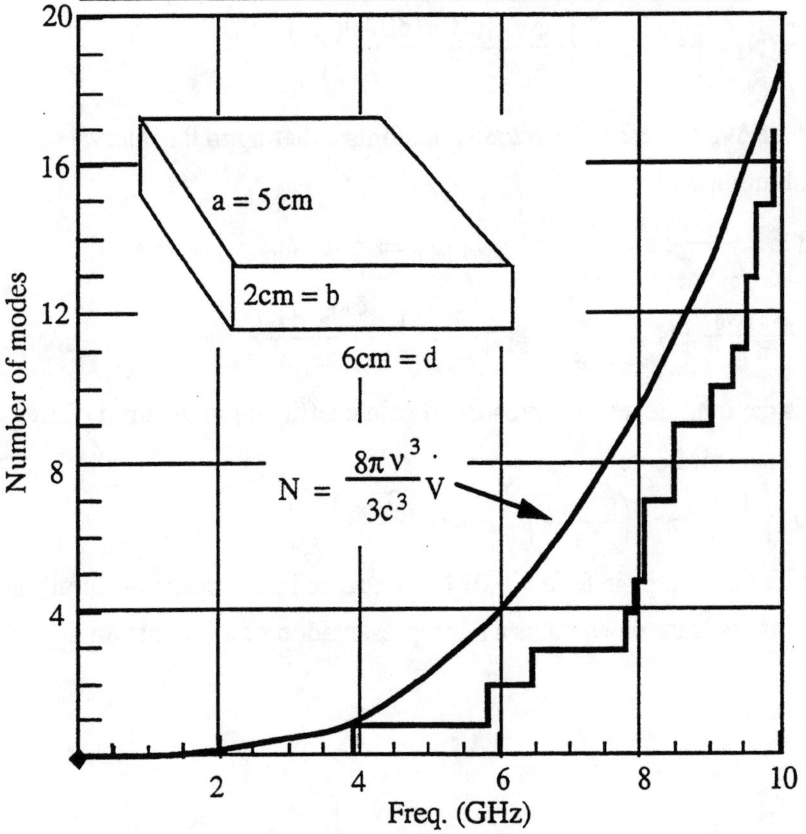

7.2

$$\left.\frac{dN_2}{dt}\right|_{stim} = B_{21}N_2\rho(\nu) = \frac{(c')^3}{8\pi h\nu^3}A_{21}N_2\rho(\nu);\ \left.\frac{dN_2}{dt}\right|_{spont} = -A_{21}N_2$$

But $\rho(\nu) = \frac{8\pi h\nu^3}{(c')^3}N_p$, where N_p= photons per mode; $\therefore\ \frac{\text{stimulated rate}}{\text{spontaneous rate}} = N_p$

7.3

$\int_0^\infty g(\nu)d\nu = 1 = K\cdot(2.667\ cm^{-1})$ or one could convert to frequency units;

$\therefore\ K\cdot(8\times10^{+10}\ Hz) = 1$; $K = 1.25\times10^{-11}\ sec = g(\nu_0)$; $\bar{\nu}_0 = 15{,}713\ cm^{-1}$; $\lambda_0 = 0.6364\ \mu m$

$\sigma_{SE} = \frac{\lambda^2}{8\pi}A_{21}g(\nu_0) = 2.01\times10^{-20}\ cm^2$; $g_2 = 3$, $g_1 = 5$, $\sigma_{abs} = 1.21\times10^{-20}\ cm^2$

7.4

$$\gamma(\nu) = \frac{A_{21}\lambda_0^2}{8\pi}\left(N_2 - \frac{g_2}{g_1}N_1\right)\int_{-\infty}^{\infty}\left\{\frac{\Delta\nu_h\,[p(f)=(df/\Delta\nu_s)]}{2\pi[(f-\nu)^2 + (\Delta\nu_h/2)^2]}\right\}$$

where the ratio $df/\Delta\nu_s$ expresses the fraction of atoms radiating in the interval df. Make the following substitutions:

$x = \frac{f-\nu}{\Delta\nu_s/2}$ and $\delta = \frac{\nu_0-\nu}{\Delta\nu_s/2}$; $a = \frac{\Delta\nu_h-\nu}{\Delta\nu_2}$; $x_{lower\ limit} \Rightarrow \delta-1$; $x_{upper\ limit} \Rightarrow \delta+1$

$$\gamma(\nu) = \frac{A_{21}\lambda_0^2}{8\pi}\left(N_2 - \frac{g_2}{g_1}N_1\right)\frac{1}{\Delta\nu_s}\left\{\frac{1}{\pi}\int_{\delta-1}^{\delta+1}\frac{a\,dx}{x^2+a^2}\right\}$$

The bold part is the inhomogeneous broadened gain coefficient in the limit of $\Delta\nu_h \ll \Delta\nu_s$. The integral is a standard one:

$$\gamma(\nu) = \gamma_0(\nu)\left\{\frac{1}{\pi}\left[\tan^{-1}\left(\frac{\delta+1}{a}\right) - \tan^{-1}\left(\frac{\delta-1}{a}\right)\right]\right\}$$

This is plotted on the next page for a = 0.01 (the extreme inhomogeneous limit), a=0.1, and a=0.5. In this last case one obtains a fair representation of a Lorentzian

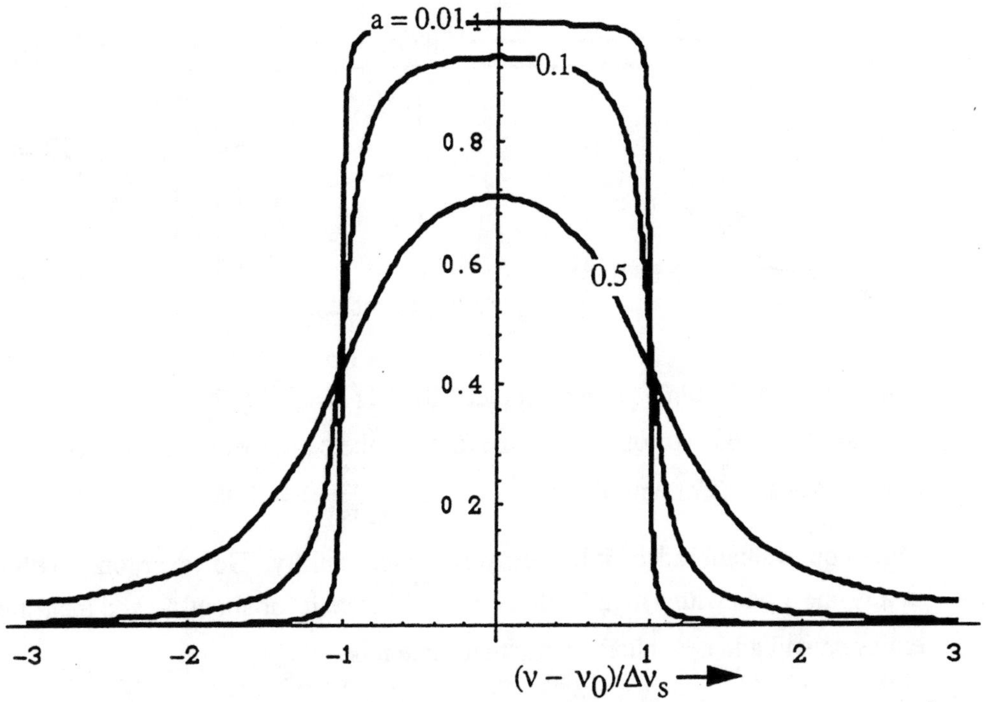

Figure for problem 7.4

7.5

The intent of this problem is to introduce some of the numerical factors associated with optical transitions. Given information: $\lambda_0 = 5000$ Å and a wave length interval of $\Delta\lambda = 1$ Å, $V = 2\ \text{cm}^3$. While λ is one of the easiest parameters to measure, frequency ν is a better theoretical variable. $\therefore \nu_0 = 600$ THz. We convert the wavelength interval into a frequency one by: $\frac{\Delta\nu}{\nu} = \frac{\Delta\lambda}{\lambda}$ or $\Delta\nu = 1.2\times10^{+11}$ Hz or $\Delta\nu = 120$ GHz or $\Delta\bar{\nu} = 4\ \text{cm}^{-1}$ (a)

There seems to be a "natural" tendency for the student to make the following mistake once, so let me make it for you in hopes that you **will NOT do the following**:

$$\Delta\nu = \frac{c}{\Delta\lambda} \quad \textbf{which is absolutely wrong}$$

(Check the numbers: If the above were correct, then $\Delta\nu = 3^{+18}$ Hz which is far greater than the central frequency of 600 THz.)

The number of modes in the volume V is: $N = [8\pi\nu^2\Delta\nu/c^3]\ V = 8.04\times10^{+10}$ modes which is the total number of ways that electromagnetic energy can appear in that wavelength interval. Now lets look at the spectral issue on a frequency scale with zero suppressed (or in the next county). The FSR = c/2d = 750 MHz

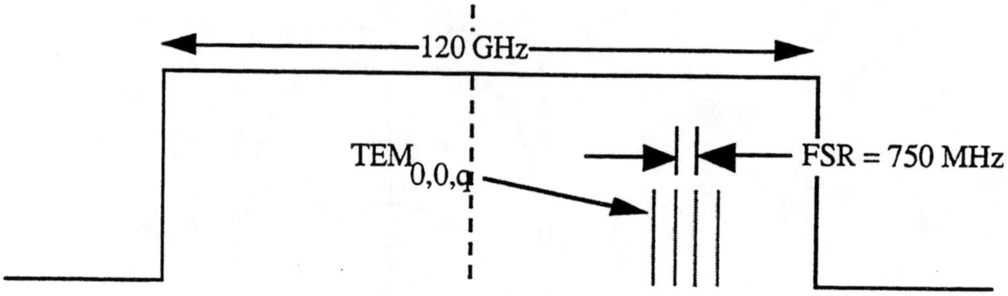

Figure for problem 7.5

The number of $TEM_{0,0,q}$ modes in that 120 GHz is = 2 x (120/0.75) = 320 modes where the extra factor of two comes from the fact that there are two polarizations.

$$\text{Probability of emission into 1 mode} = \frac{320}{8.04^{+10}} = 3.98 \times 10^{-9}$$

This is quite small, indeed it borders on an impossibility. However, once a photon appears in any one mode with a high Q, that mode will store it for about τ_p, and then stimulated emission will add new photons into that same mode.

7.6

Assume T = 300K and M = 22 AMU, 1.0 AMU = 1.67^{-27} kg;
$\Delta\nu_D = (8kT \ln 2/Mc^2)^{1/2}\nu_0 = 3.17 \times 10^{-6}\,\nu_0$

λ	ν_0	$\Delta\nu_D$	$\Delta\lambda_D$
6328Å	4.74^{14} Hz	1.5GHz	0.02Å
1.1523μm	2.6^{14}	0.823	0.0365Å
3.39μm	8.85^{13}	0.28	0.107Å

7.7

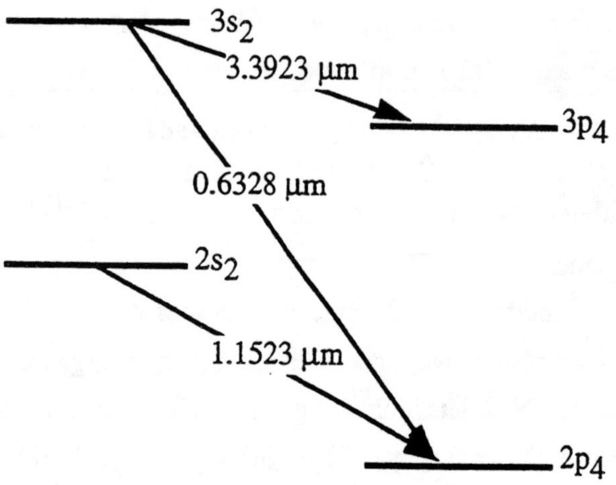

7.8

Multiply the numerator and denominator of the Lorentzian in Eq. 7.6.15 by $[(4\ln 2)^{1/2}/\Delta\nu_D]^2$ and use the substitutions suggested.

$$\frac{\Delta\nu_h/2}{\pi\,[(\nu-\nu_0-\nu_0 v_z/c)^2+(\Delta\nu_h/2)^2]}=\frac{(4\ln 2)^{1/2}}{\Delta\nu_D}\,\frac{a}{\pi\,[a^2+(\omega-y)^2]}$$

Let $\exp[-\frac{Mv_z^2}{2kT}]=e^{-y^2}$; then $dv_z=\frac{c\Delta\nu_D}{(4\ln 2)^{1/2}\nu_0}dy$;

The combined lineshape can be expressed as:

$$g(\omega)=\left[\frac{4\ln 2}{\pi}\right]^{1/2}\frac{1}{\Delta\nu_D}\left\{\tilde{g}(\omega)=\frac{a}{\pi}\int_{-\infty}^{\infty}\frac{e^{-y^2}\,dy}{a^2+(\omega-y)^2}\right\}$$

There isn't any trick in evaluating this integral numerically since it can be (and was) done on a hand calculator. To obtain the analytic approximations requires a bit of effort. Use the fact that:

$$\int_0^{\infty}e^{-ax}\cos[(\omega-y)x]\,dx=\frac{a}{a^2+(\omega-y)^2}$$ and substitute into the above.

Expand: $\cos(\omega-y)x=\cos(\omega x)\cos(yx)+\sin(\omega x)\sin(yx)$. The integration of the sine term will be zero because it is odd with respect to y. Interchanging order of integration:

$$\tilde{g}(\omega)=\int_0^{\infty}e^{-ax}\cos\omega x\left[\frac{1}{\pi}\int_{-\infty}^{+\infty}e^{-y^2}\cos(yx)dx\right];$$

The brackets $[\,]=\sqrt{\pi}\,e^{-x^2/4}$ and thus $\tilde{g}(\omega)=\frac{1}{\sqrt{\pi}}\int_0^{\infty}e^{-ax}e^{-x^2/4}\cos(\omega x)\,dx$

For small a: $e^{-ax}=1-ax$; $\tilde{g}(\omega)=\frac{1}{\sqrt{\pi}}\int_0^{\infty}e^{-x^2/4}\cos\omega x dx-\frac{a}{\sqrt{\pi}}\int_0^{\infty}x\,e^{-x^2/4}\cos\omega x\,dx$

$\therefore$ $\tilde{g}(\omega)=\frac{2}{\pi}\int_0^{\infty}e^{-t^2}\cos 2\omega t dt-\frac{4a}{\sqrt{\pi}}\int_0^{\infty}t\,e^{-t^2}\cos 2\omega t dt$ where $t=x/2$

The first integral $=\frac{\sqrt{\pi}}{2}e^{-\omega^2}$; the second integral $=1-2\omega\int_0^{\infty}e^{-t^2}\sin 2\omega t\,dt=1-2\omega\,F(\omega)$

where $F(\omega)=e^{-\omega^2}\int_0^{\omega}e^{x^2}\,dx$;

Thus we obtain $\boxed{\tilde{g}(\omega)=e^{-\omega^2}-\frac{2a}{\sqrt{\pi}}[1-2\omega F(\omega)]}$

The first term is the normal Doppler distribution whereas the second is the correction.

For large a, $e^{-y^2} \to \sqrt{\pi}\,\delta(y)$; $\therefore$ $\qquad \tilde{g}(\omega) = \frac{1}{\sqrt{\pi}} \frac{a}{a^2 + \omega^2}$

In the wings, $\omega >>$ any significant value of y; hence the original braces can be approximated;

$$\tilde{g}(\omega) = \frac{a}{\pi} \int_{-\infty}^{\infty} \frac{e^{y^2}\,dy}{a^2 + (\omega - y)^2} \text{ or } \tilde{g}(\omega) \sim \frac{a}{\pi\omega^2} \int_{-\infty}^{\infty} e^{-y^2}\,dy = \frac{a\sqrt{\pi}}{\omega^2}$$

which has the form of a Lorentzian for the variation in the wings.

7.9

One should first convert the standard "pure" lineshapes into the notation of Problem 7.9

$$g_h = \frac{\Delta\nu_h}{2\pi\left[(\nu_0 - \nu)^2 + (\Delta\nu_h/2)^2\right]} = \frac{1}{\Delta\nu_D}\left(\frac{4\ln 2}{\pi}\right)^{1/2} \left\{ \tilde{g}_h(\omega) = \frac{a\sqrt{\pi}}{\pi[a^2 + \omega^2]} = \frac{\sqrt{\pi}}{\omega^2 + 1} \text{ for } a=1 \right\}$$

$$g_D = \frac{1}{\Delta\nu_D}\left(\frac{4\ln 2}{\pi}\right)^{1/2} [\tilde{g}_D(\omega) = e^{-\omega^2}];\ \omega = \left(\frac{\nu_0 - \nu}{\Delta\nu_D}\right)(4\ln 2)^{1/2};$$

$$g_{comb} = \frac{1}{\Delta\nu_D}\left(\frac{4\ln 2}{\pi}\right)^{1/2} \tilde{g}(\omega);$$

These functions are plotted on the next page and show that all line shapes become a Lorentzian in the wings. The combined $\tilde{g}$ reaches 0.5 of the peak at $\omega \sim 1.42$ or $\nu_0 - \nu = 0.853\Delta\nu_D$ yielding a FWHM of the combined broadening of $1.7\Delta\nu_D$.

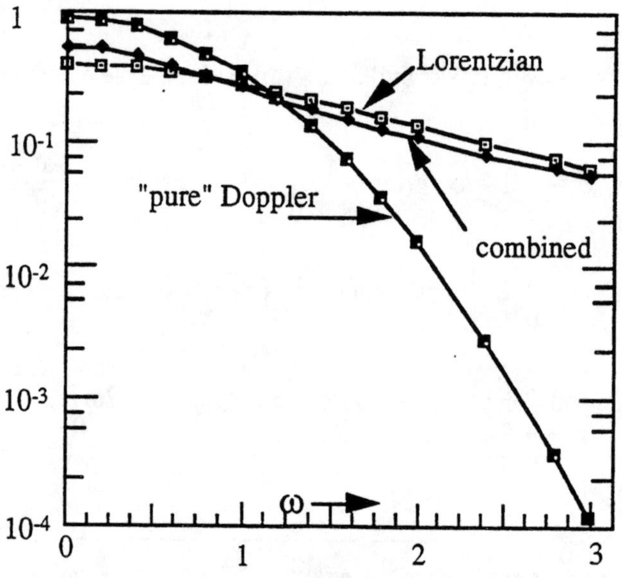

Figure for Problem 7.9

7.10

This is a reasonable model for the pulsed N_2 laser which has a very high gain and lases at 0.337 μm. Its major drawback is that it is self-terminating because the inversion can not be maintained indefinitely – fact that comes out of the analysis that follows.

$\frac{dN_2}{dt} = P_2 - \frac{N_2}{\tau_2}$ whose solution is: $N_2(t) = P_2\tau_2(1 - \exp[-t/\tau_2])$

$\frac{dN_1}{dt} = +\frac{N_2}{\tau_2} - \frac{N_1}{\tau_1}$ or $\frac{dN_1}{dt} + \frac{N_1}{\tau_1} = P_2(1 - \exp[-t/\tau_2])$

$$N_1 = P_2\tau_1\left\{1 - \frac{\tau_1/\tau_2}{\tau_1/\tau_2 - 1}e^{-t/\tau_1} + \frac{1}{\tau_1/\tau_2 - 1}e^{-t/\tau_2}\right\}$$

It is informative to consider the steady-state populations, i.e., where $t >> \tau_{2,1}$. $N_2(t\rightarrow\infty) = P_2\tau_2$ and $N_1(t\rightarrow\infty) = P_2\tau_1$. Note that since $\tau_1 > \tau_2$, we have the undesirable situation of $N_1 > N_2$ which means that the system will not lase in a steady state. However, one can obtain a transient inversion (and a laser) as the sketch below indicates.

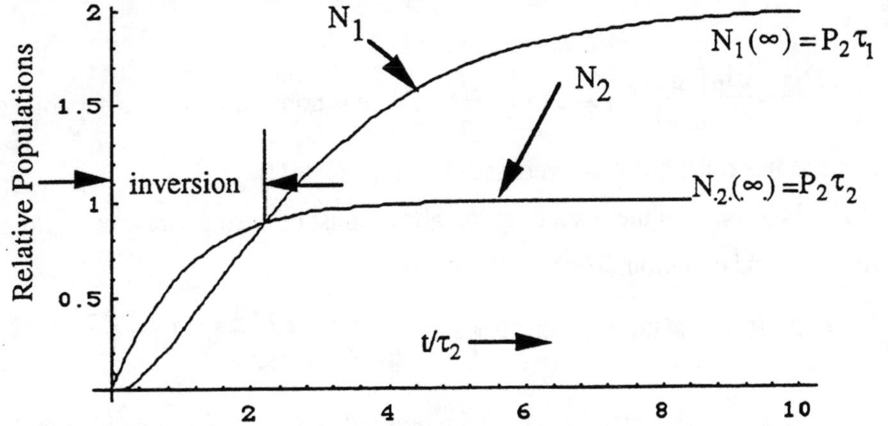

Figure for problem 7.10

$N_2(t\rightarrow\infty) = 10^{20} \times 10^{-6} = 10^{14}\ cm^{-3}$, $N_1(t\rightarrow\infty) = 10^{20} \times 2 \times 10^{-6} = 2 \times 10^{14}\ cm^{-3}$

Let $t/\tau_1 = x$; $(\tau_1/\tau_2) = 2$; $N_1 = N_2$ when $2(1 - 2e^{-x} + e^{-2x}) = (1 - e^{-2x})$;

Collect terms, multiply by e^{2x} and factor: $f(x) = [e^x - 3][e^x - 1] = 0$;

where $x = t/\tau_1$; $F(x) = 0$ at $x = 0$ (i.e.at the start) or $x = t/\tau_1 = \ln 3$; ∴ $t = 1.0986\tau_1 = 2.2\ \mu sec$

7.11

$\frac{\Delta\nu}{\nu} = \frac{\Delta E}{E} = \frac{0.08}{1.476} = 5.42\times10^{-2}$; $\nu = 3.57 \times 10^{+14}$ Hz; ∴ $\Delta\nu$(at the base) = 19.4 THz

$\int g(\nu)\,d\nu = 1 \Rightarrow \frac{1}{2}$[base]·[height= $g(\nu_0)$];

Thus $g(\nu_0) = 2 \div 1.94 \times 10^{+13} = 1.03 \times 10^{-13}$ sec

$\lambda_0 = 0.8400\ \mu m$; $\gamma(\nu_0) = \frac{1}{\tau_{sp}} \frac{\lambda_0^2}{8\pi} g(\nu_0)\ \Delta N = 10\ cm^{-1}$; $\Delta N = 1.73 \times 10^{+15}\ cm^{-3}$

7.12

A_{21} was given in the second edition as $6.56 \times 10^{+7}\ sec^{-1}$. It should have been $6.56 \times 10^{+6}\ sec^{-1}$ (see chapter 10), so let's solve the problem for both cases.

$\left\{K\cdot 0.75 + 2\left(\frac{2K}{4}\right)0.75 + 2\left(\frac{1}{2}K\right)0.75\right\} \times 10^9 = 1$;

$(3.5\ K)\ 0.76 \times 10^{+9} = 1$ or $K = 3.8 \times 10^{-10}$ sec

$\sigma = A_{21} \frac{\lambda_0^2}{8\pi} K = 4.04 \times 10^{-12}\ cm^2$(with $A_{21} = 6.56 \times 10^{+7}$) $= 4.04 \times 10^{-13}\ cm^2$ (with the correct value); $g(\nu)\ d\nu$ = probability of spontaneous emission into $d\nu$ at ν

$g(\nu)$ = relative strength of stimulated or absorption

7.13

(a) $\frac{dN_2}{dt} = \frac{\sigma I_p}{h\nu}\left[\frac{g_2}{g_1} N_1 - N_2\right] - \frac{N_2}{\tau}$; There is no need to write a separate equation for N_1 since atoms must be conserved and thus $N_1 + N_2 = [N]$;

(b) If $I_p \to \infty$, then the bracket in the above must be zero to prevent an infinity appearing in a physical equation. Thus $N_2/N_1 = g_2/g_1$.

(c) For a steady-state situation: $N_2\left[1 + \frac{\sigma\tau}{h\nu} I_p\right] = \frac{g_2}{g_1}\frac{\sigma\tau}{h\nu} I_p N_1$ or $\frac{N_2}{N_1} = \frac{(g_2/g_1)\cdot(I_p/I_s)}{1 + (I_p/I_s)}$

where $I_s = \frac{h\nu}{\sigma\tau}$; This ratio equals 0.5 when $I_p/I_s = 0.25$ for $g_2/g_1 = 2$; $I_s = 23.3\ W/cm^2$;

Thus $I = 5.82 W/cm^2$; (d) $N_2/N_1 = (g_2/g_1)\exp[-E/kT] = 6.25 \times 10^{-25}$; safe to ignore N_2.

7.14

(a) $\frac{dN_2}{dt} = -A_{21}N_2 + B_{12}N_1\rho(\nu) = 0$; $\rho_w(\nu) = \frac{A_{21}}{B_{12}}\frac{N_2}{N_1}$

$\rho_w(\nu) = \frac{A_{21}}{B_{12}} e^{-h\nu/kT} \Leftrightarrow \frac{8\pi h\nu^3}{c^3}\left\{\left[\frac{1}{e^{h\nu/kT}-1} \text{ for } h\nu/kT >> 1\right] \sim e^{-h\nu/kT}\right\}$

(b) In order to match the experiment at optical frequencies: $\frac{A_{21}}{B_{12}} = \frac{8\pi h\nu^3}{c^3}$

(c) $\rho_w(\nu) = \frac{8\pi h\nu^3}{c^3} e^{-h\nu/kT}$; (Wein's law);$\rho_{RJ}(\nu) = \left(\frac{8\pi\nu^2}{c^3}\right)kT$; $\rho_{Planck} = \frac{8\pi h\nu^3}{c^3}\left[\frac{1}{e^{h\nu/kT}-1}\right]$

$\frac{\rho_P}{\rho_{RJ}} = \frac{h\nu/kT}{e^{h\nu/kT}-1}$; $\frac{\rho_P}{\rho_W} = \frac{e^{h\nu/kT}}{e^{h\nu/kT}-1}$ For $h\nu/kT << 1$ $\rho_P/\rho_{RJ} \to 1$; For $h\nu/kT >> 1$ $\rho_P/\rho_W \to 1$

Chapter 8

8.1

$$\sigma = A_{21}\frac{\lambda_0^2}{8\pi}\left[g(\nu_0) = \frac{2}{\pi\Delta\nu_h}\right] = 9.68\times10^{-18}\ \mathrm{cm}^2;\ \gamma_0 = 0.05\ \mathrm{cm}^{-1} = \sigma\cdot\Delta N;$$

$\Delta N = 5.17\times10^{+15}\ \mathrm{cm}^{-3}$; $I_s = h\nu/\sigma\tau_2 = 193.5\ \mathrm{W/cm}^2$

8.2

(a) $$\ln\frac{I_{out}}{I_{in}} + \frac{I_1}{I_s}\left(\frac{I_{out}}{I_{in}} - 1\right) = \gamma_0 l_g;$$

For an input $I_1 = 1\mathrm{W/cm}^2$, $\ln(10) + \frac{I_1}{I_s}(10-1) = \gamma_0 l_g$; 1.

For the input $= 2\mathrm{W/cm}^2 = 2\,I_1$: $\ln 8 + 2\frac{I_1}{I_s}(8-1) = \gamma_0 l_g$; 2.

Subtract the two equations: $\ln(10/8) = (I_1/I_s)\,(14-9)$; 3.

Thus: $I_1/I_s = 0.0446$ and (b) $I_s = 1/0.0446 = 22.4$ watts/cm^2 4.

Substitute this result back into 1.$\gamma_0 l_g = \ln(10) + 0.0446\times 9 = 2.704$;

Hence $G_0 = e^{\gamma_0 l_g} = 14.94$ or 11.74 dB 5.

(c) Maximum extractable intensity $= (\gamma_0 l_g)\cdot I_s = 2.704\times 22.4 = 60.6\ \mathrm{W/cm}^2$

(d) If $I_{out} - I_{in} = 0.5\,[\gamma_0 l_g\cdot I_s] = 30.3\ \mathrm{W/cm}^2$ with $\ln\frac{I_0}{I_{in}} + \frac{I_0 - I_{in}}{I_s} = \gamma_0 l_g$,

Thus, we have: $\ln\frac{I_0}{I_{in}} + \frac{1}{2}\gamma_0 l_g = \gamma_0 l_g$ or $\ln\frac{I_0}{I_{in}} = \frac{2.704}{2}$ or $\frac{I_0}{I_{in}} = 3.866$

$I_{in}\,(3.866 - 1) = 30.3$ $\quad\therefore I_{in} = 10.6\ \mathrm{W/cm}^2$

8.3

$$\frac{df}{dz} = \left(\frac{\gamma_0}{1+f} - \alpha\right)f,\ \text{where } f = I/I_s \qquad 1.$$

Integrate: $$\int_{f_1}^{f_2}\frac{(1+f)\,df}{f\{1-[\alpha/(\gamma_0-\alpha)]\,f\}} = (\gamma_0-\alpha)\int_0^{l_g} dz$$

$$\ln\left[\frac{f_2}{f_1}\right] - \left[\frac{\gamma_0}{\alpha}\right]\ln\left\{\frac{(\gamma_0/\alpha - 1) - f_2}{(\gamma_0/\alpha - 1) - f_1}\right\} = (\gamma_0 - \alpha)\,l_g \qquad 2.$$

where $f_{1,2}$ = Intensity at (input,ouput)

Let $G_0 = \exp[(\gamma_0-\alpha)\,l_g]$, the net small signal gain ; $m = \gamma_0/\alpha$; $G_s = \frac{I_2}{I_1}$ (saturated gain);

Then the above becomes:

$$\ln G_s + \ln\left\{\frac{(m-1) - x}{(m-1) - G_s x}\right\}^m = \ln G_0\ \text{where } x = \frac{I_{in}}{I_s} \qquad 3.$$

For a given ratio γ_0/α, one can solve this for G_s in terms of x or one can solve for the normalized input, x, in terms of the ratio (G_0/G_s). The latter is easier.

$$x = \frac{[(G_0/G_s)^{1/m} - 1]}{[(G_0/G_s)^{(1-m)/m} G_0 - 1]}(m-1) \qquad 4.$$

For very large inputs: $\frac{dI}{dz} = \gamma_0 I_s - \alpha I$ or: $\frac{dI}{dz} + \alpha I = \gamma_0 I_s$;

$$\therefore \qquad I_{out} = (I_{in} - \frac{\gamma_0}{\alpha} I_s)\, e^{-\alpha l_g} + \frac{\gamma_0}{\alpha} I_s \qquad 5.$$

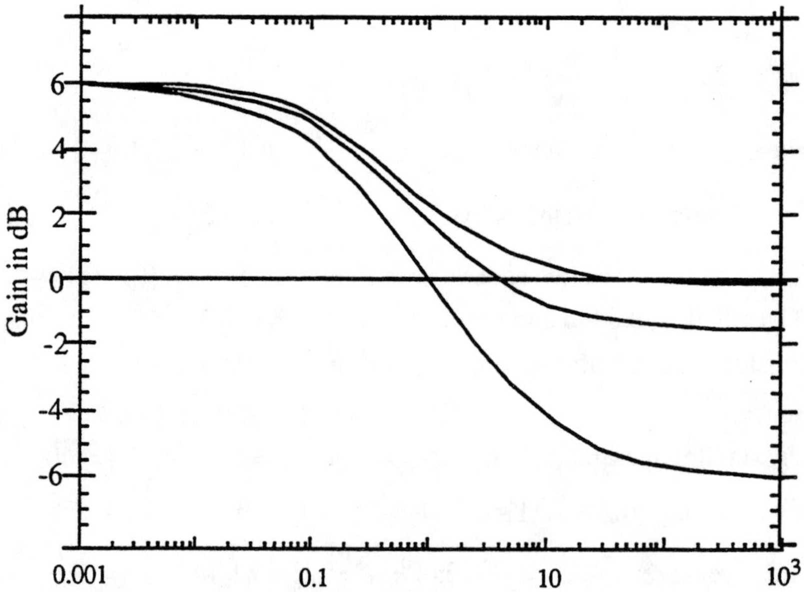

Figure for Problem 8.3

Thus the output can be less than the input i.e. the amplifier can be an attenuator of high amplitude waves.

8.4

Let $g_2 \neq g$, assume steady state.

$$\begin{bmatrix} \left(\frac{1}{\tau_2} + \frac{\sigma I_v}{h\nu}\right) & -\frac{g_2}{g_1}\frac{\sigma I_v}{h\nu} \\ -\left(\frac{1}{\tau_{21}} + \frac{\sigma I_v}{h\nu}\right) & \left(\frac{1}{\tau_1} + \frac{g_2}{g_1}\frac{\sigma I}{h\nu}\right) \end{bmatrix} \begin{bmatrix} N_2 \\ N_1 \end{bmatrix} = \begin{bmatrix} R_2 \\ R_1 \end{bmatrix}$$

$$N_2 = \frac{\left(\frac{1}{\tau_1} + \frac{g_2}{g_1}\frac{\sigma I_v}{h\nu}\right)R_2 + \left(\frac{g_2}{g_1}\frac{\sigma I_v}{h\nu}\right)R_1}{\Delta}; \quad N_1 = \frac{\left(\frac{1}{\tau_1} + \frac{\sigma I_v}{h\nu}\right)R_1 + \left(\frac{1}{\tau_{21}} + \frac{\sigma I_v}{h\nu}\right)R_2}{\Delta}$$

where $$\Delta = \left[1 + \frac{\sigma I_v}{h\nu}\left(\tau_2\left(1 - \frac{g_2}{g_1}\frac{\tau_1}{\tau_{21}}\right) + \tau_1\right)\right]\frac{1}{\tau_1\tau_2}$$

$$\therefore \qquad N_2 - \frac{g_2}{g_1} N_1 = \frac{R_2\tau_2\left(1 - \frac{g_2}{g_1}\frac{\tau_1}{\tau_{21}}\right) - R_1\tau_1\frac{g_2}{g_1}}{1 + \frac{\sigma I_\nu}{h\nu}\left[\tau_2\left(1 - \frac{g_2}{g_1}\frac{\tau_1}{\tau_{21}}\right) + \tau_1\right]}$$

Hence:
$$I_s = \frac{h\nu}{\sigma\tau_2}\left[1 - \frac{g_2}{g_1}\frac{\tau_1}{\tau_{21}} + \frac{\tau_1}{\tau_2}\right]^{-1}$$

8.5

$$\Delta\nu_n = \frac{1}{2\pi}A_{21} = 10.03 \text{ MHz}; \ \Delta\nu_p = \frac{1}{2\pi}\{A_{21} + 2\nu_{col}\}$$

$$\nu_{col} = [He]\,\sigma\left[\frac{8kT}{\pi}\left(\frac{1}{M_{He}} + \frac{1}{M_{Na}}\right)\right]^{1/2} = 1.287\times10^{+11}\ \text{sec}^{-1};$$

where [He] = density of helium

$$\therefore\ \Delta\nu_p = \frac{1}{2\pi}\{6.3\times10^{+7} + 1.287\times10^{+11}\}\text{Hz} = 40.96 \text{ GHz}$$

$$\Delta\nu_D = \left\{\frac{8kT\ln 2}{Mc^2}\right\}^{1/2}\nu_0;\ \nu_0 = \frac{c}{\lambda_0} = 5.093\times10^{+14}\ \text{Hz};\ \Delta\nu_D = 1.9 \text{ GHz};$$

$\therefore$ pressure broadening dominates; $g(\nu_0) = 2/(\pi\Delta\nu_h) = 1.554\times10^{-11}$s.

$$\sigma = A_{21}\frac{\lambda^2}{8\pi}g(\nu_0) = 1.35\times10^{-13}\ \text{cm}^2$$

$-\gamma = \sigma\left[\frac{g_2}{g_1}N_1 - N_2\right]$ and for $[N_2] = 0$, $\gamma = 414.5$ neper/cm $\Rightarrow$ 1800 dB/cm

Thus, the attenuation at low levels of intensity is 18,000 dB (no photons get through!)

$$\frac{dN_2}{dt} = 0 = -A_{21}N_2 - \frac{\sigma I}{h\nu}\left[N_2 - \frac{g_2}{g_1}N_1\right]; \qquad N_2 = \frac{\left(\frac{g_2}{g_1}\right)\frac{\sigma I}{h\nu}N_1}{A_{21} + \frac{\sigma I}{h\nu}}$$

But $N_2 + N_1 = [N_a]$;
$$N_1 = \frac{\left[A_{21} + \frac{\sigma I}{h\nu}\right][N_a]}{A_{21} + \left(1 + \frac{g_2}{g_1}\right)\frac{\sigma I}{h\nu}}; \qquad N_2 = \frac{\frac{g_2}{g_1}\frac{\sigma I}{h\nu}[N_a]}{A_{21} + \left[1 + \frac{g_2}{g_1}\right]\frac{\sigma I}{h\nu}}$$

$$\gamma = \sigma\left[N_2 - \frac{g_2}{g_1}N_1\right] = \frac{-\frac{g_2}{g_1}\sigma\,[N_a]}{1 + \left[\frac{g_1 + g_2}{g_1}\right]\frac{\sigma I}{h\nu}\tau_{21}}; \qquad I_s = \frac{h\nu}{\left[\frac{g_1}{g_1 + g_2}\right]\sigma\tau_{21}} = 472.5\ \text{W/cm}^2$$

$$\frac{dI}{dz} = \frac{\gamma_0}{1 + I/I_s} I; \; \ln\frac{I_0}{I_{in}} + \frac{I_{in}}{I_s}\left[\frac{I_0}{I_{in}} - 1\right] = \gamma_0 l_g;$$

Let's find $\frac{I_{in}}{I_s}$ to make $\frac{I_{out}}{I_{in}} = 0.5 = T$

$$\therefore \quad \frac{I_{in}}{I_s} = \frac{-414.5 - \ln 0.5}{0.5 - 1} = 827.6$$

One could solve for the input that yields a given transmission from the above equation rather than solving for T in terms of I_{in}/I_S. A graph follows.

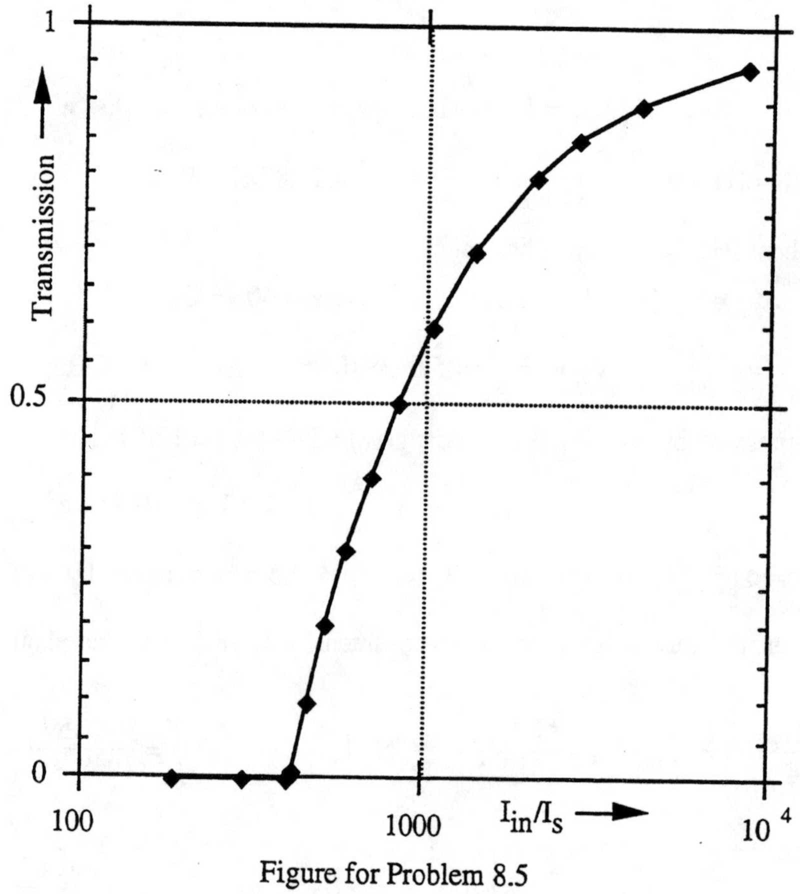

Figure for Problem 8.5

8.6

$$\frac{dI}{dz} = \frac{\gamma_0 I}{(1 + I/I_s)^{1/2}} \Rightarrow \frac{dy}{dz} = \frac{\gamma_0 y}{(1+y)^{1/2}}; \Rightarrow \quad \int_{y_i}^{y_2} \frac{(1+y)^{1/2}}{y} dy = \gamma_0 \int_0^{l_g} dz \text{ where } y = \frac{I}{I_s}$$

Let $u = (1+y)^{1/2}$, then $(u^2-1) = y$ and $dy = 2udu$

$$\int \frac{2u^2 du}{u^2-1} = 2\left[u + \frac{1}{2}\ln\left(\frac{u-1}{u+1}\right)\right];$$

$\therefore\ \gamma_0 l_g = 2\,[(y_2+1)^{1/2} - (y_1+1)^{1/2}] + \ln\left\{\frac{[(1+y_2)^{1/2}-1][(1+y_1)^{1/2}+1]}{[(1+y_2)^{1/2}+1][(1+y_1)^{1/2}-1]}\right\}$

If the input and the output intensities, normalized to to the saturation value are much less than 1, i.e. , y_1 ; $y_2 << 1$, the terms in the first bracket cancel;

$$\gamma_0 l_g \cong \ln\left\{\frac{1+y_2/2-1}{2+y_2/2}\cdot\frac{(2+y_1/2)}{1+y_1/2-1}\right\}$$

$\gamma_0 l_g \cong \ln\frac{y_2}{y_1}$ or $y_2 = y_1\exp[\gamma_0 l_g]$ which is what one would expect.

8.7

$$\sigma = A_{21}\frac{\lambda^2}{8\pi}\left[g(\nu_0) = \frac{2}{\pi\Delta\nu_h}\right] = 4.4\times10^{-14}\ \text{cm}^2;$$

$h\nu/e = 2.3$ eV; $\bar{\nu} = 18{,}552\ \text{cm}^{-1}$; $\lambda = 0.539\ \mu\text{m}$

$N_2\sigma = 0.01\ \text{cm}^{-1}$; $\therefore$ $N_2 = 2.26\times10^{+11}\ \text{cm}^{-3}$;

$$\frac{dN_2}{dt} = R_2 - N_2\left(\frac{1}{\tau_{20}} + \frac{1}{\tau_{21}}\right) = 0$$

$\therefore R_2 = 3.4\times10^{+18}\ \text{cm}^{-3}/\text{sec}; \frac{1}{\tau_2} = \frac{1}{\tau_{20}} + \frac{1}{\tau_{21}} = 1.5\times10^{+7}\ \text{sec}^{-1};$

$I_s = (h\nu/\sigma\tau_2) = 125.4\ \text{W/cm}^2$ and the Pump power $= R_2\cdot5.5\times16\times10^{-19} = 2.99\ \text{W/cm}^3$;

$\Delta\nu/\nu = \Delta\lambda/\lambda$; $\therefore$ $\Delta\lambda = 0.0968$ Å; $\Delta\bar{\nu} = (10^{10}\text{sec}^{-1})\div(3\times10^{+10}\text{cm/sec}) = 0.33\underline{3}\ \text{cm}^{-1}$

8.8

$\Delta\nu = 2\times3\times10^{+10} = 60\text{GHz}$; $\sigma = A_{21}\frac{\lambda^2}{8\pi}g(\nu_0) = 6.75\times10^{-16}\ \text{cm}^2$;

$\gamma = \frac{1}{2l_g}\ln\frac{1}{R_1R_2} = 3.045\times10^{-3}\ \text{cm}^{-1} = \left[N_2 - \frac{g_2}{g_1}N_1\right]\sigma$; $N_2 - \frac{g_2}{g_1}N_1 = 4.51\times10^{+12}\ \text{cm}^{-3}$

$\frac{dN_2}{dt} = R_2 - N_2/\tau_2$; $N_2 = R_2\tau_2$; $\tau_2^{-1} = A_{21}+k_{21}+k_{20}$; $\frac{dN_1}{dt} = (A_{21}+k_{21})N_2 - N_1/\tau_1$

$N_1 = (A_{21}+k_{21})\tau_1N_2$; $\therefore$ $N_2 = \frac{2}{3}\times10^{-7}R_2$;

$N_1 = 10^7\times50\times10^{-9}N_2 = 0.5\,N_2 = 1/3\times10^{-7}R_2$; $g_2/g_1 = 1/3$;

$N_2 - \frac{g_2}{g_1}N_1 = \left[\frac{2}{3} - \frac{1}{9}\right]\times10^{-7}R_2 = 4.51^{+12}\ \text{cm}^{-3}$; $\therefore$ $R_2 = 8.1\times10^{+19}\ \text{cm}^{-3}\text{-s}^{-1}$

8.9

$\frac{B_{12}}{B_{21}} = \frac{g_2}{g_1} = \frac{3}{5}$; $\gamma_0 = A_{21}\frac{\lambda^2}{8\pi}g(\nu)\left[N_2 - \frac{g_2}{g_1}N_1\right]$; $\int g(\nu)d\nu = 1 = \frac{1}{2}3^{+9}\ \text{Hz}\cdot g(\nu_0)$

$\therefore$ $g(\nu_0) = \frac{2}{3}\times10^{-9}$ sec; If $N_2 = N_1 = 10^{12}\ \text{cm}^{-3}$ (error in printing in 2nd Ed)

$\therefore$ $N_2 - \frac{g_2}{g_1}N_1 = \frac{2}{5}\times10^{12}\ \text{cm}^{-3}$; $\gamma_0(\nu_0) = 4.35\times10^{-2}\ \text{cm}^{-1}$

8.10

$$\frac{dI}{dz} = \frac{\gamma_0 I}{1 + \frac{I}{I_s}\bar{g}(\nu)}; \quad \bar{g}(\nu) = \frac{(\Delta\nu/2)^2}{(\nu_0 - \nu)^2 + (\Delta\nu/2)^2};$$

Integrating from input (1) to output (2)

$$\ln\frac{I_2}{I_1} + \frac{I_1}{I_s}\bar{g}(\nu)\left[\frac{I_2}{I_1} - 1\right] = \gamma_0 l_g = \ln G_0;$$

Now pick a saturated gain $(I_2/I_1) < G_0$ and solve for the input:

$$\frac{I_1}{I_s} = \frac{1}{\bar{g}(\nu)}\,\frac{\ln[G_0/G_s]}{G_s - 1}; \quad I_2 - I_1 = \frac{\gamma_0(\nu)I_s l_g}{\bar{g}(\nu)} = \gamma_0(\nu_0)I_s l_g = 23.026 \text{ W/cm}^2$$

To extract 95% of this max; $\frac{I_2 - I_1}{I_s} = \frac{0.95\gamma_0(\nu_0)I_s l_g}{I_s}$; $\therefore \ln\frac{I_2}{I_1} = 0.05\ \gamma_0(\nu_0)l_g = 0.115$

$\frac{I_2}{I_1} = 1.122 = G$ (i.e., 0.5 dB) $\therefore$ $\frac{I_1}{I_s} = 17.96$; or; $I_1 = 17.9$ watts/cm^2

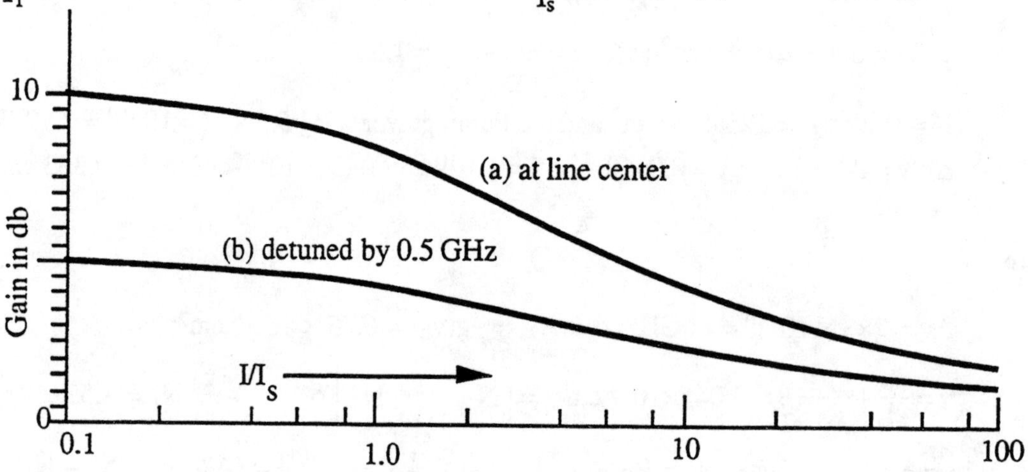

Figure for Problem 8.10

8.11

$$\frac{dN_2}{dt} = Ru(t) - \frac{N_2}{\tau_{21}}$$

$$N_2 = R\tau_{21}\{1 - \exp[-\frac{t}{\tau_{21}}]\}$$

$$\frac{dN_1}{dt} = \frac{N_2}{\tau_{21}} - \frac{N_1}{\tau_1} \text{ or}$$

$$\frac{dN_1}{dt} + \frac{N_1}{\tau_1} = R(1 - \exp[-\frac{t}{\tau_{21}}])$$

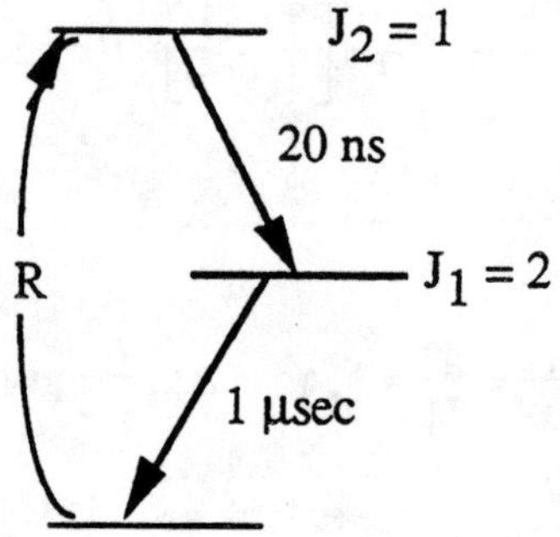

$$\therefore\ N_1 = R\tau_{21}\frac{\tau_1}{\tau_{21}}\left\{1 + \frac{1}{\tau_1/\tau_{21} - 1}\exp[-\frac{t}{\tau_{21}}] - \frac{\tau_1/\tau_{21}}{\tau_1/\tau_{21} - 1}\exp[-\frac{t}{\tau_1}]\right\}$$

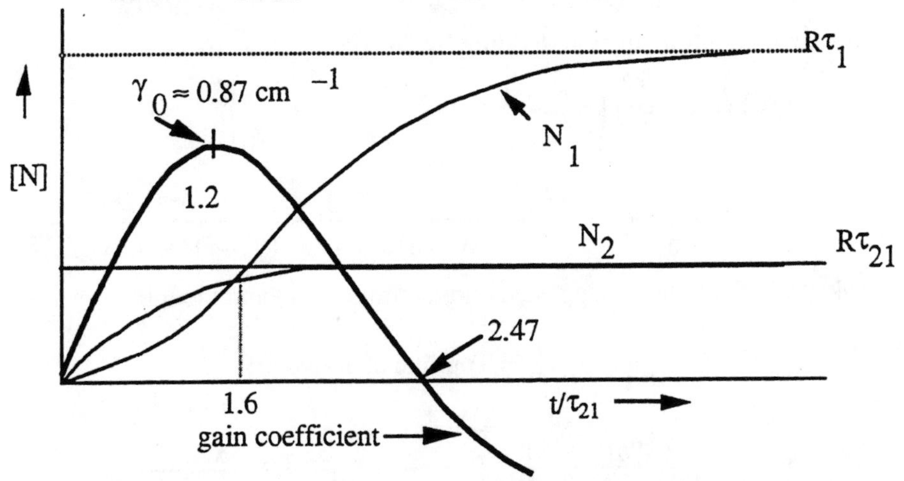

Due to unfavorable lifetime ratios, system is not suitable for CW laser, but it can and does lase with a pulsed excitation.

8.12

The side fluorescence is always proportional to $A_{21}N_2h\nu$. With N_1 small compared to N_2, the rate equations become:

$$\frac{dN_2}{dt} = 0 = R_2 - \frac{N_2}{\tau_2} - \frac{\sigma I}{h\nu_2}N_2 = R_2 - \frac{N_2}{\tau_2}\left(1 + \frac{I}{I_s}\right)$$

$$N_2 = \frac{R_2\tau_2}{1 + I/I_s} \text{ and } P = \frac{P_0}{1 + I/I_s} \text{ or } \frac{I}{I_s} = \frac{P_0}{P} - 1; \text{ where } P = \text{spontaneous power}$$

If $(P_0/P) = 2$ with $I = 100\ \text{W/cm}^2$, then $I_s = 100\ \text{W/cm}^2$

8.13

$$\tau_p = \frac{2d/c}{1 - R_1R_2T^4} = 13.1\ \text{nsec};\ \text{Is } R_1R_2T^4\exp[\gamma_0 2l_g] \overset{?}{>} 1 \text{ or}$$

$$\text{Is } \gamma_0 \overset{?}{>} \frac{1}{R_1R_2T^4} = 4.9\times10^{-3}\ \text{cm}^{-1}$$

$\therefore \gamma_0 < \alpha$; No, it will not oscillate; $\mathbf{E} = E_0\hat{\mathbf{a}}_x$

8.14

Let's start with Eq. 8.6.6

$$\gamma(\nu) = A_{21}\frac{\lambda^2}{8\pi}[N_2^0 - (g_2/g_1)N_1^0]\frac{\Delta\nu_h}{\Delta\nu_H}\times[\text{bracket}];\ \text{where } \Delta\nu_H = \Delta\nu_h[1 + I/I_s]^{1/2}$$

$$[\text{bracket}] = \left[\frac{1}{2\pi}\right]^2 \int_0^{\infty} \frac{\Delta\nu_D}{(f-\nu_0)^2 + (\Delta\nu_D/2)^2} \cdot \frac{\Delta\nu_H}{(\nu - f)^2 + (\Delta\nu_H/2)^2} df$$

Rewrite by multiplying and dividing by $2/\pi\Delta\nu_D$

$$\gamma(\nu) = A_{21} \frac{\lambda^2}{8\pi}\left(N_2^0 - \frac{g_2}{g_1} N_1^0\right) \frac{2}{\pi\Delta\nu_D} \cdot \text{"}\left\{\frac{\Delta\nu_h}{\Delta\nu_H}\right\}\text{"}$$

$$\times \int_0^{\infty} \frac{(\Delta\nu_D/2)^2}{(f - \nu_0)^2 + (\Delta\nu_D/2)^2} \frac{2}{\pi\Delta\nu_H} \frac{(\Delta\nu_H/2)^2}{(\nu - f)^2 + (\Delta\nu_H/2)^2} df$$

Make the substitutions suggested and identify $\gamma_0(\nu_0)$ and the inhomogeneous saturation law

$$\gamma_0(\nu_0) \text{"}\left\{\frac{1}{(1 + I/I_s)^{1/2}}\right\}\text{"} = \text{Top line of above}$$

$$\gamma(\nu) = \frac{\gamma_0(\nu_0)}{(1 + I/I_s)^{1/2}} \cdot \frac{1}{\pi b} \int_{-\infty}^{+\infty} \frac{a^2 b^2 \quad dx}{(x^2 + a^2)\,[(x + \delta)^2 + b^2]}$$

Follow same procedure as used in Problem 7.2 to find:

$$\gamma(\nu) = \frac{\gamma_0(\nu_0)}{(1 + I/I_s)^{1/2}} \cdot \frac{1 + [b/a]}{[\delta/a]^2 + [1 + (b/a)]^2}$$

where $\delta = (\nu_0 - \nu)$; $a = \Delta\nu_D/2$; $b = \Delta\nu_H/2$; $\Delta\nu_H = \Delta\nu_h[1 + I/I_s]^{1/2}$; substituting yields the given relationship. The following graph shows that the saturated gain coefficient falls between the extreme inhomogeneous limit and the homogeneous one.

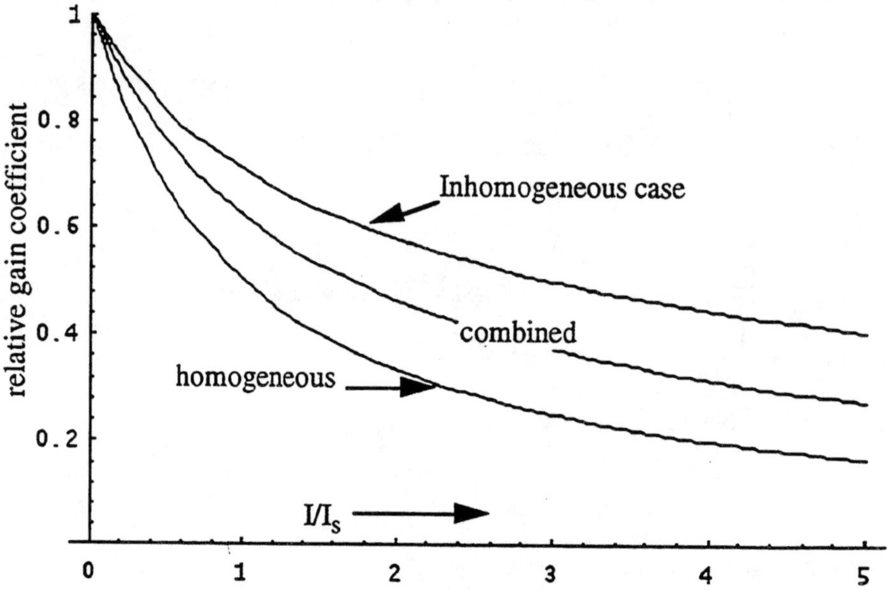

Figure for Problem 8.14

8.15

$$\sigma = A_{21}\frac{\lambda^2}{8\pi}\left[g(\nu_0) = \frac{2}{\pi\Delta\nu}\right] = 7.25\times10^{-12}\ \text{cm}^2;\ \gamma_{th} = \frac{1}{2l_g}\ln\frac{1}{R_1R_2} = 1.217\times10^{-2}\ \text{cm}^{-1}$$

$$N_2 - \frac{g_2}{g_1}N_1 = 1.68\times10^{+9}\ \text{cm}^{-3};$$

$$\frac{dN_2}{dt} = 0 = -\frac{\sigma I_p}{h\nu_p}\left(N_2 - \frac{g_2}{g_1}N_0\right) - A_2N_2 \text{ where } A_2 = A_{21}+A_{20}$$

$$\text{or } N_2 = \frac{(g_2/g_0)(\sigma I_p/h\nu)N_0}{A_2 + (\sigma I_p/h\nu_p)}; \qquad \frac{dN_1}{dt} = 0 = A_{21}N_2 - \frac{N_1}{\tau_1};\ N_1 = (A_{21}\tau_1)N_2;$$

$$N_0 = \frac{\left(A_2 + \frac{\sigma I_p}{h\nu}\right)[N]}{A_2 + \left[1 + \frac{g_2}{g_0}(1 + A_{21}\tau_1)\right]\frac{\sigma I_p}{h\nu} = D}; \qquad [N] = 10^{14}\ \text{cm}^{-3} = N_0+N_1+N_2;$$

$$N_1 = \frac{g_2}{g_1}\frac{\sigma I_p}{h\nu}\frac{[N]}{D}; \qquad N_2 = \frac{(A_{21}\tau_1)\frac{g_2}{g_0}\frac{\sigma I_p}{h\nu}[N]}{D}$$

$$\therefore\left[N_2 - \frac{g_2}{g_1}N_1\right] = \frac{\frac{g_2}{g_0}\frac{\sigma I_p}{h\nu}\left[1 - \frac{g_2}{g_1}A_{21}\tau_1\right][N]}{D} = \Delta N = 1.68\times10^{+9}\ \text{cm}^{-3} \text{ from (b)}$$

Solve for I_p; $g_2 = 1, g_1 = 3, g_0 = 5$; For $A_{21}\tau_1 = 2$ then $1 - \frac{g_2}{g_1}A_{21}\tau_1 = \frac{1}{3}$

$$\frac{\sigma I_p}{h\nu}\left\{\frac{1}{3}\frac{g_2}{g_0} - \frac{\Delta N}{[N]}\left[1 + \frac{g_2}{g_0}(1 + A_{21}\tau_1)\right]\right\} = \frac{\Delta N}{[N]}A_2;$$ The ratio $\frac{\Delta N}{[N]}$ is very small in { };

$$\therefore \qquad I_p = \frac{h\nu}{\sigma}A_2\cdot\frac{\Delta N}{N}\cdot\frac{3g_0}{g_2} = 2.14\ \text{watts/cm}^2$$

8.16

$$\int g(\nu)d\nu = 1 = K\cdot 0.6\ \text{GHz} + \frac{K}{2}\times 0.8\ \text{GHz};\ \text{(a) } K = 10^{-9}\ \text{sec}^{-1} = g(\nu_0)$$

(b) $\sigma = A_{21}\frac{\lambda_2{}^0}{8\pi n^2}g(\nu_0) = 2.85\times10^{-14}\ \text{cm}^2$

If you obtained $\sigma = 4.8\times10^{-14}\ \text{cm}^2$, you forgot the index n

(c) $\tau_p = \frac{2d_1/c + 2nd_2/c}{1 - R_1R_2T^4} = 18$ ns;

(d) $\mathbf{E} = \mathbf{E}_0\,\hat{a}_x$ the polarization with the minimum loss

(e) $\gamma_{th} = \frac{1}{2l}\ln\frac{1}{R_1R_2T^4} = 6.35\times10^{-2}\ \text{cm}^{-1}$

$$\therefore\left(N_2 - \frac{g_2}{g_1}N_1\right) = 2.23\times10^{+12}\ \text{cm}^{-3};\ N_1 = 10^{12}\ \text{cm}^{-3};\ \frac{g_2}{g_1} = \frac{3}{5};\ N_2 = 2.83\times10^{+12}\ \text{cm}^{-3}$$

8.17

If $R_2 = 0; \frac{dN_3}{dt} = R_3 - \frac{N_3}{\tau_3}; N_3 = R_3\tau_3; \frac{dN_1}{dt} = \frac{N_3}{\tau_{31}} - \frac{N_1}{\tau_1};$

$$\therefore N_1 = \frac{\tau_1}{\tau_{31}} N_3 = R_3 \frac{\tau_3}{\tau_{32}} \tau_1; \ \gamma_0 (\lambda_{31}) = R_3\tau_3 \left(1 - \frac{\tau_1}{\tau_{32}}\right)\sigma_{31}$$

$$\frac{dN_2}{dt} = R_2 - \frac{\sigma I_2}{h\nu_2}(N_2 - N_1) = 0; \ \frac{dN_1}{dt} = \frac{N_3}{\tau_3} - \frac{N_1}{\tau_1} + \frac{\sigma I_2}{h\nu}(N_2 - N_1) = 0;$$

$$\frac{\sigma I}{h\nu}(N_2 - N_1) = \frac{N_1}{\tau_1} - \frac{N_3}{\tau_3} = \frac{N_1}{\tau_1} - R_3\frac{\tau_3}{\tau_{32}}; \therefore R_2 = \frac{\sigma I}{h\nu}(N_2 - N_1) = \frac{N_1}{\tau_1} - R_3\frac{\tau_3}{\tau_{32}};$$

$$\therefore N_1 = R_2\tau_1 + R_3\frac{\tau_3}{\tau_{32}}; \ \gamma_0(\lambda_{31}) = \left\{R_3\tau_3\left(1 - \frac{\tau_1}{\tau_{32}}\right) - R_2\tau_1\right\}\sigma_{31}$$

8.18

For 13 dB gain, $G_0 = 20 = \exp[g_0 l_g] = 20$ or $\gamma_0 l_g = 2.996 \approx 3$

$\ln\frac{I_2}{I_1} + \frac{I_1}{I_s}\left(\frac{I_2}{I_1} - 1\right) = \gamma_0 l_g$ where $I_1 = 5\text{W/cm}^2$ and $I_2 = 30\text{W/cm}^2$; $\therefore \frac{I_2}{I_1} = 6$

$$\frac{I_1}{I_s} = \frac{\gamma_0 l_g - \ln\frac{I_2}{I_1}}{\frac{I_2}{I_1} - 1} = \frac{3 - \ln 6}{6 - 1} = 0.242; \text{ Thus } I_s = 20.7 \text{ W/cm}^2;$$

$I_{(extractable)} = \gamma_0 l_g \cdot I_s = 60 \text{ W/cm}^2$

8.19

$$\Delta\nu = \frac{1 - G_3(R_1R_2)^{1/2}}{\pi[G_3(R_1R_2)^{1/2}]} \cdot \frac{c}{2d}; \ G_5{}^2R_1R_2 = 1 - 9.94\times10^{-7}; \ G_s\sqrt{R_1}\,R_2 = 1 - 4.97\times10^{-7}$$

$$\Delta\nu_{osc} = \frac{4.97\times10^{-7}}{\pi[1]} \cdot 300\times10^{+6} = 47 \text{ Hz}$$

8.20

The frequency dependence of ASE is given by:

$$I(\nu, z = l_g) = \left\{\frac{8\pi h\nu^3}{c^2}\ \frac{N_2}{N_2 - (g_2/g_1)N_1}\right\}\{\exp[\gamma_0(\nu)l_g] - 1\}\frac{d\Omega}{4\pi} \text{ (See Eq. 8.7.3a)}$$

The major frequency dependence is contained in $\exp[\gamma_0(\nu)l_g] - 1$;

$$\gamma_0(\nu)l_g = \gamma_0(\nu_0)l_g \frac{(\Delta\nu/2)^2}{(\nu-\nu_0)^2 + (\Delta\nu/2)^2}; \text{ Let } \varepsilon(\nu) = |\exp[\gamma_0(\nu)l_g] - 1|; \ \delta = \frac{\nu-\nu_0}{\Delta\nu/2}$$

Find a value of δ such that : $\exp\left[\frac{\gamma_0(\nu_0)l_g}{1+\delta^2}\right] - 1 = \frac{1}{2}[\exp[\gamma_0(\nu_0)l_g - 1]$

$$\delta^2 = \left\{\frac{|\gamma_0(\nu_0)l_g|}{\ln\left[\frac{1+\exp[\gamma(\nu_0)l_g]}{2}\right]}\right\} - 1 = \frac{|\ln G_0|}{\ln\left[\frac{1+G_0}{2}\right]} - 1;\ \text{where } G_0 = \exp[\gamma_0 l_g]$$

$G_0(dB) = 10\log_{10}\exp\gamma_0 l_g = 4.343(\gamma_0 l_g)$; This leads to:

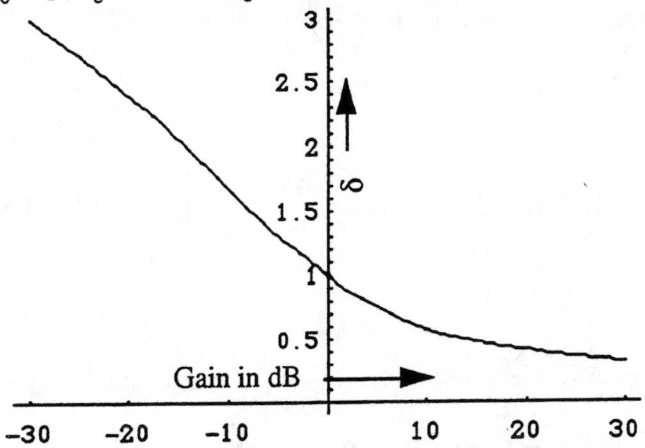

Notice that the broadening is significant when a "normal" population, i.e. an absorptive one is present. Thus lamps, such as sodium vapor arc lamps, radiate a over a significant part of the spectrum even though the D lines originate from only two excited states.

8.21

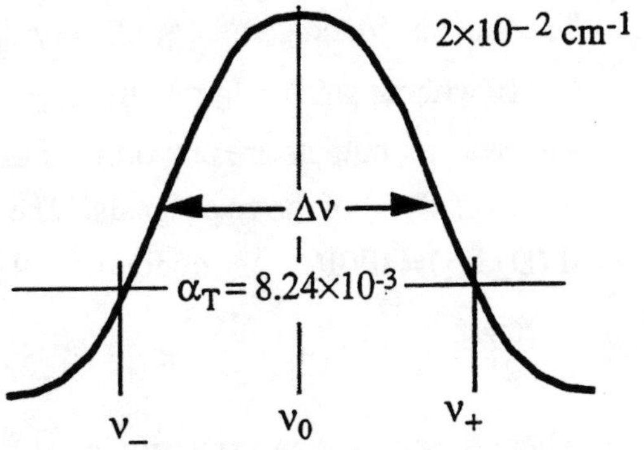

(a) $\tau_p = \frac{3d/c}{1 - R_1R_2R_3T_1T_2T_L^2} = 22.8$ ns

(b) $\Delta\omega\tau_p = 1$; $\omega = 2\pi c/\lambda_0$;

$Q = \omega/\Delta\omega; \therefore Q = 7.17\times10^{+7}$? 53.6×10^6

(c) FSR = c/3d = 200 MHz

(d) RTG = 1 for threshold

$R_1R_2R_3T_1T_2T_2^2\exp[\gamma_0(\nu_0)l_g] = 1$

$\therefore \gamma_{th}(\nu_0) = \alpha_T = 8.24^{-3}$ cm^{-1}

(e) $$\gamma_0(\nu_0)\frac{(\Delta\nu/2)^2}{(\nu\pm - \nu_0)^2 + \left(\frac{\Delta\nu_n}{2}\right)^2} = \alpha_T \;\therefore\; (\nu\pm - \nu_0) = \pm\left(\frac{\gamma_0(\nu_0)}{\alpha_T} - 1\right)^{1/2}\left(\frac{\Delta\nu_h}{2}\right)$$

$$\therefore\; \nu_+ - \nu_- = \left(\frac{\gamma(\nu_0)}{\alpha} - 1\right)^{1/2}\Delta\nu_h = 1.195\,\Delta\nu_h;\ N = \frac{\nu_+ - \nu_-}{c/3d} = 8.9;\ \text{i.e., 8 or 9 modes}$$

(f) $$\sigma = A_{21}\frac{\lambda_2^0}{8\pi}\left[g(\nu_0) = \frac{2}{\pi\Delta\nu_h}\right] = 6.08\times10^{-15}\ \text{cm}^2;$$

(g) $\sigma_{abs} = \frac{g_2}{g_1}\sigma_{SE} = \frac{3}{5}\sigma_{SE} = 3.65\times10^{-15}\ \text{cm}^2$

h(1) $z = 0$ at top Mirror;

h(2) RTPS = $q\cdot2\pi$; (double the phase shift from z=0 to the lens)

$$2\cdot\left(\frac{2\pi\nu}{c}\right)\frac{3d}{2} - 2(1+m+p)\tan^{-1}\frac{3d}{2z_0} = q\cdot2\pi \text{ or } \nu_{m,p,q} = \frac{c}{3d}\left\{q + \frac{1+m+p}{\pi}\tan^{-1}\frac{3d}{2z_0}\right\}$$

h(3) $\nu_{1,0,q} - \nu_{0,0,q} = \frac{c}{3d}\left\{\frac{1}{\pi}\tan^{-1}\frac{3d}{2z_0}\right\} = 58.04$ MHz

8.22

$$\int g(\nu)\,d\nu = 1;\ \text{Area} = g(\nu_0)\left\{\frac{1}{2}\Delta\nu + \frac{\Delta\nu}{2} + \frac{\Delta\nu}{4}\right\} = g(\nu_0)\cdot(5/4)\,\Delta\nu;\ \therefore\ g(\nu_0) = \frac{4}{5\Delta\nu}$$

8.23

$N_1 = 0$; $\frac{dN_2}{dt} = R - \frac{N_2}{\tau_2}$; $N_2 = R\tau_2$; $(N_2 - N_1)\sigma = 0.05\ \text{cm}^{-1}$; $\therefore$ $N_2 = 3.85\times10^{+15}\ \text{cm}^{-3}$;

$R_2 = 3.85\times10^{+22}\ \text{cm}^3\text{–sec} = R_1 = R_2$ (given); $h\nu/e = 3.7 - 1.2 = 2.5$ eV

$\frac{\text{Power}}{\text{Volume}} = (3.7 + 1.2) \times 1.6\times10^{-19} \times 3.85\times10^{+22} = 30.15\ \text{kW/cm}^3$;

$I_s = h\nu/\sigma\tau = 0.31\ \text{MW/cm}^2$

8.24

Define $\omega^2 = 4\ln2\,[(\nu - \nu_0)/\Delta\nu_s]^2$, a frequency normalized to the linewidth of the soure ;

The line integrated gain is: $\gamma(\omega)l_g = \gamma_0 l_g e^{-\omega^2}$; where γ_0 is the value at $\omega=0$;

Let I_1(without gain) = $I_0 e^{-\omega^2}$ then I_2(with gain) = $I_1 e^{\gamma(\omega)l_g}$;

The detector outputs are proportional to the integral over frequency band pass of the detectors (~ ∞) of the two signals. The apparent "gain" is the ratio of the two signals:

\F(D_2,D_1) = \F(\I(, ,)$I_2(\omega)d\omega$,\I(, ,)$I_1(\omega)d\omega$) = \F(\I(, ,)$e^{-\omega^2}$\b\bc\{(1 + $(\gamma_0 l_g)e^{-\alpha^2\omega^2}$ $+ \frac{(\gamma_0 l_g)^2}{2!}e^{-2\alpha^2\omega^2} + \frac{(\gamma_0 l_g)^3}{3!}e^{-3\alpha^2\omega^2}$ +..)$d\omega$, $\int e^{-\omega^2}d\omega$)

where the brace is an expansion of $e^{\gamma(\omega)l_g}$ using $\gamma(\omega)l_g = (\gamma_0 l_g)e^{-\omega^2}$. The numerator can be integrated term by term to yield:

$$\text{"Gain"} = \frac{D_2}{D_1} = \left\{1 + \frac{(\gamma_0 l_g)}{1!\sqrt{1+\alpha^2}} + \frac{(\gamma_0 l_g)^2}{2!\sqrt{1+2\alpha^2}} + \frac{(\gamma_0 l_g)^3}{3!\sqrt{1+3\alpha^2}} + \ldots\right\}$$

This series can be summed rather easily with the results given on the graph below. Note that the quantity $D_2/D_1 - 1$ is shown rather than the ratio.

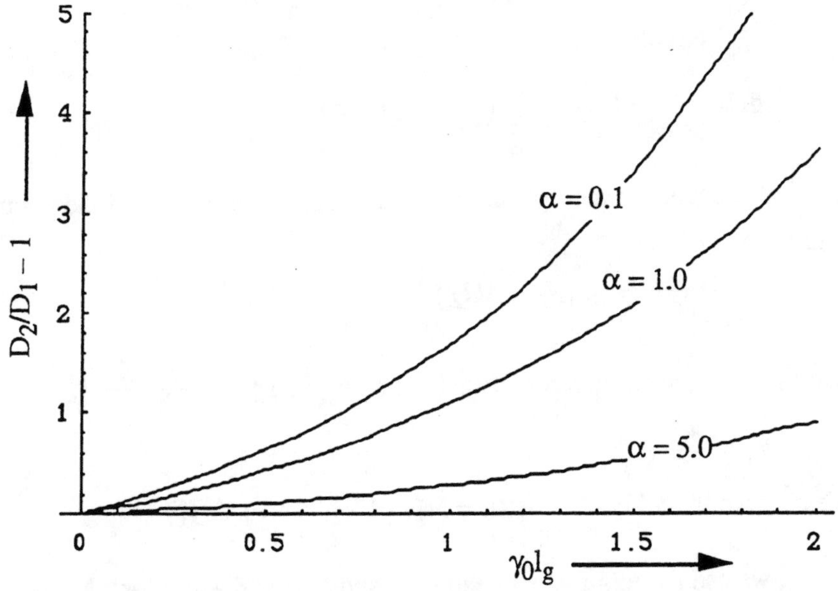

8.25

Lets start with the rate equations in the presence of stimulated emission on the 2-1 route.

$$\frac{dN_2}{dt} = P_2 - \frac{N_2}{\tau_2} - \frac{\sigma I}{h\nu}[N_2 - N_1] \quad (1); \qquad \frac{dN_1}{dt} = \frac{N_2}{\tau_{21}} - \frac{\sigma I}{h\nu}[N_2 - N_1] - \frac{N_1}{\tau_1} \quad (2)$$

which is the same as in Sec 8.3 except for the absence of pumping to the lower state. Now use 1 and 2 to express the steady-state populations in the presence of the stimulating intensity.

$$N_2 = \frac{P_2[\tau_2 + \tau_1(I/I_{s'})]}{1 + I/I_s} \quad (3); \qquad N_1 = \frac{P_2[\tau_1\phi_{21} + \tau_1(I/I_{s'})]}{1 + I/I_s} \quad (4)$$

where $I_{s'}$ is the approximate expression for the saturation intensity and that without the apostrophe is the more precise value.

$$I_s^{-1} = \frac{\sigma\tau_2}{h\nu}[1 + (\tau_1/\tau_2) - (\tau_1/\tau_{21})] \quad (5) \quad \text{and } I_{s'} = \frac{\sigma\tau_2}{h\nu} \quad (6)$$

From Eqns 3 and 4 and the above definitions, one can determine the unsaturated values of the populations and the steady state changes due to stimulated emission.

$$N_2^0 = P_2\tau_2 \quad (7); \qquad N_1^0 = P_1\tau_1\phi_{21} \quad (8); \qquad \Delta N_2 = \frac{P_2\tau_2(I/I_{s'})[1 - (\tau_1/\tau_{21})]}{1 + (I/Is)} \quad (9)$$

$$\Delta N_1 = \frac{P_2\tau_1(I/I_{s'})[1 - (\tau_1/\tau_{21})(1 - \tau_2/\tau_{21})]}{1 + (I/Is)} \quad (10)$$

The relationship between the steady-state changes in populations is:

$$\Delta N_1 = (\tau/\tau_2)\ (1 - \tau_2/\tau_{21})\ )\Delta N_2 \quad (11)$$

Now return to the differential equations and evaluate the rate of change of the populations at t=0 where $N_2(t=0)$ is equal to $N_2^0 - \Delta N_2$ and $N_1 = N_1^0 + \Delta N_1$.

$$\frac{dN_2}{dt}\text{(at t=0)} = [P_2 - \frac{N_2^0}{\tau_2}] + \frac{\Delta N_2}{\tau_2} \qquad (12);$$

$$\frac{dN_1}{dt}\text{(at t=0)} = [\frac{N_2^0}{\tau_2} - \frac{N_1^0}{\tau_1}] - \frac{\Delta N_2}{\tau_{21}} - \frac{\Delta N_1}{\tau_1} \qquad (13)$$

The first brackets on the right are zero, thus the rate of change of the population difference is given by:

$$\frac{d(N_2 - N_1)}{dt}\text{(at t=0)} = \Delta N_2 [\frac{1}{\tau_2} + \frac{1}{\tau_{21}}] + \Delta N_1 \frac{1}{\tau_1} \qquad (14)$$

Use the relationship given by Eq. 11 for ΔN_1 in 14: $\frac{d(N_2 - N_1)}{dt}\Big|_{\text{(at t=0)}} = \frac{2\Delta N_2}{\tau_2}$

(15)

We observe that: $N_2(0) - N_1(0) = N_2^0 - \Delta N_2 - [N_1^0 + \Delta N_1]$ (16)

Again, we use the relation between ΔN_2 and ΔN_1 and solve for ΔN_2 in terms of the difference of the unsaturated and saturated population inversion.

$$\Delta N_2 = \frac{\tau_2}{\tau_2 + \tau_1(1-\phi)} \{[N_2^0 - N_1^0] - [N_2(0) - N_1(0)]\} \qquad (17)$$

$$\frac{d(N_2 - N_1)}{dt}\text{(at t=0)} = \frac{2}{\tau_2 + \tau_1(1-\phi)} \{[N_2^0 - N_1^0] - [N_2(0) - N_1(0)]\} \qquad (18)$$

The pre-factor to the braces is the inverse of the slope as specified on the sketch.

$$\tau = \frac{\tau_2 + \tau_1(1-\phi)}{2} \qquad (20)$$

The above avoids the exercise of solving the differential equations which are not all that difficult but do involve long expressions and errors are easy to make. The solution for $N_2(t)$ is very easy and is given by:

$$N_2(t) = N_2^0 - \Delta N_2 \exp[-t/\tau_2] \qquad (21)$$

One has to recognize that the solution for $N_1(t)$ involves both a homogeneous part and a particular solution reflecting the fact that the source for N_1 is a time varying N_2. The functional form of the solution is given by:

$$N_1(t) = A + B \exp[-t/\tau_2] + C \exp[-t/\tau_1] \qquad (22)$$

where the boundary or initial condition is: $N_1(0) = N_1^0 - \Delta N_1$ (23)

Obviously, $A = N_1^0$ and B is given by the particular part of the solution:

$$B = -\frac{\tau_1\tau_2}{\tau_{21}(\tau_2 - \tau_1)}\Delta N_2 \qquad (24);$$

The C coefficient is evaluated by applying the initial value condition Eq.23.

$$C = \Delta N_1 + \frac{\tau_1\tau_2}{\tau_{21}(\tau_2 - \tau_1)}\Delta N_2 \qquad (25)$$

8.26

$h\nu/e = 1.38$ eV; $\nu_0 = 3.34\times10^{+14}$Hz; $\lambda_0 = 8984$Å; $h\Delta\nu/e = 0.53$ eV; $\Delta\nu = 12.8$ THz;

$\int g(\nu)d\nu = 1 = \frac{1}{2}[12.8\times10^{+12}s^{-1} = \text{base}]\cdot[g(\nu_0) = \text{height}]$; $g(\nu_0) = 7.8\times10^{-14}$ sec.;

$\sigma = \frac{1}{\tau_{sp}}\frac{\lambda_0^2}{8\pi n^2}g(\nu_0) = 3.86\times10^{-16}$ cm^2; $\gamma_{th} = \frac{1}{2l_g}\ln(1/R^2) = 3.86\times10^{-16}\Delta N$;

$\Delta N = 6.55\times10^{+16}$ cm^{-3}; $\tau_p = \frac{2nd/c}{1 - R^2} = 12.03$ ps.

8.27

$\frac{dN_2}{dt} = -A_{21}N_2 - \frac{\sigma I}{h\nu}[N_2 - (g_2/g_1)N_1]$; If $I\to\infty$, $N_2 = g_2/g_1 N_1 = 2N_1$;

$N_2 + N_1 = N_0$; $\therefore$ $2N_1 + N_1 = N_0$; $\therefore$ $N_1 = N_0/3$; $N_2 = 2/3N_0$;

If $N_2 = 1/4\ N_0$, then $N_1 = 3/4\ N_0$ (by conservation of atoms);

$(A_{21} + \frac{\sigma I}{h\nu})N_2 = \frac{g_2\sigma I}{g_1 h\nu}N_1$ or $(A_{21} + \frac{\sigma I}{h\nu})\frac{1}{4}N_0 = 2\frac{\sigma I}{h\nu}\cdot\frac{3}{4}N_0$

$(A_{21} + \sigma I/h\nu) = 6\sigma I/h\nu$ or $\frac{5\sigma I}{h\nu} = A_{21} = 1/\tau_{21}$ or $I = \frac{1}{5}\cdot\frac{h\nu}{\sigma\tau_{21}} = 2.84$ W/cm^2

8.28

(a) $\frac{dN_2}{dt} = \frac{\sigma I_p}{h\nu}[N_2 - (g_2/g_0)N_0] - \frac{N_2}{\tau_2}$; $\frac{dN_1}{dt} = \frac{N_2}{\tau_{21}} - \frac{N_1}{\tau_1}$; $N_1 + N_2 + N_0 = [N]$;

(b),(c) For d/dt =0, we obtain: $N_2 = \frac{(g_2/g_0)I_p/I_s}{1 + I_p/I_s}N_0$; $N_1 = \frac{\tau_1}{\tau_{21}}N_2 = \frac{\tau_1}{\tau_{21}}\frac{(g_2/g_0)I_p/I_s}{1 + I_p/I_s}N_0$

We must conserve atoms: $N_0 + N_1 + N_2 = N$, the original density of active atoms. Substituting the above and solve for N_0.

$$N_0 = \frac{(1 + I_p/I_s)}{1 + (I_p/I_s)[1 + (g_2/g_0)(1 + \tau_1/\tau_{21})]}N \quad \underset{\text{large pump}}{\rightarrow} \quad \frac{1}{[1 + (g_2/g_0)(1 + \tau_1/\tau_{21})]}N$$

$$N_2 = \frac{(g_2/g_0)(I_p/I_s)}{1 + (I_p/I_s)[1 + (g_2/g_0)(1 + \tau_1/\tau_{21})]}N \qquad \frac{g_2/g_1}{[1 + (g_2/g_0)(1 + \tau_1/\tau_{21})]}N$$

$$N_1 = \frac{(\tau_1/\tau_2)(g_2/g_0)(I_p/I_s)}{1 + (I_p/I_s)[1 + (g_2/g_0)(1 + \tau_1/\tau_{21})]}N \qquad \frac{(\tau_1/\tau_2)(g_2/g_0)}{[1 + (g_2/g_0)(1 + \tau_1/\tau_{21})]}$$

N

$$N_2 - (g_2/g_1)N_1 = \frac{g_2}{g_1}\frac{I_p}{I_s}\frac{[1 - (g_2/g_1)(\tau_1/\tau_{21})]}{1 + (I_p/I_s)[1 + (g_2/g_0)(1 + \tau_1/\tau_{21})]}$$

(c) If $I_p \to \infty$; $N_2 = \frac{g_2}{g_0}N_0$; and $N_1 = \frac{\tau_1}{\tau_{21}}N_2$ always;

The maximum gain is the limit of the above expression as $I_p \to \infty$,

$$N_2 - (g_2/g_1)N_1 = \frac{g_2}{g_1}\frac{[1 - (g_2/g_1)(\tau_1/\tau_{21})]}{[1 + (g_2/g_0)(1 + \tau_1/\tau_{21})]}$$

8.29

$$\frac{dN_3}{dt} = \frac{\sigma I_p}{h\nu_p}(N_0 - N_3) - \frac{N_3}{\tau_{32}} - \frac{N_3}{\tau_{30}} = 0;$$

$$\frac{dN_2}{dt} = \frac{N_3}{\tau_{32}} - \frac{N_2}{\tau_{21}} = 0; \frac{dN_1}{dt} = \frac{N_2}{\tau_{21}} - \frac{N_1}{\tau_{10}} = 0; N_0 = N_3 \text{ if } I_p \to 0;$$

$N_2 = (\tau_{21}/\tau_{32})\, N_3 = (\tau_{21}/\tau_{32})\, N_0$; $N_1 = (\tau_{10}/\tau_{21})\, N_2 = (\tau_{10}/\tau_{21})\, N_0$;

$$N_0 + (\tau_{21}/\tau_{32})N_0 + (\tau_{10}/\tau_{21})N_0 + N_0 = N; \therefore N_0 = \frac{N}{(2 + \tau_{21}/\tau_{32} + \tau_{10}/\tau_{21})};$$

$$N_2 - N_1 = \left[\frac{\tau_{21}}{\tau_{32}} - \frac{\tau_{10}}{\tau_{21}}\right]N_0 = \frac{[\tau_{21}/\tau_{32} - \tau_{10}/\tau_{21}]\, N}{(2 + \tau_{21}/\tau_{32} + \tau_{10}/\tau_{21})}$$

8.30

$$\frac{1}{I}\frac{dI}{dz} = \frac{\gamma_0 e^{-\alpha z}}{(1 + I/I_s)};$$ Let $y = I/I_s$ as before $$\int_{I_2}^{I_1} \frac{(1 + y)}{y}\, dy = \int_{l_g}^{0} \gamma_0\, e^{-\alpha z}\, dz;$$

$$\therefore \quad \ln\frac{I_2}{I_1} + \frac{I_2 - I_1}{I_s} = \gamma_0 \frac{e^{-\alpha z}}{-\alpha}\Big|_0^{l_g} = \gamma_0 \frac{(1 - e^{-\alpha l_g})}{\alpha};$$

For maximum extractable power $I_2 \to I_1$ and the log term $\to 0$;

$$I_2 = I_1 + \gamma_0 I_s \frac{(1 - e^{-\alpha l_g})}{\alpha}$$

8.31

(a) $e^{\gamma_0 l_g} = 200$ (i.e. 23 dB gain); $\therefore$ $\gamma_0 l_g = 5.30$ or

$\gamma_0 = 5.298 \times 10^{-2}\ \text{cm}^{-1} = (N_2 - N_1)\sigma$; Thus $N_2 - N_1 = 5.29 \times 10^{+17}\ \text{cm}^3$;

(b) $R_1 R_2 e^{2\gamma_0 l_g} < 1$; $R_1 R_2 < 2.5 \times 10^{-5}$;

(c) $\ln(I_2/I_1) + (I_1/I_s)(I_2/I_1 - 1) = \gamma_0 l_g$;

with $I_s = h\nu/\sigma\tau_2 = 9.8 \times 10^{+3}\ \text{W/cm}^2$ and $I_2/I_1 = 100$;

$\therefore I_1/I_s = (5.298 - 4.605)/99 = 7.001 \times 10^{-3}$ $\therefore I_1 = 68.9\ \text{W/cm}^2$

8.32

(a) If $\gamma_0 = 0$, then $\frac{dI}{dz} = -\alpha I$ or $I_2 = I_1 e^{-\alpha l_g}$ or $T = \frac{I_2}{I_1} = e^{-\alpha l_g} = 0.85$; $\therefore \alpha l_g = 0.1625$.

For small signals, $I/I_s << 1$ or $\frac{dI}{dz} = (\gamma_0 - \alpha)I$; $\frac{I_2}{I_1} = e^{(\gamma_0 - \alpha)l_g} = 6.281 = G_0$;

$\therefore$ G_0 (in dB) = 7.98 dB;

If the intensity is such that $dI/dz = 0$, then we have a unity gain amplifier.

$\gamma_0/(1+I/I_s) - \alpha = 0$ or $I/I_s = \gamma_0/\alpha - 1 = 12.31 - 1 = 11.31$; $\therefore$ $I_1 < 181$ W/cm^2.

8.33

$$\frac{dN_3}{dt} = R_3 - \frac{N_3}{\tau_3} - \frac{\sigma I}{h\nu}N_3 + \frac{\sigma I}{h\nu}N_2 = R_3 - \frac{N_3}{\tau_3}\left(1 + \frac{I}{I_s}\right) + \frac{N_2}{\tau_3}\left(\frac{I}{I_s}\right)$$

$$\frac{dN_2}{dt} = \frac{N_3}{\tau_3}\left(1 + \frac{I}{I_s}\right) - \frac{N_2}{\tau_3}\left(\frac{I}{I_s}\right) - \frac{N_2}{\tau_2};$$

Adding the two equations: $\frac{d}{dt}(N_3 + N_2) = R_3 - \frac{N_2}{\tau_2}$

After all transients have died out, $N_2 = R_3\tau_2$ irrespective of whether the stimulating wave is present or not. What this indicates is that state 2 does not care whether it is populated by spontaneous or stimulated emission, it can only receive population from above. The assumption of N_2 in equilibrium with N_3 indicates that $dN_2/dt \approx 0$.

$$\therefore N_2\left[\frac{1}{\tau_3}\left(\frac{I}{I_s}\right) + \frac{1}{\tau_2}\right] = \frac{N_3}{\tau_3}\left[1 + \frac{I}{I_s}\right]; \quad N_2 = N_3\frac{\tau_2}{\tau_3}\frac{[1 + I/I_s]}{\left[1 + (\tau_2/\tau_3)\,(I/I_s)\right]} \approx N_3\frac{\tau_2}{\tau_3}(1 + I/I_s)$$

$$\therefore \frac{dN_3}{dt} = R_3 - \frac{N_3}{\tau_3}\left(1 + \frac{I}{I_s}\right) + \frac{N_3}{\tau_3}\left(\frac{\tau_2}{\tau_3}\right)\left(1 + \frac{I}{I_s}\right) = R_3 - \frac{N_3}{\tau_3}[(1 + I/I_s)\,(1 + \tau_2/\tau_3)]$$

or $$\frac{dN_3}{dt} + \frac{N_3}{\tau_3}\left[\left(1 + \frac{I}{I_s}\right)\left(1 + \frac{\tau_2}{\tau_3}\right)\right] \approx \frac{dN_3}{dt} + \frac{N_3}{\tau_3}\left[\left(1 + \frac{I}{I_s}\right)\right] = R_3$$

define $$\tau_s = \frac{\tau_3}{(1 + I/I_s)\,(1 + \tau_2/\tau_3)} \approx \frac{\tau_3}{1 + I/I_s}$$

If you know the steady state limits, then it is just a matter of connecting those limits by the appropriate time constants: $\tau = \tau_s$ for $0 < t < T$ and τ_3 for $t > T$.

$$\therefore N_3 = R_3\tau_3\left(\frac{1}{1 + I/I_s} - e^{-t/\tau_s}\right) \text{for } t < T; \quad N_3 = R_3\tau_3\left(1 - \frac{1}{1 + I/I_s}e^{-(t-T)/\tau_3}\right) \text{for } t > T$$

The fact that $\frac{d(N_3+N_2)}{dt} = R_3 - \frac{N_2}{\tau_2} \approx \frac{dN_3}{dt}$ indicates that: $N_2 = R_3\tau_2 - \frac{dN_3}{dt}$

Hence, when N_3 decreases (dN_3/dt is negative), N_2 will increase but return to $R_3\tau_2$. When dN_3/dt is positive, N_2 will decrease but return to $R_3\tau_2$, similar to the differentiation by an RC circuit. A sketch of the two populations and the spontaneous is shown below.

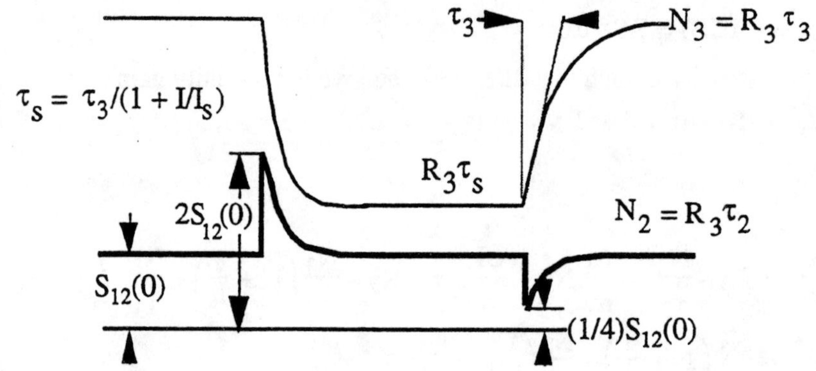

8.34

(a) $\frac{dN_3}{dt} = \frac{\sigma_p I_p}{h\nu}(N_0 - N_3) - \frac{N_3}{\tau_3}$ $\quad \frac{dN_2}{dt} = \frac{N_3}{\tau_3} - \frac{N_2}{\tau_2}$ $\quad \frac{dN_1}{dt} = 0.6\frac{N_2}{\tau_2} - \frac{N_1}{\tau_1}$

(b) For steady state; $N_3 = R_3\tau_3$; $N_2 = \frac{\tau_2}{\tau_3}N_3 = R_3\tau_2$; $N_1 = \frac{0.6\tau_1}{\tau_2}N_2$

For $N_2 = 10^{19}\ \text{cm}^{-3} = R_3\tau_3$ and $\tau_2 = 250\ \mu\text{sec}$:

$R_3 = 10^{19} \div 250 \times 10^{-6}\ \text{cm}^{-3}\text{sec}^{-1} = 4 \times 10^{+22}\ \text{cm}^{-3}\text{–sec}^{-1}$

Cost of pumping the upper state = 2eV per state;

$P = 2 \times 4 \times 10^{+22} \times 1.6 \times 10^{-19} = 12.8 \times 10^{+3}\ \text{W/cm}^3$

8.35

(a) $N_0 + N_1 + N_2 = [N] = N_0[1 + N_1/N_0 + N_2/N_0] = N_0(11/8)$

$\therefore N_0 = \frac{8}{11}[N] = 1.6 \times 10^{+20}\ \text{cm}^{-3}$; $N_1 = \frac{1}{4}N_0 = 4 \times 10^{+19}\ \text{cm}^{-3}$; $N_2 = 2 \times 10^{+19}\ \text{cm}^{-3}$

(b) $\alpha = (N_1 - N_2)\sigma = 2 \times 10^{+19} \times 3 \times 10^{-20} = 0.6\ \text{cm}^{-1}$

(c1) $\frac{dN_2}{dt} = R_2 - \left(\frac{N_2 - N_2^0}{\tau_2}\right)$ and $\frac{dN_1}{dt} = \left(\frac{N_2 - N_2^0}{\tau_2}\right) - \left(\frac{N_1 - N_1^0}{\tau_1}\right)$

(c2) For steady state: $N_2 - N_2^0 = R_2\tau_2$; $N_1 - N_1^0 = R_2\tau_1$;

$(N_2 - N_1) - N_2^0 \qquad N_1^0 = R_2(\tau_2 - \tau_1)$

For optical transparency: $\quad N_2 = N_1$; $R_2 = \frac{N_1^0 - N_2^0}{\tau_2 - \tau_1}$

(c3) Obviously $\tau_2 > \tau_1$ for the above to make sense or

$N_2 - N_1 = R_2(\tau_2 - \tau_1) - (N_1^0 - N_2^0)$; $(N_2 - N_1)\sigma = \gamma = R_2(\tau_2 - \tau_1)\sigma - (N_1^0 - N_2^0)\sigma$

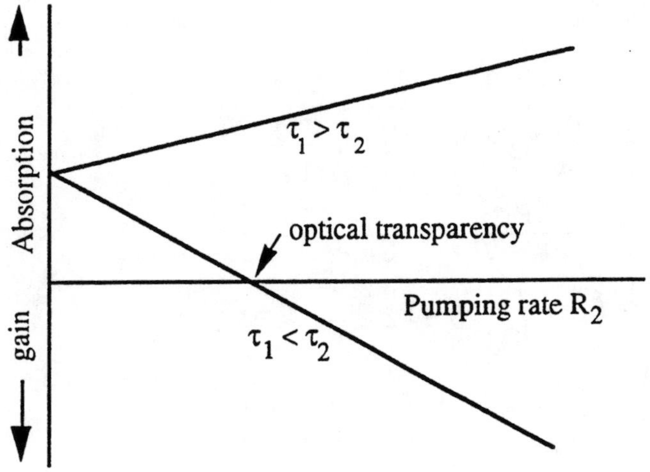

Figure for Problem 8.36

8.36

$$\frac{dN_a}{dt} = \frac{-N_a}{\tau_a} + r_{ba}N_b - r_{ab}N_a; \qquad \frac{dN_b}{dt} = \frac{-N_b}{\tau_b} - r_{ba}N_b - r_{ab}N_a$$

$$\frac{d(N_a + N_b)}{dt} = -(N_a + N_b)\left[\frac{N_a}{N_a + N_b}\frac{1}{\tau_a} + \frac{N_b}{N_a + N_b}\frac{1}{\tau_b}\right] = -\frac{(N_a + N_b)}{\tau_{eff}}$$

$$\frac{1}{\tau_{eff}} = \frac{N_a}{N_a + N_b}\frac{1}{\tau_a} + \frac{N_b}{N_a + N_b}\frac{1}{\tau_b} = \frac{1}{\tau_a}\left(\frac{1}{1 + N_b/N_a}\right) + \left(\frac{N_b/N_a}{1 + N_b/N_a}\right)\frac{1}{\tau_b}$$

$$= 10^3\left(\frac{1}{1 + 1/9}\right) + \left(\frac{1/9}{1 + 1/9}\right)10^4 = 10^3[0.9 + 1.0] = 1.9\times10^{+3}\ \text{sec}^{-1}$$

For T=600K, exp–ΔE/kT) = 1/3;

$$\frac{1}{\tau_{eff}} = 10^3\left(\frac{1}{1 + 1/3}\right) + \left(\frac{1/3}{1 + 1/3}\right)10^4 = 10^3\left(\frac{3}{4}\right) + \left(\frac{1}{4}\right)10^4 = 3.25\times10^3\ \text{sec}^{-1}$$

8.37

$\int g(\nu)d\nu = 1$; Hence; $1/2K\cdot3\times10^{+9} = 1$; $\therefore$ $K = 6.67\times10^{-10}$ sec; $\lambda_0 = 1/\bar{\nu} = 0.8\ \mu m$;

$\gamma_0 = 1/2l_g \ln(1/R_1R_2) = 3.19\times10^{-2}\ cm^{-1} = \sigma\Delta N$; $\sigma = A_{21}\frac{\lambda^2}{8\pi n^2}g(\nu_0) = 5.6\times10^{-14}\ cm^2$;

$\Delta N = 5.69\times10^{+11}\ cm^{-3}$

$$\frac{1.25}{3\times10^{+9}} = \frac{0.25}{x}$$

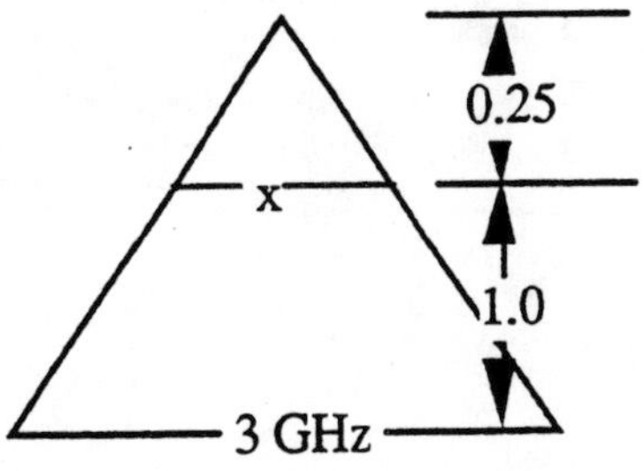

$x = 3\times10^{+9}\ 0.25/1.25 = 600$ MHz;

$k_0(d-l)) + k_0nl = q\pi$;

$\nu = c/2[nl+(d-l)]\cdot q$

Thus $\Delta\nu = c/2[nl+(d-l)] = 441$ MHz;

$\therefore$ 1 mode

8.38

$$\frac{dN_2}{dt} = P_2 - \frac{N_2}{\tau_2} - \frac{\sigma I}{h\nu} N_2 = P_2 - \frac{1}{\tau_2}\left(1 + \frac{\sigma \tau_2}{h\nu} I\right) N_2$$

(a) $\therefore \; N_2(\text{s.s.}) = \frac{P_2 \tau_2}{1 + I/I_s}; \; \therefore \; \frac{S_0}{S_1} = 1 + \frac{I}{I_s}$

(b) $\frac{dN_2}{dt} + \left[\frac{1}{\tau_2}\left(1 + \frac{I}{I_s}\right)\right] N_2 = P_2 \quad \therefore \; \tau_a = \frac{\tau_2}{1 + I/I_s}$

(c) $\frac{dN_2}{dt} + \frac{1}{\tau_2} N_2 = P_2 \quad \therefore \; \tau_b = \tau_2$

9.1

Given: $\lambda_0 = 6328$ Å; $\nu_0 = 4.743\times10^{+14}$ Hz ; T = 573 K;

(a) $\Delta\nu_D = \left[\frac{8kT}{Mc^2}\ln 2\right]^{1/2}\nu_0 = 1.81$ GHz

(b) $N_{B.B.} = \frac{8\pi\nu^2\Delta\nu}{c^3}V = 3.793\times10^{+18}$ modes;

(c) FSR = c/2d = 150 MHz; $N_L = \frac{1.809}{0.15} = 12$ (or 13) × 2 for both polarizations

(d) probability $= \frac{N_L}{N_{B.B.}} = 3.173\times10^{-8}$ (× 2 for two polarizations)

(e) E_2 = 166,658.484 $cm^{-1} \Rightarrow$ 20.66 eV; E_1 = 150,855.7$cm^{-1} \Rightarrow$ 18.70 eV

(f) $\eta_{Q.E.} = \frac{1.96}{20.66} = 9.47\%$;

(g) $g(\nu_0) = \left(\frac{4\ln 2}{\pi}\right)^{1/2}\frac{1}{\Delta\nu_D} = 5.193\times10^{-10}$ sec ; $\sigma = A_{21}\frac{\lambda^2}{8\pi}g(\nu_0) = 5.43\times10^{-13}$ cm^2

(using $A_{21} = 6.56\times10^{+6}$ sec^{-1})

(h) $[N_2 - (g_2/g_1) N_1]\,\sigma = 0.05$ m^{-1}; i.e.,5% $m^{-1} \Rightarrow 5\times10^{-4}$ cm^{-1}

$(N_2 - (g_2/g_1) N_1) = 9.22\times10^{+8}$ cm^{-3} ; $(g_2/g_1) = 3/5$;

$N_2 = 9.22\times10^{+8} + (3/5)N_1 = [9.22\times10^{+8} + 6\times10^9]$ $cm^{-3} = 6.92\times10^9$ cm^{-3}

Note: $N_1 > N_2$! but there is gain.

9.2

(a)

Transition	eV	THz	$\bar{\nu}$ (cm^{-1})	Å
2→0	3.4	823	27424	3646
2→1	2.3	556	18552	5390
1→0	1.1	266	8876	11271

(b) $\frac{1}{\tau_2} = (A_{21}+A_{20}) = 7\times10^{+7}$ sec^{-1} $\tau_2 = 14.3$ ns;

(c) $\phi_{21} = \frac{A_{21}}{A_{21}+A_{20}} = 0.71$; $\tau_1 = \frac{1}{A_{10}} = 10$ ns

(d) $N_2 = N_2(0)\exp[-t/\tau_2]$; $\frac{dN_1}{dt} = -\frac{N_1}{\tau_1} + A_{21}N_2$; $\frac{dN_1}{dt} + \frac{N_1}{\tau_1} = \frac{\phi_{21}}{\tau_2}N_2(0)\exp[-t/\tau_2]$

Homogeneous solution: $N_1 = A\exp[-t/\tau_1]$ Particular solution: $B\exp[-t/\tau_2]$

$\left(\frac{1}{\tau_1} - \frac{1}{\tau_2}\right)B = \frac{\phi_{21}}{\tau_2}N_2(0)$; $B = \frac{\phi_{21}}{\tau_2/\tau_1 - 1}N_2(0)$;

$N_1 = A\exp[-t/\tau_1] + \frac{\phi_{21}}{\tau_2/\tau_1 - 1}N_2(0)\exp[-t/\tau_2]$; at t = 0, $N_1 = 0$

$\therefore\ N_1 = \frac{\phi_{21}}{\tau_2/\tau_1 - 1}N_2(0)\,\{\exp[-t/\tau_2] - \exp[-t/\tau_1]\}$

(e) The pump must produce N_2 just as fast as it decays and it costs 3.4 eV to produce each upper state.

(1) Power = (3.4 eV)×(1.6×10^{-19}joule/eV)×($N_2 = 10^{14}$ cm^{-3})×(decay rate of state 2 = 1/14.2ns) = 3.84 kW/cm^3.

(2) A steady-state for N_1 is obtained when $A_{21}N_2 - (N_1/\tau_1) = 0$ and thus $N_1 = (A_{21}\tau_1)N_2 = 5\times10^{13}$ cm^{-3}.

(3) The power radiated spontaneouesly by the atoms in state 2 is given by: $P_{sponT} = h\nu_{21}A_{21}N_2 = 1.84$ kW/cm^3

(4) The quantum efficiency is $\eta_{qe} = (E_2 - E_1)/E_2 = 67.7\%$

9.3

$\mathbf{E} = E_0\mathbf{a_x}$ (yields min loss);

$$\frac{P_{out}}{T_2} = P_{inc} = \frac{1}{2}\frac{E_0^2}{\eta_0}\int_0^{\infty}\int_0^{2\pi} \exp\left[\frac{2r^2}{w^2}\right] r\,dr\,d\phi = \frac{1}{2}\frac{E_0^2}{\eta_0}\left(\frac{\pi w_0^2}{2}\right) = 80 \text{ watts}$$

Since R >> d, beam does not spread much over distance d; $\therefore E_0^+ = 979.8$ V/cm

9.4

(a) $\alpha l = 0.01$ (for 1 way); $\alpha = 2\times10^{-4}$ cm^{-1}; $R_1R_2\, e^{(\gamma-\alpha)2l_g} = 1$

$\gamma_{th} = \alpha + \frac{1}{2l_g}\ln\frac{1}{R_1R_2} = 1.456\times10^{-3}$ cm^{-1};$\gamma = \Delta N\sigma = 10^{14}\times10^{-16}$ cm^{-1} $= 10^{-2}$ cm^{-1}

$\therefore \frac{\Delta N}{\Delta N_t} = \frac{10^{-2}}{1.456^{-3}} = 6.87$; Follow the photons in space and time

– Space –	– Time –
$\frac{dI}{dz} = (\gamma-\alpha)I$	$\frac{dN_p}{dt} = \left\{\frac{G^2R_1R_2 - 1}{2d/c}\right\} N_p$
$I = I(0)\exp[(\gamma_0-\alpha)z]$	$G = \exp[(\gamma_0-\alpha)l_g] = 1.63$
$(\gamma_0-\alpha)z = \ln 10^5 = 11.51$	$\therefore\ \tau_p = 2.38$ nsec
or $z = \frac{11.51}{0.01 - 2^{-4}} = 1.17\times10^{+3}$ cm	$N_p \approx N_p(0)\exp[+t/\tau_p]$
$\Delta t = z/c = 39.2$ nsec	$\exp[t/\tau_p] = 10^5 \quad t \approx 11.51\times2.38$ t = 27.4 ns (close to the answer at the left)

(c) $I_s = \frac{h\nu}{\sigma\tau_2} = 1.99$ kW/cm^2; $\frac{I^+}{I_s} = \frac{1}{2}\left(\frac{\gamma_0}{\alpha_T} - 1\right) = 2.935$; $I^+ = 5840$ W/cm^2

$I_{out} = T_2 \cdot I^+ = 5.84$ W/cm^2

9.5

(a) $\tau_p = \frac{2d/c}{1 - R_1R_2} = 4.17$ nsec;

(b) $R_1R_2 \exp[2\gamma_0 l_g] = 1$; $\gamma = \Delta N\sigma = \frac{1}{2l_g} \ln \frac{1}{R_1R_2} \Delta N = 1.37\times10^{+16}$ cm^{-3}

(c) Since $I < I_s$, ignore saturation;;$G_0 = \exp[\gamma_0 l_g] = 7.39$ for $\Delta N = 2\times10^{17}$ cm^{-3};

Open up the cavity and follow the photons in space; $N_p(z) = N_p(0) \exp[(\gamma_0-\alpha)z]$;
$\gamma_0 = 0.2$ cm^{-1} ; $\alpha = 1.37\times10^{-2}$ cm^{-1}; Now $I_s = 20$ kW/cm^3 = $h\nu\cdot c\, N_{ps}$; ∴ N_{ps} = $2.41\times10^{+12}$ photons/cm^2

$$(\gamma_0-\alpha)l_g = \ln\left\{\frac{(1/2)\cdot 2.4\text{x}10^{12}}{10^8}\right\} = 9.4;\ \gamma_0 = 2\times10^{+17}\text{ cm}^{-3}\times10^{-18}\text{ cm}^2 = 0.2\text{ cm}^{-1}$$

$$\alpha = \frac{1}{2l_g}\ln\frac{1}{R_1R_2} = 1.37\times10^{-2}\text{ cm}^{-1};\quad (\gamma-\alpha) = 1.86\times10^{-1}\text{ cm}^{-1};\quad \therefore\ z = 50.46\text{ cm}$$

∴ $\Delta t = (z/c) = 1.68$ ns (the actual time is longer because saturation was neglected)

9.6.

$\exp[(\gamma_0-\alpha)l_g] = 4$ for a 6dB amplifier.; $(\gamma_0-\alpha)l_g = 1.386$; $(\gamma_0-\alpha) = 0.1386$ cm^{-1}
$\gamma_0 = 0.1486$ cm^{-1} (since $\alpha = 0.01$ cm^{-1}); $I_s = h\nu/\sigma\tau_2 = 8.49\times10^{+3}$ w/cm^2 ; $\nu = 395$ THz

$N_2 - g_2/g_1\, N_1 = 0.1486 \div 2\times10^{-20}$ cm^2 = $7.43\times10^{+18}$ cm^{-3}

$$\frac{dy}{dz} = \gamma_0 \frac{y}{1+y} - \alpha y \text{ where } y = \frac{I}{I_s};\ \frac{dy}{dz} = -\alpha y\frac{\{y - [(\gamma_0/\alpha) - 1]\}}{y};\ \text{Separate variables:}$$

$$\frac{(1+y)\,dy}{y^2 - [(\gamma/\alpha) - 1]\,y} = dz \text{ or } \left\{\frac{A}{y} + \frac{B}{y - [\gamma/(\alpha-1)]}\right\} = -\alpha\, dz$$

where: $A = -\frac{1}{(\gamma/\alpha) - 1}$; $B = \frac{1}{(\gamma/\alpha) - 1}$; let $m = \frac{\gamma_0}{\alpha} - 1 = 1.386$;

$$\int_{y_1}^{y_2} \frac{dy}{y - m} - \int_{y_1}^{y_2} \frac{dy}{y} = -(\gamma_0 - \alpha) \int_0^{l_g} dz\ \ \ln\left\{\frac{y_2 - m}{y_1 - m}\right\} - \ln\frac{y_2}{y_1} = -(\gamma_0 - \alpha)l_g;$$

Now $y_2 = \frac{I_2}{I_s} = 2\cdot y_1 = 2\cdot\frac{I_1}{I_s}$

$$\ln\left\{\frac{y_1y_2 - m}{y_2y_1 - m}\right\} = -(\gamma_0 - \alpha)l_g;\text{ or } \frac{1}{2}\cdot\left\{\frac{2y_1 - m}{y_1 - m}\right\} = \exp[-(\gamma_0 - \alpha)l_g] = 0.25$$

Solve for $y_1 = 4.62$; ∴ $I_1 = 39.2$ kW/cm^2

9.7

$\overline{\nu} = E_2 - E_1 = 19{,}581.1$ cm^{-1}; Thus $\lambda_0 = 5107$ Å i.e ($\nu = 587$ THz)and $\Delta\lambda = 0.0304$ Å
$g_2 = 2J_2+1 = 4$; $g_1 = 2J_1+1 = 6$; $g(\nu_0) = (2/\pi\Delta\nu)$;
$\sigma = (A_{21}\lambda_0^2/8\pi)\, g(\nu_0) = 6.42\times10^{-14}$ cm^2

$$\eta_{Q.E.} = \frac{E_2-E_1}{E_2} = 63.6\%;\ \gamma_0 l_g = \ln\left\{\frac{1}{R_1R_2R_3R_4T_{w1}T_{w2}}\right\};$$

$\gamma_0 = 2.72^{-2}\ cm^{-1}$; $\therefore\ \Delta N = 4.23\times10^{+11}\ cm^{-3}$;(g) $\mathbf{E} = E_0\hat{a}_x$ (max gain to loss)

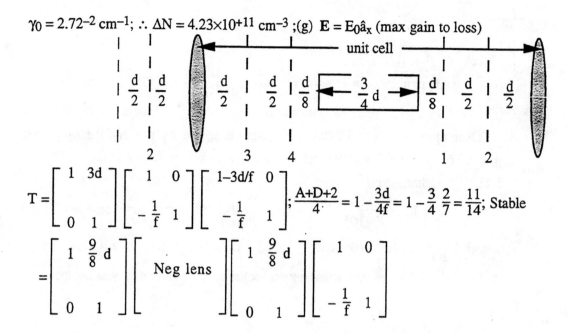

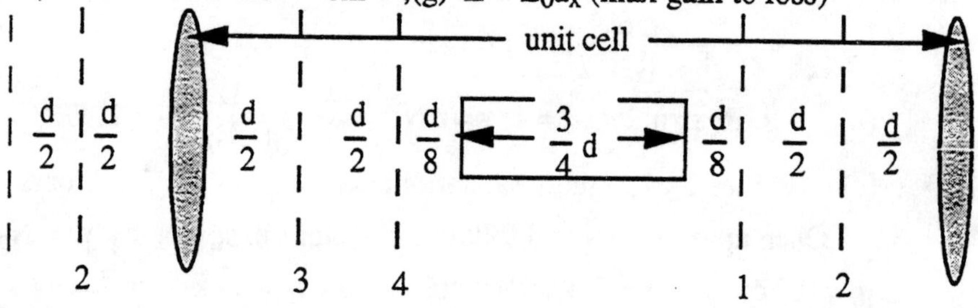

$$T = \begin{bmatrix} 1 & 3d \\ 0 & 1 \end{bmatrix}\begin{bmatrix} 1 & 0 \\ -\frac{1}{f} & 1 \end{bmatrix}\begin{bmatrix} 1-3d/f & 0 \\ -\frac{1}{f} & 1 \end{bmatrix};\ \frac{A+D+2}{4} = 1 - \frac{3d}{4f} = 1 - \frac{3}{4}\frac{2}{7} = \frac{11}{14};\ \text{Stable}$$

$$= \begin{bmatrix} 1 & \frac{9}{8}d \\ 0 & 1 \end{bmatrix}\begin{bmatrix} & \text{Neg lens} & \end{bmatrix}\begin{bmatrix} 1 & \frac{9}{8}d \\ 0 & 1 \end{bmatrix}\begin{bmatrix} 1 & 0 \\ -\frac{1}{f} & 1 \end{bmatrix}$$

9.8

$$\sigma = A_{21}\frac{\lambda_0^2}{8\pi}g(\nu_0) = 4.05\times10^{-14}\ cm^2;\ \gamma_{th} = \frac{1}{l_g}\ln\frac{1}{R_1R_2R_3R_4} = 5.98\times10^{-2}\ cm^{-1}$$

$$N_2 - \frac{g_2}{g_1}N_1 = 1.48\times10^{+12}\ cm^{-3};\ I_s = \frac{h\nu}{\sigma\tau_2}\ \text{since } \tau_1 << \tau_2\ I_s = 6.8\ \text{watts/cm}^2$$

$$\Delta\lambda/\lambda = \Delta\nu/\nu;\ \nu = 375\ \text{THz};\ \Delta\lambda = 0.043\ \text{Å}$$

$$I_{OUT} = T_4\left\{\frac{\gamma_0 l_g - \alpha_T l_g}{1 - \exp[-\alpha_T l_g]}\right\};\ \alpha_T l_g = \gamma_{th}\ l_g;\ \therefore\ I_{out} = 3.13\ \text{watts/cm}^2$$

9.9

$$R_1R_2R_3R_4T_aT_b\exp[\gamma_{th}l_g] = 1;$$

$\gamma_{th} = 1.573\times10^{-2}\ cm^{-1} = N_2\sigma$; $N_{2th} = 7.36\times10^{+18}\ cm^{-3}$ (at threshold)

$$\frac{dN_2}{dt} = R_{02} - \frac{N_2}{\tau_2} = 0;\ R_{02} = \frac{N_2}{\tau_2} = 5.1\times10^{+20}cm^{-3}/sec;$$

Power/Volume $= 3.2\times1.6\times10^{-19}\cdot R_{02} = 262$ watts/cm^3;

$$\frac{dN_2}{dt} = R_2 - N_2\left[\frac{1}{\tau_2} + \frac{\sigma I}{h\nu}\right]$$

Now $N_2 = N_{2th}$ (i.e.the inversion is clamped at threshold) $= R_{20}\tau_2$ with the excess going into stimulated emission

Use by Stimuted Emission $N_{2th}\left(\frac{\sigma I}{h\nu}\right) = R_2 - R_{20}{=}0.5R_{20} = \frac{N_{2th}}{\tau_2}$;

$I^+ = \frac{h\nu}{\sigma}\left[\frac{R_2 - R_{20}}{N_{2th}}\right] = 4.23\times10^{+3}$ kW/cm^2; $I_{out} = 0.2\,I = 847$ W/cm^2;

If one uses Eq. 9.2.6, the output is 987 W/cm^2

9.10

$\ln\frac{I_2}{I_1} + \frac{I_1}{I_s}\left[\frac{I_2}{I_1} - 1\right] = 3\gamma_{th}l_g$; where $\exp[\gamma_{th}l_g] = \frac{1}{\Pi R_j} = 2.786$ $\gamma_{th}l_g = 1.02$

$\frac{I_2}{I_1} = \frac{1}{\pi R_j}\frac{I_1}{I_s} = \frac{3\gamma_0 l_g - \ln(1/\Pi R)}{(I_2/I_1) - 1} = 1.15$; $I_1 = 5.74$ W/cm^2; $I_2 = 15.98$ W/cm^2,

$I_{out} = 0.3\,I_2 = 4.79$ W/cm^2; Approx: $\frac{I}{I_s} = \left[\frac{\gamma_0}{\alpha} - 1\right] = 2$

$I^+ = 10$ watts/cm^2; $I_{out} = (T_3)I^+ = 2$ Watts/cm^2 – close even though approximations are not justified.

In the spirit of the high Q approximation, one assumes that the intensity is uniform throughout the cavity. Hence it is not necessary to multiply by all of the reflection factors to obtain the output.

9.11

(a) $\sigma_{abs} = \frac{g_2}{g_0} A_{20}\frac{\lambda^2}{8\pi} g(\nu_0)$; $g(\nu_0) = 6.37\times10^{-11}$ s; $\frac{g_2}{g_0} = \frac{5}{3}$;

$\frac{h\nu_{20}}{e} = 4.1$ eV; $\nu = 990$THz; $\lambda_0 = 3030$ Å; $\sigma_{abs} = 3.88\times10^{-15}$ cm^2;

(b) $\sigma_{stim} = A_{21}\frac{\lambda^2}{8\pi} g(\nu_0) = 8.87\times10^{-16}$ cm^2; (at $\lambda_0 = 0.592$ µm)

(c) $1/\tau_2 = A_{20} + A_{21} + k_{21} = 6.1\times10^{+6}$ sec^{-1} ;$\tau_2 = 0.164$ µs

$\frac{dN_1}{dt} = 0 = A_{21}N_2 - \frac{N_1}{\tau_1}$; $\frac{N_2}{N_1} = \frac{1}{A_{21}\tau_1} = 100$;

$R_1R_2T_w^4 \exp[\gamma_{th}2l_g] = 1$;$\gamma_{th} = 1.33\times10^{-2}$ cm^{-1};

(d) $N_2 - \frac{g_2}{g_1}N_1 = 1.5^{+13}$ cm^{-3};

(e) $\frac{dN_2}{dt} = \frac{\sigma_p I_p}{h\nu_p}(N_0 - N_2) - \frac{N_2}{\tau_2} - \frac{\sigma_{21}I_{21}}{h\nu_{21}}\left(N_2 - \frac{g_2}{g_1}N_1\right)$

$\frac{dN_1}{dt} = \frac{N_2}{\tau_{21}} + \frac{\sigma_{21}I_{21}}{h\nu_{21}}\left[N_2 - \frac{g_2}{g_1}N_1\right] - \frac{N_1}{\tau_1}$;

At threshold, stimulated emission is small.($I_{21} = 0$)

$N_2 = \left(\frac{\sigma I_p}{h\nu_p} N_0\right)\tau_2 \overset{\Delta}{=} R_2\tau_2$; $N_1 = \frac{\tau_1}{\tau_{21}} N_2$; $\Delta N = 1.5\times10^{+13}\ cm^{-3}$ from (d); $N_0 = 10^{17}\ cm^{-3}$

$N_2 - \frac{g_2}{g_1} N_1 = \left(\frac{\sigma I_p}{h\nu_p} N_0\right)\tau_2\left(1 - \frac{g_2}{g_1}\frac{\tau_1}{\tau_{21}}\right)$; Solve for $I_p = 1.57\ W/cm^2$

(g) Above threshold, $N_2 - \frac{g_1}{g_2} N_1$ saturates at the threshold value. Thus substitute the value of the pump to be $I_p' = 10\times I_p$(at threshold) and use the threshold inversion density of $1.5\times10^{+14}\ cm^{-3}$.

$\therefore I_{21} = I^+ + I^- \approx 2I^+ = \frac{h\nu_{21}}{\sigma_{21}\tau_2\left[1 - \frac{g_2}{g_1}\frac{\tau_1}{\tau_{21}}\right]} \cdot \frac{I_p'}{I_{p(th)}} \approx 10 \times I_s$; $I^+ \approx 5I_s$;

$I_{out} = 0.1\ I^+$; $I_s = 2.3\ kW/cm^2$; $\therefore\ I_{out} \approx 1.15\ kW/cm^2$

Due to fast stimulation on $2 \to 1$, $N_2 - (g_2/g_2)N_1$ is clamped at threshold and the net pumping to 2 is equal to that of 1 and all of the pumping to 2 ends as population in 1.

$\frac{dN_1}{dt} = \frac{\sigma_p I_p}{h\nu_p} N_0^0 - \frac{N_1}{\tau_1}$; $N_0 + N_2 + N_1 = N_0^0$; Now $N_2 - \frac{g_2}{g_1} N_1 = 1.5^{+13}\ cm^{-3} << N_0^0$;

$N_2 \approx \frac{g_2}{g_1} N_1 = \frac{5}{3} N_1$; $N_0 = N_0^0 - N_1 - \frac{g_2}{g_1} N_1 = N_0^0 - \left(\frac{g_2+g_1}{g_1}\right) N_1$

$$N_1 = \frac{\frac{\sigma_0 I_p \tau_1}{h\nu_p} N_0^0}{1 + \left[\frac{g_1+g_2}{g_1}\frac{\sigma I_p}{h\nu}\tau_1\right]};\ N_0 = N_0^0 - \left(\frac{g_2+g_1}{g_1}\right) N_1 = \frac{N_0^0}{1 + \left[\frac{g_2+g_1}{g_1}\right]\frac{\sigma I_p}{h\nu}\tau_1} = 0.7\ N_0^0$$

$\therefore\ I_p = 272\ watts/cm^2$

9.12

$\gamma_{th} = \frac{1}{2l_g}\ln\frac{1}{R_1R_2} = 1.756\times10^{-3}\ cm^{-1}$; $N_2 - \frac{g_2}{g_1} N_1 = 1.756\times10^{+13}\ cm^{-3}$;

$I_s = \frac{h\nu}{\sigma\tau_2} = 3.2\ watts/cm^2$

(b) Laser oscillates at the cavity made with highest gain to loss ratio.

(c) $\frac{I^+}{I_s} = \frac{1}{2}\left[\frac{\gamma_0}{\alpha} - 1\right] = 0.25$; $I^+ = 0.8\ watts/cm^2$

(d) $\frac{I^+}{I_s} = \frac{\gamma_0 l_g - \frac{1}{2}\ln(1/R_1R_2)}{(1 - \sqrt{R_1R_2})(1 + \sqrt{R_2/R_1})} = 0.221$; $I^+ = 0.7073\ watts/cm^2$;

for $\gamma_0 l_g = 1.5 \times (1/2)\ \ln(1/R_1R_2)$

9.13 Figure 9.20 was inspired by this paper

9.14

$$\alpha_T l_g \quad \alpha_d l_d + \ln\frac{1}{R_1R_2R_3} + \ln\frac{1}{R_2{=}1 - T_2} = 1.0 + 0.061 + \ln\frac{1}{R_2{=}1 - T_2}$$

Left out of problem specifications in 2nd Edition: $l_d = 2.0$ cm; $l_g = 10$ cm

Use Eq. 9.2.6 for the self–consistent theory: $\frac{I_{out}}{I_s} = T_2\left\{\frac{\gamma_0 l_g - \alpha_T l_g}{1 - \exp[-\alpha_T l_g]}\right\}$;

High Q approx; $\frac{I_{out}}{I_s} = T_2\left\{\frac{\gamma_0 l_g}{\alpha_T l_g} - 1\right\} \approx T_2\left\{\frac{g_0}{L+T_2} - 1\right\}$

$\gamma_0 l_g = 2$; $T_2(\max) = -L + (g_0 L)^{1/2} = 0.396$ where $L = 1.061$

The graph shows that the presence of the loss makes the vertical scale in error, but that the prediction for the maximum is still good.

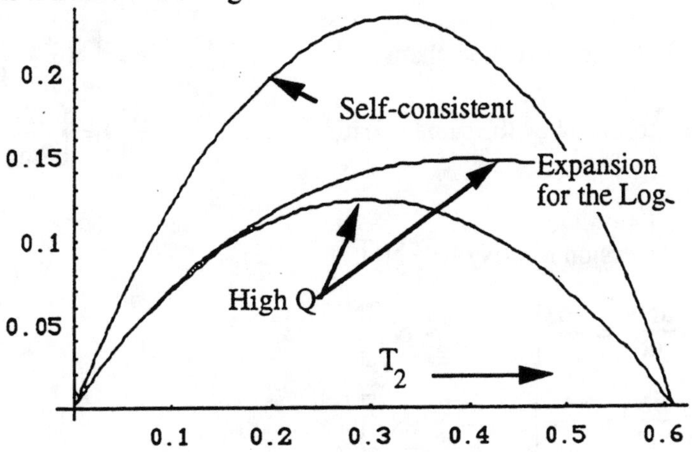

9.15

$$\gamma_{th} l_g = \ln\frac{1}{R_1R_2R_3R_4T_w^2} = \alpha_T l_g;\quad \left[\gamma_0 l_g - \ln\frac{1}{R_1R_2R_3R_4T_w^2}\right] \geq \ln\frac{1}{R_2} = \text{coupling loss where}$$

the log term inside the brackets represents the internal loss and the right-hand side represents the coupling loss, whereas the sum of the two log terms represent $\alpha_T l_g$.

$\alpha_{int} l_g \gamma_0 l_g = 0.9320$; $\therefore\ R_3 > e^{-0.6941} = 0.4995$;

(b) $\frac{I_{out}}{I_s} = T_3\left\{\frac{\gamma_0 l_g - \ln[1/R_1R_2R_3R_4T_w^2] - \ln(1/R_2)}{1 - \exp[-\alpha_T l_g]}\right\}$; (c) $\frac{I_{out}}{I_s} = T_3\left[\frac{\gamma_0}{\alpha_T - 1}\right]$

These functions are graphed below and show a much closer agreement than in problem 9.14 because there isn't a large residual loss.

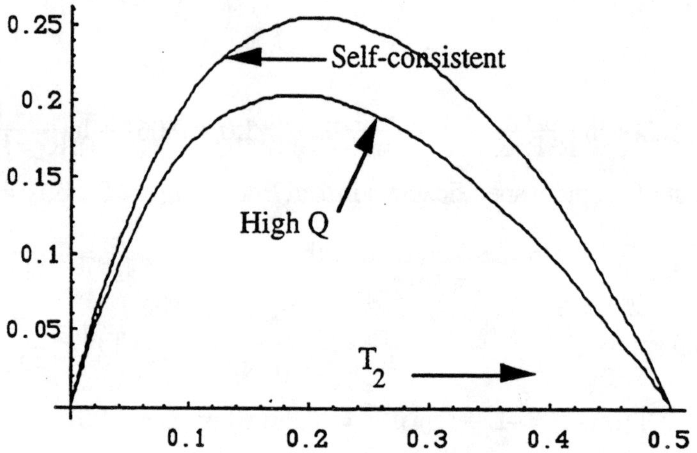

9.16

The definition of inversion changes to: $n = \left[N_2 - \frac{g_2}{g_1} N_1\right] Al_g$;

but the photons obey the same equation. $\frac{dN_p}{dt} = \left[\frac{n}{n_{th}} - 1\right]\frac{N_p}{\tau_p}$

For the inversion $n = [N_2 - \frac{g_2}{g_1} N_1]$:

$$\frac{dN_2}{dt} = \frac{-\sigma I}{h\nu}\left[N_2 - \frac{g_2}{g_1} N_1\right];$$

$$\frac{dN_1}{dt} = \frac{+\sigma I}{h\nu}\left[N_2 - \frac{g_2}{g_1} N_1\right]$$

Multiply the the equation for N_1 by g_2/g_1, subtract from the equation for N_2, multiply by Al_g and by 1 in the form of $(\tau_{RT}/2)\div(\tau_{RT}/2)$:

$$\frac{d}{dt}\left\{\left(N_2 - \frac{g_2}{g_1} N_1\right) Al_g\right\} = -\left(\frac{g_1+g_2}{g_1}\right)\left\{\left(N_2 - \frac{g_2}{g_1} N_1\right)\sigma l_g\right\} \times \frac{(I^+ + I^-)\, A(\tau_{RT}/2)}{h\nu}\frac{2}{\tau_{RT}}$$

where τ_{RT} = time for a round-trip and thus $\tau_{RT}/2$ = time for one-way passage.

The number of photons inside the cavity is given by: $N_p = (I^+ + I^-)\, A(\tau_{RT}/2)$

Thus: $$\frac{dn}{dt} = -\left[1 + \frac{g_2}{g_1}\right]\frac{n}{n_{th}}\frac{N_p}{\tau_p}$$

$$\therefore\ N_p\,(\max) = \frac{n_i - n_{th}}{(1 + g_2/g_1)} - \frac{\eta_{th}}{(1 + g_2/g_1)} \ln\frac{n_i}{n_{th}}; \qquad w_p = \frac{n_i h\nu}{(1 + g_2/g_1)}\eta_{xtn}$$

9.17

One should always start each problem with an energy level diagram showing how the atoms get to the upper state and how the atoms return. **The most important fact is that atoms must be conserved and thus:**

$N_1 + N_2 = N_0 = 1.58\times10^{19}\ cm^{-3}$ always

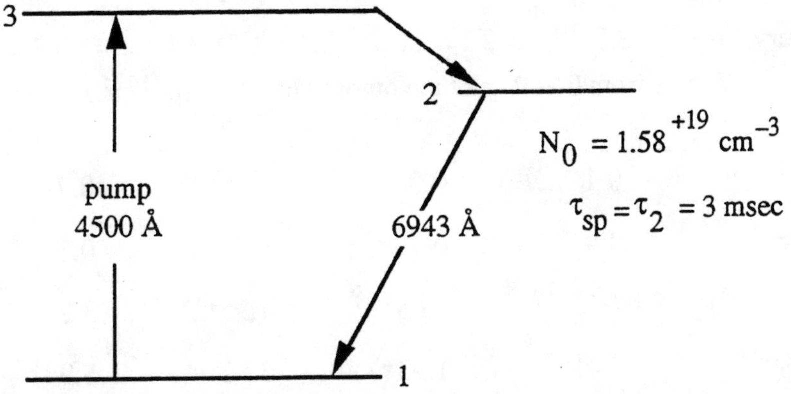

For $N_2 = 10^{19}\ cm^{-3}$, $N_1 = 0.58\times10^{+19}\ cm^{-3}$ assuming that nothing resides in state 3.

(b) $\quad P_{spont} = \dfrac{N_2V}{\tau_{sp}} \cdot h\nu_{laser} = 14.3$ kW;

This power must be supplied by absorption on the $1 \rightarrow 3$ route. In the best of all worlds, all of the atoms pumped to 3 would transfer to state 2 – the fraction that does so is called the quantum efficiency of the pump. For ruby, that efficiency is 70%, but for this problem, we can assume it to be 100%

(a) $\quad P_{pump} = \dfrac{\lambda_{31}}{\lambda_{21}} P_{spont} = 22.1$ kW. (It would be 31.6 kW for the real system)

$$\tau_{R.T.} = \frac{2l_g n_g}{c} + \frac{2(d - l_g)}{c} = \frac{2x15x1.78}{c} + \frac{2x5}{c} = 2.1\times10^{-9}\ s;$$

$$2g_{th} = \ln\frac{1}{R_1} + \ln\frac{1}{R_2} = 5.13\times10^{-2} + 0.357 = 0.408$$

The first log term is internal loss (per round-trip), last is the external value. The photon lifetime is given by:

$$\frac{1}{\tau_p} = \frac{<\alpha_T>2d}{\tau_{R.T.}} = 19.4^{+9}\ s^{-1};\ \tau_p = 5.15\ ns;\ \eta_{cpl} = 0.357/0.408 = 0.875$$

$$P(max) = \eta_{cpl} \cdot \frac{h\nu}{\tau_p}\left\{\frac{n_i - n_{th}}{2} - \frac{n_{th}}{2}\ln\left(\frac{n_i}{n_{th}}\right)\right\}$$

$n_i = 15\ cm \times 1\ cm^2 \times [(10^{19} - 0.58x10^{19})cm^{-3}] = 6.3\times10^{+19}$ atoms

$\gamma_{th} = \dfrac{1}{2l_g}\ln\dfrac{1}{R_1R_2} = 1.36^{-2}\ cm^{-1} = (N_2 - N_1)_{th}\,\sigma;$

$(N_2 - N_1)_{th} \cdot A \cdot l_g = n_{th} = 1.61^{+19}$ atoms; Thus $n_1/n_{th} = 3.92$; and $\eta_{xtn} = 0.98$;

(c) Hence $P(max) = \dfrac{0.351}{0.408} \cdot \dfrac{2.86\times10^{-19}}{5.15\times10^{-9}}\left\{1.24\times10^{+19}\right\} = 603$ MW

(d) $W_{out} = \eta_{cpl}\eta_{xtn} \cdot (h\nu n_i/2) = 7.72$ Joules

(e) $\Delta t \sim \frac{W}{P_{max}} = 12.8$ ns; If one uses Fig. 9.10, the peak is 0.8 at T = 2.4 and the FWHM interval is $\Delta T = 3.8 - 1.7 = 2.1 = \Delta t/\tau_p$; $\therefore \Delta t = 2.1 \times 5.15$ ns = 10.8 ns

(f) Vary T from $0 \rightarrow 1$, plot the output ; $n_i = 6.3\times10^{+19}$ atoms for all cases.

$T_2 \Rightarrow$	0.1	0.3	0.5	0.7	0.75
$R_2 \Rightarrow$	0.9	0.7	0.5	0.3	0.25
$\Delta N(cm^{-3})$	4.11+17	1.08+18	1.95+18	3.29+18	3.77+18
$1/\tau_p(s^{-1})$	7.41+7	1.93+8	3.52+8	5.94+8	6.8+8
n_{th}(atoms)	6.16+18	1.61+19	2.93+19	4.94+19	5.66+19
P_{out}(MW)	303	603	528	130	32
n_i/n_{th}	10.2	3.91	2.15	1.28	1.11
η_x	1.0	0.98	0.81	0.38	0.176
W(Joules)	6.075	7.72	6.8	3.27	1.53

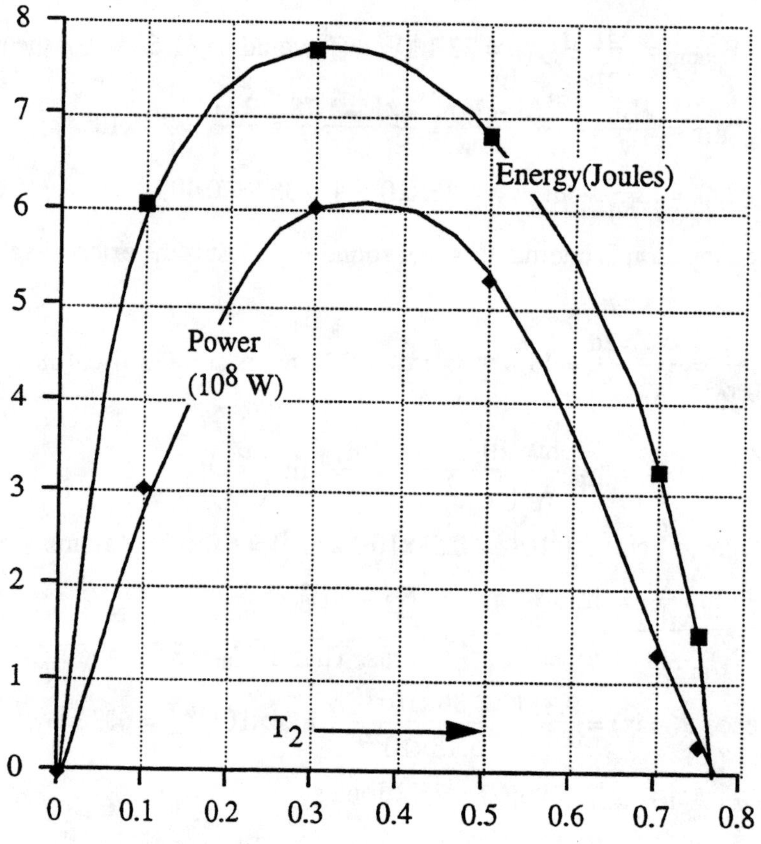

9.18

The difference here from 9.17 is that $g_2 \neq g_1$ and hence all of the equations for Q–switching must be re–examined (see Problem 9.16). Furthermore, the absorption cross–section is given, not the stimulated one. $N_2 + N_1 = N_0 = 1.58^{+19}\ \text{cm}^{-3}$

$\therefore N_1 = 0.58\times10^{+19}\ \text{cm}^{-3}$; (a)$P_{spont} = \dfrac{h\nu N_2 \cdot Vol}{\tau_{sp}} = 9.53$ kW

(b) $P_{pump} = \dfrac{1}{0.9}\,\dfrac{6943}{4500}\,P_{spont} = 16.4$ kw;

(c) $\tau_{RT}' = 2\left[\dfrac{12}{c} + \dfrac{2.35\text{x}8}{c} + \dfrac{1.78\text{x}10}{c}\right] = 3.24$ ns

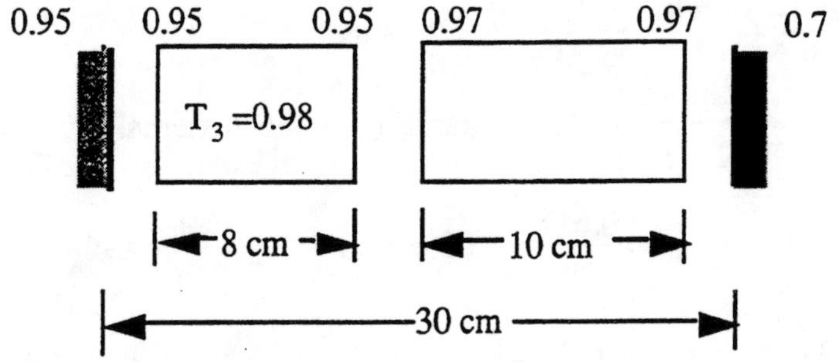

$\sigma_{STIM} = \dfrac{g_1}{g_2}\sigma_{abs} = 2.65\times10^{-20}\ \text{cm}^2$;

$\gamma_{th} = \dfrac{1}{2l_g}\ln\dfrac{1}{R_1T_a^2T_b^2T_c^2T_d^2T_s^2} + \ln(1/R_2) = 2.09\times10^{-2}\ \text{cm}^{-1} + 1.78\times10^{-2} = 3.87\times10^{-2}\ \text{cm}^{-1}$

$1/\tau_p = (1 - R_1T_a^2T_b^2T_c^2T_d^2T_s^2)/\tau_{RT} = 1.67\times10^{+8}\ \text{sec}^{-1}$;

$(N_2 - N_1)_{th} = 1.52\times10^{+18}\ \text{cm}^{-3}$

$n_{th} = 1.52^{+19}$ atoms; $n_i = (N_2 - \frac{g_1}{g_2}N_1)Al_g = \left(10^{19} - \frac{1}{2}\times 0.58\times10^{+19}\right)10 = 7.1\times10^{+19}$

atoms$\therefore \dfrac{n_i}{n_{th}} = 4.66\ \therefore\ n_{xtr} = 0.99$;

$$P_{out} = \frac{\alpha_{exT}}{\alpha_T}\frac{h\nu}{\tau_p}\left\{\frac{n_i - n_{th}}{(1 + g_2/g_1)} - \frac{n_{th}}{(1 + g_2/g_1)}\ln\frac{n_i}{n_{th}}\right\}$$

$$= \frac{1.78}{3.87}\cdot\frac{2.86\times10^{-19}}{6\times10^{-9}}\cdot\left\{\frac{1.69\times10^{+19}}{1.5}\right\} = 474\ \text{MW}$$

$W = \eta_{cpl}\dfrac{n_i h\nu}{(1 + g_2/g_1)}n_{xtn} = 6.16$ Joules; $\Delta t = \dfrac{W}{P} = 13.0$ nsec

9.19

$n_i/n_{th} = 3$ and $n_i = 10^{18}$ atoms was given.

$N_p(max) = \dfrac{n_i - n_{th}}{2} - \dfrac{n_{th}}{2}\ln\dfrac{n_i}{n_{th}}$; $\therefore N_p(max) = 1.51\times10^{+17}$ photons

$h\nu = 1.988\times10^{-19}$ Joule; $1/\tau_p = (5 + 2 + 1)\times10^{+7}\ \text{sec}^{-1}$;$\tau_p = 12.5$ ns

$$\eta_{cpl} = \frac{5\times10^7\ s^{-1}}{(5+2+1)\times10^7\ s^{-1}} = 0.675$$

$P(max) = \eta_{cpl} h\nu \cdot \frac{N_p(max)}{\tau_p} = 1.5$ MW; $\eta_{xtn} = \frac{n_i - n_f}{n_i} = 0.944$ for $n_i/n_{th} = 3$

$\therefore W(out) = h\nu \frac{n_i}{2} \eta_x \cdot \eta_{cpl} = 58.6$ mJ

$$\Delta t = \frac{w_{out}}{P_{MAX}} = \frac{58.6\times10^{-3}}{1.5\times10^{+6}} = 37.4 \text{ ns}$$

9.20

$[C_r] = 1.58\times10^{+19}$ cm^{-3} $N_3 = 0$; $(N_2-N_1)\, Al_g = 6.3\times10^{+19}$ atoms $= N_i$

$\tau_{R.T.} = \frac{2n_r l_g}{c} + \frac{2n_s l_s}{c} + \frac{2(d-l_g-l_s)}{c} = 2.18$ ns,

$\alpha_T 2d = \ln\left[\frac{1}{R_1 T_R^4 T_Q^4}\right] = 0.255(\text{internal}) + 0.3567(\text{external})$; $\therefore \frac{1}{\tau_p} = \frac{2\alpha_T d}{\tau_{R.T.}}$; $\tau_p = 3.56$ns

$\gamma_{th} \cdot 2l = \alpha_T \cdot 2d$; $\gamma_{th} = \frac{0.617}{30} = 2.039^{-2}$ cm^{-1}; $n_{th} = \frac{\gamma_{th}}{\sigma} \cdot A \cdot l_g = 2.408^{+19}$ atoms

$n_i/n_{th} = 2.616$; $\therefore \eta_{xtn} = 0.91 = n_i - n_f/n_i$; $\therefore n_f = 5.67^{+18}$ atoms; $\eta_{cpl} = \frac{\alpha_{ext}}{\alpha_{total}}$

$W_{out} = \eta_{cpl} \cdot \left[n_x \frac{n_i h\nu}{2}\right] = 4.78$ Joules;

$P_{(MAX)} = \eta_{cpl} \cdot \left\{\frac{h\nu}{\tau_p}\left[\frac{n_i - n_{th}}{2} - \frac{n_i}{2} \ln\frac{n_i}{n_{th}}\right]\right\} = 368$ MW; $\Delta t \approx \frac{W_0}{P_{MAX}} = 12.96$ nsec

From Fig. 9.4, $\Delta T = 3$; $n_i/n_{th} = 2.5$ (close); $\therefore \Delta t = 3\tau_p = 10.7$ nsec (reasonable)

9.21

The basic equations become

$$\frac{dN_p}{dT} = \left(\frac{n}{n_{th}} - 1\right) N_p \text{ (as before);} \quad 1.$$

Since $N_1 = 0$ always, one photon added changes the inversion n by 1 and the time dependent equation for the inversion becomes:

$$\frac{dn}{dT} = -\frac{n}{n_{th}} N_p \quad 2.$$

Now follow the same procedure as before and divide 1 by 2 to obtain:

$$\frac{dN_p}{dn} = -1 + \frac{n_{th}}{n} ;$$

To obtain the energy, integrate between the initial and final conditions:

$$\int_{N_{pi}\approx 0}^{N_{pf}\approx 0} dN_p = 0 = -\int_{n_i}^{n_f} dn + n_{th} \int_{n_i}^{n_f} \frac{dn}{n} \text{ or } 0 = (n_i - n_f) - n_{th} \ln\left(\frac{n_i}{n_f}\right) \quad 3.$$

which is the conventional equation for the extraction efficiency, η_{xtn} ;

For the given condition of $n_i = 4n_{th}$ one obtains $\eta_{xtn} = 0.98$

On first evaluates threshold: $\gamma_{th} = \frac{1}{2l_g}\ln\frac{1}{R_1R_2T_Q^2} = 0.027\ \text{cm}^{-1}$;

$N_{2th} = 2.7\times10^{+15}\ \text{cm}^{-3}$ using $\sigma = 10^{-18}\ \text{cm}^2$

(Note: There was a mistake in the printing of σ in 2nd Ed)

$n_i = 4N_2\cdot 10\text{cm}\times 0.75\text{cm}^2 = 8.09\times10^{+17}$ atoms;

For this case every atom in state 2 yields a photon

$$W = \eta_{xtn}\cdot n_i\cdot h\nu\ \frac{\ln[1/R_2]}{\ln[1/R_1R_2T_Q^2]}$$

$$W = 0.98\times(8.09\times10^{17}\text{atoms})\times(2.5\ \text{eV}\times1.6\times10^{-19}\text{J/eV})\frac{0.223}{0.539} = 0.131\ \text{J}$$

9.22

Input: $I_1T_1 = 50\ \text{mJ/cm}^2$; $T_1 = 100$ ns; $\therefore\ I_1 = 0.5\ \text{MW/cm}^2$;

$G_0 = 10$ and $w_s = 100\ \text{mJ/cm}^2$

$I_2(t) = I_1\dfrac{e^x}{e^x + G_0^{-1} - 1}$ where $x = \dfrac{I_1t}{w_s}$; at $t = 0$; $x = 0$; $I_2 = G_0I_1 = 5\text{MW/cm}^2$;

Find a time such that: $\dfrac{e^x}{e^x - 0.9} = 0.5$; or $4e^x = 4.5$; $x = 0.1178$; $\dfrac{I_1t_{1/2}}{w_s} = 0.1178$

$\therefore\ t_{1/2} = 11.78$ ns; $w_{(MAX)} = \gamma_0\, l_g\, w_s$; $\exp[\gamma_0 l_g] = 10$; $\therefore\ \gamma_0 l_g = 2.3$; $w_{(MAX)} = 230\ \text{mJ/cm}^2$

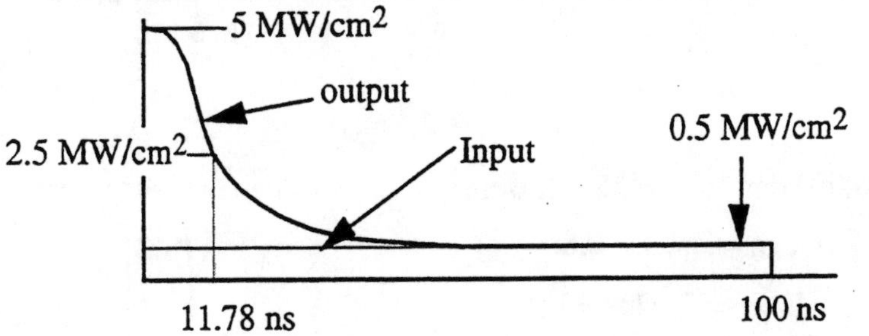

Figure for problem 9.22

9.23.

$\lambda_0 = 5889\text{Å}$; $w_s = h\nu/2\sigma = 16.86\ \mu J/cm^2$; $G_0 = 10^{-3}$

$I_1(t) = I_0 \sin^2\pi t/T = \frac{I_0}{2}(1 - \cos 2\pi t/T)$ where $I_0 = 2w_0/T$

$\therefore\ w_1(t) = \frac{I_0}{2}\left(t - \frac{T}{2\pi}\sin\frac{2\pi t}{T}\right) = w_0\left(\frac{t}{T} - \frac{1}{2\pi}\sin\frac{2\pi t}{T}\right)$ where $w_0 = I_0T/2$;

Apply 9.6.11 for $w_0/w_s = 0.11862$, 1.1862 and 11.862. Result plotted below.

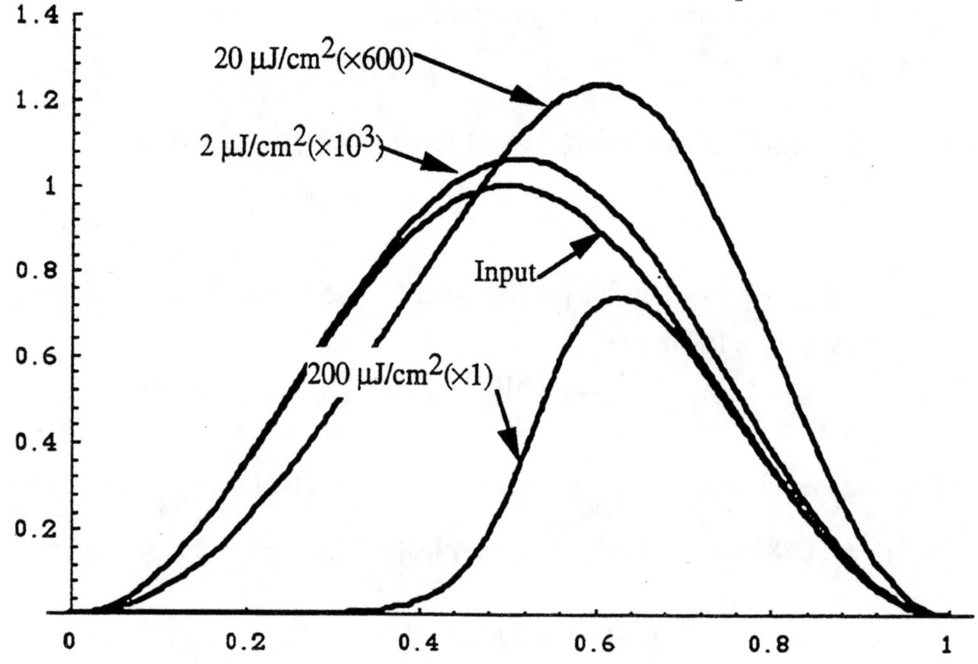

9.24

$\gamma_0 = 0.005\ cm^{-1}$; $I_s = 25$ watts/cm^2;

$R_1 = 0.98$; $g_0 = 2\gamma_0 l_g = 0.8$;

$\alpha_{mt}2l_g = \ln\frac{1}{R_1} = 2.02^{-2} = L$;

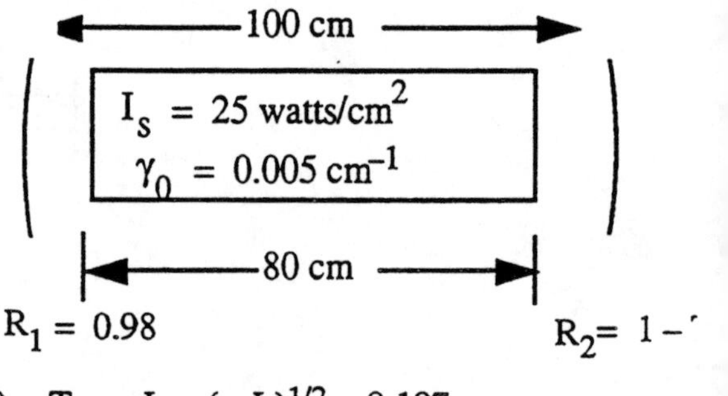

(Use the simple theory to find the optimum coupling) $\therefore\ T_2 = -L + (g_0L)^{1/2} = 0.107$

i.e., $R_2 = 0.893$; $\frac{I_{out}}{I_s} = \frac{1}{2}\{g_0^{1/2} - L^{1/2}\}^2 = 0.283$; $I_{out} = 7.07$ watts/cm^2

For the Rigrod (exact) analysis: $\frac{I_0}{I_s} = T_2\left\{\frac{\gamma_0 l_g - \frac{1}{2}\ln\frac{1}{R\text{–}1R_2}}{(1 - \sqrt{R_1R_2})(1 + \sqrt{R_2/R_1})}\right\}$

Simple $\frac{I_0}{I_s} = \frac{T_2}{2}\left\{\frac{\gamma_0 2l_g}{\ln\frac{1}{R_1} + \ln\frac{1}{1 - T_2}} - 1\right\}$; Very simple: $\ln\frac{1}{1 - T_2} \approx T_2$

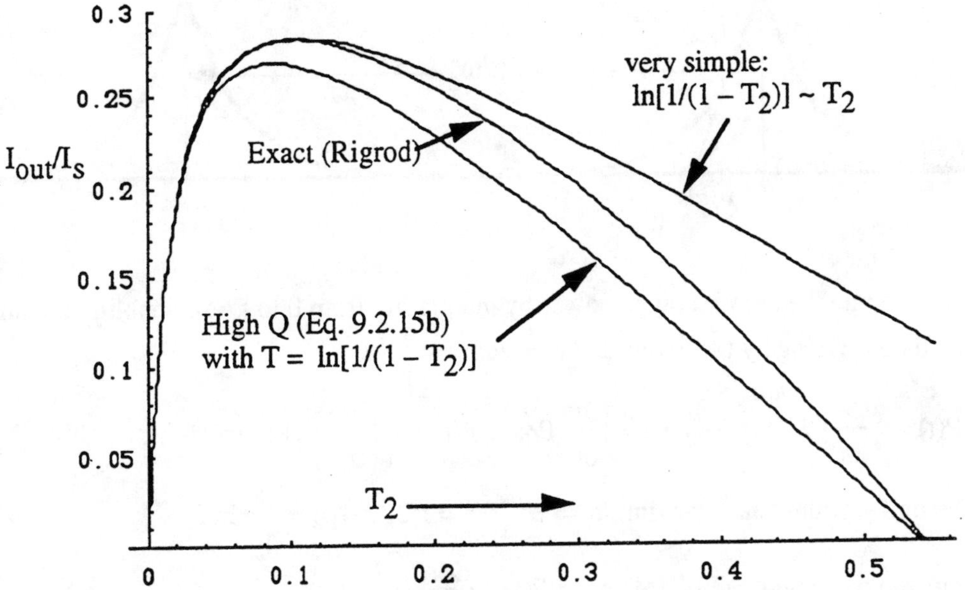

9.25

Let's consider the case in which the spectral representation of the power is the square of a Lorentzian:

$$P = P_0 \Sigma \left\{ \frac{(\Delta\omega/2)^2}{(n\omega_c)^2 + (\Delta\omega/2)^2} \right\}^2$$

where the summation is over all positive and negative values of n The first task is to obtain an expression for the electric field, which when squared yields this power.

$$e(t) = \left(\frac{2\eta_0 P_0}{A}\right)^{1/2} e^{j(\omega_0 t)} \Sigma\, e^{j(n\omega_c)t} \frac{(\Delta\omega/2)^2}{(n\omega_c)^2 + (\Delta\omega/2)^2}$$

Now we follow the prescription of the book and let $x = n\omega_c$ and convert to an integral

$$\frac{e(t)}{\left(\frac{2\eta_0 P_0}{A}\right)^{1/2} e^{j\omega_0 t}} = \frac{1}{\omega_c} \int_{-\infty}^{+\infty} \frac{(\Delta\omega/2)^2}{x^2 + \left(\frac{\Delta\omega}{2}\right)^2} e^{jxt}\, dx = \frac{2}{\omega_c} \int_0^{\infty} \frac{\left(\frac{\Delta\omega}{2}\right)^2}{x^2 + \left(\frac{\Delta\omega}{2}\right)^2} \cos xt\, dx$$

Now we use the Fourier cosine pair (formula 33.18 in MHB)

If: $f(x) = \frac{1}{x^2+b^2}$ then: $F_c(\alpha) = \frac{\pi e^{-b\alpha}}{2b}$ $b = \left(\frac{\Delta\omega}{2}\right)^2$ and $\alpha = t$

$$\therefore e(t) = \left(\frac{2\eta_0 P_0}{A}\right)^{1/2} \left(\frac{\pi}{2} \frac{\Delta\omega}{\omega_c}\right) e^{j\omega_0 t} e^{[-\Delta\omega t]/2}; \text{ Hence: } P(t) = P_0 \frac{\pi^2}{4} \left(\frac{\Delta\omega}{\omega_c}\right)^2 e^{-\Delta\omega t}$$

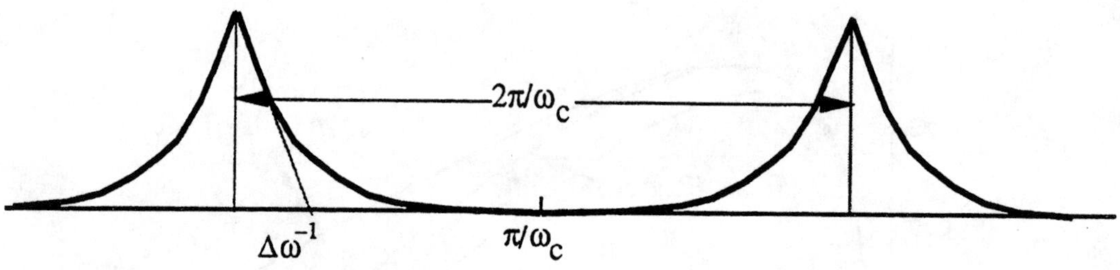

We compute the time averaged power by integrating from 0 to π/ω_c, doubling the answer, and then dividing by the period $2\pi/\omega_c = 2d/c$

$$\langle P(t)\rangle = \frac{\omega_c}{2\pi}\cdot 2\int_0^{\pi/\omega_c} p(t)dt = \left(\frac{\pi}{4}\right)\frac{\Delta\omega}{\omega_c}P_0;\ \therefore\ P(t) = \pi\left(\frac{\Delta\omega}{\omega_c}\right)\langle P\rangle\, e^{-\Delta\omega t}$$

The half–width at half–maximum $\Rightarrow e^{\Delta\omega t_{1/2}} = 1/2;\ \therefore\ t_{1/2} = \frac{1}{\Delta\omega}\ln 2$

Thus the pulse width (FWHM) $\Delta t_p = 2t_{1/2} = \frac{2\ln 2}{\Delta\omega}$

9.26

$$P(\omega) = P_0\sum_{-N}^{+N}\frac{\sin^2(n\pi\omega_c/\Delta\omega)}{(n\pi\omega_c/\Delta\omega)^2},\ \text{where } (n\pi\omega_c/\Delta\omega) = \pi n/N.$$

The spectral content of the power appears as shown below.

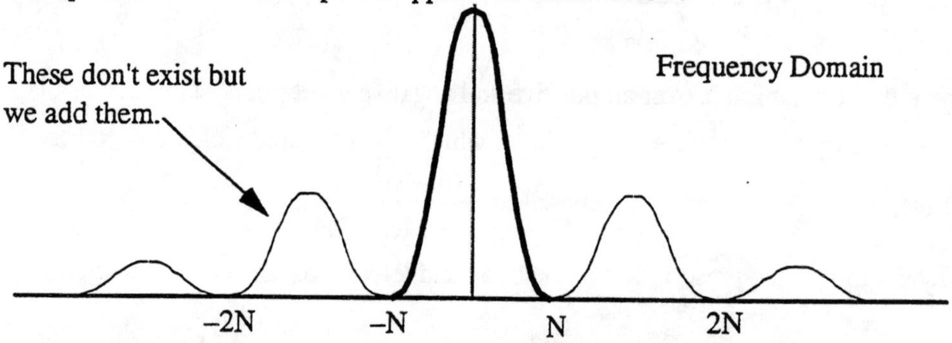

The time domain representation is a result of the following mathematics. The first step is to generate an expression for the electric field.

$$\frac{e[t]}{\left(\frac{2\eta_0 P_0}{A}\right)^{1/2} e^{j\omega_0 t}} = \sum_{-\infty}^{\infty}\frac{\sin\left(\frac{n\pi\omega_c}{\Delta\omega}\right)}{\left(\frac{n\pi\omega_c}{\Delta\omega}\right)} e^{jn\omega_c t}\cdot 1;\ \text{Let } n\omega_c = x;\ dx = \omega_c \text{ and } \frac{dx}{\omega_c} = 1$$

$$\frac{e[t]}{\left(\frac{2\eta_0 P_0}{A}\right)^{1/2} e^{j\omega_0 t}} = \frac{1}{\omega_c} \int_{-\infty}^{+\infty} \frac{\sin\left(\frac{\pi x}{\Delta\omega}\right)}{\left(\frac{\pi x}{\Delta\omega}\right)} e^{jxt}\, dx$$

From "Mathematical Handbook", p. 175; #33.7 and 33.8, the Fourier transform pair:

$$\text{If: } f(y) = \begin{cases} 1 \text{ if } y < b \\ 0 \text{ if } y > b \end{cases} \text{ then } F(\alpha) = \frac{2\sin(b\alpha)}{\alpha}$$

Let $x = \alpha$, $t = y$, $b = \pi/\Delta\omega$;

The field becomes: $$\frac{e(t)}{\left(\frac{2\eta_0 P_0}{A}\right)^{1/2} e^{j\omega_0 t}} = \frac{\Delta\omega}{\omega_c} \left\{ \frac{1}{2\pi} \int_{-\infty}^{+\infty} \frac{2\sin b\alpha}{\alpha} e^{j\alpha y}\, d\alpha \right\}$$

where the { } = F(α). Hence: $$\frac{e(t)}{\left(\frac{2\eta_0 P_0}{\Delta}\right)^{1/2} e^{j\omega_0 t}} = \frac{\Delta\omega}{\omega_c} \begin{cases} 1 \text{ for } |t| < \pi/\Delta\omega \\ 0 \text{ for } |t| > \pi/\Delta\omega \end{cases}$$

or $$p(t) = \frac{e^2(t)}{2\eta_0} = \left(\frac{\Delta\omega}{\omega_c}\right)^2 P_0 \begin{cases} 1 \text{ for } |t| < \pi/\Delta\omega \\ 0 \text{ for } |t| > \pi/\Delta\omega \end{cases}$$

Thus if one displayed the output of the laser using a fast detector and a fast oscilloscope, one would obtain the following time dependence. There are two points to be noted:

1. If a slow detector were used, the sharp edges would be rounded due to the slow transit time of the carriers or the stray capacitance.
2. The writing speed of the oscilloscope can also lead to a display with rounded corners.

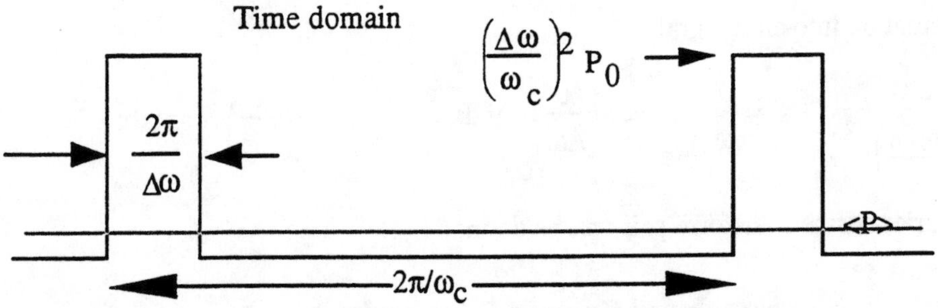

$$\text{Average power} = \frac{\omega_c}{2\pi} \int_{-\pi/\omega_c}^{+\pi/\omega_c} p(t)\, dt = \left(\frac{\Delta\omega}{\omega_c}\right)^2 P_0 \cdot \frac{2\pi}{\Delta\omega} \cdot \frac{\omega_c}{2\pi} = \left[\frac{\Delta\omega}{\omega_c}\right] P_0$$

Notice this factor ($\Delta\omega/\omega_c$) again,which is more–or–less the number of modes locked together.

There is a tendency for the student to use the power spectrum directly and not take the time to obtain an expression for the electric field. The Fourier transform is not applicable to the power; it is only applicable to linear systems.

9.27

The power spectrum was given to be:

$$P(\omega) = P_0 \sum_{-\infty}^{+\infty} \text{sech}^2\left(\frac{n\omega_c}{\Delta\omega}\right)\delta(\omega - [\omega_0 + n\omega_c])$$

which is a nice "bell-shaped" curve in the angular frequency domain and is sketched in the diagram below.

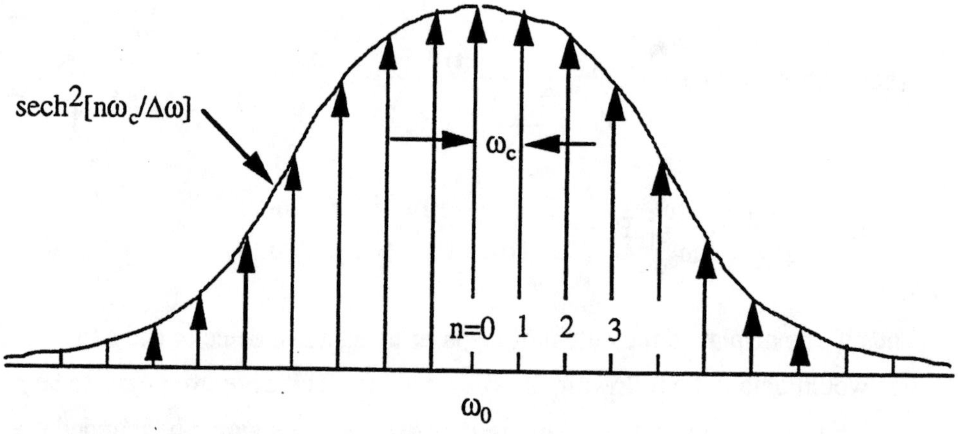

The electric field associated with that power spectrum is:

$$e(t) = \left(\frac{2\eta_0 P_0}{A}\right)^{1/2} e^{j\omega_0 t} \sum_{-\infty}^{+\infty} \text{sech}\left(\frac{n\omega_c}{\Delta\omega}\right) e^{jn\omega_c t} e^{j\phi_n(t)}$$

and $\phi_n(t) = 0$ for a mode-locked laser. Let $x = n\omega_c$, $dx/\omega_c = 1$ as in the text, and convert the summation into an integral.

$$\frac{e(t)}{\left(\frac{2\eta_0 P_0}{A}\right)^{1/2}} e^{-j\omega_0 t} = \frac{1}{\omega_c}\int_{-\infty}^{+\infty} \text{sech}\left(\frac{x}{\Delta\omega}\right) e^{jxt}\, dx = \frac{2}{\omega_c}\int_0^{\infty} \text{sech}\left(\frac{x}{\Delta\omega}\right) \cos xt\, dx$$

The Fourier cosine transform pair can be defined by:

$$F_c(\alpha) = \int_0^{\infty} f(y) \cos\alpha y\, dy \text{ and } f(y) = \frac{2}{\pi}\int_0^{\infty} F_c(\alpha) \cos\alpha y\, d\alpha$$

(Use MHB 33.48, page 178) If $f(y) = \text{sech}\, by$, then $F_c(\alpha) = \frac{\pi}{2b}\text{sech}\left(\frac{\pi\alpha}{2b}\right)$

Let $x = y$, $\alpha = t$, with $b = \dfrac{1}{\Delta\omega}$ and that pair fits our problem

$$\frac{e(t)}{\left(\frac{2\eta_0 P_0}{A}\right)^{1/2}} e^{-j\omega_0 t} = \frac{2}{\omega_c} \cdot \frac{\pi}{2b} \operatorname{sech}\left(\frac{\pi\alpha}{2b}\right) = \pi \frac{\Delta\omega}{\omega_c} \operatorname{sech}\left(\frac{\pi\Delta\omega t}{2}\right)$$

The instantaneous power is given by $[e(t)e^*(t)/2\eta_0]A$: $p(t) = P_0\pi^2 \left(\frac{\Delta\omega}{\omega_0}\right)^2 \operatorname{sech}^2\left(\frac{\pi\Delta\omega t}{2}\right)$

This function is not periodic - a result of replacing the summation with an integral. However we know that it is periodic and thus one can not blindly trust all of the mathematics. The temporal behavior, such as would be observed with a photon detector and a fast oscilloscope, would appears as follows:

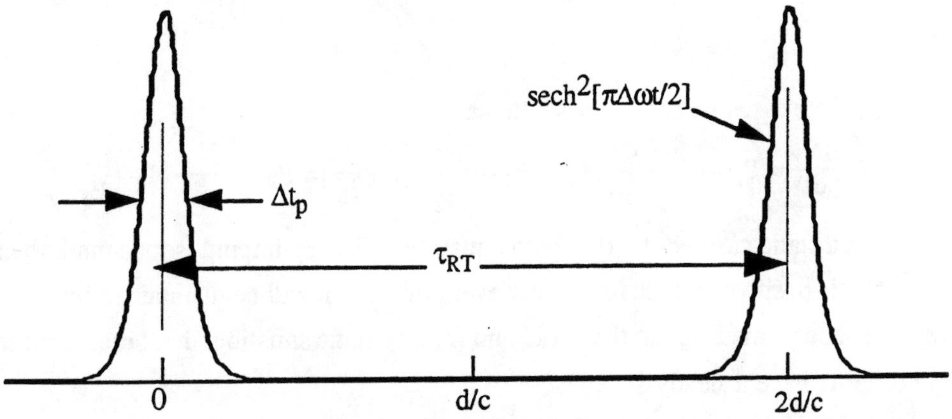

To compute the average power, <P>, integrate p(t) from ($-d/c \approx -\infty$ to $d/c \approx +\infty$ since the function is essentially zero at those times); and divide by $2\pi/\omega_c = \tau_{RT} = 2d/c$

$$\langle P\rangle = P_0\,\pi^2 \left(\frac{\Delta\omega}{\omega_c}\right)^2 \frac{\omega_c}{2\pi} \int_{-\infty}^{+\infty} \operatorname{sech}^2\left(\frac{\pi\Delta\omega t}{2}\right) dt$$

Now $\int \operatorname{sech}^2 ax = \dfrac{\tanh ax}{a}$ and if we let $a = \dfrac{\pi\Delta\omega}{2}$

$$\langle P\rangle = 2\left(\frac{\Delta\omega}{\omega_c}\right) P_0 = 200 \text{ mW for } P_0 = 10 \text{ mW and } \Delta\omega/\omega_c = 10$$

Thus the instantaneous power can be expressed as:

$$\boxed{p(t) = P_0\pi^2 \left(\frac{\Delta\omega}{\omega_0}\right)^2 \operatorname{sech}^2\left(\frac{\pi\Delta\omega t}{2}\right) = \frac{\langle P\rangle\pi^2}{2} \frac{\Delta\omega}{\omega_c} \operatorname{sech}^2\left(\frac{\pi\Delta\omega t}{2}\right)}$$

The peak of the instantaneous power $= \dfrac{\langle P\rangle\pi^2}{2}\left(\dfrac{\Delta\omega}{\omega_c}\right) = 9.87$ watts

The pulse width is found by $\text{sech}^2\left(\frac{\pi\Delta\omega t_{1/2}}{2}\right) = \frac{1}{2}$ or $\text{sech}\ at_{1/2} = \frac{1}{\sqrt{2}}$ where $a = \frac{\pi\Delta\omega}{2}$

$$\frac{2}{e^{at_{1/2}} + e^{-at_{1/2}}} = \frac{1}{\sqrt{2}} \text{ or } e^{2at_{1/2}} - 2\sqrt{2}e^{at_{1/2}} + 1 = 0$$

this is a quadratic equation for $e^{at_{1/2}}$ and its solution is $e^{at_{1/2}} = \sqrt{2} \pm 1$. Only the + sign obeys the obvious condition that $e^{at_{1/2}} > 1$. Thus $at_{1/2} = \ln(1 + \sqrt{2}) = 0.881$

$$\therefore \ \Delta t_p = 2t_{1/2} = \frac{2 \times 0.881}{a} = \frac{1.12}{\Delta\omega} = 0.179 \text{ ns.}$$

It should be noted that $\Delta\omega$ is not the FWHM of the power spectrum but it is close. The actual FWHM = 1.763 $\Delta\omega$.

9.28

(a) The rate equation should be written as:

$$\frac{dN_2}{dt} = P_2 - \frac{N_2}{\tau_2}\frac{\sigma I}{h\nu}N_2 = P_2 - \frac{N_2}{\tau_2}[1 + \frac{I}{I_S}] = P_2 - \frac{N_2}{\tau_2}[1 + \left(\frac{E}{E_S}\right)^2] \qquad 2.$$

(b) For a static case, $\partial/\partial t = 0$ in both equations. If the pumping is too small, then the [ ] in Eq. 1 is positive and the field will never build-up- it will be maintained by the spontaneous emission. At threshold and for any static situation, that bracket must be zero in order to have a steady-state laser.

$$[1 - (c/n)\ \tau_p\ \gamma(t)\ ] = 0 \text{ or } \gamma(t) = 1/[(c/n)\tau_p] = N_2\sigma \qquad 3.$$

We relate the gain coefficient to the pumping rate by: $N_2\sigma = \frac{P_2\tau_2\sigma}{[1 + (E/E_S)^2]}$ 4

At threshold, E = 0, which specifies the threshold pumping rate:

$$P_2(\text{th}) = \frac{1}{\tau_2\sigma(c/n)\tau_p} \qquad 5.$$

The saturated gain of any CW laser is clamped at threshold. Thus, the denominator of equation 5 must increase from 1 to make the population equal to the threshold value.

$$[1 + \left(\frac{E}{E_S}\right)^2] = \frac{P_2}{P_2(\text{th})} = m \text{ or } \frac{I}{I_S} = m - 1 \qquad 6.$$

The output is $T_2/2$ times the internal intensity with the factor of 2 coming from the fact that the I refers to both the forward and reverse intensities: $(I_{out}/I_S) = (T_2/2)\ (m - 1)$ 7.

9.29

$$\frac{dN_2}{dt} = \frac{\sigma I_p}{h\nu_p}(g_0/g_2\, N_0 - N_2) - \frac{N_2}{\tau_2} \qquad \text{where } 1/\tau_2 = 1/\tau_{21} + 1/\tau_{20};$$

$$\frac{dN_1}{dt} = \frac{N_2}{\tau_{21}} - \frac{N_1}{\tau_{10}} = 0; \text{ and atoms must be conserved} \qquad N_1 + N_2 + N_0 = [N];$$

$$N_1 = \frac{\tau_{10}}{\tau_{21}} N_2;\ N_2 = \frac{(g_0/g_2)(I/I_s)}{1 + I/I_s} N_0; \qquad \text{where } I_s = \frac{h\nu_p}{\sigma_p \tau_2};$$

$$N_0 + N_1 + N_2 = N_0\left[1 + \frac{(g_0/g_2)(\tau_{10}/\tau_{21})(I_p/I_s)}{1 + I_p/I_s} + \frac{(g_0/g_2)(I_p/I_s)}{1 + I_p/I_s}\right] = [N]$$

$$N_0 = \left\{\frac{1 + I_p/I_s}{1 + [1 + (g_0/g_2)(1 + \tau_{10}/\tau_{21})](I_p/I_s)}\right\}[N] \rightarrow \frac{1}{[1 + (g_0/g_2)(1 + \tau_{10}/\tau_{21})]}[N]$$

$$N_2 = \left\{\frac{(g_0/g_2)(I_p/I_s)}{1 + [1 + (g_0/g_2)(1 + \tau_{10}/\tau_{21})](I_p/I_s)}\right\}[N] \rightarrow \frac{g_0/g_2}{[1 + (g_0/g_2)(1 + \tau_{10}/\tau_{21})]}[N]$$

$$N_1 = \left\{\frac{(g_0/g_2)(\tau_{10}/\tau_{21})(I_p/I_s)}{1 + [1 + (g_0/g_2)(1 + \tau_{10}/\tau_{21})](I_p/I_s)}\right\}[N] \rightarrow \frac{(g_0/g_2)(\tau_{10}/\tau_{21})}{[1 + (g_0/g_2)(1 + \tau_{10}/\tau_{21})]}[N]$$

where the arrows indicate the limits for an infinite pump. To obtain $N_2 > (g_2/g_1)N_1$, we require $(g_0/g_2) > (g_0/g_1)(\tau_{10}/\tau_{21})$, which is reasonable enough, but that result is independent of the pump intensity, implying gain even with I_p=0. Of course, that is ridiculous and is caused by the neglect of any thermal populations in (1,2). But it does show that it is relatively easy to obtain an inversion on 2 – 1.

For an inversion on 1-0, $N_1 > (g_1/g_0)N_0$ and we require:

$$g_0/g_2(\tau_{10}/\tau_{21})(I_p/I_s) > 1 + (I_p/I_s);$$

$$\therefore \qquad (I_p/I_s) > \frac{1}{(g_0/g_2)(\tau_{10}/\tau_{21}) - 1}.$$

Obviously one must have $(g_0/g_2)(\tau_{10}/\tau_{21}) > 1$ to even hope for an inversion on $1 \rightarrow 0$. One can never obtain an inversion on $2 \rightarrow 0$ since the limiting ratio $N_2/N_0 = g_2/g_0$ even at infinite pump.

9.30.

Using the model of Sec. 9.2.3

$$\frac{1}{I^+}\frac{dI^+}{dz} = \frac{\gamma_0 e^{-\alpha z}}{1 + (I^+ + I^-)/I_s} = -\frac{1}{I^-}\frac{dI^-}{dz} \qquad 1.$$

Let's first compute the threshold value of γ_0 and thus saturation is not important. For the positive going wave:

$$\ln\frac{I_2^+}{I_1^+} = \frac{\gamma_{th}}{\alpha}(1 - e^{-\alpha l_g}) \qquad 2.$$

where (2,1) indicate the value at the (right, left) ends of the gain cell.

And for the negative wave

$$\ln\frac{I_1^-}{I_2^-} = \frac{\gamma_{th}}{\alpha}(1 - e^{-\alpha l_g}) \qquad 3.$$

Now $I_2^- = R_2 T_b^2 I_2^+$ and $I_1^+ = R_1 T_a^2 I_1^-$ 4.

Adding (2) and (3) yields

$$\ln\left[\frac{I_2^+ I_1^-}{I_1^+ I_2^-}\right] = 2\frac{\gamma_{th}}{\alpha}(1 - e^{-\alpha l_g}) \qquad 5.$$

Substituting (4) yields:

$$\ln\left[\frac{1}{R_1 R_2 T_a^2 T_b^2}\right] = \frac{2\gamma_{th}}{\alpha}(1 - e^{-\alpha l_g}) \qquad 6.$$

Threshold value :(a) $\rightarrow$

$$\gamma_{th} l_g = \left\{\frac{1}{2}\ln\left[\frac{1}{R_1 R_2 T_a^2 T_b^2}\right]\right\}\frac{\alpha l_g}{1 - e^{-\alpha l_g}} \qquad 7.$$

The only change in the saturated behavior is the right hand side of all differential equations and their solutions. For instance, 9.2.21(a) becomes:

$$\ln\left[\frac{f(2)}{f(1)}\right] + [f(2) - f(1)] + k^2\left[\frac{1}{f(1)} - \frac{1}{f(2)}\right] = \frac{\gamma_0(1 - e^{-\alpha l_g})}{\alpha} \qquad 8.$$

where k^2 is still given by 9.2.19(a) - (c) and the relation 9.2.20 applies also. (They are derivable from (4) above). Thus 9.2.3 becomes

$$\frac{I_{out}}{I_s} = \frac{T_b T_2\left\{\gamma_0 l_g\left[\frac{1 - e^{-\alpha l_g}}{\alpha l_g}\right] - \frac{1}{2}\ln\left[\frac{1}{R_1 R_2 T_a^2 T_b^2}\right]\right\}}{\left[1 - \sqrt{T_a^2 T_b^2 R_1 R_2}\right]\left[1 + \sqrt{T_b^2 R_2 / T_a^2 R_1}\right]} \qquad 9.$$

This can also be expressed as: (answer to Part b):

$$\frac{I_0}{I_s} = \frac{T_b T_2\left[(\gamma_0 - \gamma_{th}) l_g\right]\left[\frac{1 - e^{-\alpha l_g}}{\alpha l_g}\right]}{\left[1 - \sqrt{T_a^2 T_b^2 R_1 R_2}\right]\left[1 + \sqrt{T_b^2 R_2 / T_a^2 R_1}\right]} \qquad 10.$$

If we assume a simple rate equation for upper state and recognize that all lasers have the upper state clamped at the threshold value (presuming $N_1 = 0$)

$$\frac{dN_2(z)}{dt} = \eta_p\left\{\frac{\sigma_p I_p^{(th)}(z)}{h\nu_p}\right\} N_0 - \frac{N_2}{\tau_2} \quad \text{(for threshold)} \qquad 11.$$

where η_p=pumping efficiency and we assume the pump decreases exponentially with z

$$N_2(z) = \eta_p \left\{\frac{\sigma_{21}\tau_2}{h\nu_p}\right\} N_0\, I_p^{th}(0)\ e^{-\alpha z} \qquad 12.$$

Multiplying by σ_{21} (of the laser transition) allows one to evaluate the threshold value of the pump at z = 0.

$$\gamma_{th}(z{=}0) \;=\; N_2^0(0)\,\sigma_{21} \;=\; \eta_p \left\{\frac{\sigma_{21}\tau_2}{h\nu_p}\right\} I_p^{th}(0)\, N_0\, \sigma_{21} \qquad 13.$$

where the superscript on I_p implies the threshold value. One can rewrite Eq. (13) in more convenient terms

$$\gamma_{th} \;=\; N_2^0(0)\,\sigma_{21} \;=\; \eta_p \left(\frac{\sigma_{21}\tau_2}{h\nu_{21}}\right)\left(\frac{h\nu_{21}}{h\nu_p}\right)(N_0\sigma_p)\, I_p^{th}(0) \qquad 14.$$

The first parenthesis is I_s^{-1}, the second is the quantum efficiency, and the third is the absorption coefficient of the pump. One can also use this for all values of pumping intensity because the effects of stimulated emission on the populations have been included in Eq. 1.

$$\gamma_0 l_g = \eta_p \eta_{qe}\,(\alpha l_g)\,\frac{I_p(0)}{I_s} \qquad 15.$$

For a pump beam of area A, the absorbed power is: $P_{abs} = I_p(0)\, A(1 - e^{-\alpha l_g})$ 16.

Thus the efficiency is:

$$\eta = \frac{I_{out}A}{P_{abs}} = \frac{T_bT_2}{\left[1 - \sqrt{T_a^2T_b^2R_1R_2}\,\right]\left[1 + \sqrt{T_b^2R_2/T_a^2R_1}\,\right]}\,\eta_p\,\eta_{qe}\left(\frac{I_p(0) - I_p^{th}(0)}{I_p(0)}\right)$$

The first factor can be identified with the coupling efficiency and the expression reduces to:

$$\eta = \eta_c\eta_p\eta_{qe}\left(\frac{I_p(0) - I_p^{th}(0)}{I_p(0)}\right) \qquad 17.$$

While the above is restricted to systems similar to YAG with virtually zero lower state lifetime, almost all lasers obey this relation. The "differential" or "slope efficiency" is the product of the first three factors and the "wall plug" efficiency includes that of the pump.

9.31

The secret to this problem is to start the mathematics with the physics in mind by writing equations in the format which is most meaningful from a physical sense. For instance, it makes sense to group the quantities $\gamma_0-\alpha$ together because there isn't an easy way of measuring each of them separately - only the difference can be determined.

$$\frac{df}{dz} = \frac{[(\gamma_0-\alpha) - \alpha f]f}{1 + f} \quad \text{or} \quad \frac{(1+f)df}{f\left[1 - (\alpha_0/\gamma_0-\alpha)\, f\right]} = (\gamma_0 - \alpha)dz \qquad 1.$$

$$\text{Expanding: } \frac{1 + f}{(f\,[1 - \delta f])} = \frac{A}{f} + \frac{B}{1 - \delta f} \quad \text{where } \delta = \frac{\alpha}{\gamma_0 - \alpha};\ A = 1;\ B = \delta + 1 \qquad 2.$$

Now integrate between the input (1) and the output (2):

$$\int_{f_2}^{f_1} \frac{df}{f} + (\delta + 1) \int_{f_2}^{f_1} \frac{df}{1 - \delta f} = (\gamma_o - \alpha) \int_0^{l_g} dz \qquad 3.$$

$$\ln \frac{f_2}{f_1} + \frac{\delta + 1}{\delta} \ln \left\{ \frac{1 - \delta f_1}{1 - \delta f_2} \right\} = (\gamma_0 - \alpha)\, l_g \qquad 4.$$

Lets make sure that the expression reduces to a familiar result if $\delta = 0$:

$$\lim_{\delta \to 0} [\text{Equation 4}] \to \ln \frac{f_2}{f_1} + f_2 - f_1 = \gamma_0 l_g$$

For maximum extractable intensity $f_2 = f_1 + \Delta f$, where f_1 must be large. (In other words, we only **add** the extractable intensity.) We use the expansion $\ln(1+x) \approx x$ in the various terms of equation 4.

$$\ln \frac{f_2}{f_1} = \ln \left(1 + \frac{\Delta f}{f_1}\right) \approx \frac{\Delta f}{f_1}; \text{ and } \qquad \left(\frac{\delta + 1}{\delta}\right) \ln (1 - \delta f_1) = -(\delta + 1)\, f_1 \qquad 5a$$

$$-\left(\frac{\delta + 1}{\delta}\right) \ln (1 - \delta f_2) = +(\delta + 1)\, f_2 = (\delta + 1)(f_1 + \Delta f) \qquad 5b$$

Thus Eq. 4 becomes:

$$\frac{\Delta f}{f_1} - (\delta + 1)\, f_1 + (\delta + 1)\, f_1 + (\delta + 1)\, \Delta f = (\gamma_0 - \alpha)\, l_g \qquad 6.$$

The second and third terms of Eq. 6 cancel, and the first is small:

$$\Delta f \left\{ \frac{1}{f_1} + (\delta + 1) \right\} = (\gamma_0 - \alpha)\, l_g \approx \Delta f(\delta + 1) \qquad 7.$$

$$\delta + 1 = \frac{\alpha}{\gamma_0 - \alpha} + 1 = \left(\frac{\gamma_0}{\gamma_0 - \alpha}\right) \qquad 8.$$

$$\therefore \Delta f = \frac{(\gamma_0 - \alpha) l_g}{\gamma_0/(\gamma_0 - \alpha)} = \frac{(\gamma_0 - \alpha)^2}{\gamma_0}\, l_g \qquad 9.$$

If $\alpha = 0$, then the maximum extractable power is $\gamma_0 l_g I_s$. Thus, we rewrite Eq. 9 as:

$$\Delta I = (\gamma_0\, l_g)\, I_s) \left(\frac{\gamma_0 - \alpha}{\gamma_0}\right)^2 \quad \text{(ans. to part (a))} \qquad 10.$$

Note that if α were 20% of γ_0, then one can only extract 64% of the value for $\alpha = 0$.

When this is used as a laser one must return to Eq. 4, insert the self-consistency requirement, and solve for f_2.

$$f_1 = [T_a\, T_b\, \Pi R_j]\, f_2 \qquad 11.$$

Return to Eq. 4 and abbreviate various factors in terms of their physical significance. Let

$$\ln \frac{1}{T_a\, T_b\, \Pi R_j} \equiv (\gamma_{th} - \alpha)\, l_g \stackrel{\Delta}{=} g_{th}. \quad 12(a) \text{ and } (\gamma_0 - \alpha)\, l_g \stackrel{\Delta}{=} g_0 \qquad 12.$$

where all g's are the **net** small signal gain coefficient times the length of the medium. Eq. 4 becomes

$$\ln\left\{\frac{1 - f_2\delta e^{-g_{th}}}{1 - f_2\delta}\right\} = (g_0 - g_{th})\frac{\delta}{\delta+1} \qquad 13.$$

Solve for f_2: $$f_2 = \frac{1}{\delta}\frac{\{\exp[(g_0 - g_t)\,\delta/(\delta+1)] - 1\}}{\{\exp[(g_0 - g_{th})\,\delta/(\delta+1)] - \exp[-g_{th}]\}} \qquad 14.$$

The output intensity is $T_bT_2I_sf_2$

$$I_{out} = T_bT_2I_s\frac{\{\exp[(g_0 - g_t)\,\delta/(\delta+1)] - 1\}}{\{\exp[(g_0 - g_{th})\,\delta/(\delta+1)] - \exp[-g_{th}]\}} \qquad 15.$$

If we assume δ is small, then $e^x = 1 + x$ and thus exp[ ] = 1 + [ ].

$$I_{out} = T_bT_2T_s\left(\frac{1}{\delta+1}\right)\frac{\{g_0 - g_{th}\}}{\{1 - e^{-g_{th}}\}} \qquad 16.$$

re-inserting the definition of $\delta+1$

$$I_{out} = T_bT_2T_s\left(\frac{\gamma_0 - \alpha}{\gamma_0}\right)\frac{\{\gamma_0 - \gamma_{th}\}}{\{1 - e^{-(\gamma_{th} - \alpha)l_g}\}} \qquad 17.$$

which has the same functional form as before but with a correction factor. This analysis should point out to you the detrimental effects of an unsaturable loss in the gain medium. Such a loss could be scattering in the gain medium due to crystal imperfections, "dust" in the gas, or absorption by an impurity.

9.32

The following is the laser cavity which is analyzed:

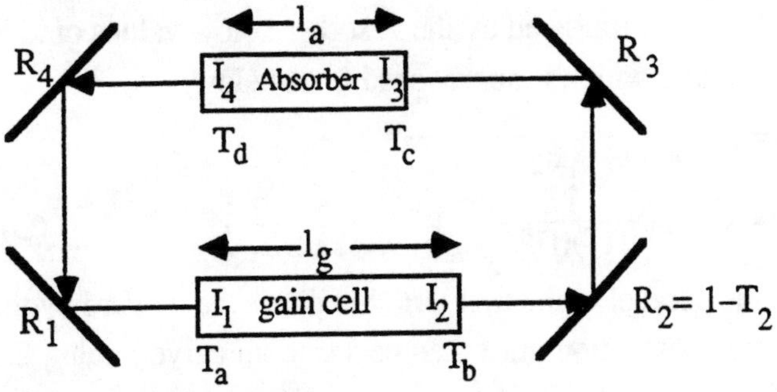

Integrating along the path of the gain cell yields:

$$\ln\left(\frac{I_2}{I_1}\right) + \frac{I_2}{I_{sg}} - \frac{I_1}{I_{sg}} = \gamma_0 l_g = g_0 \text{ or } y = x + g_0 - \ln\left(\frac{y}{x}\right) \text{ where } x = \frac{I_1}{I_{sg}} \text{ and } y = \frac{I_2}{I_{sg}}$$

or $$(y - x) = g_0 - \ln\left(1 + \frac{y-x}{x}\right) \qquad 1.$$

As we shall see, it will be more convenient to use y–x as the dependent variable rather than y alone. Eq. 1 indicates that $y = I_2/I_{sg}$ is always less than $[x = I_1/I_{sg}] + g_0$ since $y = I_2/I_1 > 1$.

In the absorber:

$$\ln\left(\frac{I_4}{I_3}\right) + \frac{I_4}{I_{sa}} - \frac{I_3}{I_{sa}} = -\alpha_0 l_a = a_0 \qquad 2.$$

Self-consistency requires that: $I_3 = T_b T_c R_2 R_3 I_2$ 3.

and $I_4 = \frac{I_1}{T_a T_d R_1 R_4}$ 4.

One can combine the last two equations with (2) and eliminate I_3 and I_4:

$$y = \frac{x}{(\Pi T)(\Pi R)} + \frac{a_0}{R_2 R_3 T_b T_c} \frac{I_{sa}}{I_{sg}} - \frac{I_{sa}}{I_{sg}} \ln\left(\frac{x}{y} \frac{1}{(\Pi T)(\Pi R)}\right) \quad 5.$$

If $a_0=0$, then $y(\Pi T)(\Pi R)=x$. For $a_0 \neq 0$, then $y(\Pi T)(\Pi R)>x$ to make up for the additional loss, saturated or otherwise. Thus the logarithmic term is positive and Eq. 5 shows that:

$$y < \frac{x}{(\Pi T)(\Pi R)} + \frac{a_0}{R_2 R_3 T_b T_c} \frac{I_{sa}}{I_{sg}}$$

or $$y-x < x\left(\frac{1}{(\Pi T)(\Pi R)-1}\right) + \frac{a_0}{R_2 R_3 T_b T_c} \frac{I_{sa}}{I_{sg}} \quad 6.$$

and y approaches this asymptotic limit from below. It is useful to consider asymptotes in the $(I_2 - I_1, I_1)$ plane, both normalized to the saturation intensity of the gain cell (hence the (y-x,x) plane):

If $I_{1,2} << I_{sg}$; $y = x\,e^{g_0}$ or $y-x = x(e^{g_0} - 1)$ (A) 7.

If $I_{1,2} >> I_{sg}$ $y - x = g_0$ (B) 8.

Thus, curve B is just a straight line displaced from $y-x = 0$ upwards by the added value g_0 with the y axis intercept being g_0. If the attenuator can not be saturated and $I_{3,4} << I_{sa}$;

$$I_4 = I_3 \exp(-\alpha_0 l_a) \text{ or } y = x \frac{e^{+g_0}}{(\Pi T)(\Pi R)}$$

or $$y - x = x\left\{\frac{e^{+g_0}}{(\Pi T)(\Pi R)} - 1\right\} \quad \text{(C)} \quad 9.$$

which is the curve followed by the absorber at low values of x. Equation 6 is another asymptotic curve which is approached from below.

$$y = \frac{x}{(\Pi T)(\Pi R)} + \frac{a_0}{R_2 R_3 T_b T_c} \frac{I_{sa}}{I_{sg}}$$

or $$y - x = x\left(\frac{1}{(\Pi T)(\Pi R)} - 1\right) + \frac{a_0}{R_2 R_3 T_b T_c} \frac{I_{sa}}{I_{sg}} \quad \text{(D)} \quad 10.$$

This is a line parallel to the first term but displaced upward by the second additive term. The saturated absorption must then be a smooth curve joining C and D at the extremes.

The graphical solution is shown below.

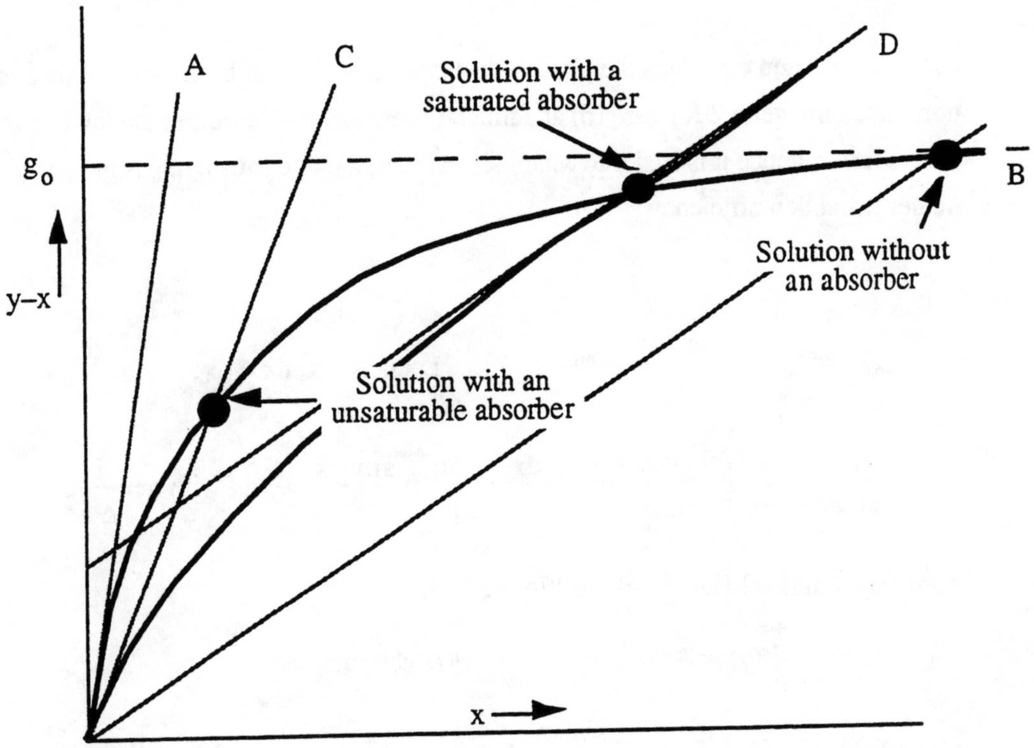

9.33

a. $E_2 = 8 \times 8066\ cm^{-1} = 64{,}528\ cm^{-1}$; $\eta_{QE} = 16{,}753/64528 = 25.9\%$

b. (1/2)(base)(height) = 0.5 $(8\ cm^{-1} \times 3 \times 10^{10}\ cm/sec)(g(\nu_0))$; $g(\nu_0) = 8.33 \times 10^{-12}$ s

$\sigma = A_{21}(\lambda^2/8\pi)g(\nu_0) = 5.91 \times 10^{-17}\ cm^2$

c. $\frac{dN_2}{dt} = R - \frac{\sigma I}{h\nu}[N_2 - (g_2/g_1)N_1] - \frac{N_2}{\tau_2}$; $\frac{dN_1}{dt} = \frac{\sigma I}{h\nu}[N_2 - (g_2/g_1)N_1] + \frac{N_2}{\tau_2} - \frac{N_1}{\tau_1}$

For a threshold calculation, one can neglect the stimulated emission terms.

$N_2 = R\tau_2$; $N_1 = R\tau_1$; but $\tau_2 = \tau_1 = \tau = 10\ \mu s$; $g_2/g_1 = 1/2$; $\gamma_{th} = \sigma[N_2 - (g_2/g_1)N_1] = \sigma R\tau/2$;

$S = \Pi R \cdot \Pi T = 0.734$; $\gamma_{th} = (1/2l_g)\ln(1/S) = 1.55 \times 10^{-2}\ cm^{-1}$

d. $N_2[1 + I/I_s] - [(g_2/g_1)I/I_s]N_1 = R\tau$; and $N_2[1 + I/I_s] - [1 + (g_2/g_1)I/I_s]N_1 = 0$

where $I_s = h\nu/\sigma\tau$; Solve for $[N_2 - (g_2/g_1)N_1]$:

$[N_2 - (g_2/g_1)N_1] = \frac{R\tau(g_2/g_1)}{1 + I/I_s}$ and we have re-derived the saturation law: $\gamma = \frac{\gamma_0}{1 + I/I_s}$

9.34

$G_0 = 6$ dB $\rightarrow 0.6 = \log_{10}(e^{\gamma_0 l_g})$; $G_0 = 3.98$; $\gamma_0 l_g = 1.382$; $S = R_1R_2R_3R_4T_aT_b = 0.279$;

$\gamma_{th}l_g = 1.276$; $\frac{I_4}{I_s} = \frac{(\gamma_0 - \gamma_{th})l_g}{1 - 1/G_0} = 0.147$; $I_{out} = 0.6\ I_4$; $I_s = 37.8\ W/cm^2$ for $\lambda_0 = 1.05\ \mu m$.

$I_{out} = 3.33\ W/cm^2$

9.35

The infinite pump equalizes the population between 3 and 0 in both cases. However, atoms accumulate in 2 for case (b) at a much faster rate. Furthermore, the lower state decays faster, hence it is easier to establish an inversion and thus n_i/n_{th} is greater yielding a greater extraction efficiency.

9.36

$$e(t) = E_0 e^{j\omega_0 t} \sum_{-\infty}^{+\infty} \frac{\sin n\omega_c/\Delta\omega}{n\omega_c/\Delta\omega} e^{jn\omega_c t}; \qquad \text{Let } n\omega_c = x;\ dx = \omega_c;$$

$$\frac{e(t)}{E_0 e^{j\omega_0 t}} = \int_{-\infty}^{+\infty} \frac{\sin(x/\Delta\omega)}{(x/\Delta\omega)} e^{jxt} \frac{dx}{\omega_c} = \frac{\Delta\omega}{\omega_c} \int_{-\infty}^{+\infty} \frac{\sin ax}{x} e^{jxt}\, dx \text{ with } a = \frac{1}{\Delta\omega}.$$

From Mathematical Handbook, p. 176, #33.17:

$$F(\alpha) = \int_{-\infty}^{+\infty} f(y)\, e^{-j\alpha y}\, dy;\ f(y) = \frac{1}{2\pi} \int_{-\infty}^{+\infty} F(\alpha) e^{j\alpha y}\, d\alpha.$$

For $f(y) = 1\ |y| < b$; $\therefore F(\alpha) = \frac{2\sin b\alpha}{\alpha}$. Let $\alpha = x$, $b = a$, $y = t = 0\ |y| > b$;

$$\therefore \frac{e(t)}{E_0\, e^{j\omega_0 t}} = \frac{\Delta\omega}{\omega_c} \cdot \int \left[\frac{\sin b\alpha}{\alpha}\right] e^{j\alpha y}\, d\alpha = \frac{2\pi}{2}\left(\frac{\Delta\omega}{\omega_c}\right)\left[\frac{1}{2\pi}\int_{+\infty}^{-\infty} \frac{2\sin b\alpha}{\alpha} e^{j\alpha y}\, d\alpha\right]$$

$$= \pi\frac{\Delta\omega}{\omega_c}\left\{\begin{bmatrix} 1 & \Delta\omega t<1 & \text{or } t<\frac{1}{\Delta\omega} \\ 0 & \Delta\omega t>1 & \text{or } t>\frac{1}{\Delta\omega} \end{bmatrix} = f(t)\right\};$$

$$I(t) = \frac{e(t)\cdot e^*(t)}{2\eta_0} = \frac{E_0^2}{2\eta_0}\left(\frac{\pi\Delta\omega}{\omega_c}\right)^2 f^2(t) = I_0 f^2(t)$$

(a,b) Thus, the repetition frequency is c/2d, period is 2d/c = 5 nsec (d=75 cm).

(c) Peak intensity is $\frac{E_0^2}{2\eta_0}\left(\frac{\pi\Delta\omega}{\omega_c}\right)^2 = 8.18 \times 10^{+4}\ \text{W/cm}^2 = I_0$.

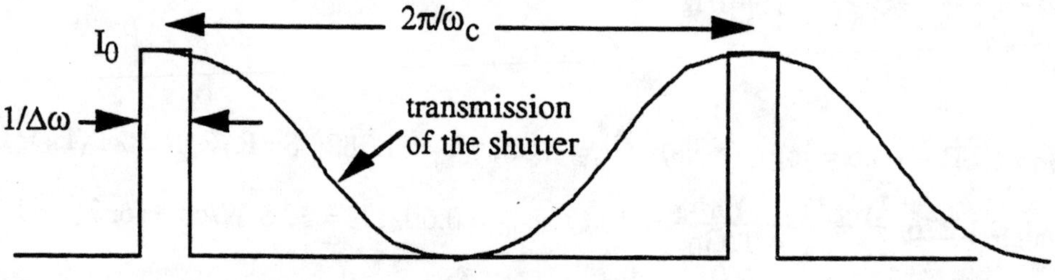

(d) Energy transmitted by the shutter

$$T = \int_{-1/2\Delta\omega}^{1/2\Delta\omega} I_0 \cos^2(\pi t/T)\, dt = \frac{I_0}{2}\left[t + \frac{1}{\omega_c}\sin \omega_c t\right]_{-1/2\Delta\omega}^{1/2\Delta\omega}$$

$$= \frac{I_0}{2}\left[\frac{1}{\Delta\omega} + \frac{2}{\omega_c}\sin\frac{\omega_c}{2\Delta\omega}\right] = \frac{I_0}{\Delta\omega}\left\{1 - \frac{1}{12}\left[\frac{\omega_c}{\Delta\omega}\right]^2\right\} \text{ where } \sin x = x - x^3/3!;$$

The term subtracting from 1 is the loss: Loss =0.00013

9.37

(a) $\sigma = A_{21}\frac{\lambda_2}{8\pi n^2}\left(\frac{2}{\pi\Delta\nu_h}\right)$; $\Delta\nu_h = 5 \times 3 \times 10^{+10}$ Hz $= 0.150$ THz; $\frac{2}{\pi\Delta\nu_h} = 4.24\times10^{-12}$ s

$\therefore \sigma = 2.9\times10^{-19}$ cm^2; $I_s = \frac{h\nu}{\sigma\tau_2} = 2.5 \times 10^{+3}$ W/cm^2

(b) R.T.G. ≥ 1; $\therefore \gamma_0 = \frac{1}{l_g}\ln\frac{1}{(\Pi R)T^2} = 0.48$ cm^{-1}; $\gamma_0 l_g = 0.856$;

(c) $\ln\frac{I_2}{I_1} + \frac{I_2}{I_s}\left[1 - \frac{I_1}{I_2}\right] = \gamma_0 l_g = 3 \times 0.856$;

Thus $\frac{I_2}{I_s} = \frac{(\gamma_0 - \gamma_{th})l_g}{1 - e^{-\gamma_{th}l_g}} = 2.976$; $I_2 = 5.95$ kW/cm^2; $I_{out} = T_b \cdot T_2 I_2 = 2.92$ kW/cm^2

9.38

(a) $2d/c = 4$ ns; $\therefore d = 60$ cm

(b) From Graph $\Delta t_{1/2} = 0.4$ ns; $e^{-(t_{1/2}/\tau)^2} = 1/2$;

Thus $t_{1/2} = (\ln 2)^{1/2}\tau$ and $\Delta t_{1/2} = (4\ln 2)^{1/2}\tau$; $\tau = \Delta t_{1/2}/(4\ln 2)^{1/2} = 0.6\,\Delta t_{1/2} = 0.24$ nsec

(c) $\langle I \rangle = I_0 \frac{c}{2d}\int_{-\infty}^{+\infty} e^{-(t/\tau)^2}\, dt = I_0 \frac{c}{2d}\sqrt{\pi}\tau = I_0\sqrt{\pi}\frac{\tau}{2d/c}$; $\frac{I_p}{\langle I \rangle} = \frac{2d/c}{\sqrt{\pi}\tau} = 9.4$

(d) $e(t) = E_0\, e^{-(1/2)(t/\tau)^2}$ and is periodic with $T = 2d/c$;

$F(\omega) = E_0 \int_{-\infty}^{+\infty} e^{-(1/2)(t/\tau)^2} e^{j\omega t}\, dt = 2E_0 \int_{-\infty}^{+\infty} e^{-(1/2)(t/\tau)^2} \cos\omega t\, dt$; $\therefore b = 1/2\tau^2$; $x = t$; $\alpha = \omega$;

Thus: $F(\omega) = \sqrt{\frac{\pi}{2}}\,\tau\, e^{-(\omega^2\tau^2)/2}$; $f^2(\omega) = \frac{\pi}{2}\tau^2 e^{-(\omega\tau)^2}$

9.39

With no excitation $N_2 = 0$, $N_1 + N_0 = [N] = N_0[1 + e^{-\Delta E/kT}]$; $N_0 = 0.769[N]$;

$N_1 = 0.231[N] = 6.93^{+19}$ cm^{-3}; $\alpha = [(N_2{=}0) - N_1]\sigma = 6.93$ cm^{-1};

For an infinitely strong pump, $N_2 = N_0$; $N_0[2 + e^{-\Delta E/kT}] = [N]$;

$N_0 = N_2 = 0.435\,[N] = 1.3\times10^{+20}$ cm^{-3}; $N_1 = 3.92\times10^{+19}$ cm^{-3}; $\gamma_{max} = 36.3$ cm^{-1}

9.40

$S = R_1R_2R_3R_4T_aT_b = 0.551$; $\gamma_{th}l_g = 0.596$; $\gamma_{th} = 0.397\ cm^{-1}$; $\Delta N = 3.97^{+17}\ cm^{-3}$; $I_s =$ $15.94\ kW/cm^2$; $\frac{I_2}{I_s} = \frac{(\gamma_0 - \gamma_{th})l_g}{1 - S} = 0.343$; $\frac{I_{out}}{I_s} = 0.068$; $I_{out} = 1.09\ kW/cm^2$

9.41

For oscillation $G_0^2R_1R_2 > 1$, thus $G_0 < 1/\sqrt{R_1R_2} = 40$ i.e max gain =16 dB

9.42

(a) $\sigma(\nu) \propto g(\nu)$ and $\int g(\nu)d\nu = 1 = \frac{1}{2}(8\times10^{+9})\ g(\nu_0)$; $g(\nu_0) = 0.25$ ns

(b) $\exp[\gamma_0(\nu_0)l_g] = (1/S)$; $\therefore \gamma(\nu_0) = (1/l_g)\ln(1/S) = (1/l_g)\cdot[\ln 1.25 \approx 0.25] = 0.025$
$[N_2 - (g_2/g_1)N_1]\sigma = 0.025\ cm^{-1}$; $N_2 - \frac{g_2}{g_1}N_1 = 2.5\times10^{+16}\ cm^{-3}$

(c)

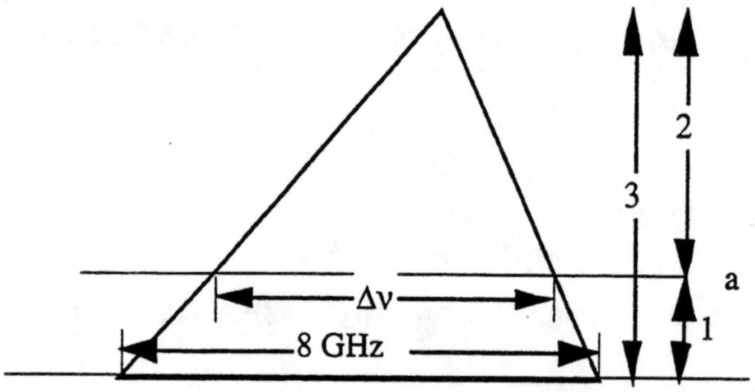

$\Delta\nu = \frac{2}{3}\cdot 8\ GHz = 5.3\ GHz$

9.43

$\tau_{RT} = 150\ cm/3\times10^{+10} = 50\times10^{-10} = 5ns$; (a) $\tau_p = \frac{5\times10^{-9}}{1 - 0.975} = \frac{5\times10^{-9}}{.025} = 200ns$

(b) $0.97\ e[\gamma_0 l_g] > 1 \quad \therefore \gamma_0 l_g = \ln\frac{1}{0.975} = \ln\frac{1}{1 - 0.025} \approx 0.025$

$\gamma_0 = \frac{0.025}{20} = 1.25\times10^{-3}\ cm^{-1} = \Delta N\sigma$; $\Delta N = 1.25\times10^{+11}\ cm^{-3}$

(c) $\frac{5(\Delta\nu/2)^2}{(\nu_\pm - \nu_0)^2 + (\Delta\nu/2)^2} = 1$; $\quad 5(\Delta\nu/2)^2 = (\nu_\pm - \nu_0)^2 + (\Delta\nu/2)^2$

or $(\nu_\pm - \nu_0)^2 = 4(\Delta\nu/2)^2$; $\therefore \nu_\pm = \nu_0 \pm \Delta\nu$; $\nu_+ - \nu_- = 2\Delta\nu = 6\ GHz$

$FSR = \frac{c}{2d} = \frac{3\times10^{+10}}{3\times50} = \frac{1000\ MHz}{50} = 200\ MHz$

$\therefore \quad N = \frac{6\times10^{+9}}{2\times10^{+8}} = 30$ modes

9.44

$\int g(\nu)d\nu = 1; \qquad g(\nu_0) = 3.33\times10^{10}$ s;

$$\sigma = A_{21}\frac{\lambda^2}{8\pi}\cdot g(\nu_0) = \frac{6^{+4}\cdot(0.6^4)^2}{8\pi}\cdot 3.33\times10^{10} = 2.86\times10^{+15}\ \text{cm}^2$$

$$I_s = \frac{h\nu}{\sigma\tau_2} = \frac{6.62\times10^{34}\ \text{joulesec}\times 3\times10^{+10}\ \text{cmsec}^1}{0.6\times10^4\ \text{cm}\times 2.86\times10^{15}\ \text{cm}^2\ \times 3.9\times10^6\ \text{sec}} = 29.6\ \text{watts/cm}^2$$

$$\gamma_{th} = \frac{1}{l_g}\ln\left(\frac{1}{\Pi R}\right) = \frac{1}{20}\ln\left\{\frac{1}{0.95\cdot0.6\cdot0.9\cdot0.85}\right\} = 4.15\times10^{-2}\ \text{cm}^{-1}$$

$$[N_2 - (g_2/g_1)\ N_1]_{th} = \frac{4.15\times10^{-2}\ \text{cm}^1}{2.86\times10^{15}\ \text{cm}^2} = 1.45\times10^{+13}\ \text{cm}^{-3};$$

(b) Path length = 2(40+30)cm = 140 cm ∴ FSR $= \frac{c}{\text{perimeter}}$ = 214.3 MHz; For a small signal inversion density= $5\times10^{+13}$ cm^{-3}, the system is pumped to $5\times10^{+13}/1.45\times10^{+13}$ = 3.45 times threshold.

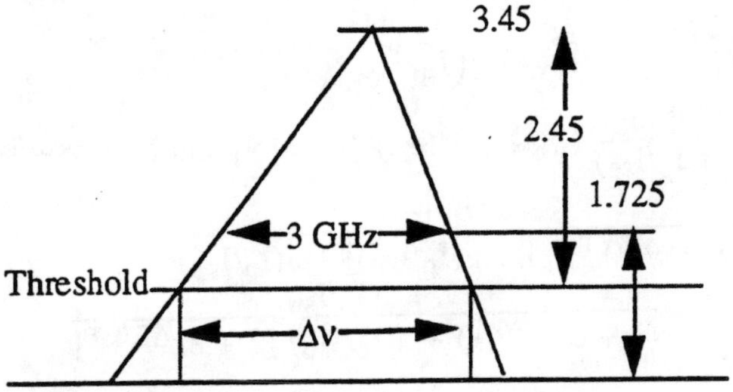

Use similar triangles: $\frac{3}{3.45/2} = \frac{\Delta\nu}{2.45}$ ∴ $\Delta\nu$ = 4.26 GHz

Thus: $N = \frac{4.26\ \text{GHz}}{0.214\ \text{GHz}}$ = 19 or 20 modes

(c) $$\frac{[N_2 - g_2/g_1 N_1]^0}{1 + I/I_s} = \frac{\Delta N^0}{4} = 1.25\times10^{+13}\ \text{cm}^3$$

(d) $I_1 = R_1R_2R_3R_4I_2 = (S = 0.436)\ I_2$

$$\ln\frac{I_2}{I_1} + \frac{I_2}{I_s}\left[1 - \frac{I_1}{I_2}\right] = \gamma_0 l_g = 3.45\ \gamma_{th}l_g; \qquad \gamma_{th}l_g = \ln\left(\frac{1}{\Pi R}\right)$$

$$\frac{I_2}{I_s} = \frac{2.45\ \gamma_{th}l_g}{1 - 0.436} = \frac{2.45\times 20\ \text{cm}\times 0.0415\ \text{cm}^{-1}}{0.564} = 3.61$$

$I_{out} = T_2I_2 = 0.4\ (3.61 \times 29.6\ \text{W/cm}^2) = 42.7\ \text{W/cm}^2$

9.45

Case (a)

$$\frac{dN_2}{dt} = \left(\frac{\sigma_p I_p}{h\nu_{30}}\right)N_0 - \frac{N_2}{\tau_2} = 0;\ N_2 = \frac{I_p}{I_{sp}}N_0;\ \gamma = (N_2 - N_1)\sigma_{21};\ I_{sp} = h\nu_{30}/\sigma_p\tau_2;$$

$N_1 = [e^{-\Delta E/kT}]N_0$; $N_1 + N_2 + N_0 = [N]$; $N_0\,(e^{-\Delta E/kT} + I_p/I_{sp} + 1) = [N]$

$$\therefore N_0 = \frac{[N]}{(1 + I_p/I_{sp} + e^{-\Delta E/kT})}[N]; \qquad N_2 = \frac{I_p/I_{sp}}{(1 + I_p/I_{sp} + e^{-\Delta E/kT})}[N]$$

$$N_1 = \frac{e^{-\Delta E/kT}}{(1 + I/I_{sp} + e^{-\Delta E/kT})}[N];$$

$$\boxed{\gamma_0(\nu) = \sigma_{21}\frac{[N]}{(1 + I/I_{sp} + e^{-\Delta E/kT})}\left\{\frac{I_p}{I_{sp}} - e^{-\Delta E/kT}\right\}};$$

Optical transparency: $\frac{I_p}{I_{sp}} = e^{-\Delta E/kT} = 0.22$; and for $I/I_{sp} \rightarrow$ large,

$$\boxed{\frac{\gamma_0(\nu)}{[N]\sigma_{21}} \rightarrow 1}$$

Case (b)

$$\frac{dN_2}{dt} = \frac{E_3}{E_2}\left(\frac{\sigma_p I_p}{h\nu_{30}}\right)(N_0 - N_2) - \frac{N_2}{\tau_2} = 0;$$

$$\frac{N_2}{\tau_2}\left(1 + a\frac{I_p}{I_{sp}}\right) = a\left(\frac{I_p}{I_{sp}}\right)\frac{N_0}{\tau_2}; \qquad a = \frac{E_3}{E_2}$$

$$N_2 = \frac{a(I_p/I_{sp})}{1 + a(I_p/I_{sp})}N_0;\ N_1 + N_2 + N_0 = [N] \text{ and } N_0\left\{e^{-\Delta E/kT} + \frac{a(I_p/I_{sp})}{1 + a(I_p/I_{sp})} + 1\right\} = [N]$$

$$\frac{N_0}{[N]} = \frac{1 + a(I_p/I_{sp})}{(1 + e^{-\Delta E/kT})\,[1 + a(I_p/I_{sp})] + a(I_p/I_{sp})}$$

$$= \frac{1 + a(I_p/I_{sp})}{(1 + e^{-\Delta E/kT}) + a(I_p/I_{sp})\,[2 + e^{-\Delta E/kT}]}$$

$$\frac{N_1}{[N]} = \frac{[1 + a(I_p/I_{sp})]\,e^{-\Delta E/kT}}{(1 + e^{-\Delta E/kT}) + a(I_p/I_{sp})\,[2 + e^{-\Delta E/kT}]}; \quad \frac{N_2}{[N]}$$

$$= \frac{a(I_p/I_{sp})}{(1 + e^{-\Delta E/kT}) + a(I_p/I_{sp})\,[2 + e^{-\Delta E/kT}]}$$

$$\gamma_0 = (N_2 - N_1)\sigma_{21} = [N]\sigma_{21}\frac{a(I_p/I_{sp}) - [1 + a(I/I_{sp})]\,e^{-\Delta E/kT}}{(1 + e^{-\Delta E/kT}) + a(I_p/I_{sp})\,[2 + e^{-\Delta E/kT}]}$$

$$\boxed{\gamma_0 = [N]\sigma_{21}\frac{[a(I_p/I_{sp})\,[1 - e^{-\Delta E/kT}] - e^{-\Delta E/kT}]}{(1 + e^{-\Delta E/kT}) + a(I_p/I_{sp})\,[2 + e^{-\Delta E/kT}]}}$$

at transparency: $$I_p/I_{sp} = \frac{E_2}{E_3}\cdot\frac{e^{-\Delta E/kT}}{1 - e^{-\Delta E/kT}} = 0.255$$

For $I_p/I_{sp} >> 1$ $$\boxed{\frac{\gamma_0}{[N]\sigma_{21}} = \frac{1 - e^{-\Delta E/kT}}{2 + e^{-\Delta E/kT}}} \rightarrow 0.35$$

At $I_p = 0$, $\gamma_0/[N]\sigma_{21} = -0.1802$ for both cases

9.46

If $e(t) = E_0 \exp\{j[\omega_0 + \Delta\omega t/T]t\} \exp[-t^2/2\tau_p^2]$

$$= E_0 \exp[+j\omega_0 t] \left\{\exp\left[-1/2\tau_p^2 - j\Delta\omega/T\right]t^2\right\} = \exp[+j\omega_0 t] \exp[-at^2]$$

where $a = 1/2\tau_p^2 - j\,\Delta\omega/T$;

Thus the envelope of the spectra around ω_0 is given by:

$$F(\omega) = E_0 \int_{-\infty}^{+\infty} \exp[-j\omega t] \exp[-at^2]\, dt; \text{ where } \omega \text{ is measured with respect to } \omega_0$$

$$= E_0 \left\{ \int_{-\infty}^{0} \exp[-j\omega t'] \exp[-at'^2]\, dt' + \int_{0}^{\infty} \exp[-j\omega t] \exp[-at^2]\, dt \right\}$$

$$= 2E_0 \int_0^{\infty} \exp[-at^2] \cos\omega t\, dt = 2F_c(\omega);$$

Use Mathematical Handbook, p. 176 $F_c(\alpha) = \int_0^{\infty} f(x) \cos\alpha x\, dx$;

Let $x = t$; $f(x) = \exp[-at^2]$; $\alpha = \omega$ and use transform 33.41

If $f(x) = \exp[-bx^2]$; $\quad F_c(\alpha) = \frac{1}{2}\sqrt{\frac{\pi}{b}} \exp[-\alpha^2/4b]$; $\quad b = a = \frac{1}{2\tau_p^2} - j\frac{\Delta\omega}{T}$

Thus $F(\omega) = 2\left\{\frac{1}{2}\sqrt{\frac{\pi}{a}} \exp[-\omega^2/4a]\right\}$; (Remember, a is a complex quantity)

$$a = \frac{1}{2\tau_p^2} - j\frac{\Delta\omega}{T} = \frac{1}{2\tau_p^2}[1 - j2(\Delta\omega\tau_p^2/T)] = \frac{1}{2\tau_p^2}[1 + 4(\Delta\omega\tau_p^2/T)^2]^{1/2} \exp -j \tan^{-1}[2(\Delta\omega\tau_p^2/T)]$$

$$\frac{1}{a} = \frac{2\tau_p^2[1 + j2(\Delta\omega\tau_p^2/T)]}{[1 + 4(\Delta\omega\tau_p^2/T)^2]^{1/2}} = \frac{2\tau_p^2}{[1 + 4(\Delta\omega\tau_p^2/T)^2]^{1/2}} \exp +j \tan^{-1}[2(\Delta\omega\tau_p^2/T)];$$

$$\frac{1}{4a} = \frac{\tau_p^2}{2[1 + 4(\Delta\omega\tau_p^2/T)^2]^{1/2}} \exp +j \tan^{-1}[2(\Delta\omega\tau_p^2/T)]$$

$$\frac{1}{a^{1/2}} = \frac{\sqrt{2}\tau_p}{[1 + 4(\Delta\omega\tau_p^2/T)^2]^{1/4}} \exp +j \frac{1}{2} \tan^{-1}[2(\Delta\omega\tau_p^2/T)]$$

$$\text{Thus: } E_0 F(\omega) = E_0 \frac{\sqrt{2\pi}\tau_p}{[1 + 4(\Delta\omega\tau_p^2/T)^2]^{1/2}} \exp +j \frac{1}{2} \tan^{-1}[2(\Delta\omega\tau_p^2/T)]$$

$$\times \exp\left[-\frac{2(\omega\tau_p)^2}{4[1 + 4(\Delta\omega\tau_p^2/T)^2]} - j\frac{2(\omega\tau_p)^2 \Delta\omega/T}{[1 + 4(\Delta\omega\tau_p^2/T)^2]}\right] = E_0|F(\omega)|\exp[-j\theta(\omega)];$$

where:

$$\boxed{|E(\omega)| = \frac{\sqrt{2\pi}E_0\tau_p}{[1 + 4(\Delta\omega\tau_p^2/T)^2]^{1/4}} \cdot \exp\left[-\frac{(\omega\tau_p)^2}{2[1 + 4(\Delta\omega\tau_p^2/T)^2]}\right]}$$

and

$$\theta(\omega) = \left\{ \frac{(\omega\tau_p^2)(\Delta\omega/T)}{[1 + 4(\Delta\omega\tau_p^2/T)^2]} - \frac{1}{2}\tan^{-1}\frac{2\Delta\omega\tau_p^2}{T} \right\}$$

The spectral distribution is proportional to $E(\omega)\cdot E^*(\omega) \propto |F(\omega)|^2 = S(\omega)$

$$S(\omega) = |E(\omega)|^2 = \frac{2\pi(E_0\tau_p)^2}{[1 + 4(\Delta\omega\tau_p^2/T)^2]^{1/2}} \cdot \exp\left[- \frac{(\omega\tau_p)^2}{[1 + 4(\Delta\omega\tau_p^2/T)^2]} \right]$$

$$(\text{FWHM})_\omega = \frac{2\,(\ln 2)^{1/2}}{\tau_p}[1 + 4(\Delta\omega\tau_p^2/T)^2]; \qquad (\text{FWHM})_t = 2\,(\ln 2)^{1/2}\,\tau_p$$

Note: If the product of the chirp parameter and τ_p equals 1, $\Delta\omega\tau_p = 1$, the spectral width broadens by a factor of $\sqrt{5}$, whereas the time domain signal remains unchanged.

$$(\text{FWHM})_\omega \cdot (\text{FWHM})_t = 4\,(\ln 2)\,[1 + 4(\Delta\omega\tau_p^2/T)^2]$$

$$(\text{FWHM})_\nu \cdot (\text{FWHM})_t = \frac{4\,(\ln 2)}{2\pi}[1 + 4(\Delta\omega\tau_p)^4] = 0.44\cdot[1 + 4(\Delta\omega\tau_p^2/T)^2]$$

9.47

Case (a)

$$\frac{dN_2}{dt} = \frac{\sigma_p I_p}{h\nu_p}\left(\frac{g_2}{g_1}N_1 - N_2\right) - \frac{N_2}{\tau_2} = 0;$$

Thus $\dfrac{N_2}{N_1} = \dfrac{g_2}{g_1}\dfrac{I_p/I_{sp}}{1 + I_p/I_{sp}}$ where $I_{sp} = \dfrac{h\nu_p}{\sigma_p\tau_2}$

$\lim\limits_{I_p\to\infty}\dfrac{N_2}{N_1} = \dfrac{g_2}{g_1}$; optical transparency at $I_p \to \infty$! To obtain 75% of this limit:

$$\frac{N_2}{N_1} = \frac{3}{4}\frac{g_2}{g_1} = \frac{g_2}{g_1}\frac{I_p/I_{sp}}{1 + I_p/I_{sp}} \quad \text{or} \quad \frac{I_p}{I_{sp}} = 3$$

Case (b)

$$\frac{N_2}{N_0} = \frac{g_2}{g_0}\frac{I_p/I_{sp}}{1 + I_p/I_{sp}} \text{ from case (a) ; } \frac{N_1}{N_0} = \frac{g_2}{g_0}\exp[-\Delta E/kT]$$

For optical transparency on $2 \to 1$, $N_2 - (g_2/g_1)\,N_1 = 0$

$$\text{or } \frac{1}{N_0}\left\{\frac{g_2}{g_0}\left[\frac{I_p/I_{sp}}{1 + I_p/I_{sp}}\right] - \frac{g_2}{g_1}\frac{g_1}{g_0}\cdot\exp\left[-\frac{\Delta E}{kT}\right]\right\} = 0 \text{ or}$$

$$\frac{I_p}{I_{sp}} = \frac{1}{\exp\left[\frac{\Delta E}{kT}\right] - 1} \approx \exp\left[-\left(\frac{\Delta E}{kT}\right)\right] \qquad \text{if } \Delta E >> kT$$

Case (c)

$$\frac{N_3}{N_0} = \frac{g_3}{g_0}\left[\frac{I_p/I_{sp}}{1 + I_p/I_{sp}}\right] \text{ from case (a) ; } \frac{dN_2}{dt} = \frac{N_3}{\tau_3} - \frac{N_2}{\tau_2} = 0 \;\therefore\; \frac{N_2}{N_3} = \frac{\tau_2}{\tau_3}$$

$$\therefore \quad \frac{N_2}{N_0} = \frac{g_3}{g_0}\cdot\frac{\tau_2}{\tau_3}\cdot\left[\frac{I_p/I_{sp}}{1 + I_p/I_{sp}}\right] ; \; \frac{N_1}{N_0} = \frac{g_1}{g_0}\exp\left[-\frac{\Delta E}{kT}\right]$$

$$\left(N_2 - \frac{g_2}{g_1}N_1\right) = \frac{1}{N_0}\left\{\frac{g_3}{g_0}\frac{\tau_2}{\tau_3}\left[\frac{I_p/I_{sp}}{1 + I_p/I_{sp}}\right] - \frac{g_2}{g_1}\frac{g_1}{g_0}\exp\left[-\left(\frac{\Delta E}{kT}\right)\right]\right\} = 0$$

or
$$\frac{I_p}{I_{sp}} = \frac{1}{\frac{g_3}{g_2}\frac{\tau_2}{\tau_3}\exp\left[\frac{\Delta E}{kT}\right] - 1} \approx \frac{g_2}{g_3}\frac{\tau_3}{\tau_2}\exp\left[-\left(\frac{\Delta E}{kT}\right)\right]$$

Case (d)

$$\frac{N_3}{N_1} = \frac{g_3}{g_1}\,\frac{I_p/I_{sp}}{1 + I_p/I_{sp}};\; \frac{N_2}{N_1} = \frac{g_3}{g_1}\cdot\left[\frac{I_p/I_{sp}}{1 + I_p/I_{sp}}\right] \text{ by (a)} \rightarrow \text{(c)}$$

$N_2 - \frac{g_2}{g_1}N_1 = 0$ at optical transparency ; $\frac{N_2}{N_1} = \frac{g_2}{g_1} = \frac{g_3}{g_1}\cdot\frac{I_p/I_{sp}}{1 + I_p/I_{sp}}$

or:
$$\frac{I_p}{I_{sp}} = \frac{1}{\left(\frac{g_3}{g_2}\frac{\tau_2}{\tau_3} - 1\right)} \approx \frac{g_2}{g_3}\frac{\tau_3}{\tau_2} \text{ if a favorable lifetime ratio (independent of kT)}$$

Case(e)

One has to be a bit careful because of the fast interchange of populations between 2 and 1.

$$\frac{dN_3}{dt} = \frac{\sigma_p I_p}{h\nu_p}\left[\frac{g_3}{g_0}N_0 - N_3\right] - \frac{N_3}{\tau_3} - r_{32}N_3 + r_{23}N_2 = 0;$$

$\frac{dN_2}{dt} = + r_{32}N_3 - r_{23}N_2 - \frac{N_2}{\tau_2} = 0$; where the rates r_{32} and r_{23} are related by the Boltzmann factor so as to keep $N_2/N_3 = (g_2/g_3)\exp[-(E_2 - E_3)/kT]$. If we add the two equations one obtains:

$$\frac{d(N_3+N_2)}{dt} = \frac{\sigma_p I_p}{h\nu_p}\left[\frac{g_3}{g_0}N_0 - N_3\right] - \frac{N_3}{\tau_3} - \frac{N_2}{\tau_2} = 0; \text{ with } \frac{N_2}{N_3} = \frac{g_2}{g_1}e^{-\Delta E_{23}/kT}$$

Thus we can define an effective lifetime by:

$$\boxed{\frac{1}{\tau_{eff}} = \frac{1}{\tau_3} + \frac{g_2}{g_3}\frac{1}{\tau_2}e^{-\Delta E_{23}/kT}}$$

This is the lifetime that goes into the pump saturation intensity for this case. With this modification, we can use the results from the prior cases.

$$\frac{N_3}{N_0} = \frac{g_3}{g_0}\left[\frac{I_p/I_{sp}}{1 + I_p/I_{sp}}\right]; \qquad \frac{N_2}{N_0} = \frac{g_2}{g_0}\left[\frac{I_p/I_{sp}e^{-\Delta E_{23}/kT}}{1 + I_p/I_{sp}}\right]; \qquad \frac{N_1}{N_0} = \frac{g_1}{g_0}e^{-\Delta E_{10}/kT}$$

To obtain $N_2 - (g_2/g_1)N_1 = 0$;

$$\boxed{\frac{I_p}{I_{sp}} = \frac{e^{-(\Delta E_{10}-\Delta E_{23})/kT}}{1 - e^{-(\Delta E_{10}-\Delta E_{23})/kT}}}$$

9.48

9.6.1(b) becomes: $\frac{dI}{dz} = \left[N_2(z,t) - \left(\frac{g_2}{g_1}\right)N_1(z,t)\right]\frac{\sigma I(z,t)}{h\nu} - \alpha_0 I(z,t)$

9.6.2(a)becomes: $\frac{\partial N_2}{\partial t} = \frac{-\sigma I}{h\nu}\left[N_2 - \left(\frac{g_2}{g_1}\right)N_1\right] = \frac{-(1+g_2/g_1)\sigma I}{h\nu}N_2 \frac{-(g_2/g_1)\sigma I}{h\nu}N$

where $N_1 + N_2 = N \quad \therefore N_1 = N - N_2$

9.6.2(b) becomes: $\frac{\partial N_2}{\partial t} + \left[\frac{(1+g_2/g_1)\sigma I}{h\nu}\right]N_2 = \left[\frac{(1+g_2/g_1)\sigma}{h\nu}\right]I\,\frac{(g_2/g_1)N}{(1+g_2/g_1)}$

9.6.3(b)becomes: $w_s = \frac{h\nu}{\sigma(1+g_2/g_1)} \qquad \therefore \frac{dN_2}{dt} + \dot{u}\,N_2 = \frac{(g_2/g_1)}{1+g_2/g_1}N\,\dot{u}$

$\therefore$ 9.6.5 becomes: $\quad N_2(z,t) = \frac{(g_2/g_1)N}{(1+g_2/g_1)} + Ke^{-u(z,t)}$

Initial conditions: $[N_2^0 + N_1^0 = N]$ and $N_2^0 - (g_2/g_1)N_1^0 = \Delta N^0$;

Multiply the first by (g_2/g_1), add, and solve:

$N_2^0 = \frac{(g_2/g_1)}{1 + g_2/g_1}N + \frac{1}{1 + g_2/g_1}\Delta N^0$; The last term is K.

The rest of section 9.6 remains as is provided one uses the gain coefficient with the degeneracies in the usual manner.

10.1

The Q–switch model of Chapter 9 neglects any pumping on the time scale of the pulse. Here, one will supply populations to the other on a typical time scale of the Q–switch pulse. Furthermore, one must now account for the degeneracies.

10.2

$A_{21} = \phi/\tau$; ($\tau = 255\ \mu s$); $n = 1.81623$; $\sigma = A_{21} \dfrac{\lambda^2}{8\pi n^2}\left(\dfrac{2}{\pi\Delta\nu}\right)$;

$\Delta\nu = c\Delta\overline{\nu}$; Upper (2) = 11507 cm^{-1}; Upper (1) = 11423 cm^{-1}; the gain evaluated below assumes the same inversion for each transition.

λ		Up	Lower (cm^{-1})	φ	σ (10^{-19} cm^2)	I_s (kW/cm^2)	γ_0 (%/cm)
1.0521	(1.0515)	2	2002	0.0383	0.946	7.83	0.77
1.0549	(1.0545)	2	2028	0.0023	0.058	128.0	0.048
1.0615	(1.0621)	1	2002	0.0799	2.51	2.93	7.52
1.06415	(1.0636)	2	2110	0.1275	2.90	2.53	5.81
1.0644	(1.0652)	1	2028	0.0533	1.44	5.08	4.33
1.0682	(1.0678)	2	2148	0.0340	0.599	12.2	1.20
1.0737	(1.0745)	1	2110	0.0657	1.65	4.49	4.94
1.0779	(1.0788)	1	2148	0.0463	0.77	9.6	2.31
1.1055	(1.1057)	2	2461	0.0145	0.16	43.5	0.32
1.1119	(1.1122)	2	2514	0.0297	0.36	19.5	0.73
1.1158	(1.1174)	1	2461	0.0356	0.42	16.9	1.25
1.1225	(1.1241)	1	2514	0.0328	0.42	17.1	1.25

The net gain at 1.06415 μm is given by:

$$\gamma(1.06415) = N_2(2)\sigma(2) + N_2(1)\sigma(1)\frac{[\Delta\overline{\nu}(1)/2]^2}{[\overline{\nu}_0(2) - \overline{\nu}_0(1)]^2 + [\Delta\overline{\nu}(1)/2]^2}$$

$$N_2(2) + N_2(1) = N_2; \quad \frac{N_2(2)}{N_2(1)} = e^{-\Delta E/kT} = 0.669;$$

$\therefore$ $N_2(2) = 0.401\ N_2$; $N_2(1) = 0.599\ N_2$; $\overline{\nu}_0(2) - \overline{\nu}_0(1) = 2.2\ cm^{-1}$.

The effective cross–section on the A transition at 1.06415 includes a 60% contribution from the wings of the A' transition:

$$\sigma = 2.9\times10^{-19} + 0.599 \times 1.44\times10^{-19}\frac{(2.1\ cm^{-1})^2}{2.2^2 + 2.1^2} = 3.31\times10^{-19}\ cm^2$$

At 77°K; $kT = 53.6\ cm^{-1}$; $\Delta E = 95\ cm^{-1}$; $e^{-\Delta E/kT} = 0.17$; $\therefore N_2(2) = 0.145\ N_2$; $N_1(1) = 0.855\ N_2$. The gains on transitions starting at $N_2(2)$ drops dramatically while those from $N_2(1)$ increase.

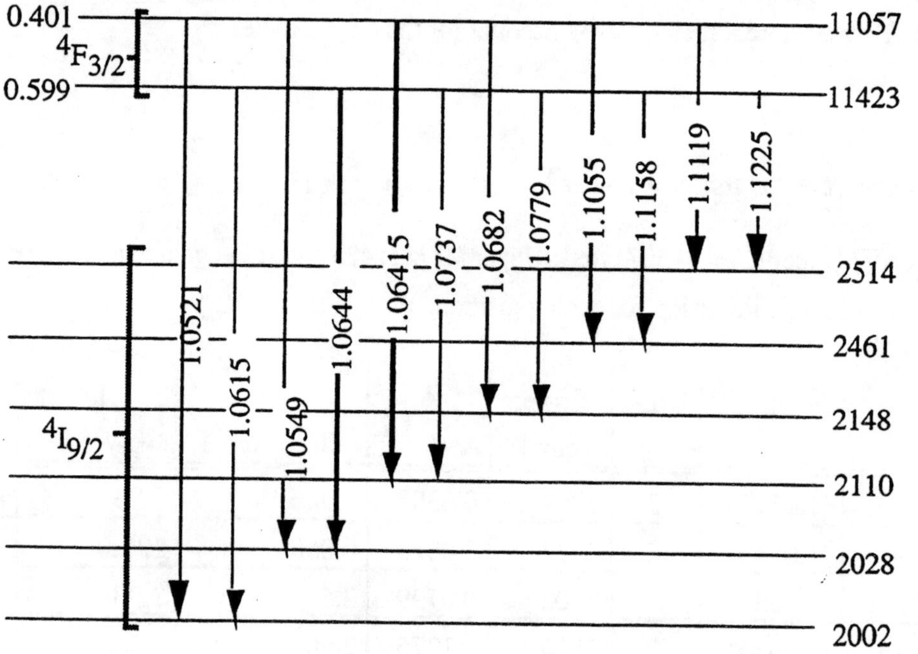

10.3

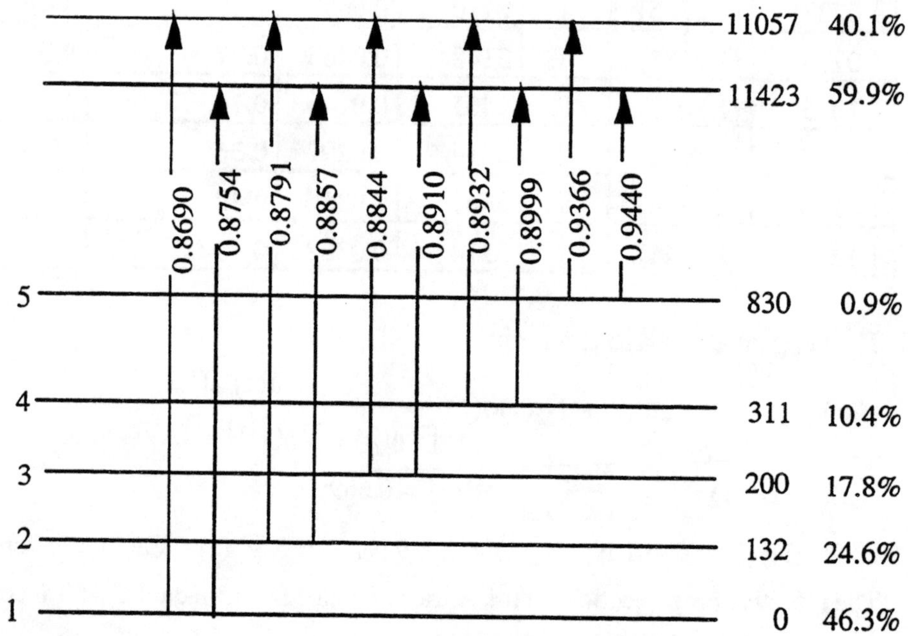

$N_1(5) + N_1(4) + N_1(3) + N_1(2) + N_1(1) = N_1$; $\frac{N_1(j)}{N_1(1)} = e^{-\Delta E_j/kT}$; $\therefore N_1(1) = 0.463\ N_1$.

Note that all wavelengths are in the region for semiconductor laser pumping.

10.4

See calculation in Prob. 10.2 at the end

10.5

Notice that table 10.4 gives the total A coefficient for the $^4F_{3/2}$ state, not A_{21}.

$$\text{Given that } \sigma = A_{21}\frac{\lambda^2}{8\pi n^2}\left(\frac{2}{\pi\Delta\nu}\right) = 3.03\times10^{-20}\ \text{cm}^2 .$$

Assume ED–2 glass. $\Delta\lambda = 260\text{Å}$; $(\Delta\nu/\nu) = (\Delta\lambda/\lambda)$;

$\nu = c/\lambda_0 = 2.83\times10^{+14}$ Hz and $\Delta\nu = 6.96\times10^{+12}$ Hz;

$$\text{Thus } A_{21} = \left[\frac{1}{\sigma}\frac{\lambda^2}{8\pi n^2}\cdot\frac{2}{\pi\Delta\nu}\right]^{-1} = 1.77\times10^3\ \text{s}^{-1};$$

$$\gamma = 0.01\ \text{cm}^{-1} = N_2\sigma \text{ (assuming } N_1 = 0);$$

$$\therefore N_2 = 3.3\times10^{+17}\ \text{cm}^{-3};\ P_f = \frac{h\nu N_2}{\tau} = 45.9\ \text{W/cm}^3$$

10.6

$$w_s = \frac{h\nu}{2\sigma}\cdot l_g = 29.2\ \text{Joules/cm}^2$$

10.7

$$\gamma_0(\nu) = \gamma_0(0)\frac{(\Delta\nu_h/2)^2}{(\nu_0-\nu)^2 + (\Delta\nu_h/2)^2}$$

$$\frac{\gamma_0(0)}{\alpha} = 1.5$$

The graphical implications are shown at the right.

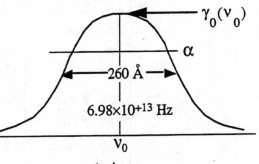

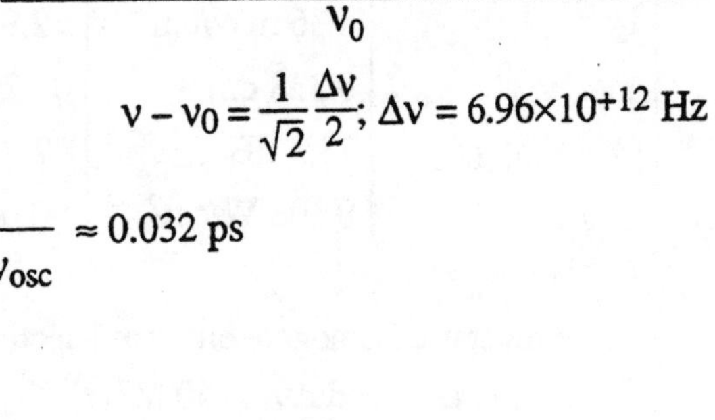

$$\nu - \nu_0 = \frac{1}{\sqrt{2}}\frac{\Delta\nu}{2};\ \Delta\nu = 6.96\times10^{+12}\ \text{Hz};$$

$$\nu_+ - \nu_- = \frac{\Delta\nu}{\sqrt{2}} = 4.92\times10^{+12}\ \text{Hz};\ \tau_p \approx \frac{1}{2\pi\Delta\nu_{osc}} \approx 0.032\ \text{ps}$$

10.8

$\frac{\Delta\nu_D}{\nu_0} = \left(\frac{8kT}{Mc^2}\right)^{1/2} = 4.14\times10^{+6}$; $g(\nu_0) = \left(\frac{4\ln 2}{\pi}\right)^{1/2}\frac{1}{\Delta\nu_0} = \frac{0.939}{\Delta\nu_D}$; $I_s = \frac{h\nu}{\sigma_h\tau_2}$; where the homogeneous line width $\Delta\nu_h$ must be used in σ_h for the saturation intensity and $\sigma_h = A_{21}\frac{\lambda^2}{8\pi}\left[\frac{2}{\pi\Delta\nu_h}\right]$

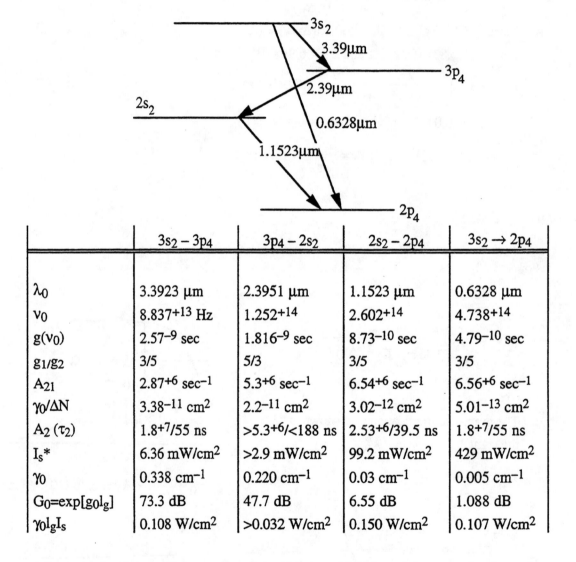

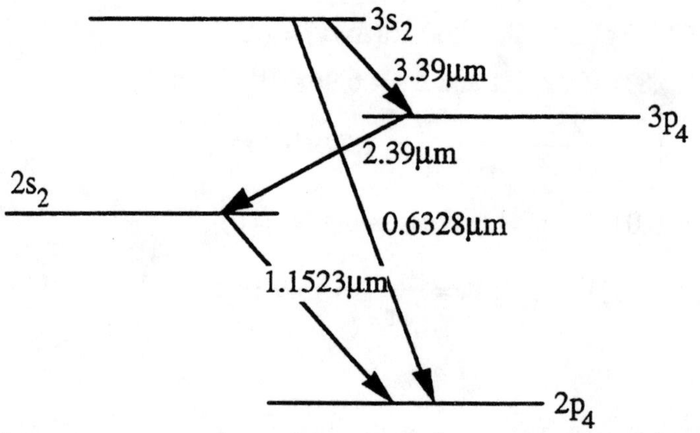

	$3s_2 - 3p_4$	$3p_4 - 2s_2$	$2s_2 - 2p_4$	$3s_2 \to 2p_4$
λ_0	3.3923 μm	2.3951 μm	1.1523 μm	0.6328 μm
ν_0	8.837^{+13} Hz	1.252^{+14}	2.602^{+14}	4.738^{+14}
$g(\nu_0)$	2.57^{-9} sec	1.816^{-9} sec	8.73^{-10} sec	4.79^{-10} sec
g_1/g_2	3/5	5/3	3/5	3/5
A_{21}	2.87^{+6} sec^{-1}	5.3^{+6} sec^{-1}	6.54^{+6} sec^{-1}	6.56^{+6} sec^{-1}
$\gamma_0/\Delta N$	3.38^{-11} cm^2	2.2^{-11} cm^2	3.02^{-12} cm^2	5.01^{-13} cm^2
A_2 (τ_2)	1.8^{+7}/55 ns	$>5.3^{+6}$/<188 ns	2.53^{+6}/39.5 ns	1.8^{+7}/55 ns
I_s*	6.36 mW/cm^2	>2.9 mW/cm^2	99.2 mW/cm^2	429 mW/cm^2
γ_0	0.338 cm^{-1}	0.220 cm^{-1}	0.03 cm^{-1}	0.005 cm^{-1}
$G_0=\exp[g_0 l_g]$	73.3 dB	47.7 dB	6.55 dB	1.088 dB
$\gamma_0 l_g I_s$	0.108 W/cm^2	>0.032 W/cm^2	0.150 W/cm^2	0.107 W/cm^2

*One must use homogeneous cross-section for the calculation of the saturation intensity. The above assumed $\Delta\nu_h = 50$ MHz.

(e) The $3s_2 \to 3p_4$ pushes a population into $3p_4$ state while the 1.15 μm pulls the population out of or depletes the $2s_2$ state.

(f) The 6401Å transition has the same upper state as the 6328Å one, but a much smaller A coefficient and thus, a smaller stimulated emission cross–section. Thus, the 6328 line dominates by using the upper state population and thus suppresses oscillation on the 6401Å line.

10.9

$\exp[\gamma_0 l_g] = 10^3$; $\gamma_0 l_g = 6.91$; $\gamma_0 = 0.0696\ \text{cm}^{-1} = \sigma\Delta N$

(a) $\sigma_D(3.39\ \mu\text{m}) = 3.38\times10^{-11}\ \text{cm}^2$ (Prob. 10.8); $\therefore\ \Delta N = 2.04\times10^{+9}\ \text{cm}^{-3}$

(b) $\sigma_D(0.6328\mu\text{m}) = 5.01\times10^{-13}\ \text{cm}^2$; $\therefore\ \gamma = 1.02\times10^{-3}\ \text{cm}^{-1} \Rightarrow 0.445$ dB/m;

(The big difference arises because of the λ^3 variation in σ – one of the λ's from Doppler effect)

(c) $\sigma_h = A_{21}\dfrac{\lambda^2}{8\pi}\cdot\dfrac{2}{\pi\Delta\nu_n}$; $\sigma_h\,(3.39) = 4.18\times10^{-10}\ \text{cm}^2$; $I_s = 2.55\ \text{mW/cm}^2$;

$\sigma_h(0.6328) = 3.33\times10^{-11}\ \text{cm}^2$; $I_s = 0.17\ \text{W/cm}^2$

10.10

$F = \dfrac{\pi\sqrt{R_1R_2}}{1-(R_1R_2)^{1/2}}$; Thus $(R_1R_2)^{1/2} = \dfrac{F}{F+\pi}$ and $(R_1R_2)^{1/2}e^{\gamma_0 l_g} = 1$ or

$\gamma_0 l_g = \ln[(R_1R_2)^{-1/2}] = \ln[1+\pi/F] \approx \pi/F$

Thus $\dfrac{F(\lambda)}{F(6328)} = \dfrac{A_{21}(6328)}{A_{21}(\lambda)}\dfrac{(0.6328)^3}{(\lambda)^3}$ where λ is in μm. The extra factor of λ comes from expressing the Doppler width in terms of wavelength.

λ	$A_{21}(\times 10^6)$	$F(\lambda)/F(0.6328)$
0.7304	0.48	8.89
0.6401	0.6	10.6
0.6351	0.7	9.27
0.6294	1.35	4.94
0.6118	1.28	5.67
0.6046	0.68	11.0
0.5939	0.56	14.2
0.5433*	0.59	17.6

*Green He–Ne

10.11

Cd+ (Ion) Laser Energy Levels (relative to Helium)

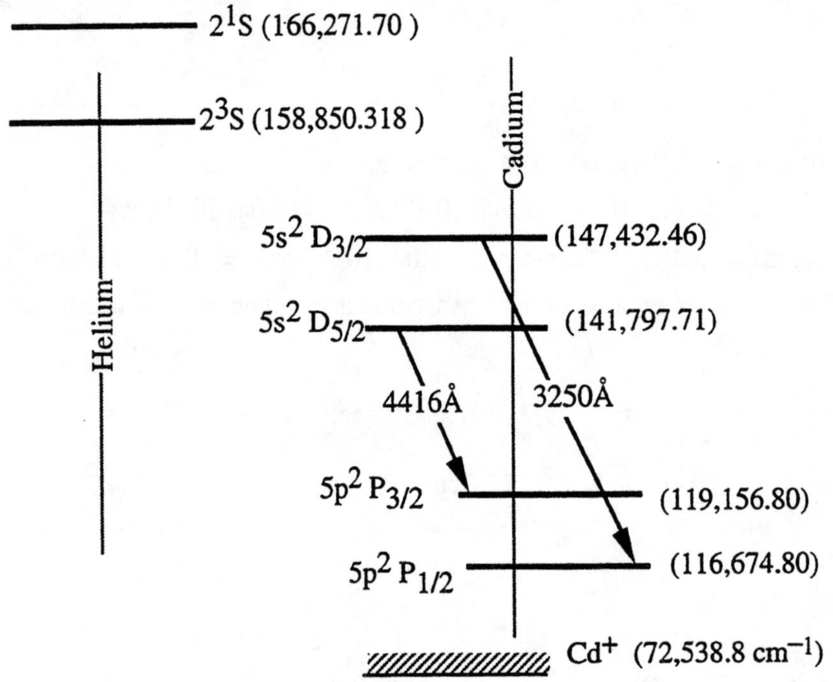

10.12

Pick the reaction: $He(2^3S) + Cd \rightarrow Cd(5s^2D_{3/2}) + He + e(K.E)$;
e(K.E.) = 159,850.318 − 147,432.46 = 12,417.86 $cm^{-1} \Rightarrow$ 1.54 eV

10.13

4p $^2D_{5/2}{}^0$ = 158,731.2cm^{-1}; 4s $^2P_{3/2}$ = 138,244.51cm^{-1} with the latter two being relative to the ionization potential of Argon, IP(Ar) = 127,109.9 cm^{-1};
Upper state = 285,841.10 cm^{-1}; Lower state = 265,354.41cm^{-1};
$\overline{v}$ = 20,486.69 (λ_0 = 488 nm); $\eta = \frac{20\,487}{285\,841} = 7.2\%$

10.15

See Table 10.6 for data for N_2; $\omega_e = 2359.1$; $\omega_e x_e = 14.456$; $\omega_e y_e = 0.0075\ cm^{-1}$

$$G(\upsilon) = \omega_e\left(v+\frac{1}{2}\right) - \omega_e x_e\left(v+\frac{1}{2}\right)^2 + \omega_e y_e\left(v+\frac{1}{2}\right)^3 ;$$

Let <E> = average energy stored in vibration where $\langle E\rangle = \dfrac{\sum_{1}^{8} \Delta G_{\upsilon}\, e^{-\Delta G_V/kT}}{\sum_{0}^{\infty} e^{-\Delta G_V/kT}}$

v	G(v)	$\Delta G_V = G(\upsilon) - G(0)$	N_V/N_T		
			T = 500	1000	1500
0	1175.94		0.999	0.965	0.892
		2330.2			
1	3506.15		1.23×10^{-3}	3.39×10^{-2}	9.56×10^{-2}
		4631.6			
2	5807.52		1.65×10^{-6}	1.24×10^{-3}	1.05×10^{-2}
		6904.1			
3	8080.09			4.73×10^{-5}	1.19×10^{-3}
		9147.96			
4	10,323.9				1.39×10^{-4}
		11,363.1			
5	12,539.0				
		13,549.5			
6	14,725.5				
		15,707.3			
7	16,883.27				
		17,836.6			
8	19,012.52		<E> = 1.54J	45.3J	281J

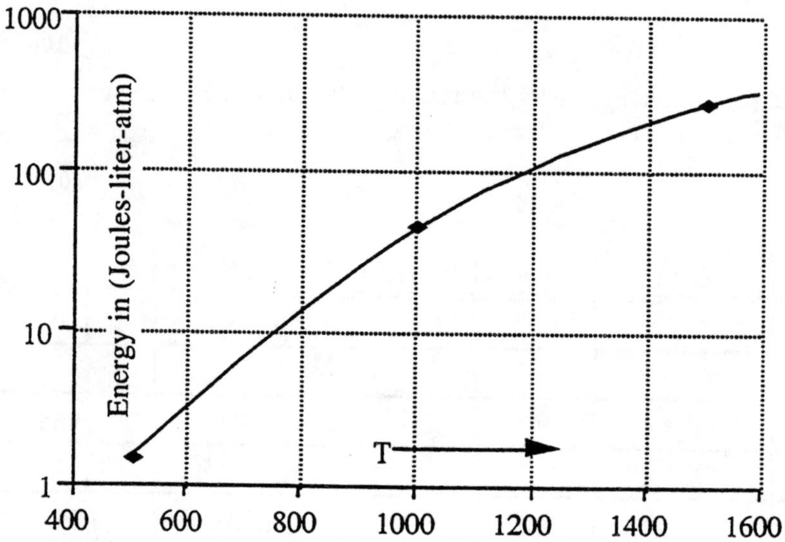

10.15

$B = 0.387\ cm^{-1}$; $A_{21}(P) = 0.34\ sec^{-1}$; $A_{21}(R) = 0.33\ sec^{-1}$; $T = 500$ K; $kT = 347.8\ cm^{-1}$

P(22): $\therefore J_L = 22$; $J_u = 21$; R(20): $\therefore J_L = 20$; $J_u = 21$

$\lambda(P(22)) = 10.611385\ \mu m$; $\lambda(R(20)) = 10.246625\ \mu m$

(see Ch. 15 Handbook of Lasers, p. 331)

$$\sigma(P) = A_{21}\frac{\lambda^2}{8\pi}\cdot\frac{2}{\pi\Delta\nu_h} = 2.85^{-17}\ cm^2;\ \sigma(R) = 2.58^{-17}\ cm^2;$$

$$\gamma(\nu) = \sigma\left\{(2J_\upsilon+1)\frac{hcB}{kT}\left[N_{v'}\exp\left(\frac{-hcBJu(J_\upsilon+1)}{kT}\right) - N_{v''}\exp\left(\frac{-hcBJ\upsilon(J_L+1)}{kT}\right)\right]\right\}$$

See Ch. 15.3.5 $[N_{v''}] = 10^{15}\ cm^{-3}$; $N_{v'} = 1.1\times10^{+15}\ cm^{-3}$;

$[hcBJ_\upsilon(J_v+1)]/kT = 0.514$; $(2J_v+1)[hcB]/kT = 4.78^{-2}$; where:

$$N_{v'}\exp\left[\frac{hcBJ_v(J+1)}{kT}\right] - N_{v''}\exp\left[\frac{hcBJ_v(J_v+1)}{kT}\right] = 8.84\times10^{+13}\ cm^{-3};$$

$$N_{v'}\exp\left[\frac{hcBJ_v(J_v+1)}{kT}\right] - N_{v''}\exp\left[\frac{hcBJ_v(J_v+1)}{kT}\right] = 3.12\times10^{+13};$$

$$\sigma(2J_v+1)\frac{hcB}{kT} = 1.36\times10^{-18}\ cm^2;$$

$\gamma(P(22)) = 1.36\times10^{-18}\ (8.84\times10^{+13}) = 1.2\times10^{-4}\ cm^{-1}$;

$\gamma(R(20)) = 1.36\times10^{-18}\ (3.12\times10^{+13}) = 4.2\times10^{-5}\ cm^{-1}$

10.16

Data: $\omega_{32} = 10^8\ sec^{-1}$; $\omega_{23} = 0.021\ \omega_{32}$ (Boltzmann factor);

$A_{30} = 10^7\ sec^{-1}$; $A_{21} = 10^8\ sec^{-1}$; $A_{20} = 2\times10^7\ sec^{-1}$; $A_{10} = 8\times10^8\ sec^{-1}$;

Let's start with the rate equations:

$$\frac{dN_3}{dt} = R_1 - (A_{30}+\omega_{32})N_3 + \omega_{23}N_2 = 0 \qquad (1)$$

$$\frac{dN_2}{dt} = \omega_{32}N_3 - (A_{20}+A_{21}+\omega_{23})N_2 - \frac{\sigma I}{h\nu}(N_2-N_1) = 0 \qquad (2)$$

$$\frac{dN_1}{dt} = A_{21}N_2 + \frac{\sigma I}{h\nu}(N_2-N_1) - A_{10}N_1 = 0 \qquad (3)$$

Add (1) to (3) : $\frac{d}{dt}(N_1+N_2+N_3) = R_1 - A_{30}N_3 - A_{20}N_2 - A_{10}N_1$ (4)

Equation 4 applies under all circumstances – large or small signal. Assume small signal so as to neglect stimulated emission. $\therefore N_1^0 = \frac{A_{21}}{A_{10}} N_2^0$ from (3) (5)

Substitute into (4): $A_{30}N_3^0 + (A_{20}+A_{21})\, N_2^0 = R_1$ (6)

Re–write (1) $(A_{30}+\omega_{32})N_3^0 - \omega_{23}N_2^0 = R_1$ and then subtract (6)

$$\therefore (A_{20}+A_{21}+\omega_{23})N_2^0 = \omega_{32}N_3^0 \text{ or } N_3^0 = \frac{(A_{20}+A_{21}+\omega_{23})N_2^0}{\omega_{32}} \qquad (7)$$

Substitute back into (6): $\left[\frac{A_{30}(A_{20}+A_{21}+\omega_{23})+\omega_{32}(A_{20}+A_{21})}{\omega_{32}}\right] N_2^0 = R_1$

$$\therefore N_2^0 = \frac{\omega_{32}}{A_{30}(A_{20}+A_{21}+\omega_{23}) + \omega_{32}(A_{20}+A_{21})} R_1 \qquad (8)$$

$$N_3^0 = \frac{(A_{20}+A_{21}+\omega_{23})}{A_{30}(A_{20}+A_{21}+\omega_{23})+\omega_{32}(A_{20}+A_{21})} R_1 \qquad (9)$$

$$N_1^0 = \frac{A_{21}}{A_{10}} \frac{\omega_{32}}{A_{30}(A_{20}+A_{21}+\omega_{23}) + \omega_{32}(A_{20}+A_{21})} R_1 \qquad (10)$$

Now assume saturation as specified in part (c). $\therefore \boxed{N_1^s = N_2^s}$; (11)

Eq. 4 becomes: $A_{30}N_3^s + (A_{20}+A_{10})N_2^s = R_1$ (12)

and (1) remains $(A_{30}+\omega_{32})N_3^s - \omega_{23}N_2^s = R_1$ (13)

$$\therefore N_3^s = \frac{(A_{20}+A_{10}+\omega_{23})}{\omega_{32}} N_2^s \qquad (14)$$

$$N_1^s = N_2^s = \frac{\omega_{32}}{A_{30}(A_{20}+A_{10}+\omega_{23}) + \omega_{32}(A_{20}+A_{10})} R_1 \qquad (15)$$

$$N_3^s = \frac{A_{20}+A_{10}+\omega_{23}}{A_{30}(A_{20}+A_{10}+\omega_{23}) + \omega_{32}(A_{20}+A_{10})} R_1 \qquad (16)$$

For a transfer laser: $\omega_{32} = 10^8 \text{ sec}^{-1} >> A_{30}$; $\omega_{23} = 0.02\, \omega_{32} << A_{20}+A_{21}$; (17)

$$\therefore N_2^0 = \frac{R_1}{A_{20}+A_{21}}; \quad N_1^0 = \frac{A_{21}}{A_{10}} N_2^0; \therefore \gamma = (N_2^0 - N_1^0)\sigma = \frac{R_1}{A_{20}+A_{21}}\left(1 - \frac{A_{21}}{A_{10}}\right)\sigma \qquad (18)$$

For values of the A's; $\gamma = 0.01$ when $R_1 = 1.5\text{x}10^{22}$ cm^{-3} sec^{-1}.

(c) Stimulated emission decreases the population in 2 and thus decreases the spontaneous rate out of 2. This decrease in spontaneous rate out of 2 is equal to the stimulated rate from 2 to 1. It is easier to compute the change in spontaneous rather than the laser power. Change in spontaneous rate out of 2:

$$\Delta p_{sp} = (A_{20}+A_{21})[N_2^0 - N_2^s] = (A_{20}+A_{21})\left[\frac{1}{A_{20}+A_{21}} - \frac{1}{A_{20}+A_{10}}\right]R_1$$

$$= \left(1 - \frac{A_{20}+A_{21}}{A_{20}+A_{10}}\right)R_1 = \left(\frac{A_{10}-A_{21}}{A_{20}+A_{10}}\right)R_1 = 0.8537\ R_1 \qquad (19)$$

This change produces a stimulated 1.8 eV photon at the cost of (4.3 eV)xR_1

$$\therefore \eta = \frac{1.8\text{x}0.8537}{4.3} = 35.7 \qquad (20)$$

10.17

Let $\frac{\gamma_0(\nu_0)}{\alpha} = k = 3$; $\gamma_0(\nu) = \gamma_0(\nu_0)\exp\{-4\ln 2\,[(\nu-\nu_0)/\Delta\nu_D]^2\}$;

$$\exp\{-4\ln 2\,[(\nu-\nu_0)/\Delta\nu_D]^2\} = \frac{1}{3}\ \frac{\nu_\pm - \nu_0}{\Delta\nu_D/2} = 1.259;$$

$\nu_+ - \nu_0 = 1.259\ (\Delta\nu_D/2) = 6.29\times10^{+9}$ Hz; $\nu_+ - \nu_- = 12.59$ GHz;

FSR = $c/2d = 150$ MHz; $\therefore (\nu_+ - \nu_-)/\text{FSR} = 83.9$;

Thus there is 1 mode at line center, 41 modes on each side.

(b) Let $I(\nu) = I_0\exp\{-4\ln 2\,[(\nu-\nu_0)/\Delta\nu_{osc}]^2\}\exp[-2r^2/w_0^2]$; $\Delta\nu_{osc}$ = freq. interval over which modes are $> \frac{1}{2} I_0$; $w_0 = 2$ mm;

$I_\nu/I_s \approx [(\gamma_0(\nu)/\alpha)^2 - 1]$ since the laser is inhomogeneous broadened;

$K^2\exp\{-8\ln 2[(\nu-\nu_0)/\Delta\nu_D]^2\} - 1 = K^2/2 - 1/2$;

Thus: $\Delta\nu_{osc} = \Delta\nu_D\left\{\frac{\ln[2K^2/(K^2+1)]}{2\ln 2}\right\} = 0.651\ \Delta\nu_D$

$$\frac{\langle I\rangle}{I_0} = \frac{1}{2}\left(\frac{\pi}{\ln 2}\right)^{1/2}\left(\frac{\Delta\nu_{osc}}{\Delta\nu_c}\right);\ \text{Now } P_0 = I_0\int_0^\infty \exp[-(2r^2/w_0^2)]\,r dr = I_0\frac{\pi w_0^2}{2};\ I_0 = \frac{2P_0}{\pi w_0^2};$$

$$P_0 = 2\langle P\rangle\left(\frac{\ln 2}{\pi}\right)^{1/2}\left(\frac{\Delta\nu_c}{\Delta\nu_{osc}}\right) = 0.141\text{ watts};\ P_{MAX} = \left(\frac{\pi}{\ln 2}\right)^{1/2}\left(\frac{\Delta\nu_{osc}}{\Delta\nu_c}\right)\langle P\rangle = 354\text{ watts};$$

$\Delta t_{1/2} = 4\ln 2/\Delta\omega_{osc} = 0.135$ ps

10.18

The energy stored in the gas before lasing: E = [N] (2300 + 2200 + 2100 + 2000 = 8600 [N] (E in cm^{-1}). After lasing, all populations are equal. E = [N]/5) ( ) = 1720 [N] (E in cm^{-1}); $\Delta E \rightarrow$ stimulation emission – 6480 (cm^{-1}).

For [N] = $2.69\times10^{+19}$ cm^{-3} (Standard Temperature and Pressure),

$\Delta E = (1.743\times10^{+23})\times(\text{ E in cm}^{-1})/\text{cm}^3 \rightarrow 3.46 \text{ J/cm}^3$

10.19

$$\gamma_0(\nu) = \gamma_0(\nu_0)\left[\bar{g}(\nu) = \exp[-(4\ln 2)\left(\frac{\nu - \nu_0}{\Delta\nu_D}]\right)^2]\right];\ \bar{g}(\nu_\pm) = \frac{1}{4} = \exp[-4\ln 2]\left(\frac{\nu_\pm - \nu_0}{\Delta\nu_D}\right)^2$$

$$\left(\frac{\nu_\pm - \nu_0}{\Delta\nu_D}\right)^2 = \frac{\ln 4}{4\ \ln 2} = \frac{2\ \ln 2}{4\ \ln 2} = \frac{1}{2};\ \nu_+ - \nu_0 = \frac{\Delta\nu_D}{\sqrt{2}};\ \nu_+ - \nu_- = \sqrt{2}\Delta\nu_D = 2.12\text{ GHz}$$

$\Delta\nu_c = \frac{c}{2d} = 150$ MHz; $\therefore$ N = 14 (or 15) modes; $\Delta t \approx \frac{\tau_{RT}}{N} = 0.48$ ns

10.20

$$\frac{dN_2}{dt} = P_2 - \frac{N_2\phi}{\tau} + N_2\frac{(1-\phi)}{\tau};\ \therefore N_2 = P_2\tau.$$

For a threshold calculation: $\gamma_0 = \frac{1}{2l_g}\ln\frac{1}{R_1R_2T_a^2T_b^2} = 1.84\times10^{-2}\text{ cm}^{-1}$;

$\therefore N_2$ (threshold) $= 1.84\times10^{+13}\text{ cm}^{-3}$. Spontaneous power $= \frac{h\nu N_2\phi}{\tau}V$;

$$P_{sp} = \frac{h\nu N_2\phi}{\tau}VN_{2(th)}\cdot\frac{1}{N_{2(th)}} = 790\left(\frac{P_2}{P_{2th}}\right)\text{watts};$$

$$I_s = \frac{h\nu}{\sigma\tau_2} = 7.95\text{ kW/cm}^2;\ P_{LASER} = \frac{T_2I_s}{2}\left(\frac{P_2}{P_{2th}} - 1\right) = 994\left(\frac{P_2}{P_{2th}} - 1\right)$$

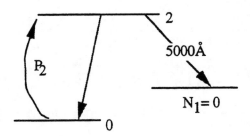

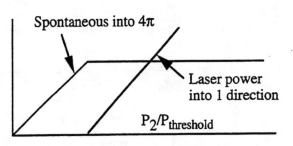

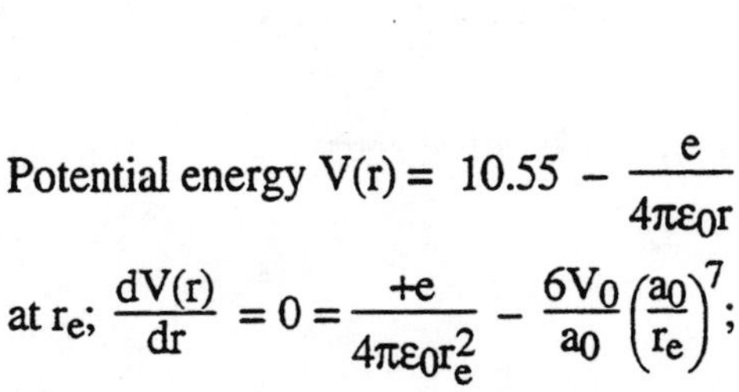

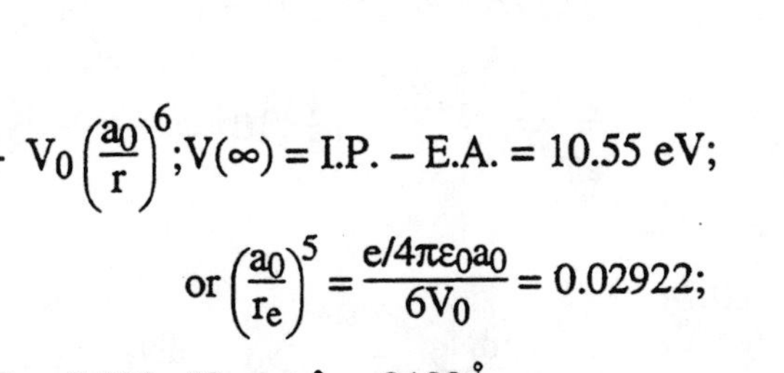

10.21

$$\text{Potential energy } V(r) = 10.55 - \frac{e}{4\pi\varepsilon_0 r} + V_0\left(\frac{a_0}{r}\right)^6;\ V(\infty) = \text{I.P.} - \text{E.A.} = 10.55\text{ eV};$$

$$\text{at } r_e;\ \frac{dV(r)}{dr} = 0 = \frac{+e}{4\pi\varepsilon_0 r_e^2} - \frac{6V_0}{a_0}\left(\frac{a_0}{r_e}\right)^7;\qquad \text{or } \left(\frac{a_0}{r_e}\right)^5 = \frac{e/4\pi\varepsilon_0 a_0}{6V_0} = 0.02922;$$

$r = 2.03\ a_0 = 3.04$ Å; $h\nu/e = 6.612 - 0.789 = 5.823$ eV $\therefore\quad \lambda = 2129$Å

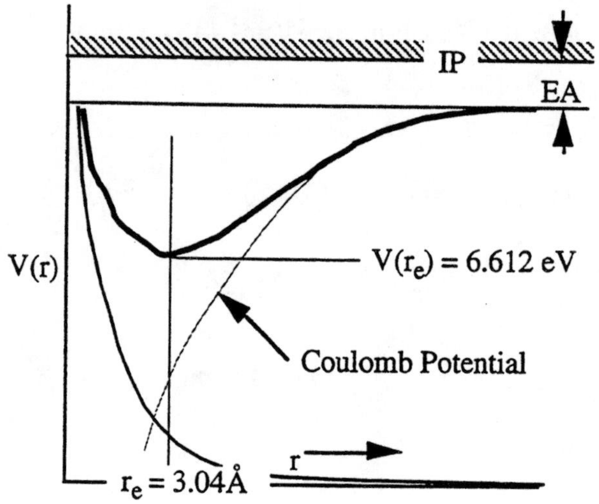

10.22

$E = 75\ \text{MeV} = (\gamma - 1)(m_0c^2/e)$; $m_0c^2/e = 0.511$ MeV

$\therefore (\gamma - 1) = 146.8$ or $\gamma = 147.8$; $\gamma = (1 - \beta^2)^{-1/2}$; $1 - \beta^2 = 1/\gamma^2$

$\beta^2 = 1 - 1/\gamma^2 = 0.99995$; $\beta = 0.99998$; $\qquad a_w = \dfrac{(cB_0)\,\Lambda_0}{2\pi(m_0c^2/e)} = 2.8031$

$$\lambda_0 = \frac{\Lambda}{2\gamma^2}[1 + a_w^2] = 6.17\ \mu\text{m}$$

10.23

$$\frac{dN_a}{dt} = \frac{-N_a}{\tau_a} + r_{ba}N_b - r_{ab}N_a; \quad \frac{dN_b}{dt} = -\frac{N_b}{\tau_b} - r_{ba}N_b - r_{ab}N_a$$

$$\therefore \quad \frac{d(N_a+N_b)}{dt} = -(N_a + N_b)\left[\frac{N_a}{N_a + N_b}\frac{1}{\tau_a} + \frac{N_b}{N_a + N_b}\cdot\frac{1}{\tau_b}\right] = -\frac{(N_a + N_b)}{\tau_{eff}}$$

where $$\frac{1}{\tau_{eff}} = \frac{N_a}{N_a + N_b}\frac{1}{\tau_a} + \frac{N_b}{N_a + N_b}\frac{1}{\tau_b} = \frac{1}{\tau_a}\left(\frac{1}{1 + N_b/N_a}\right) + \left(\frac{N_b/N_a}{1 + N_b/N_a}\right)\frac{1}{\tau_b}$$

$$= 10^3\left(\frac{1}{1 + 1/9}\right) + \left(\frac{1/9}{1 + 1/9}\right)10^4 = 10^3[0.9 + 1.0] = 1.9\times10^{+3}\ \text{sec}^{-1}$$

For T=600K, $e^{-\Delta E/kT} = 1/3$; $\dfrac{1}{\tau_{eff}} = 10^3\left(\dfrac{1}{1 + 1/3}\right) + \left(\dfrac{1/3}{1 + 1/3}\right)10^3$

$$\frac{1}{\tau_{eff}} = 10^3\left(\frac{3}{4}\right) + \left(\frac{1}{4}\right)10^4 = 10^3\ [0.75 + 2.5] = 3.25\times10^3\ \text{sec}^{-1}$$

10.24

(a) $\dfrac{dN_b}{dt} = P_b - \dfrac{N_b}{\tau_b}$; $\dfrac{dN_a}{dt} = P_a - \dfrac{N_a}{\tau_a}$; add the two equations

$$\frac{d[N_a+N_b]}{dt} = (P_a+P_b) - \frac{N_b}{\tau_b} - \frac{N_a}{\tau_a} = P_a + P_b - [N_a+N_b]\left\{\frac{N_a}{N_a+N_b}\frac{1}{\tau_a} + \frac{N_b}{N_a+N_b}\frac{1}{\tau_b}\right\}$$

\f(d[$N_a + N_b$],dt) = (P_a+P_b) – \F([$N_a + N_b$],τ_{eff}) where \f(1,τ_{eff}) = \f(b,1+b) \f(1,τ_b) +

$$\frac{1}{1+b}\frac{1}{\tau_a} = \frac{1}{\tau_a}\left[\frac{b}{1+b}\frac{\tau_a}{\tau_b} + \frac{1}{1+b}\right]$$

and $b = N_b/N_a = \exp[-\Delta E/kT]$ where $\Delta E = 46\ cm^{-1}$

(b) At T = 4K; $kT = 2.782\ cm^{-1}$; $e^{-\Delta E/kT} = 6.6\times10^{-8}$ $\therefore$ $\tau = \tau_a$

at T = 100K; $kT = 69.33\ cm^{-1}$; $e^{-\Delta E/kT} = 0.515$

$\tau = 1.2886\ \tau_a = 1.58$ ms; $\therefore$ $\tau_a = 1.23$ ms and $\tau_b = 3.59$ ms

(c) $N^* = N_a + N_b + {}^2T_{1a} + {}^2T_{1b} + {}^2T_{1c} + {}^4T_{2a} + {}^4T_{2b} + {}^4T_{2c}$

$$N^* = N_a\left\{1 + \frac{N_b}{N_a} + \frac{{}^2T_{1a}}{N_a} + \ldots + \frac{{}^4T_{2a}}{N_a} + \ldots\right\} = N_a Z(T)$$

$\frac{N_b}{N_a} = \frac{g_b}{g_a} e^{-\Delta E_{ba}/kT} = e^{-\Delta E/kT}$ and so on: Note $\frac{{}^4T_s}{N_a} = 2\,e^{-\Delta E/kT}$

at 300K, this leads to the fractions indicated in Table III of reference 1.

(d) At high temperatures, the ${}^2T_1$ and ${}^4T_2$ states become populated

$$\frac{d[\Sigma N]}{dt} = P - \Sigma N\left\{\frac{N_a}{\Sigma N}\frac{1}{\tau_a} + \frac{N_b}{\Sigma N}\frac{1}{\tau_b} + \frac{\Sigma^4 T_2}{\Sigma N}\frac{1}{\tau_c}\right\}$$ where $\tau_c = 10\ \mu$sec;

$\frac{\Sigma^4T_2}{\Sigma N} = 3.64\times10^{-2}$; $\frac{N_a}{\Sigma N} = 0.5006$; $\frac{N_b}{\Sigma N} = 0.4015$

$= P - \Sigma N(4.16\times10^{+3})$; $\therefore$ $\tau = 240\ \mu$sec (Excellent agreement with Fig.5 of the cited paper)

(e) For optical transparency $[N_{upper}] = \frac{g_{upper}}{g_{lower}}[N_{lower}]$

(1) For the R_1 $N_a = \frac{1}{2}[{}^4A_2]$ but $N_a = 0.5006N^*$ $\therefore$ $N^* = [{}^4A_2]$

But $N^* + [{}^4A_2] = [Cr]^\circ = 2\,[{}^4A_2]$ $\therefore$ $[{}^4A_2] = \frac{1}{2}[Cr]^\circ = 1.1\times10^{+19}\ cm^{-3}$

$\therefore$ $N^* = 1.1\times10^{+19}\ cm^{-3}$ $N_a = 5.5\times10^{+18}\ cm^3$

(2) For optical transparency on the 2→1 transition

$\Sigma^4T_2 = N_1$ $N_1 = e^{-\Delta E/kT}[{}^4A_2] = 8.9^{-5}\,[{}^4A_2]$

$\therefore$ $\Sigma^4T_2 = 3.64\times10^{-2}N^* = 8.9\times10^{-5}[{}^4A_2]$ $\therefore$ $N^* = 2.44\times10^{-3}[{}^4A_2]$

$N^* + [{}^4A_2] = [Cr]^\circ$; $[{}^4A_2] = 2.19\times10^{+19}\ cm^{-3}$; $N_1^* = 1.95\times10^{+15}\ cm^{-3}$

10.25

$$\tau_{RT} = \frac{2}{c}\{(n{=}1)\cdot 15\ cm + (n{=}2.3)\cdot 5\ cm + (n{=}1.816)\cdot 10\ cm\} = 2.98\ ns$$

$S = R_1R_2T^8 = 0.701$; $\tau_p = \frac{\tau_{RT}}{1-S} = 9.97$ ns

Threshold inversion density: $S\exp[2\gamma_{th}l_g] = 1$; $\gamma_{th} = \frac{1}{2l_g}\ln\frac{1}{S} = 1.78\times10^{-2}\ \text{cm}^{-1}$

$A_{21} = \frac{0.0799}{255\times10^{-6}\ \text{sec}} = 313.3\ \text{sec}^{-1}$; $\Delta\bar{\nu} = 3.6\ \text{cm}^{-1}$; $\Delta\nu = 108$ GHz

$\sigma = A_{21}\frac{\lambda^2}{8\pi n^2}\frac{2}{\pi\Delta\nu} = 2.51\times10^{-19}\ \text{cm}^2$;

The transition is from 11,423 to 2002 cm^{-1}, hence:

$[^4F_{3/2}]_{lower} = 7.09\times10^{+16}\text{cm}^{-3}$; $[^4F_{3/2}]_{upper} = 4.73\times10^{+16}\text{cm}^{-3}$;

$[^4F_{3/2}]_{threshold} = 3.54\times10^{+17}\ \text{cm}^{-3}$

$n_{th} = 7.67\times10^{+17}$ atoms; $n_i = 3n_{th} = 2.3\times10^{+18}$ atoms; $h\nu = 1.869\times10^{-19}$ Joules

From Fig. 9.13, $\eta_{xtn} = 0.941$; coupling efficiency: $\eta_{coup} = \frac{0.2}{1 - S} = \frac{0.2}{0.299} = 0.669$

$[^4F_{3/2}]_{final} = 2.09\times10^{+16}\ \text{cm}^{-3}$; $W_{out} = \eta_{xtn}\,\eta_{cpl}\frac{n_i h\nu}{2} = 135.3$ mJ

From Fig. 9.14: $\Delta t_{1/2}/\tau_p = 5.5 - 2.3 = 3.2$ units $\quad\therefore\ \Delta t_{1/2} = 31.9$ ns

$$P_{out}\,(\max) = \eta_c\left\{\frac{n_i - n_{th}}{2} - \frac{n_{th}}{2}\ln\frac{n_i}{n_{th}}\right\}\frac{h\nu}{\tau_p} = 4.33\ \text{MW};$$

Note: $W/P_{max} = 31.2$ ns (very close to the numerical integration answer)

If $N_1=0$, then all factors of 2 disappear and thus the answers for W and P increase by a factor of 2.

10.26

a(1) Probably the most drastic assumption of this model is the neglect of stimulated emission by the pump (at 1.48 μm) back to 1. If the pump were at 0.98 μm, then the assumption of $\tau_{32} \ll \tau_{21} = \tau$ is sufficient to justify it. It is debatable whether it is legitimate for a 1.48 μm pump.

a(2) $$\frac{dN_2}{dt} = \frac{\sigma_p I_p}{h\nu_p}N_1 - \frac{\sigma_s I_s}{h\nu_s}(N_2 - N_1) - \frac{N_2}{\tau} = 0;\ N_2 = \frac{S+P}{1+S}N_1;\ N_1 + N_2 = N;$$

$\left[\frac{1+2S+P}{1+S}\right]N_1 = N$ where: $I_{sp} = h\nu_p/(\sigma_p\tau)$, $I_{ss} = h\nu_s/\sigma_s\tau$, $S = I_s/I_{ss}$ and $P = I_p/I_{sp}$;

$$\therefore\ N_1 = \frac{1+S}{1+2S+P}N;\qquad N_2 = \frac{S+P}{1+2S+P}N;\qquad (N_2 - N_1) = \frac{(P-1)}{1+2S+P}N$$

$$\frac{dS(z)}{dz} = \left[\frac{P(z)-1}{1+2S(z)+P(z)}\right]\alpha_s S(z);\ \alpha_s = N\sigma_s \qquad (1)$$

and $$\frac{dP(z)}{dz} = -\left[\frac{1+S(z)}{1+2S(z)+P(z)}\right]\alpha_p P(z);\ \alpha_p = N\sigma_p \qquad (2)$$

(b) Divide (1) by (2): $\frac{dS}{dP} = \frac{(P(z)-1)}{1+S(z)}\frac{\alpha_s}{\alpha_p}\frac{S(z)}{P(z)}$ or

$$\int_{S_1}^{S_2}\left[\frac{1+S}{S}\right]dS = -\frac{\alpha_s}{\alpha_p}\int_{P_1}^{P_2}\left[\frac{P-1}{P}\right]dP;$$ where 1 = input plane; 2 = output plane;

$$\ln\frac{S_2}{S_1} + S_1\left[\frac{S_2}{S_1-1}\right] = \frac{\alpha_s}{\alpha_p}\left\{(P_1-P_2) - \ln\frac{P_1}{P_2}\right\}.$$

Now $G \triangleq S_2/S_1$ = gain; $T \triangleq P_2/P_1$ = saturated transmission of pump;

$$\therefore \quad \ln G + S_1(G-1) = \frac{\alpha_s}{\alpha_p}\left[(P_1-P_2) - \ln\frac{P_1}{P_2}\right] \tag{3}$$

$$\ln G + S_1(G-1) = \frac{\alpha_s}{\alpha_p}\left[P_1(1-T) - \ln\frac{1}{T}\right] \tag{4}$$

(c) For a small signal, $S = I_s/I_{ss} \to 0$ and $G \to G_0$;

$$\ln G_0 = \frac{\alpha_s}{\alpha_p}\left[(P_1-P_2) - \ln\frac{P_1}{P_2}\right] = \frac{\alpha_s}{\alpha_p}\left[\frac{I_{p1}-I_{p2}}{I_{sp}} - \ln\frac{P_1}{P_2}\right] \tag{5}$$

(d) If $P = I_{p1}/I_{sp} \to 0$, $I_{p2}=I_{p1}\exp[-\alpha_p L]$; Eq. 5 $\to \ln G_0 = -\alpha_s L$;

or $\quad G_0 = \exp[-\alpha_p L] < 1$ as one would expect.

(e) For optical transparency; $G_0 = 1$. Thus from Eq. 5, we have:

$$0 = \frac{\alpha_s}{\sigma_p}\left[P_{10} - P_{20} - \ln\frac{P_{10}}{P_{20}}\right] \text{ or } P_{10} - P_{20} = \ln\frac{P_{10}}{P_{20}} \tag{6}$$

which only applies at optical transparency. Just because the signal is small, the pump need not be (and is usually large), and thus saturation of the absorption must be included.

(f) For S small throughout the length L, Eq. 2 can be approximated by:

$$\text{Eq. 2} \Rightarrow \frac{dP}{dz} \approx -\frac{\alpha_p P}{1+P}; \quad \int_{P_1}^{P_2}\left[\frac{1+P}{P}\right]dP = -\alpha_p\int_0^L dz$$

$$\text{or} \quad (P_1-P_2) + \ln\frac{P_1}{P_2} = \alpha_p L \tag{7}$$

(g) Eq. 7 applies in all cases for $S<<1$; it also applies to OT. Now:

$$\ln\frac{P_{10}}{P_{20}} = \alpha_p L - (P_{10}-P_{20}) \text{ from (7);}$$

Substitute into (6): $$\boxed{(P_{10}-P_{20}) = +\frac{\alpha_p L}{2}} \tag{8}$$

(h) Substitute (7) into (5).

$$\ln G_0 = (\alpha_s/\alpha_p)[2(P_1-P_2) - \alpha_p L] = (2\alpha_s/\alpha_p)[(P_1-P_2) - (\alpha_p L/2)].$$

Use Eq. 8 $$\boxed{\ln G_0 = \frac{2\alpha_s L}{\alpha_p L}[(P_1-P_2) - (P_{10}-P_{20})]} \tag{9}$$

i(1) For a fixed length and increasing P_1, the transmission starts with a net attenuation, crosses transparency, and then saturates at the maximum possible gain of $G_0 = \exp \alpha_s L$ as shown in the (b) part of the following figure.

i(2) Let's first assume that the pump is large enough to provide gain at the input to the fiber. Most of the pump would be wasted since little is absorbed for short lengths. If we kept the pump power fixed at the input and increased the length, one would absorb more of the pump and the gain should increase. Eventually, most of the pump will have been absorbed and the remaining length contributes an attenuation rather than gain. If the length is too long, the net gain will be less than 1. This is shown in part (a).

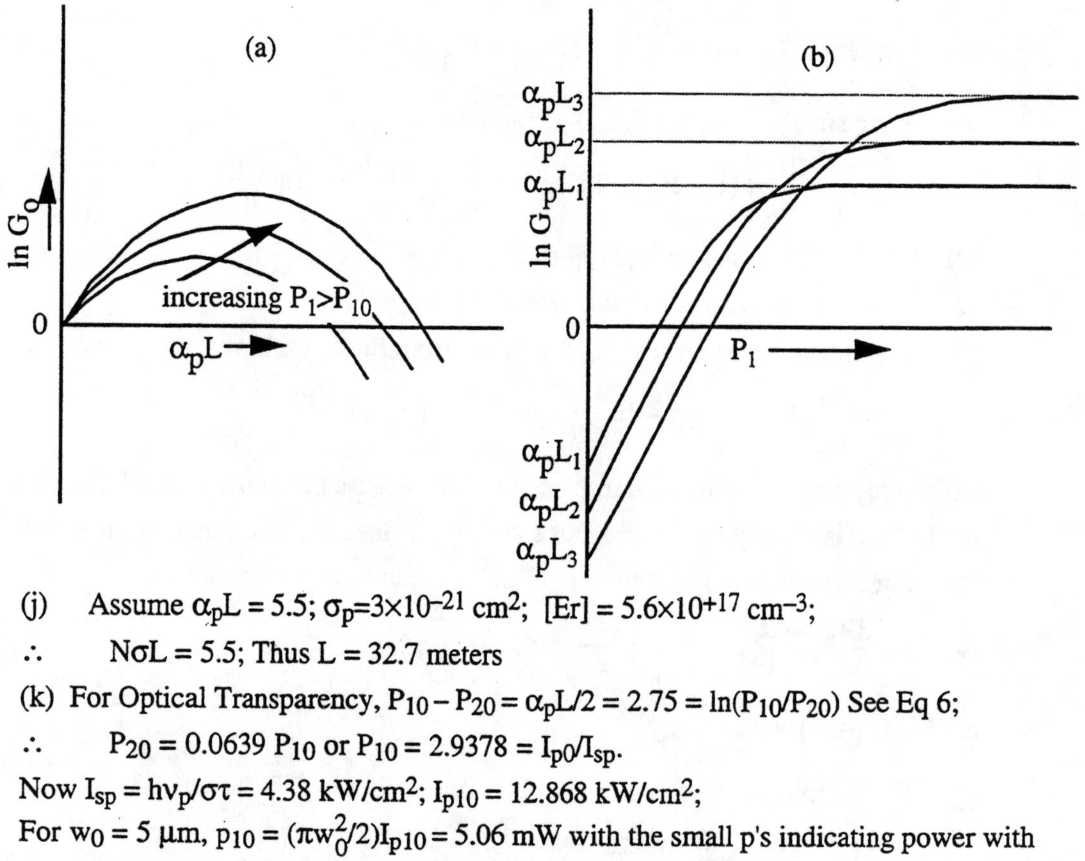

(j) Assume $\alpha_p L = 5.5$; $\sigma_p = 3\times10^{-21}$ cm^2; [Er] = $5.6\times10^{+17}$ cm^{-3};

$\therefore$ $N\sigma L = 5.5$; Thus L = 32.7 meters

(k) For Optical Transparency, $P_{10} - P_{20} = \alpha_p L/2 = 2.75 = \ln(P_{10}/P_{20})$ See Eq 6;

$\therefore$ $P_{20} = 0.0639\ P_{10}$ or $P_{10} = 2.9378 = I_{p0}/I_{sp}$.

Now $I_{sp} = h\nu_p/\sigma\tau = 4.38$ kW/cm^2; $I_{p10} = 12.868$ kW/cm^2;

For $w_0 = 5\ \mu$m, $p_{10} = (\pi w_0^2/2) I_{p10} = 5.06$ mW with the small p's indicating power with the capital P indicating power normalized to the saturation value:

$p_{abs} = (1-0.0639) p_{10} = 4.73$ mW

(l) If $P_1 = 10 \times P_{10} = 29.378$, then Eq. 7 states that $P_2 = 24.077$

Use a "solve" key on a calculator to find:

$$\ln(P_1/P_2) = 0.19899;\ P_2 = 0.81956\ P_1;\ P_1 - P_2 = 0.18044\ P_1;$$

and $p_1 - p_2 = 9.12$ mW; $p_1 = 50.6$ mW and thus: $p_2 = 41.43$ mW

(m) $\ln G_0 = (2\alpha_s/\alpha_p)\left[P_1 - P_2 - (\alpha_p L/2)\right]$ by Eq. 9

$$\ln G_0 = 2 \cdot \frac{5\times10^{-21}}{3\times10^{-21}} [0.18044 \times 29.378 - 2.75] = 8.503;\ \therefore\ G_0 = 4.93\times10^{+3} \Rightarrow 36.9 \text{ dB}$$

(n) As the signal gets bigger, stimulated emission returns atoms from 2→1 increasing the population in 1. This increases the absorption of the pump, negating the depletion of state 2 by the signal.

10.27

$$\frac{d(\Delta N)}{dt} = \frac{\Delta N_b - \Delta N}{\tau} - \frac{\sigma(I_1 + I_2)}{h\nu}\Delta N$$

or
$$\frac{d(\Delta N)}{dt} + \frac{1}{\tau}\left[1 + \frac{I_1 + I_2}{I_s}\right]\Delta N = \frac{\Delta N_0}{\tau}; 0 < t < T;$$

$$\Delta N = \frac{\Delta N^{\circ}}{1 + (I_1 + I_2)/I_s} + A\exp\left\{-\left[1 + \frac{I_1 + I_2}{I_s}\right]\frac{t}{\tau}\right\};$$

at t=0
$$\Delta N - \Delta N_a = \frac{\Delta N_0}{1 + (I_1 + I_2)/I_s} + A;$$

$$A = \Delta N_a - \frac{\Delta N^{\circ}}{1 + (I_1 + I_2)/I_s};$$

$$\Delta N = \frac{\Delta N^{\circ}}{1 + (I_1 + I_2)/I_s}\left\{1 - \exp\left[-\left(1 + \frac{I_1 + I_2}{I_s}\right)\frac{t}{\tau}\right]\right\} + \Delta N_a \exp\left[-\left(1 + \frac{I_1 + I_2}{I_s}\right)\frac{t}{\tau}\right]$$

For $0 < t' < T$,

$$\Delta N = \frac{\Delta N^{\circ}}{1 + I_1/I_s}\{1 - \exp[-(1 + I_1/I_s)(t/\tau)\} + \{\Delta N_b \exp[-(1 + I_1/I_s)(t/\tau)\}$$

At t=T, $\Delta N = \Delta N_b$; at t' = T, $\Delta N = \Delta N_a$;

Define $\varepsilon_1 = \exp[-(1 + I_1/I_s)(T/\tau)]$; $\varepsilon_2 = \exp[-(I_2/I_s)(T/\tau)]$; $a = I_1/I_s$, $b = I_2/I_s$;

$$\Delta N_b = \frac{\Delta N_0}{1 + a + b}(1 - \varepsilon_1\varepsilon_2) + \varepsilon_1\varepsilon_2\Delta N_a;$$

and
$$\Delta N_a = \frac{\Delta N_0}{1 + a}(1 - \varepsilon_1) + \varepsilon_1\Delta N_b$$

$$\Delta N_b = \frac{\Delta N_0}{1 + a + b}(1 - \varepsilon_1\varepsilon_2) + \frac{\varepsilon_1\varepsilon_2(1 - \varepsilon_1)\Delta N_0}{1+a} + \varepsilon_1^2\varepsilon_2\Delta N_b;$$

or
$$\Delta N_b = \frac{\Delta N_0}{1-\varepsilon_1^2\varepsilon_2}\left\{\frac{1 - \varepsilon_1\varepsilon_2}{1 + a + b} + \frac{\varepsilon_1\varepsilon_2(1 - \varepsilon_1)}{1 + a}\right\};$$

Therefore:
$$\Delta N_a - \Delta N_b = \frac{\Delta N_0}{1 - \varepsilon_1^2\varepsilon_2}(1 - \varepsilon_1)(1 - \varepsilon_1\varepsilon_2)\left\{\frac{1}{1 + a} - \frac{1}{1 + a + b}\right\}$$

Hence the difference between the two levels is given by:

$$\boxed{\Delta N_a - \Delta N_b = \Delta N_0\left[\frac{(1 - \varepsilon_1)(1 - \varepsilon_1\varepsilon_2)}{1 - \varepsilon_1^2\varepsilon_2}\right]\left\{\frac{b}{(1 + a)(1 + a + b)}\right\}}$$

For $\tau >> T$, $\varepsilon_1 = 1 - (1 + a)\frac{T}{\tau}$ thus $1 - \varepsilon_1 = (1 + a)\frac{T}{\tau}$;

and $\varepsilon_1^2 = 1 - 2(1 + a)\dfrac{T}{\tau}$; $\varepsilon_2 = 1 - b\dfrac{T}{\tau}$;

$\varepsilon_1^2 = 1 - 2(1 + a)\dfrac{T}{\tau}$; $1 - \varepsilon_1 \approx (1 + a)\dfrac{T}{\tau}$; $\varepsilon_1\varepsilon_2 = 1 - (1 + a + b)\dfrac{T}{\tau}$;

$$\varepsilon_1^2\varepsilon_2 = 1 - (2 + 2a + b)\frac{T}{\tau};\ \therefore \frac{(1 - \varepsilon_1)(1 - \varepsilon_1\varepsilon_2)}{1 - \varepsilon_1^2\varepsilon_2} = \frac{(1 + a)(1 + a + b)}{(2 + 2a + b)}\frac{T}{\tau}$$

(b)
$$\Delta N_a - \Delta N_b = \frac{(1 + a)(1 + a + b)}{2 + 2a + b}\frac{T}{\tau}\frac{b}{(1 + a)(1 + a + b)}\Delta N_0$$

$$\approx \left[\frac{b}{2 + 2a + b}\Delta N_0\right]\frac{T}{\tau};$$

$\therefore$ For $\tau \ll T$, $\varepsilon_{1,2} \ll 1$;

$$\Delta N_a - \Delta N_b = \left[\frac{b}{(1 + a)(1 + a + b)}\right]\Delta N_0$$

(c) Obviously, the case of $\tau \gg T$ minimizes the changes in the inversion.

Chapter 11

11.1

Given that $n_e = p = 5\times10^{18}$ cm^{-3} and that T = 0K, then all levels up to the maximum in the conduction band are filled

(a) $n_e = \frac{1}{3\pi^2}\left\{\frac{2m_e^*\Delta E_c}{\hbar^2}\right\}^{3/2} = 5\times10^{+24}$ m^{-3}; $\therefore$ $\Delta E_c = 0.1596$ eV $= 2.55\times10^{-20}$ joules

There are two type of holes, light and heavy, whose bands are emptied to ΔE_v.

(b) $p = \frac{1}{3\pi^2}\left\{\frac{2m_{hh}\Delta E_v}{\hbar^2}\right\}^{3/2} + \frac{1}{3\pi^2}\left\{\frac{2m_{lh}\Delta E_v}{\hbar^2}\right\}^{3/2} = 5\times10^{+24}$ m^{-3}; $\therefore$ $\Delta E_v = 0.0189$ eV

(c) $p_{hh} = \frac{1}{3\pi^2}\left\{\frac{2m_{hh}}{\hbar^2}\Delta E_v\right\}^{3/2} = 4.8\times10^{+18}$ cm^{-3};

$p_{lh} = \frac{1}{3\pi^2}\left\{\frac{2m_{lh}}{\hbar^2}\Delta E_v\right\}^{3/2} = 0.2\times10^{+18}$ cm^{-3} $\therefore$ most of the holes are heavy holes;

(d) $m_e^* v^2/2 = e\Delta E_c$; $\therefore$ $v = 9.15\times10^{+5}$ m/s $= 9.15\times10^{+7}$ cm/s

11.2

(a) $\frac{dn}{dt} = G - \beta np$ and $n = p$; $G = \frac{10^3 \text{ joules/sec/cm}^3}{hc/\lambda = 3.855\times10^{-19}\text{joules}} = 2.59\times10^{+21}\frac{\text{e - h pairs}}{\text{cm}^3\text{–sec}}$

$n = (G/\beta)^{1/2} = 3.6\times10^{+15}$ cm^{-3} $= 3.6\times10^{+21}$ m^{-3} $= \frac{1}{3\pi^2}\left\{\frac{2m_e^*}{\hbar^2}\Delta E_c\right\}^{3/2}$ since T = 0

(b) $\therefore F_n - E_c = \Delta E_c = 1.28$ meV and $E_v - F_p = \Delta E_v = \frac{m_e}{m_h}\Delta E_c = 0.156$ meV

11.3

Start with Eq. 11.2.8 $\rho_c(E_2) = \frac{1}{2\pi^2}\left\{\frac{2m_e}{\hbar^2}\right\}^{3/2}(E_2 - E_c)^{1/2}$;

$$\rho_v(E_1) = \frac{1}{2\pi^2}\left\{\frac{2m_{hh}}{\hbar^2}\right\}^{3/2}(E_v - E_1)^{1/2}$$

$E_2 - E_c = \frac{m_h}{m_h + m_e}(h\nu - E_g)$ and $E_v - E_1 = \frac{m_e}{m_h + m_e}(h\nu - E_g)$

Substitute the above into: $\rho_{jnt} = \frac{1}{2}\left[\frac{1}{\rho_c(E_2)} + \frac{1}{\rho_v(E_1)}\right]^{-1}$ and identify $m_r = \frac{m_e m_h}{m_e + m_h}$

$$\rho_c(E_2) = \frac{1}{2\pi^2}\left[\frac{2m_e}{\hbar^2}\right]^{3/2}\left(\frac{m_h}{m_e + m_h}\right)^{1/2}(h\nu - E_g)^{1/2}$$

$$\rho_v(E_1) = \frac{1}{2\pi^2}\left[\frac{2m_h}{\hbar^2}\right]^{3/2}\left(\frac{m_e}{m_e + m_h}\right)^{1/2}(h\nu - E_g)^{1/2}$$

$$\therefore \quad \rho_{jnt} = \frac{1}{4\pi^2}\left\{\frac{2}{\hbar^2}\right\}^{3/2}(m_r)^{1/2}\left[\frac{1}{m_e} + \frac{1}{m_h}\right]^{-1}(h\nu - E_g)^{1/2} = \frac{1}{4\pi^2}\left[\frac{2m_r}{\hbar^2}\right]^{3/2}(h\nu - E_g)^{1/2}$$

11.4

An inversion requires that the probability of the states at E_2 being occupied be greater than the probability that the states at E_1 are occupied, or:

$$f_n(E_2) = \frac{1}{\exp\left[\frac{E_2 - F_n}{kT}\right] + 1} > f_v(E_1) = \frac{1}{\exp\left[\frac{E_1 - F_p}{kT}\right] + 1}$$

Thus: $$\exp\left[\frac{E_2 - F_n}{kT} + 1\right] < \exp\left[\frac{E_1 - F_p}{kT} + 1\right];$$

$$E_2 - F_n < E_1 - F_p \text{ or } (E_2 - E_1) = h\nu < F_n - F_p$$

Note: E_2, E_1 are absolute energies, not relative to band edges.

11.5

Ignore light holes

$$E_2 - E_c = \frac{m_h}{m_e + m_h}(h\nu - E_g) = \Delta E_c = \frac{0.55}{0.55 + 0.067} \times 0.05 = 0.04457 \text{ eV}$$

$$E_v - E_1 = \frac{m_e}{m_e + m_h}(h\nu - E_g) = 0.00543 \text{ eV}$$

$$N = \frac{1}{3\pi^2}\left\{\frac{2m\Delta E_c}{\hbar^2}\right\}^{3/2} = 7.4\times10^{+23}\ \text{m}^{-3} = 7.4\times10^{+17}\ \text{cm}^{-3}$$

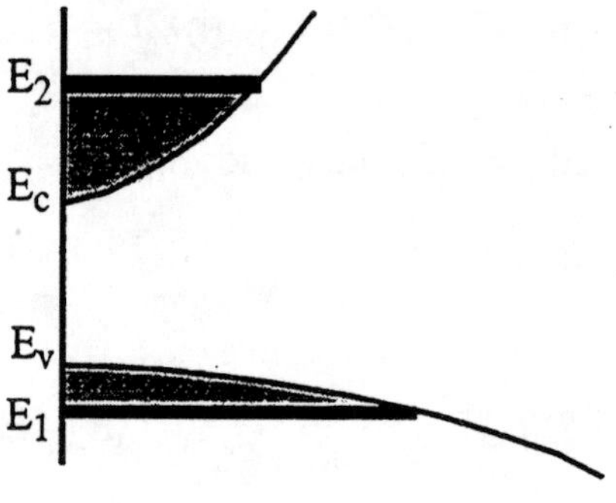

11.6

$N = N_0 + \Delta N(t)$; $J = J_0 + \Delta J(t)$; and $P = P_0 + \Delta P(t)$; Equating AC variables and neglecting products:

$$\frac{d\Delta N}{dt} = \frac{\Delta J}{ed} - \left(\frac{1}{\tau_s} + AP_0\right)\Delta N - A[N_D - N_{tr}]\Delta P$$

Now $$A(N_0 - N_{tr}) = \frac{1}{\tau_p} - \frac{\beta N_0}{P_0\tau_s} \approx \frac{1}{\tau_p};\ \therefore \frac{d\Delta N}{dt} = \frac{\Delta J}{ed} - \left(\frac{1}{\tau_s} + AP_0\right)\Delta N - \frac{\Delta P}{\tau_p}$$

Likewise: $$\frac{d\Delta N}{dt} = A[N_0 - N_{tr}]\Delta P + AP_0\Delta N - \frac{\Delta P}{\tau_p} + \beta\frac{\Delta N}{\tau_s};$$

The first and third terms cancel leaving: $$\frac{d\Delta P}{dt} = \left[AP_0 + \frac{\beta}{\tau_s}\right]\Delta N$$

11.7

The answers to parts (a) and (c) are given in the text. Theory predicts $\omega^2 = (AP_0/\tau_p)$ But τ_p varies directly with length. Pick $P_0 = 2$ mW.

l_g	ω_{meas}	ω_{pred}
120 μm	7.2 GHz	7.2* GHz
165 μm	6.3	6.14
284 μm	4.2	4.6

*i.e., forcing a fit on this point and then using it to predict the others. (Reasonable predictions).

11.8

(a) Pick P_0 as being the power in +z direction at M_1; $\therefore$ $P_0\, e^{-\alpha z}\, e^{+\int\gamma dz} = P_{inc}$ on M_2;
Let $T = e^{-\alpha z}$ and $G = e^{+\int\gamma dz}$; Note: it is note necessary to evaluate this integral.
Then the output power at $M_2 = (1 - R_2)TGP_0$ and the power incident on $M_1 = R_2T^2G^2P_0$
Thus the output at $M_1 = (1 - R_1)R_2T^2G^2P_0$;

$\therefore \dfrac{P_1}{P_2} = \left(\dfrac{1 - R_1}{1 - R_2}\right)R_2GT$ However, $G^2T^2R_1R_2 = 1$ for CW laser;

$$\boxed{\frac{P_1}{P_2} = \left(\frac{1 - R_1}{1 - R_2}\right)\left(\frac{R_2}{R_1}\right)^{1/2}}$$

(b) G only measures the ratio of output to input of the active region. Hence, the answer is independent of the saturation law or possible nonuniformity along z.

(c) A"soft." transition is a gradual evolution from a LED to a laser.

(d) Use the following diagram and chase the power around the cavity and demand sel-consistency:

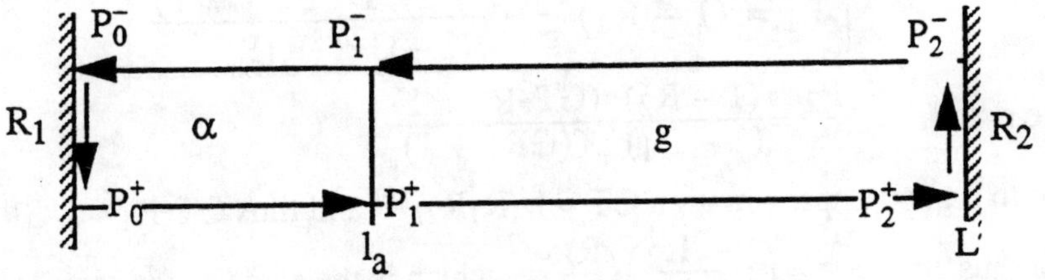

$$\frac{dP^+}{dz} = -\alpha P^+ \qquad \text{in the loss region} \qquad (1)$$

$$P^+(z) = P_0^+\, e^{-\alpha z} \text{ and thus } P_1^+ = T\cdot P_0^+ \text{ where } T = e^{-\alpha l_g} \qquad (2)$$

In the gain region: $\dfrac{dP^+}{dz} = g_0P^+ + s$ (3)

where s = spontaneous power added per unit of length.

or $P^+(z) = A_1e^{+g(z-l_g)} - s/g$ at $z = l_g$. $P^+(z{=}l_g) = P_1^+$ is given by Eq. 2 and thus

$$A_1 = TP_1^+ + s/g$$

Thus $P^+(l_g<z<L) = TP_1^+(0) + (s/g)\, e^{g(z-l_g)} - (s/g)$

at z=L $\boxed{P_2^+ = GP_1^+ + (G-1)(s/g) = GTP_0^+ + (s/g)(G-1)}$ (4)

where $G = e^{g(L-l_g)}$

The output power is:

$$P_2 = (1-R_2)P_2^+ = (1-R_2)[GTP_0^+ + (s/g)(G-1)] \quad (5)$$

and the reflected power

$$P_2^- = R_2P_2^+ = R_2[GTP_0^+ + (s/g)(G-1)] \quad (6)$$

Now examine the reverse wave using P_2^- as the input and apply the first equality part of (4)

$$P_1^- = GP_2^- + (G-1)(s/g) = G^2TR_2\, P_0^+ + (s/g)(G-1)(GR_2+1) \quad (7)$$

and the wave incident on M_1 is given by:

$$P_0^- = TP_1^- = G^2T^2R_2\, P_0^+ + (s/g)(G-1)T(GR_2+1) \quad (8)$$

Now demand self-consistency: $P_0^+ = R_1P_0^-$ (9)

which allows one to solve for P_0^+

$$\therefore \quad P_0^+ = \frac{s}{g}\frac{(G-1)(TR_1)(GR_2+1)}{1-G^2T^2R_1R_2} \quad (10)$$

Note that this implies that $G^2T^2R_1R_2 < 1$ to avoid the absurdity of an infinite power.

Substitute (10) into (5) to obtain

$$\therefore \quad \boxed{P_2 = (1-R_2)\frac{s}{g}\frac{(G-1)(GT^2R_1+1)}{1-G^2T^2R_1R_2}} \quad (11)$$

Now

$$P_1 = \frac{1-R_1}{R_1}P_0^+ \text{ with } P_1^+ \text{ given by (10)}$$

Thus

$$\boxed{P_1 = (1-R_1)\frac{s}{g}\frac{(G-1)\,T\,(GR_2+1)}{(1-G^2T^2R_1R_2)}} \quad (12)$$

The ratio $\dfrac{P_2}{P_1} = \dfrac{(1-R_2)}{(1-R_1)}\dfrac{(GT^2R_1+1)}{T(GR_2+1)}$ (13)

But to a good approximation $GT \approx 1/(R_1R_2)^{1/2}$ and thus $GT^2R_1 \approx 1/GR_2$

and thus $\dfrac{P_2}{P_1} \approx \left(\dfrac{1-R_2}{1-R_1}\right)\left(\dfrac{R_1}{R_2}\right)^{1/2}$ which is the same as for part (a) (14)

11.9

Resonance: $\Rightarrow q \cdot \lambda_q = 2n_{eff}d$; Mean spacing between peaks at 8723Å is 2.66Å (where ± 3 modes from center were chosen);

$$\text{Now } n(\lambda) = n(\lambda_0) + \frac{dn}{d\lambda}(\lambda - \lambda_0)$$

$$(q-1)\,\lambda_{q-1} = 2d\left[n(\lambda_0) + \frac{dn}{d\lambda}(\lambda_{q-1} - \lambda_0)\right];$$

$$q\,\lambda q = 2d\left[n(\lambda_0) + \frac{dn}{d\lambda}(\lambda_q - \lambda_0)\right]$$

Subtract:

$$\Delta\lambda = \lambda_{q-1} - \lambda_q = \frac{\lambda_0}{q - 2d\,(\partial n/\partial\lambda)}; \qquad \text{Now } q = \frac{2nd}{\lambda_0};$$

$$\therefore \quad \Delta\lambda = \frac{\lambda_0}{(2nd/\lambda_0) - 2d(\partial n/\partial\lambda)} = \frac{\lambda_0^2}{2d[n(\lambda_0) - \lambda_0(\partial n/\partial\lambda)]}$$

The [ ] in denominator can be considered as the effective or group index.
For $\Delta\lambda = 2.66$Å; $d = 380^{-4}$ cm; $\lambda_0 = 8723$Å $= 0.872$ μm;
$n_{eff} = 3.764$ whereas $n = 3.6$; $\therefore\ \lambda_0\,(\partial n/\partial\lambda) = -0.164$; $(\partial n/\partial\lambda) = -\,0.1878\ \mu m^{-1}$

11.10

(a) For $E_t = E_0\, e^{-(x/w_x)^2} e^{-(y/w_y)^2}$; $P = \frac{1}{2}\frac{E_0^2}{\eta_0}\iint_{+\infty}^{-\infty} e^{-2(x/w_x)^2} e^{-2(y/w_y)^2}\,dx\,dy$

$$P = \frac{1}{2}\frac{E_0{}^2}{\eta_0}\left[\frac{w_x w_y}{2}\right]\left\{\int_{-\infty}^{\infty} e^{-U^2}\,dU\right\}^2 = \frac{E_0^2}{2\eta_0}\left[\frac{\pi w_x w_y}{2}\right];\ \therefore\ E_0 = 21.9\text{ kV/cm (field radiated)}$$

(b) This field comes from insuring continuity of E on either side of the air-index boundary.
$E_0 = (1 + \Gamma)\,E^+$ where E^+ = the wave incident on the index-air boundary, and

Γ = the <u>field</u> reflection coefficient is approximate by the Fresnel formula:

$$= \frac{\eta_0 - \eta_0/n}{\eta_0 + \eta_0/n} = 0.565$$

$$\therefore \quad E^+ = \frac{E_0}{1+\Gamma} = 14\text{ kV/cm}\ ;\ E^- = \Gamma E^+ = 7.9\text{ kV/cm}$$

(c) $\tan\frac{\theta}{2} = \frac{\lambda}{\pi w}$; $\tan\frac{\theta_\perp}{2} = 0.278$; for $\lambda = 873$ nm; $\therefore\ \theta_\perp = 31.04°$;

$\tan\frac{\theta_{||}}{2} = 0.0278$; $\theta_{||} = 3.18°$

11.11 and 11.12 Easy reading papers

11.13

$$\frac{dn}{dt} = G - \beta n^2 - \frac{n}{\tau_D}; \quad \text{(a) } \beta n^2 > \frac{n}{\tau_D}; \quad \therefore \qquad n > (1/\beta\tau_D) = 1.9\times10^{+18}\ \text{cm}^{-3}$$

$$\text{(b)} \qquad G = \beta n^2 + \frac{n}{\tau_D}\Big|_{n = 3\times10^{+18}} = 2.95\times10^{+27}\ \text{(e–h pairs)/(cm}^3\text{–sec)}$$

This is also equal to the absorbed photons per unit of volume = $(P_p/h\nu)$;
Since $h\nu_p/e = 2.41$ eV, $\therefore$ $P = 1.14 \times 10^{+9}$ W/cm^3, which is a lot!

11.14

$$\text{(a)} \qquad \frac{(\hbar k_e)^2}{2m_e^*} = \frac{(\hbar\cdot\pi/L_z)^2}{2m_e^*} = E_{1e} - E_c = 56.1\ \text{meV};$$

$$\text{For the 2nd band } \frac{(\hbar\cdot 2\pi/L_z)^2}{2m_e^*} = E_{2e} - E_c = 224.1\ \text{meV}$$

$$\text{(b)} \qquad n_c = \frac{1}{2\pi^2}\left(\frac{2m_e^*}{\hbar^2}\right)\left(\frac{\pi}{L_z}\right)\Delta E \text{ or } \Delta E = 17.89\ \text{meV, for the QW}$$

$$= \frac{1}{3\pi^2}\left(\frac{2m_e^*\Delta E}{\hbar^2}\right)^{3/2} \text{ or } \Delta E = 34.3\ \text{meV for the bulk semiconductor}$$

$$\text{(c)} \qquad \frac{\hbar k_h}{2m_{hh}} = E_v - E_{1hh} = 6.86\ \text{meV};\ E_v - E_{1lh} = 56.1\ \text{meV}$$

(d)

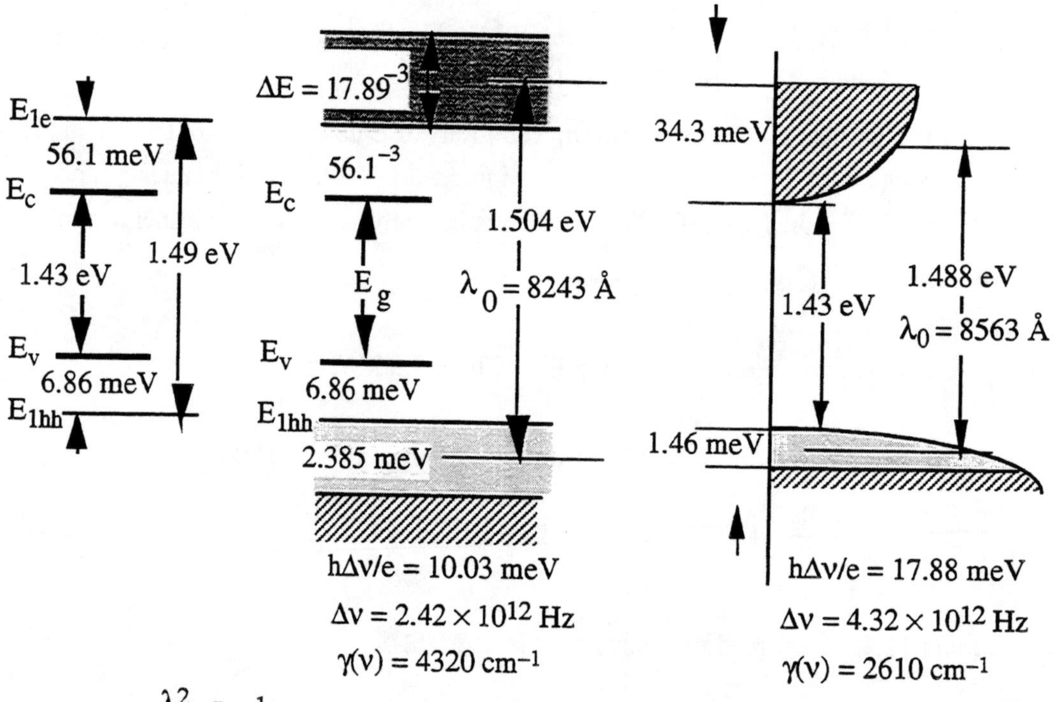

where $\gamma(\nu) = \frac{\lambda^2}{8\pi n^2}\frac{n_c}{\tau}\frac{1}{\Delta\nu}$ was used to compute the gain coefficient.

11.15

$\nu_0 = 3.57\times10^{+14}$ Hz; $\Delta\nu_{Base} = 1.02\times10^{+13}$ Hz; and $\int_0^\infty g(\nu)d\nu = 1$;

$\therefore\ g(\nu_0) = 2/\Delta\nu_{Base} = 1.99\times10^{-13}$ s;

For threshold $R_1R_2\exp[(\gamma_0-\alpha)2l_g] = 1; \therefore\quad \gamma_0 = \alpha + \frac{1}{2l_g}\ln\frac{1}{R_1R_2} = 27.7\ \text{cm}^{-1}$

$\gamma_0 = \frac{\lambda_0^2}{2\pi n^2}\frac{n_e}{\tau}g(\nu_0) = 4.26\times10^{-15}n_e = 27.7\ \text{cm}^{-1}; \therefore\quad n_e = 6.5\times10^{+15}\ \text{cm}^{-3}; \lambda_0 = 8400\text{Å}$

11.16

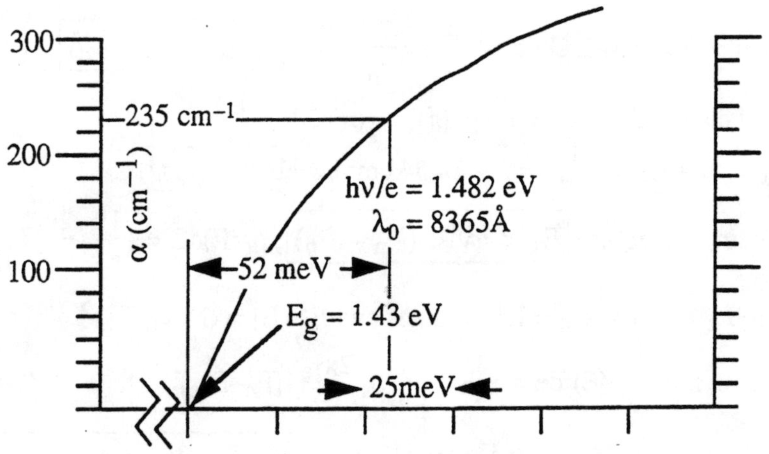

11.17

$E_{1e} = \frac{[\hbar(n\pi/L_z)]^2}{2m_e^*} = 78.04$ meV for n=1, $E_{2e} = 0.3122$ eV for n=2, which will not be confined even with the help of assuming an infinite well formula for the confined energy. $E_{hh} = 9.51$ meV using the same formula but with the heavy-hole mass. The actual energy is closer to the band edges because the tail of the wave function penetrates into the "forbidden" region and thus it "knows" that there isn't an infinite well.

11.18

For L_z=50Å between 20% AlGaAs; $R_e^2 = 1.77968; R_e = 1.33405 < \pi/2$;

$\therefore$ only 1 confined electron state; $R_h^2 = 7.86656$; $R_h = 2.80474$; 2 hole states;

$x^2\tan^2 x + x^2 - R^2 = 0$

$x_{1e} = 0.865157$; $\boxed{E_{1e} = 68.2\ \text{meV}}$;

$x_{1h} = 1.14879$; $\boxed{E_{1h} = 14.6\ \text{meV}}$

$-x\cot x = \sqrt{R^2-x^2}$; or $\left(\frac{x}{\tan x}\right)^2 - R^2 + x^2 = 0$;

$x_{2hh} = 2.22524$; $\boxed{E_{2hh} = 54.9\ \text{meV}}$

$\boxed{E = 1.50684 = h\nu/e \text{ or } \lambda = 8227.6\text{Å}}$;

$\rho_c(E) = \frac{1}{2\pi^2}\left(\frac{2m_e^*}{\hbar^2}\right)\left(k_z = \frac{2x_{1e}}{L_z}\right)$ for a finite barrier

$$\therefore \quad n_c = \int_{E_{c1}+E_{1e}}^{E_{c2}} \rho(E)dE = \frac{1}{2\pi^2}\left(\frac{2m_e^*}{\hbar^2}\right)\left(\frac{2x_{1e}}{L_z}\right)\cdot(E_{c2} - E_{c1} - E_{1e})$$

$$= 2.89\times10^{+24}\ \text{m}^{-3} = 2.89\times10^{+18}\ \text{cm}^{-3}$$

11.19

$$\tau_p = \frac{2hd/c}{1 - e^{-\alpha 2d}R_1R_2} = \frac{2nd/c}{1 - 0.289} = \boxed{13.5\ \text{ps}}$$

$\text{FSR} = \frac{c}{2nd} = 104.2\ \text{GHz} \qquad \frac{\Delta\lambda}{\lambda} = \frac{\Delta\nu}{\nu_0} \qquad \boxed{\therefore\ \Delta\lambda = 2.51\ \text{Å}}$

Threshold condition: $R_1R_2 \exp[\gamma_{th} - \alpha_s)\cdot 2d] = 1$;

$\therefore \gamma_{th} = \alpha_s + \frac{1}{2d}\ln\frac{1}{R_1R_2} = 2 + 14.54\ \text{cm}^{-1} = \boxed{16.54\ \text{cm}^{-1}}$

For gain, we require $\boxed{E_g < h\nu < (F_n - F_p)}$; $\rho_c(E)dE = \frac{1}{2\pi^2}\left(\frac{2m_e^*}{\hbar^2}\right)\left(\frac{2x_{1e}}{L_z}\right)dE$

where $L_z = 100$ Å, $x_{1e} = 1.13$ radians and $E > E_1 = (\hbar 2x_{1e}/L_z)^2$

For T=0; $n = \int_{E_1}^{F_n} \rho(E)\,de = \frac{1}{2\pi^2}\left(\frac{2m_e^*}{\hbar^2}\right)\left(\frac{2x_{1e}}{L_z}\right)[F_n - E_{1e}]$

For $n = 1.0\times10^{+24}\ \text{m}^{-3} = 1.0\times10^{+18}\ \text{cm}^{-3}$; $\boxed{\therefore\ F_n - E_1 = 50\ \text{meV} = 8\times10^{-21}\ \text{joules}}$

If $n = p = 2\times10^{+18}$, recombination dominates;

For pumping by absorption of 5145 Å radiation and with $\beta = 2\times10^{-10}\ \text{cm}^3/\text{sec}$

$p/h\nu = \beta n^2 + n/\tau_D \qquad \therefore\ p = \text{Power/Volume} = 385\ \text{MW/cm}^3$

11.20

(a) $\frac{e^{-\Delta E_v/kT}}{1 + e^{-\Delta E/kT}} = \boxed{0.0177}$

(b) $.0177\times10^{+20} = \boxed{1.77\times10^{+18}\ \text{cm}^3}$

(c) $N_1\sigma_{abs} = 20 \quad \therefore \boxed{\sigma = 1.17\times10^{-17}\ \text{cm}^2}$

(d) $N_3/N_2 = 5.87^{-6} = e^{-0.312/kT}$

(e) $\boxed{N_2 \approx 1.77\times10^{+18}\ \text{cm}^{-3}}$ The general approach would be to sum the populations in all of the states and invoke the condition that $N_2 = N_1$. The population in 3 is very small and can be ignored. Even if one summed N_1 and N_2, it will be a small fraction of the active atom population. Hence the above can be stated without arithmetic.

(f) $\frac{P/v}{h\nu_{30}} = \frac{n_2}{\tau_{21}}; \quad \therefore \boxed{\frac{P}{V} = 471\ \text{MW/cm}^3}$

Chapter 12

12.1

This is a very nice paper to assign to the students for reading. Most of the answers are covered in the text with a slightly different notation.

12.2

$$g_1 = 1 - \frac{d}{R_1} = \frac{5}{8}; \qquad g_2 = 1 + \frac{3}{2} = \frac{5}{2}; \qquad g_1 g_2 = \frac{25}{16}$$

The one-way survival factor due to diffraction:

$$s = \frac{1 - [1 - (g_1g_2)^{-1}]^{1/2}}{1 + [1 - (g_1g_2)^{-1}]^{1/2}} = \frac{1 - 3/5}{1 + 3/5} = \frac{1}{4}$$

Thus to reach threshold: $G_0 s = 1$, $G_0 = 4$;

In order to label the diagram as shown below, one must first find the point P where the "rays" originate, and then use similar triangles. The point P is 1 meter to the right of M_2 and thus the beam diameter $2a_1$ is given by:

$$\frac{2a_1}{4 \text{ meter}} = \frac{2.5 \text{ cm}}{1.25 \text{ meter}}; \; 2a_1 = 8 \text{ cm which is also the beam size at the bottom.}$$

The beam comes back parallel to the axis through the hole, and then expands going back to the slicer. Ignoring the differences in top and bottom for the distance along the z axis to the slicer, we obtain the beam size on the top:

$$\frac{2a_T}{1.25 \text{ meter}} = \frac{2.5 \text{ cm}}{1 \text{ meter}}; \; 2a_T = 3.12 \text{ cm}$$

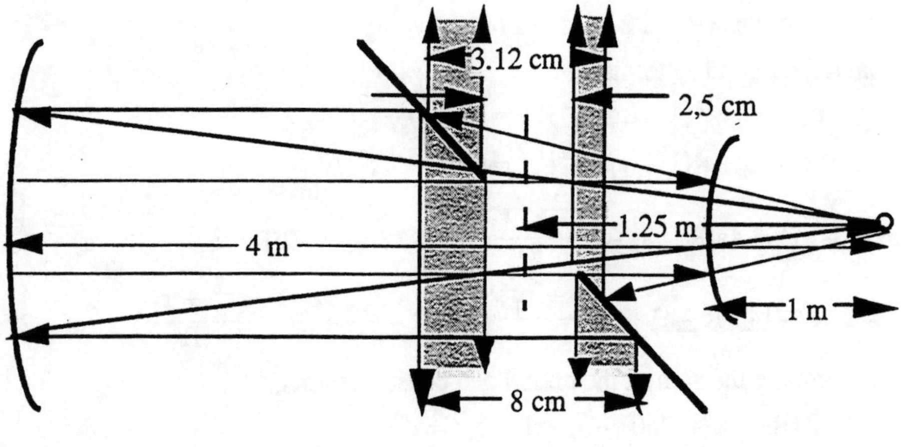

12.3

$$g_1 = 1 - \frac{d}{R_1} = 1 + 1 = 2; \qquad g_2 = 1 - \frac{d}{R_2} = 1 - \frac{1}{3} = \frac{2}{3}; \qquad g_1 g_2 = \frac{4}{3}; \qquad S = \frac{1 - \frac{1}{2}}{1 + \frac{1}{2}} = \frac{1}{3}$$

$$\therefore\ G = 3 = \exp[\gamma_0 l_g] \text{ and } \gamma_0 = \frac{1}{80} \ln 3 = 1.37 \times 10^{-2}\ \text{cm}^{-1}$$

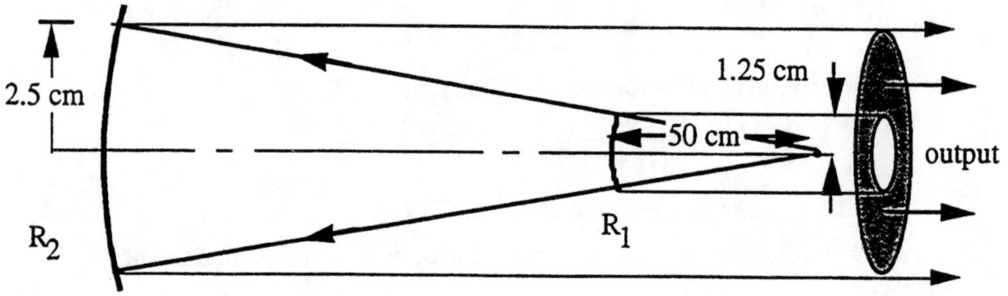

12.4

$$R^2 = (x_2 - x_1)^2 + (y_2 - y_1)^2 + (z_2 - z_1)^2$$
$$= x_2^2 + y_2^2 + (z_2 + a)^2 \qquad \rightarrow (R = \text{radius of } M_2)^2$$
$$+ x_1^2 + y_1^2 + (z_1 - a)^2 \qquad \rightarrow (R = \text{radius of } M_1)^2$$
$$- \mathbf{2a(z_2 - z_1)} - 2a^2 \qquad \rightarrow \text{(left over from above)}$$
$$-2x_1x_2 - 2y_1y_2 - \mathbf{2z_1z_2} \qquad \rightarrow \text{(left over from above)}$$

where $a = R - d/2$ to save a bit on typing;

Expand the z_1 and z_2 terms:

$$z_2 = -a + R[1 - (r_2/R)^2]^{1/2} \approx (R - a) - r_2^2/2R;$$
$$z_1 = -a + R[1 - (r_1/R)^2]^{1/2} \approx (R - a) - r_1^2/2R$$

$$\mathbf{2a(z_2 - z_1)} = 4a(R - a) - \frac{a[r_2^2 + r_1^2]}{R}; \text{ and } \mathbf{2z_1z_2} \approx -2(R - a)^2 + (R - a)\frac{r_2^2 + r_1^2}{R};$$

$$R^2 = 2R^2 - [\underline{4a(R - a)} + \frac{a(r_2^2 + r_1^2)}{R}] + \{\underline{2(R - a)^2} - (R - a)\frac{r_2^2 + r_1^2}{R}\} - \underline{2a^2} - 2x_1x_2 - 2y_1y_2$$

Now compute the sum of the underlined constant terms;

$$2\,[R^2 - a^2 - 2a(R - a) + (R - a)^2] = d^2$$

$$R^2 = d^2 - 2x_1x_2 - 2y_1y_2 - (R - 2a)\frac{(r_1^2) + r_2^2}{R}$$

Now $a = R - (d/2)$; hence $2a/R = \frac{2R - d}{R} = 2 - d/R$; Thus $1 - 2a/R = -[1 - d/R] = -g$

$$\therefore \qquad R^2 = d^2 - 2x_1x_2 - 2y_1y_2 + g[r_1^2 + r_2^2];$$

Expand R by the binomial theorem:

$$R = d\left\{1 - \frac{x_1x_2}{d^2} - \frac{y_1y_2}{d^2} + g\left[\frac{r_1^2 + r_2^2}{2d^2}\right]\right\};$$

$$u(x_2) = \left(\frac{j2k}{4\pi d}\right)^{1/2} \int u(x_1)\, e^{-jkR}\, dx_1$$

$$\boxed{u(x_2) = \left(\frac{j}{\lambda d}\right)^{1/2} e^{-jkd} \int_{M_1} u(x_1) \exp\left\{-j\frac{k}{2d}\left[g(x_1^2 + x_2^2) - 2x_1x_2\right]\right\} dx}$$

12.5

The wave incident on M_2 in terms of the field reflected from M_1 is given by:

$$E^+(x_2,y_2) = \frac{k}{2\pi b} e^{-j(kb-\pi/2)} \iint E_r(x_1,y_1) \exp\left[+j\frac{kx_1x_2}{b}\right] \exp\left[+j\frac{ky_1y_2}{b}\right] dx_1dy_1$$

The field reflected from M_2 is given by:

$$E_r(x_2,y_2) = \Gamma_0 \exp[-t^2(x_2^2 + y_2^2)]\, E^+(x_2,y_2)$$

where t = taper parameter (L^{-1}). Factor the field as before:

$$\sigma_x f_r(x_2) = \left\{\frac{k}{2\pi b} e^{-j(kb-\pi/2)}\right\}^{1/2} \Gamma_0^{1/2} \exp[-t^2x_2^2] \int f_r(x_1) \exp\left[+j\frac{kx_1x_2}{b}\right] dx_1$$

Choose $f_r(x_1) = \exp[-x_1^2/w^2]$ with w to be determined;

$$\text{The integral } I = \int \exp\left[-\frac{x_1^2}{w^2} - j\frac{kx_1x_2}{b}\right] dx = \sqrt{\pi}\, w \exp\left[-\left(\frac{kwx_2}{2b}\right)^2\right]$$

$$\sigma f_r(x_2) = \left\{\frac{k}{2\pi b} e^{-j(kb-\pi/2)}\right\}^{1/2} \Gamma_0^{1/2} \exp\left\{-\left[t^2 + \left(\frac{kw}{2b}\right)^2\right] x_2^2\right\}$$

Doing the same thing for y and re-combining leads to:

$$\frac{E_r(x_2,y_2)}{E_0} = \left\{\frac{k}{2\pi b} \pi w^2 \Gamma_0 e^{-j(kb-\pi/2)}\right\} \left\{\exp\left[-\left\{t^2 + \left(\frac{kw}{2b}\right)^2\right\}(x_2^2+y_2^2)\right]\right\}$$

The first bracket is the eigenvalue $\sigma_x\sigma_y$; and the second expressses the field variation as :$\exp\{-[x_2^2+y_2^2]/w^2\}$ allowing us to solve for the spot-size w.

$$\frac{1}{w^2} = t^2 + \left(\frac{kw}{2b}\right)^2 \quad \text{but} \quad w_s^2 = \frac{2b}{k} = \frac{\lambda b}{\pi} \quad \text{and thus:}$$

$$\frac{1}{w^2} = t^2 + \frac{w^2}{w_s^2} = \frac{m^2}{w_s^2} + \left(\frac{w^2}{w_s^4}\right) \text{since } t^2 = \frac{m^2}{w_s^2};$$

$\therefore$ $(w/w_s)^4 + m^2(w/w_s)^2 - 1 = 0$ whose solution is: $\boxed{\left[\frac{w}{w_s}\right]^2 = \frac{-m + \sqrt{m^2 + 4}}{2}}$

For m = 1 $(w/w_s)^2 = 0.618$; $(w/w_s) = 0.786$

The field reflected from M_2 can be written as:

$$E_r(x_2,y_2) = E_0(w/w_s)^2\Gamma_0 \exp[-r^2/w^2]\, e^{-j(kb-\pi/2)}$$

where $(w/w_s)^2\Gamma_0 = 0.6056$ for $\Gamma_0 = 0.98$. The required gain is $G = (1/0.6056)^2 = 2.73$

The field incident on M_2 is given by:

$$E^+(x_2,y_2) = E_r(x_2,y_2) \div \Gamma(r)$$

leading to: $E^+(x_2,y_2) = (w/w_s)E_0 \exp\left\{-[(1/w)^2 - t^2]r^2\right\} e^{-j(kb-\pi/2)}$

$E_{trans} = [1 - \Gamma(r)]E^+(r) = (w/w_s)E_0 \exp\left\{-[(1/w)^2 - t^2]r^2\right\} e^{-j(kb-\pi/2)}(1 - \Gamma_0\exp[-(tr)^2])$

where it is assumed that field reflection coefficient is a negative value at $r = 0$

The output intensity is:

$$I_{out} = \frac{E_t \cdot E_t^*}{2\eta_0} = \frac{E_0^2}{2\eta_0}\left(\frac{w}{w_s}\right)^2 \left\{\exp\left[-\left(\frac{1}{w^2} - t^2\right)r^2\right] - \Gamma_0 \exp[-r^2/w^2]\right\}^2 \quad \text{(plotted below)}$$

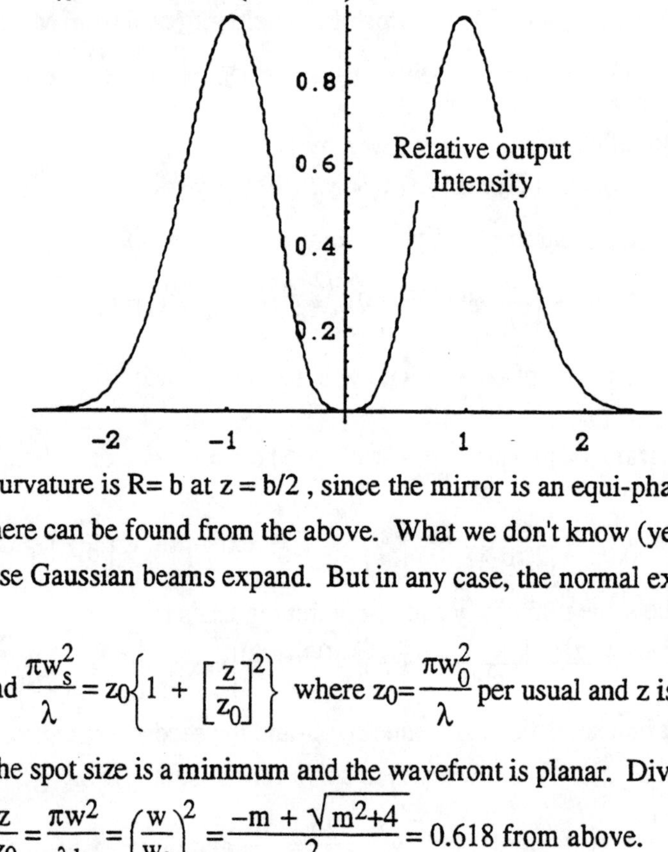

The radius of curvature is $R = b$ at $z = b/2$, since the mirror is an equi-phase surface, and the spot–size there can be found from the above. What we don't know (yet) is the plane from which these Gaussian beams expand. But in any case, the normal expansion laws apply.

$$R = \frac{z^2 + z_0^2}{z} \text{ and } \frac{\pi w_s^2}{\lambda} = z_0\left\{1 + \left[\frac{z}{z_0}\right]^2\right\} \text{ where } z_0 = \frac{\pi w_0^2}{\lambda}$$ per usual and z is measured from a plane where the spot size is a minimum and the wavefront is planar. Dividing:

$$\therefore \quad \frac{\pi w_s^2}{\lambda R} = \frac{z}{z_0} = \frac{\pi w^2}{\lambda b} = \left(\frac{w}{w_s}\right)^2 = \frac{-m + \sqrt{m^2+4}}{2} = 0.618 \text{ from above.}$$

$$\left(\frac{w}{w_0}\right)^2 = 1 + \left(\frac{z}{z_0}\right)^2 = 1.382; \; w_0 = 0.7236\, w^2 = 0.4472\, w_s^2; \; \therefore \; z_0 = 0.4472\, b$$

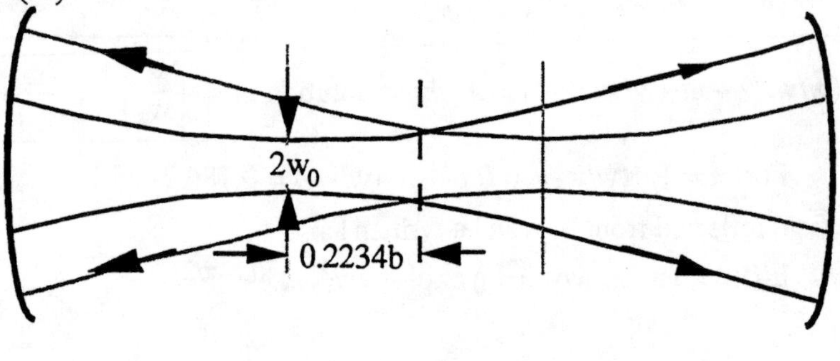

12.6

For $l_g = 500\ \mu m$; $\gamma_{net} l_g = 3.638$; $\gamma_{th} l_g = \ln\frac{1}{\sqrt{R_1 R_2}} = 1.022$; $\therefore\ (\gamma_{net}/\gamma_{th}) = 3.56$

Area $= 10\ \mu m \times 500\ \mu m = 5\times10^{-5}\ cm^2$; For $j = 10^3 A/cm^2$, $I = 10^3 \times 5 \times 10^{-5} = 50mA$

Thus the threshold current would be: $I_{th} = 50/3.56 = 14.04$ mA

The matrix for a beam emerging from an index n to air is: $\mathbf{T} = \begin{bmatrix} 1 & 0 \\ 0 & n \end{bmatrix}$;

Thus $\frac{1}{q_2} = \frac{C + D\left(\frac{1}{q_1}\right)}{A + B\left(\frac{1}{q_1}\right)} = \frac{n}{q_1}$; Now $\frac{1}{q_1} = \frac{1}{R_1} - j\frac{\lambda_0/n}{\pi w_1^2}$ hence: $\frac{1}{q_2} = \frac{n}{R_1} - j\frac{\lambda_0}{\pi w_1^2}$;

Thus the spot size remains the same ($w_2 = w_1$) and R_2 (air) = R (inside)/n = 101.9 μm

(c) For expansion in free space: $\mathbf{T} = \begin{bmatrix} 1 & z \\ 0 & 1 \end{bmatrix}$

$$\frac{1}{q(z)} = \frac{0 + 1(1/q_2)}{1 + z(1/q_2)} = \frac{\frac{1}{R_2} - j\frac{\lambda_0}{\pi w_2^2}}{\left[1 + \frac{z}{R_2}\right] - j\frac{\lambda_0 z}{\pi w_2^2}} = \frac{1}{R(z)} - j\frac{\lambda_0}{\pi w^2(z)};\ \text{Solving for w}$$

$$w^2(z) = w_2^2\left\{\left(1 + \frac{z}{R_2}\right)^2 + \left(\frac{\lambda_0 z}{\pi w_2^2}\right)\right\};\ \text{For the far-field } z >> R_2\left(\frac{\lambda_0 z}{\pi w_2}\right)^2 >> 1$$

$$w(z) \approx w_2\left[\left(\frac{1}{R_2}\right)^2 + \left(\frac{\lambda_0}{\pi w_2^2}\right)\right]^{1/2} z$$

$$\frac{dw(z)}{dz} = \tan\theta \approx \theta = w_2\left[\left(\frac{1}{R_2}\right)^2 + \left(\frac{\lambda_0}{\pi w_2^2}\right)^2\right]^{1/2} z$$

For $R_{2y} = 101.9\mu m$, $w_3 = 5.22\mu m$; $(\theta_y/2) = 4.15°$ and $\theta_y = 8.3°$ (5.87° for $R_2 = \infty$)

For $R_{2x} = \infty$; $w_x = 0.862\mu m$; $(\theta_x/2) = 17.8°$; $\theta_x = 35.5°$

12.7

This is a fundamental paper which the students should be encouraged to read. Most of the questions are answered in the text or in the other problems.

12.8

$$\frac{\partial}{\partial z}\begin{bmatrix} E_1 \\ E_2 \\ E_3 \end{bmatrix} = -j\begin{bmatrix} \beta_0 & \kappa & \kappa \\ \kappa & \beta_0 & \kappa \\ \kappa & \kappa & \beta_0 \end{bmatrix}\begin{bmatrix} E_1 \\ E_2 \\ E_3 \end{bmatrix}$$

Assume $E_n = E_n^{(k)} \exp[-j\beta_k z]$

$$-j\begin{bmatrix} \Delta\beta & \kappa & \kappa \\ \kappa & \Delta\beta & \kappa \\ \kappa & \kappa & \Delta\beta \end{bmatrix}\begin{bmatrix} E_1^{(k)} \\ E_2^{(k)} \\ E_3^{(k)} \end{bmatrix} = 0; \text{ where } \Delta\beta = \beta_0 - \beta_k;$$

The determinate $\Delta = 0$ for a non-trivial solution.

$$\Delta = (\Delta\beta - \kappa)^2(\Delta\beta + 2\kappa)=0;$$

The non-degenerate solution is: $\Delta\beta = -2\kappa$ or $\beta_3 = \beta_0 + 2\kappa$;

Substitute $\Delta\beta = -2\kappa$ back into the matrix and find that $E_1 = E_2 = E_3$ i.e. all in phase, which is the most desirable situation. The other two solutions are degenerate and one needs to employ special mathematical techniques or change the approach to the problem.

Let's squeeze the top element closer to the base so that the coupling between 1 and (2,3) becomes $\kappa+\delta$, but the coupling between 2 and 3 remains as κ. The eigenvalue equation becomes:

$$\begin{bmatrix} \Delta\beta & \kappa+\delta & \kappa+\delta \\ \kappa+\delta & \Delta\beta & \kappa \\ \kappa+\delta & \kappa & \Delta\beta \end{bmatrix}\begin{bmatrix} E_1^{(k)} \\ E_2^{(k)} \\ E_3^{(k)} \end{bmatrix} = 0;$$

$$\Delta = (\Delta\beta)^3 - (3\kappa^2 + 4\kappa\ 2\delta^2)\,\Delta\beta + 2\kappa(\kappa + \delta)^2 = 0$$

A lucky guess or many trials with synthetic division yields the fact that the determinant can be factored into: $\Delta = (\Delta\beta - \kappa)[\Delta\beta^2 + \kappa\Delta\beta - 2(\kappa + \delta)^2]$

Thus $\Delta\beta_1 = \kappa$; $\qquad \Delta\beta_{2,3} = \dfrac{-\kappa \pm \{\kappa^2 + 8(\kappa + \delta)^2\}^{1/2}}{2}$;

If $\delta \to 0$, $\Delta\beta_2 = \kappa$ (degenerate with β_1) from the plus sign and $\Delta\beta_2 = -2\kappa$ from the negative sign. We substitute these solutions (with finite δ) back into the eigenvalue equation to find the relationship between the components; let $\delta \to 0$; and then assume that each solution carries the same power (3 units), one finds:

$\Delta\beta_1 = \kappa$; $\qquad E_1=0,\ E_2 = -E_3 \ \rightarrow\ [0,(3/2)^{1/2},-(3/2)^{1/2}]$

$\Delta\beta_2 = \dfrac{-\kappa + \{\kappa^2 + 8(\kappa + \delta)^2\}^{1/2}}{2}$; $\qquad E_1 = -2E_2 = -2E_3 \ \rightarrow\ [-\sqrt{2},1/\sqrt{2},1/\sqrt{2}]$

$\Delta\beta_3 = \dfrac{-\kappa - \{\kappa^2 + 8(\kappa + \delta)^2\}^{1/2}}{2}$; $\qquad E_1 = E_2 = E_3 \ \rightarrow\ [1,1,1]$

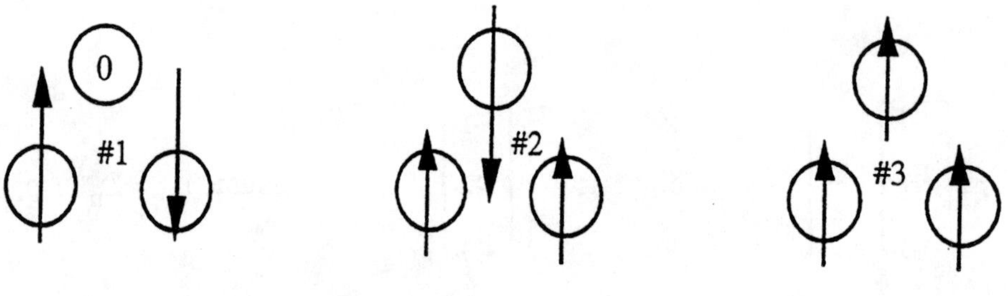

There are purely mathematical techniques for taking care of the degenerate cases, but the above has a nice physical basis to it since one could never make something with perfect symmetry anyway.

12.9

$N = 4;\ \theta = k\pi/5;\ A_l^{(k)}\ \sin[l\left[\frac{k\pi}{N+1}\right];\ \beta_k = \beta_0 + 2\kappa\cos\theta$

For $k = 1,\ \theta = \pi/5 \rightarrow 36°;\ \beta_1 = \beta_0 + 1.61803\kappa;$

$A_1^{(1)} = 0.588;\ A_2^{(1)} = 0.951;\ A_3^{(1)} = 0.951;\ A_4^{(1)} = 0.588$

For $k = 2,\ \theta = 2\pi/5 \rightarrow 72°;\ \beta_2 = \beta_0 + 0.61803\kappa;$

$A_1^{(2)} = 0.951;\ A_2^{(2)} = 0.588;\ A_3^{(2)} = -0.588; A_4^{(2)} = -0.951$

For $k = 3,\ \theta = 3\pi/5 \rightarrow 108°;\ \beta_3 = \beta_0 - 0.61803\kappa;$

$A_1^{(3)} = 0.951;\ A_2^{(3)} = -0.588;\ A_3^{(3)} = -0.588;\ A_4^{(3)} = 0.951$

For $k = 4,\ \theta = 4\pi/5 \rightarrow 144°;\ \beta_4 = \beta_0 - 1.61803\kappa;$

$A_1^{(4)} = 0.588;\ A_2^{(4)} = -0.951;\ A_3^{(4)} = 0.951;\ A_4^{(4)} = 0.588$

12.10

The supermode solutions are either the in-phase or out-of-phase addition of the individual facet fields:

$$E(x_1,y_1,z=0) = A\exp[-(x_1/w_x)^2\left\{\exp[-\left(\frac{y_1-a}{w_y}\right)^2] \pm \exp[-\left(\frac{y_1+a}{w_y}\right)^2]\right\} \qquad 1.$$

The distance between the facet plane and the observation points is given by:

$$R(z) = \{(x_2-x_1)^2 + (y_2-y_1)^2 + z^2\}^{1/2} \approx z\left[1 + \frac{(x_2-x_1)^2}{2z^2} + \frac{(y_2-y_1)^2}{2z^2}\right]$$

$$R(z) \approx z + \frac{x_2^2 + y_2^2}{2z} - \frac{x_1x_2}{z} - \frac{y_1y_2}{z} + \frac{x_1^2 + y_1^2}{2z} \qquad 2.$$

Assume $k(x_1^2 + y_1^2)/2z << \pi/2$, so that it can be neglected since it amounts to ignoring a factor of the form $\cos[k(x_1^2+y_1^2)/2z]$ which remains close to 1 if the inequality is obeyed for all values of the variables of integration. Thus, the Fresnel integral becomes in the Fraunhofer limit.

$$E(x_2,y_2,z) = \left[\frac{\exp[-j(kz-\pi/2)]}{\lambda_0 z}\right]\left[\exp[-j\frac{k(x_2^2+y_2^2)}{2z}\right]$$

$$\times\int_{-\infty}^{+\infty}\int_{-\infty}^{+\infty} E(x_1,y_1,z=0)\exp[-j\frac{ky_1y_2}{z}]\exp[+j\frac{kx_1x_2}{z}]\,dx_1dy_1 \qquad 3.$$

The first bracket in (3) suggests that the field appears to be originating at $z = 0$ as a spherical wave; the second factor indicates that the wavefront is curved with a radius of curvature equal to z; and the last integral describes the variation of the amplitude of the field at the far field plane where $z \rightarrow \infty$. One can observe this far–field pattern at a finite distance by the use of a simple lens located a distance $z = f$, and observing the pattern at $z = 2f$. However, the mathematical handstands required to show this fact require more complexity than we deserve.

The last integral can be broken up into two parts along x_1 and lastly along y_1

$$I_x = \int_{-\infty}^{+\infty} \exp - \left(\frac{x_1}{w_y}\right)^2 \exp\left[+j\,\frac{kx_1x_2}{z}\right] dx_1 \qquad 4.$$

Now we employ the standard technique for the evaluation of this integral: complete the square in the exponent by multiplying and dividing by a factor which is a function of x_2 alone and thus is independent of the variable of integration x_1

$$\left\{\left(\frac{x_1}{w_y}\right)^2 - j2\left(\frac{x_1}{w_y}\right)\left(\frac{kw_yx_2}{2z}\right) - \left(\frac{kw_yx_2}{2z}\right)^2 + \left(\frac{kw_yx_2}{2z}\right)^2\right\}$$

$$= \left\{\left[\frac{x_1}{w_y} - jk\frac{w_yx_2}{2z}\right]^2 + \left[\frac{kw_yx_2}{2z}\right]^2\right\} \qquad 5.$$

Let $u = \frac{x_1}{w_y} - jk\frac{w_yx_2}{2z}$ then $du = \frac{dx_1}{w_y}$

$$I_x = w_x \exp - \left[\frac{kw_yx_2}{2z}\right]^2 \int_{-\infty}^{+\infty} \exp\,[-u^2]\,du \;=\; \sqrt{\pi}\, w_x \exp - \left[\frac{kw_1x_2}{2z}\right]^2 \qquad 6.$$

The evaluation of the y integral proceeds along a similar line except that we must shift the centroid of integration.

$$I_y = \int_{-\infty}^{+\infty} \exp[-\left[\frac{y_1 \pm a}{w_x}\right]^2]\exp[-j\frac{ky_1y_2}{z}]\,dy_1 \qquad 7.$$

Let $y' = y_1 \pm a$; $dy' = dy_1$. Fortunately, the limits remain the same and $ky_1y_2/z = ky'y_2/z \pm kay_2/a$ and thus, the exponential of the latter term comes out of the integral.

$$I_y = \exp \pm j\frac{kay_2}{z} \int_{-\infty}^{+\infty} \exp\left[-\left(\frac{y'}{w_x}\right)^2\right]\exp\left[+j\,\frac{ky'y_2}{z}\right]dy'$$

$$= \exp\left[\pm j\,\frac{kay_2}{z}\right]\exp\left[-\frac{kw_yy_2}{2z}\right]^2 \sqrt{\pi}\, w_y \qquad 8.$$

Hence the far field patterns for the two modes are given by:

$$E(x_2,y_2) = \left[\frac{\pi w_x w_y}{\lambda_0 z}\right] \exp[-j(kz - \pi/2)] \exp\left[-j\frac{k(x_2^2 + y_2^2)}{2z}\right]$$

$$\times\left\{\exp-\left[\frac{kw_x x_2}{2z}\right]^2 \exp-\left[\frac{kw_y y_2}{2z}\right]^2\right\}\times\left\{\exp\left[+j\frac{kay_2}{z}\right] \pm \exp\left[-j\,\frac{kay_2}{z}\right]\right\} \qquad 9.$$

The far–field intensity pattern is given by:

$$I(x_2,y_2) \propto \left[\frac{2\pi w_x w_y}{\lambda_0 z}\right]\left\{\exp -2\left[\left(\frac{y_2}{w_{2y}}\right)^2+\left(\frac{x_2}{w_{2x}}\right)^2\right]\right\}\begin{Bmatrix}\cos^2(kay_2/z)\\ \sin^2(kay_2/z)\end{Bmatrix}\begin{Bmatrix}\text{symmetric}\\ \text{anti-symmetric}\end{Bmatrix} \qquad 10.$$

The first exponential factor describes an elliptical beam:

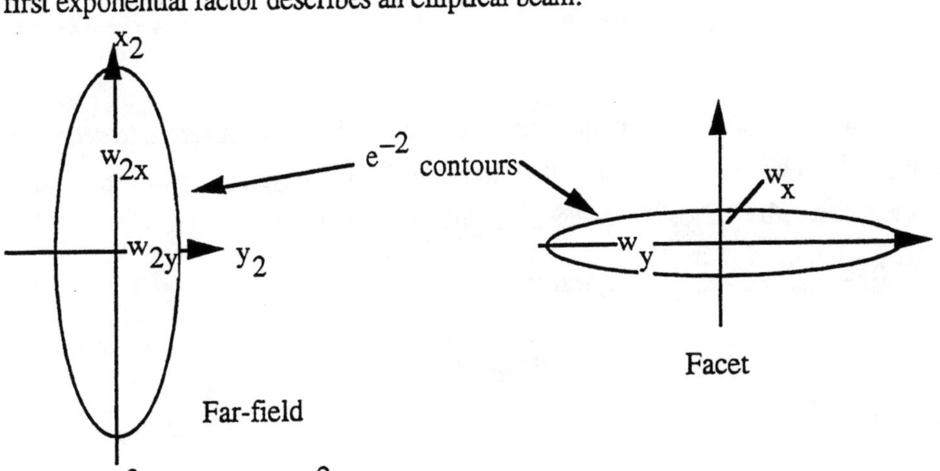

$$\text{where } w_{2x} = \frac{2z}{kw_x} \text{ and } w_{2y} = \frac{2z}{kw_y} \qquad 11.$$

Usually $w_x << w_y$, hence the far field spot–sizes are in the reverse order $w_{2x} >> w_{2y}$.

The last brace in Eq. 10 indicates the presence of "fringes" in this far–field pattern. For the symmetric mode, the first zero appears at

$$\frac{kay_2}{z} = \frac{\pi}{2} \qquad 12.$$

$$\text{Since } a = w_y,\ y_{20} = \frac{\pi}{2}\left[\frac{z}{kwy1}\right] = \frac{\pi}{4}\left(\frac{2z}{kwy1}\right) \text{or} \left[\frac{y_{20}}{w_{2y}}\right] = \frac{\pi}{4} \qquad 13.$$

$$\text{and} \qquad \frac{y_{20}}{w_{2y}} = \frac{\pi}{2} \quad \text{for the anti-symmetric mode} \qquad 14.$$

However, the intensity of the symmetric mode is down by exp $[-\pi/2] = 0.208$ at the first zero and the anti-symmetric is down by exp$[-\pi] = 0.0432$. A sketch of the intensity for the two modes is shown below. Thus, there is a single main lobe on the axis for the symmetric mode. For the anti-symmetric mode, the intensity goes to zero at $y_2 = 0$ and 1.571 (and other points where the Gaussian envelope is insignificant). It is plotted below.

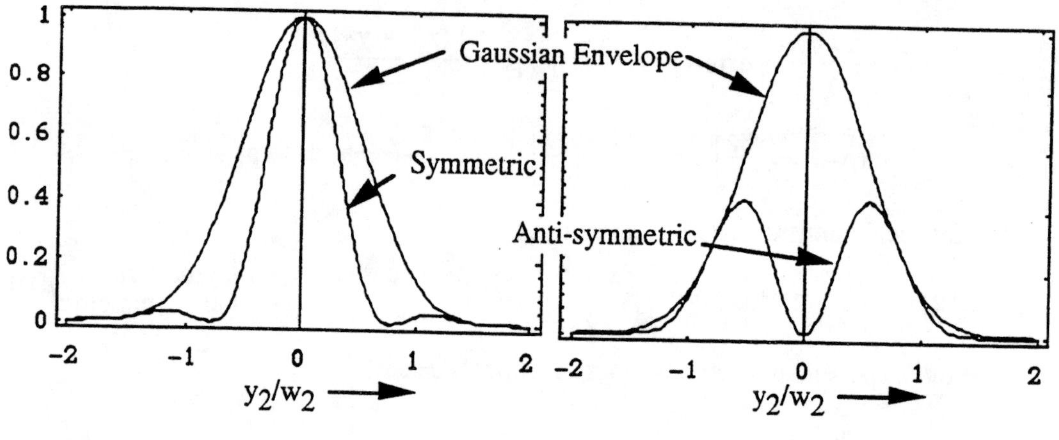

From an operational standpoint, one states that the in-phase supermode generates the single far–field beam whereas the out–of–phase supermode yields a two-lobe beam.

One can use the "zeros" to define an angular spread

$$\theta = \frac{dy_0}{dz} = \frac{\pi}{2kw_y} \quad \text{(symmetric)} \qquad 15a.$$

$$= \frac{\pi}{kw_y} \quad \text{(anti-symmetric)} \qquad 15b.$$

12.11

We start with the wave equation

$$\nabla^2 E + \frac{\omega^2}{c^2}\left\{\varepsilon'\left[1 + \left(\frac{r}{L_1}\right)^2\right] + j\varepsilon''\left[1 - \left(\frac{r}{L_1}\right)^2\right]\right\} E = 0 \qquad 1.$$

Abbreviate the terms $\omega\sqrt{\varepsilon'}/c = \beta$ and $\omega^2\varepsilon''/c^2 = \gamma_0\beta$ and assume $\gamma_0 << \beta$.

$$\nabla^2 E + \left\{\beta^2\left[1 + \left(\frac{r}{L_1}\right)^2\right] + j\gamma_0\beta\left[1 - \left(\frac{r}{L_2}\right)^2\right]\right\} E = 0 \qquad 2.$$

Now we follow the ploy used in Chapter 3 for the Hermite-Gaussian beam modes: Assume circular symmetry and that the field can be expressed as a correction factor times the propagator for a uniform plane wave.

$$E = \psi(r,z)\exp\left[\frac{\gamma_0}{2} - j\beta\right]z \qquad 3.$$

yielding: $$\nabla_t^2\psi - j2\beta\frac{\partial\psi}{\partial z} + \beta^2\left(\frac{r}{L_1}\right)^2\psi - j\gamma_0\beta\left(\frac{r}{L_2}\right)^2\psi = 0 \qquad 4.$$

Let $\psi = \exp -j\left[P(z) + \frac{\beta r^2}{2q(z)}\right]$ 5.

$$\nabla_t^2\psi = \left\{\frac{-\beta^2 r^2}{q^2} - j\,\frac{2\beta}{q}\right\}\psi \text{ and } -j2\beta\frac{\partial\psi}{\partial z} = \left\{-2\beta P' + \frac{\beta^2 r^2 q'}{q^2}\right\}\psi \qquad 6.$$

Substitute, add $\beta^2\left(\frac{r}{L_1}\right)^2\psi - j\gamma_0\beta\left(\frac{r}{L_2}\right)^2\psi$ and collect factors of r^2 and r^0:

$$\left\{\beta^2\left[\frac{q'-1}{q^2} + \frac{1}{L_1^2} - \frac{j\gamma_0}{\beta L_2^2}\right] r^2 - 2\beta\left[P' + \frac{j}{q}\right] r^0\right\}\psi = 0 \qquad 7.$$

Each coefficient of (r^2, r^0) must vanish since the expression must be valid for all r.

$$\frac{q'-1}{q^2} = -\frac{1}{L_1^2} + j\frac{\gamma_0}{\beta L_2^2} \text{ and } P' = -\frac{j}{q} \qquad 8.$$

One can solve Eq. 8 without any further assumptions but the arithmetic mess is dismaying to say the least. It should be recognized that $1/L_1$ is a measure of the index **anti-guiding**, whereas $1/L_2$ is a measure of gain **guiding**. Let's look for solutions where the complex beam parameter, q, is independent of z, i.e., $q' = 0$.

$$\therefore \quad \frac{1}{q^2} = \frac{1}{L_1^2} - j\frac{\gamma_0}{\beta L_2^2} \triangleq \frac{1}{a^2}\exp(-j\theta) \qquad 9a.$$

where $$\frac{1}{a^2} = \left[\left(\frac{1}{L_1^2}\right) + \left(\frac{\gamma_0}{\beta L_2^2}\right)\right]^{1/2} \text{ and } \theta = \tan^{-1}\left[\frac{\gamma_0}{\beta}\left(\frac{L_1}{L_2}\right)^2\right] \qquad 9b.$$

Hence: $$\frac{1}{q} = \pm\frac{1}{a}\exp(-j\,\theta/2) = +\frac{1}{a}\left[\cos(\theta/2) - j\sin(\theta/2)\right] \qquad 10.$$

The positive root must be chosen to insure that the field vanishes at $r \to \infty$. One can re-insert Eq. 10 into Eq. 5 to identify the spot-size and the radius of curvature of the phase front

$$\exp -j\frac{\beta r^2}{2q}$$
$$= \left\{\exp -j\left[\frac{\beta r^2\cos\theta/2}{2a}\right]\right\}\left\{\exp -\left[\frac{\beta r^2\sin\theta/2}{2a}\right]\right\} \triangleq \left\{\exp -j\left[\frac{\beta r^2}{2R}\right]\right\}\left\{\exp-\left[\left(\frac{r}{w}\right)^2\right]\right\} \qquad 11b.$$

Thus, $$w^2 = \frac{2a}{\beta\sin\theta/2} \qquad 12a$$

and $$R = \frac{a}{\cos\theta/2} \qquad 12b.$$

Return to Eq. 8 to solve for P(z): $-j\,P(z) = -\frac{1}{a}(\cos\theta/2 - j\sin\theta/2)\,z$ 13.

Now let's combine $\exp -jP(z)$ with the uniform plane wave propagator.

$\{\exp[(\gamma_0/2) - j\beta)z]\}\{\exp[-j\,P(z)]\}$

$$= \left\{\exp\left[\frac{\gamma_0}{2} - \frac{\cos\theta/2}{a}\right]\right\}\left\{\exp -j\left[\beta - \frac{\sin\theta/2}{a}\right]\right\} \qquad 14.$$

Thus, we see that the "net" or modal gain coefficient is given by:

$$\boxed{\frac{\gamma}{2} = \frac{\gamma_0}{2} - \frac{\cos\theta/2}{a}}$$ 15.

The modal phase constant is: $\boxed{\beta = \beta_0 - \frac{\sin\theta/2}{a}}$ 16.

The only intrinsic assumption made was that of $q' = 0$. Now is the time to ask whether these expressions could represent an active medium and whether the system could lase. Obviously, we would require that the modal gain coefficient be positive if this were to be a laser medium. $\frac{\gamma_0}{2} > \frac{\cos(\theta/2)}{a}$ 17a

For the parameters of the problem: $\lambda_0 = 1.06\ \mu m$, $n = 1.73$,
$\beta = 2\pi n/\lambda_0 = 1.025 \times 10^{+5}\ cm^{-1}$, $\gamma_0 = 0.1\ cm^{-1}$, $L_1 = 100$ cm, $L_2 = 0.1$ cm.

$$\frac{1}{q^2} = 10^{-4} - j\,0.9752 \times 10^{-4} = 1.397 \times 10^{-4}\ \exp{-j(0.7728 \text{ radians} \rightarrow 44.28°)}$$

$\therefore$ $a = 84.61$ cm. $\theta/2 = 0.3864$ rad $= 22.14°$

$$\gamma = \gamma_0 - \frac{2\cos(\theta/2)}{a} = 0.1 - 0.0219 = 0.0781\ cm^{-1}$$ 18.

$$w_1^2 = \frac{2a}{\beta \sin\theta/2} = 4.379 \times 10^{-3} cm^2;\ w = 0.06617\ cm = 0.662\ mm$$

$$R_1 = \frac{a}{\cos\theta/2} = 91.34\ cm\ (large)$$ 19.

The situation with the field and the gain coefficient is shown on the sketch below.

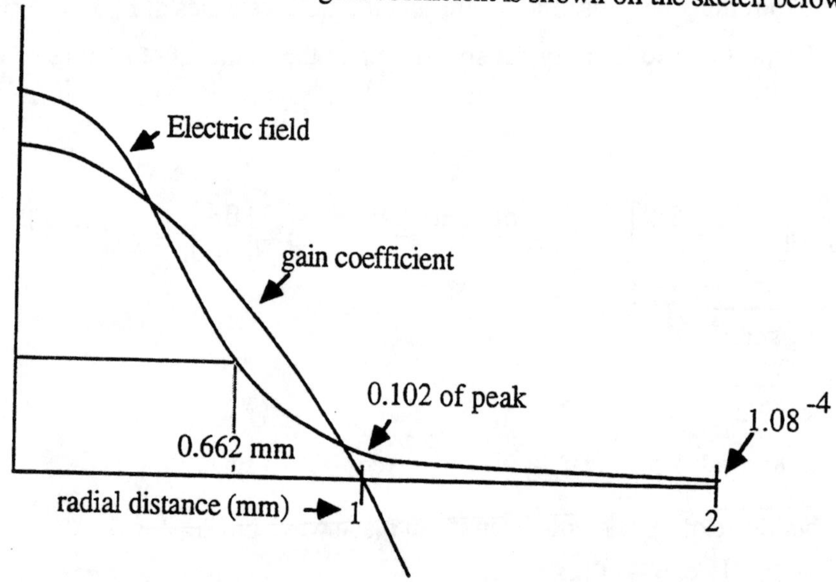

The beam emerges from a dielectric slab and thus one must use the ABCD matrix to compute the emerging parameters

$$T = \begin{bmatrix} 1 & 0 \\ 0 & n \end{bmatrix}$$ 20.

$$q_2 = \frac{Aq_1 + B}{Cq_1 + D} \text{ or } \frac{1}{q_2} = \frac{n}{q_1} = n\left(\frac{1}{R_1} + j\frac{\lambda_0}{\pi\, n\, w^2}\right);$$

$$R_2 = \frac{R_1}{n} = 52.8 \text{ cm};\ w_2^2 = w_1^2$$

where the 1 subscript refers to the beam parameters in the rod and 2 to that in the air gap. Now we know the complex beam parameters at the exit plane but we would prefer to know the plane at which the wavefront would be planar as shown on the diagram below.

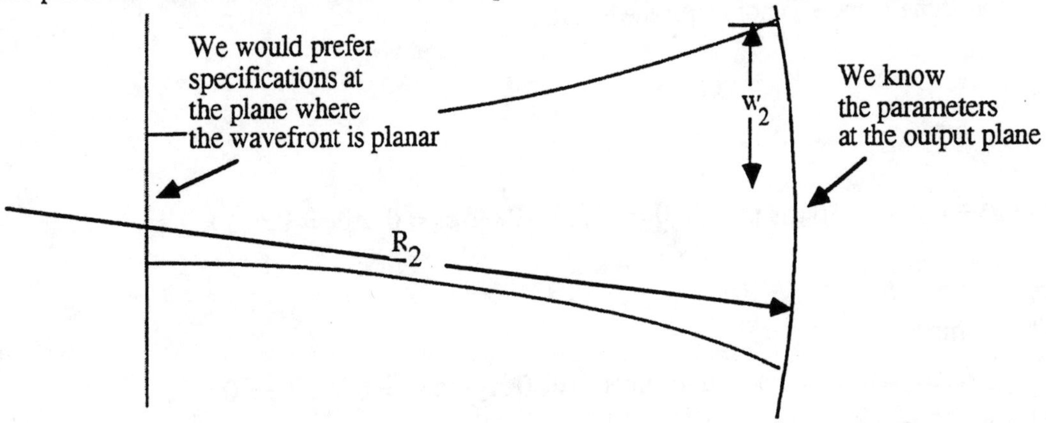

The beam parameters expand according to:

$$z_2 = \frac{\pi w_2^2}{\lambda_0} = \frac{\pi w_0^2}{\lambda_0}\left[1 + \left(\frac{z}{z_0}\right)^2\right] = \frac{z_0^2 + z^2}{z_0} = 1.298 \times 10^{+4} \text{ cm};$$

and $\quad R_2 = \dfrac{z^2 + z_0^2}{z} = 52.80 \text{ cm}$

Dividing; $\left(\dfrac{z}{z_0}\right) = \dfrac{z_2}{R_2} = 245.8;\ z_0\left(1 + \left(\dfrac{z}{z_0}\right)^2\right) = z_2;$

and $\quad z_0 = \dfrac{z_2}{1 + (z_2/R_2)^2} = 0.2149 \text{ cm}$

We can now solve for the hypothetical distance z:

$$z = z_0\left(\frac{z_2}{R_2}\right) = R_2\left[\frac{(z_2/R_2)^2}{1 + (z_2/R_2)^2}\right] \approx R_2 = 52.8 \text{ cm}$$

The beam propagates to the mirror, represented by a lens, and then back to the entrance and must reproduce its spot-size and radius of curvature in the opposite direction. The ABCD parameters for a mirror (lens) plus two equal lengths d are:

$$T = \begin{bmatrix} 1 - d/f & d(2 - d/f) \\ -1/f & 1 - d/f \end{bmatrix} \quad \text{where: } f = \frac{R}{2} \qquad 21.$$

For the entering complex beam parameter to be the same as that exiting the rod, we require

$$\frac{1}{q_3} = \frac{1}{q_2} = -\frac{(A-D)}{2B} - j\frac{\left[1-\left(\frac{A+D}{2}\right)^2\right]^{1/2}}{2B} \qquad \text{Eq. (5.3.5)} \rightarrow \quad 22.$$

i.e., the complex beam parameter after propagating to and reflection by the mirror and propagating to the entrance must be equal to that exiting the rod. But since $A = D$ for this system, one can only do so if $R_2 = \infty$, which is not true.

One can still use a mirror successfully but the above analysis suffers from the assumption of $q' = 0$. To correct it one would have to retreat to Eq. 8a and solve for $q(z)$. The arithmetic mess is not worth the effort.

12.12

(a) $$\Delta = \begin{bmatrix} \Delta\beta_k & \kappa & 0 \\ \kappa & \Delta\beta_k & \kappa \\ 0 & \kappa & \Delta\beta_k \end{bmatrix} = 0 \Rightarrow \Delta\beta_k{}^3 - 2\kappa^2\Delta\beta_k = 0,\ \Delta\beta_k = 0, \pm\sqrt{2}\kappa.$$

(b) Solution 1.

$\Delta\beta_k = 0$; Use line 1 to evaluate: $\Rightarrow 0\cdot A_1 + \kappa A_2 = 0;\ \therefore A_2 = 0$

Use line 2:$\Rightarrow \kappa A_1 + 0\cdot(A_2{=}0) + \kappa A_3 = 0;\ \therefore A_3 = -A_1;$

Relative amplitudes of the modes: (1,0,-1)

Solution 2.

$\Delta\beta_k = \sqrt{2}\,\kappa$; Use line 1to evaluate: $\Rightarrow \sqrt{2}\,\kappa A_1 + \kappa A_2 = 0 \therefore A_2 = -\sqrt{2}A_1$

Use line 3:$\Rightarrow \kappa A_2 + \sqrt{2}\,\kappa A_3 = 0$; $A_3 = -1/\sqrt{2}\,A_2 = A_1;$

Relative amplitudes: $(1, -\sqrt{2}, 1)$

Solution 3.

$\Delta\beta_k = -\sqrt{2}\,\kappa$; Use line 1: $\Rightarrow -\sqrt{2}\,\kappa A_1 + \kappa A_2;\ \therefore A_2 = \sqrt{2}$

Use line 3:$\Rightarrow \kappa A_2 - \sqrt{2}\,\kappa A_3 = 0;\quad A_3 = 1/\sqrt{2}A_2 = A_1;$

Relative amplitudes: $(1, \sqrt{2}, 1)$

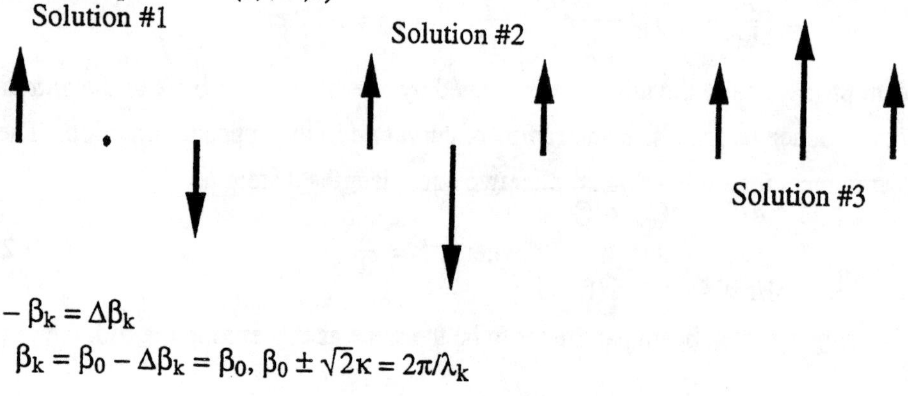

(c) $\beta_0 - \beta_k = \Delta\beta_k$

$\therefore \quad \beta_k = \beta_0 - \Delta\beta_k = \beta_0,\ \beta_0 \pm \sqrt{2}\kappa = 2\pi/\lambda_k$

$$\beta_k l_g = q\pi \Rightarrow \beta_0 l_g \pm \sqrt{2}\kappa l_g = q\pi;\ \frac{2\pi n l_g}{\lambda_k} \pm \sqrt{2}\,\kappa l_g = q\pi \text{ or}$$

$$\frac{1}{\lambda_k} = \frac{q}{l_g/2} \mp \frac{\kappa}{\sqrt{2}n} = \frac{1}{\lambda_0} \mp \frac{\kappa}{\sqrt{2}n};$$

$$\frac{1}{\lambda_3} - \frac{1}{\lambda_1} = \frac{\sqrt{2}\kappa}{n} = \frac{\lambda_1 - \lambda_3}{\lambda_1\lambda_3};\ \frac{1}{\lambda_2} = \frac{1}{\lambda_0};\ \frac{1}{\lambda_1} \times \frac{1}{\lambda_3} = \frac{1}{\lambda_0^2} - \frac{\kappa^2}{2n^2} \approx \frac{1}{\lambda_0^2};$$

$$\therefore \quad \frac{\lambda_1 - \lambda_3}{\lambda_0} = \lambda_0\left(\frac{\sqrt{2}\kappa}{n}\right)$$

(d) One could use the Fresnel integral directly, but a simpler approach is to expand each Gaussian and allow interference to occur. In the far–field $z >> z_0$

$$\therefore \frac{1}{q_x} \to \frac{1}{z} - j\frac{z_0}{z^2} \text{ and } w^2 = w_0^2\left(\frac{z}{z_0}\right)^2 \text{ with } z_0 = \pi w_0^2/\lambda \text{ and } R_x = z$$

Thus the far–field of any Gaussian (with $z >> z_{0x,y}$)

$$E = E_0\left(\frac{\sqrt{z_{0x}z_{0y}}}{z}\right)e^{-j(kz - \pi/2)} \exp[-\left[\frac{x\, z_{0x}}{w_0\, z}\right]^2] \exp[-\left[\frac{y\, z_{0y}}{w_0\, z}\right]^2]\cdot\exp\left[-j\,\frac{k(x^2+y^2)}{2z}\right]$$

One must remember that x or y is measured from the axis ($\pm$a,0) of the Gaussians. Drop the terms involving y (as being of no interest) and also the geometric phase shift, $kz-\pi/2$.

$$E_{ff}(x_2) = A_1 \exp[-\frac{(x_2 - a)^2}{w_0^2}\left(\frac{z_0}{z}\right)^2]\cdot\exp[-j\frac{k}{2z}(x_2 - a)^2] = A_1(x_2)e^{-j\phi_f(x_2)}$$

$$+ A_2 \exp[-\frac{x_2^2}{w_0^2}\left(\frac{z_0}{z}\right)^2]\cdot\exp[-j\frac{k}{2z}x_2^2] = A_2(x_2)e^{-j\phi_2(x_2)}$$

$$+ A_3 \exp[-\frac{(x_2 + a)^2}{w_0^2}\left(\frac{z_0}{z}\right)^2]\cdot \exp[-j\frac{k}{2z}(x_2 + a)^2] = A_3(x_2)e^{-j\phi_3(x_2)}$$

The intensity in the far field is given by:

$$I = E_T\cdot E_T^*/2n_0$$
$$= A_1^2 + A_2^2 + A_3^2$$
$$+ 2A_1A_2\cos[\phi_1(x_2) - \phi_2(x_2)] + 2A_1A_2\cos[\phi_1(x_2) - \phi_3(x_2)\,]$$
$$+ 2A_2A_3\cos[\phi_2(x_2) - \phi_3(x_2)\,]$$

Hence it is just a matter of plotting the above functions after reducing the mathematical clutter.

Let: $\dfrac{z}{z_0} = m$ and $\dfrac{x_2 \pm a}{w_0}\cdot\dfrac{z_{0x}}{z} = \left(\dfrac{x_2 \pm a}{m w_0}\right)$

$$\frac{k}{2z}(x_2 \pm a)^2 = \frac{k w_0^2}{2z}\left(\frac{x_2 \pm a}{w_0}\right)^2 = \frac{z_0}{z}\left(\frac{x_2 \pm a}{w_0}\right)^2 = m\left(\frac{x_2 \pm a}{m w_0}\right)^2$$

$$\phi_1 - \phi_2 = m\left[\frac{1}{m w_0}\right]^2[x_2^2 - 2ax_2 + a^2 - x_2^2] = -\frac{a}{w_0}\left[\frac{2x_2 - a}{m w_0}\right]$$

$$\phi_2 - \phi_3 = m\left[\frac{1}{m w_0}\right]^2[x_2^2 - x_2^2 + 2ax_2 - a^2] = -\frac{a}{w_0}\left[\frac{2x_2 + a}{m w_0}\right]$$

$$\phi_1 - \phi_3 = m\left[\frac{1}{mw_0}\right]^2 [x_2^2 - 2ax_2 + a^2 - x_2^2 - 2ax_2 - a^2] = -\frac{a}{w_0}\left[\frac{4ax_2}{mw_0}\right]$$

Now set the ratio $a/w_0 = 1$ and use a normalized variable in the far field given by $u = x_2/mw_0$ and let $m \to \infty$ in obvious places.

$$A_1(x_2) = \exp\left[-\left(\frac{x_2 - w_{0x}}{mw_{0x}}\right)^2\right] = A_1 \exp[-(u-1/m)^2] \to A_1 e^{-u^2}$$

$$A_2(x_2) = A_2 \exp[-u^2] \text{ and } A_3(x_2) = A_3 \exp[-(u+1/m)^2] \to A_3 \exp -u^2$$

$$\phi_1 - \phi_2 = -\frac{2x_2}{mw_{0x}} + \frac{w_{0x}}{mw_{0x}} = -2u + \frac{1}{m} \to -2u\ ;\ \phi_2 - \phi_3 = -2u - \frac{1}{m} \to -2u;\ \phi_1 - \phi_3 = -4u$$

$$\boxed{I = e^{-2u^2}\{A_1^2 + A_2^2 + A_3^2 + 2(A_1A_2 + A_2A_3)\cos(2u) + 2A_1A_3\cos(4u)\}}$$

Solution 1. $A_1 = 1, A_2 = 0, A_3 = -1$

$$I_1 = A_1^2 e^{-2u^2}\{2 - 2\cos 4u\} = 2A_1^2 e^{-2u^2}(1 - \cos 4u)$$

Solution 2. $A_1 = 1, A_2 = -\sqrt{2}, A_3 = 1$

$$I_3 = A_1^2 e^{-2u^2}\{4 - 4\sqrt{2}\cos 2u + 2\cos 4u\}$$

Solution 3. $A_1 = 1, A_2 = \sqrt{2}, A_3 = 1$

$$I_3 = A_1^2 e^{-2u^2}\{4 + 4\sqrt{2}\cos 2u + 2\cos 4u\}$$

These functions are plotted in the following graph.

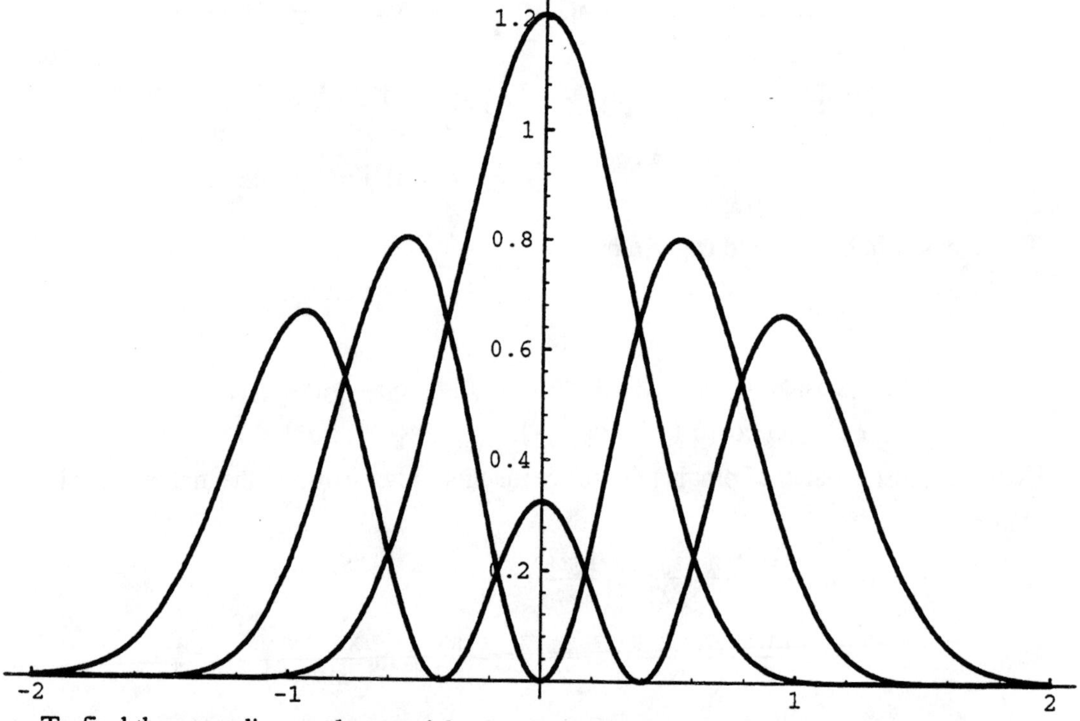

To find the spreading angle one picks the place where the intensity is down from the peak by e^{-2}. Those values are ~ 0.65, 1.2 and 1.5 for solution 3, 1, and 2 respectively. Since the horizontal axis is scaled according to the far-field spot-size of a **single** Gaussian (which would spread as $\theta \sim 2\lambda/\pi w_0 = 1.24°$ for the numerical values given), the real x_2

coordinate would expand as [ ]$\cdot\lambda z/\pi w_0$, where [ ] indicates the e^{-2} values given above. Thus we can define an "effective" spot-size as being w_0' or $1.54\cdot w_0$ for solution 3 (and sure enough, the near field looks like a "fatter" Gaussian), $0.833\cdot w_0$ for 1 (an equivalent near field Gaussian is smaller than one) and $0.66\cdot w_0$ for 2 (an even smaller equivalent near field Gaussian). Thus the spreading angle would be the [ ] times that of a single Gaussian, or 0.8°, 1.49°, and 1.86°. If the aperture Gaussian were much smaller - say 5μm – then all of the above numbers would be multiplied by 5.

12.13

The beam emerges from a dielectric slab; hence, one must use the ABCD matrix to compute the emerging parameters

$$T=\begin{bmatrix}1 & 0\\ 0 & n\end{bmatrix} \text{and } q_2=\frac{Aq_1+B}{Cq_1+D} \text{ or } \frac{1}{q_2}=\frac{n}{q_1}=n\left[\frac{1}{R_y}+j\frac{\lambda_0}{\pi n w_y^2}\right];$$

$$R_2=\frac{R_1}{n};w_2^2=w_y^2$$

where the y subscript refers to the beam parameters in the rod and 2 to that in the air. Now we know the complex beam parameters at the exit plane but we would prefer to know the plane at which the wavefront would be planar. The distance from the output plane to that imaginary surface is the astigmatic distance.

The beam parameters expand according to:

$$z_2=\frac{\pi w_y^2}{\lambda_0}=\frac{\pi w_0^2}{\lambda_0}\left[1+\left(\frac{z}{z_0}\right)^2\right]=\frac{z_0^2+z^2}{z_0};\ R_2=\frac{z^2+z_0^2}{z}=\frac{R_y}{n}$$

$$\text{Dividing;}\left(\frac{z}{z_0}\right)=\frac{z_2}{R_2};\ z_0\left[1+(z/z_0)^2\right]=z_2;\ \text{Thus } z_0=\frac{z_2}{1+(z_2/R_2)^2}=0.2149\text{ cm}$$

We can now solve for the hypothetical distance z:

$$z=z_0\left(\frac{z_2}{R_2}\right)=R_2\left[\frac{(z_2/R_2)^2}{1+(z_2/R_2)^2}\right]=\left[\frac{\pi w_y}{\lambda_0}\right]\left[\frac{(\pi n w_y^2)/(\lambda_0 R_y)}{1+[(\pi n w_y^2)/(\lambda_0 R_y)]^2}\right]$$

Note that if $R_y\rightarrow\infty$, $z=0$; Recall Eq. 3.4.2 : $\tan\theta/2=dw/dz|_{z\rightarrow\infty}=\lambda_0/\pi w_0$

$$\text{Thus } \theta=2\tan^{-1}\left\{\left[\frac{\lambda_0}{\pi w_y}\right]\left[1+\left[\frac{\pi n w_y^2}{\lambda_0 R_y}\right]^2\right]^{1/2}\right\}$$

The first bracket is the expansion if $R_y=\infty$. Obviously the astigmatism increases the expansion angle.

12.14

$$E_T(z) = E^+ e^{(g_0 - j\beta)(z + L/2)} + E^- e^{-(g_0 - j\beta)(z - L/2)}$$

$$\frac{\omega\mu_0}{\beta_0} H_T(z) = E^+ e^{(g_0 - j\beta)(z + L/2)} - E^- e^{-(g_0 - j\beta)(z - L/2)}$$

at $z = +L/2$; $\Gamma = E^-/[E^+ e^{(g_0 - j\beta)L}]$; $\therefore$ $E^- = [\Gamma e^{(g_0 - j\beta)L}]\, E^+$
at $z = -L/2$; $E^+ = E_{inc} = E_0$; $E_r = E^- e^{(g_0 - j\beta)L} = E_0 \Gamma\, e^{2(g_0 - j\beta)L}$

(a) $$E_T(z) = E_0\{e^{(g_0 - j\beta)(z + L/2)} + [\Gamma e^{(g_0 - j\beta)L}]\, e^{-(g_0 - j\beta)(z - L/2)}\}$$

$$\frac{\omega\mu_0}{\beta_0} H_T(z) = E_0\{e^{(g_0 - j\beta)(z + L/2)} - [\Gamma e^{(g_0 - j\beta)L}]\, e^{-(g_0 - j\beta)(z - L/2)}\}$$

(b) $$\mathbf{E} \times \mathbf{H}^* = \frac{\beta_0}{\omega\mu_0} E_0^2 \{e^{2g_0(z+L/2)} - (\Gamma^2 e^{2g_0L})\, e^{-2g_0(z-L/2)} + 2\, j\, \Gamma_0\, e^{2g_0L} \sin[2\beta_0(z-L/z)]\}$$

(c) $R = \Gamma^2 e^{4g_0L}$ at $z = +L/2$; $P^+ = \dfrac{\beta}{\omega\mu_0} E_0^2 \{e^{2g_0L} - \Gamma^2 e^{2g_0L}\}$

$\therefore T = e^{2g_0L}(1 - \Gamma^2)$

(d) $\Gamma^2 e^{4g_0L} > e^{2g_0L} - \Gamma^2 e^{2g_0L}$;

$\Gamma^2 e^{2g_0L}(e^{2g_0L} + 1) > e^{2g_0L}$;

or $\Gamma^2 > 1/(e^{2g_0L} + 1)$

12.15

(a) When $\delta > \kappa$, $(pL)^2 = (\kappa l)^2 - (\delta L)^2 < 0$, For $pL = jy$ and $(\delta L)^2 = (\kappa L)^2 + y^2$ and $\sinh pL \rightarrow j \sin y$; $\cosh pL \rightarrow \cos y$; yielding the expressions given.

(b) When $\sin y = 0$, $R = 0$, and $T = 1$, $y = m\pi$
or $(m\pi)^2 = (\delta L)^2 - (\kappa L)^2$; $\therefore (\delta L/\pi)^2 = m^2 + (\kappa L/\pi)^2$

(c) Setting $T = 1/2$ yields: $\dfrac{y^2}{y^2\cos^2 y + [(\kappa L)^2 + y^2]\sin^2 y} = \dfrac{1}{2}$

or $2y^2 = y^2\cos^2 y + y^2\sin^2 y + (\kappa L)^2\sin^2 y \;\; \therefore \left[\dfrac{\sin y}{y}\right]^2 = \left[\dfrac{1}{\kappa L}\right]^2$

(d) $\delta = \beta_0 - \beta_m$; $\beta_m = \pi/\Lambda \triangleq 2\pi\nu_B n_0/c$; $\beta = 2\pi\nu n_0/c$

$\delta L/\pi = (\nu_0 - \nu_B)\dfrac{[2n_0 L]}{c} = (\nu_0 - \nu_B) \div [c/2n_0 L]$

(e) For $\kappa L = 3$, $y = 2.2789$ $\quad (\delta L)_{1/2} = \pm\, 3.7674$

$\kappa L = 4$, $y = 2.4746$ $\quad (\delta L)_{1/2} = \pm\, 4.7036$

For $\kappa L = 4$. The structure reflects over a band $\delta L/\pi = 4$ with $R > 50\%$.

Now $2nL = 2nN\Lambda$ and $\Lambda = \lambda_B/2n_0$; $\therefore 2n_0 L = N\lambda_B$

$$\frac{1}{\lambda_-} - \frac{1}{\lambda_+} = \frac{4}{N\lambda_B}; \quad \frac{\lambda_+ - \lambda_-}{\lambda_B^2} = \frac{4}{N\lambda_B}; \quad \therefore \lambda_+ - \lambda_- = \frac{4\lambda_B}{N}$$

If $\lambda_B = 1.55\mu m$ and $N = 10^3$; $\therefore \lambda_+ - \lambda_- = 62$ Å

$\therefore$ $\qquad \lambda_+ = 1.5531\ \mu m$ and $\lambda_- = 1.5469$ Å

The narrow 3 dB pass band: $\Delta_{3dB}(\delta l_g/\pi) = 0.1 \therefore \lambda_+ - \lambda_- = \dfrac{0.1\lambda_B}{N} = 1.55$ Å

The 10 db pass–band is 4.65 Å

$$\kappa L = \frac{\omega}{c}\frac{n_1}{2} L = \frac{2\pi}{\lambda_B} \cdot \frac{n_1}{4n} 2nL = \frac{2\pi}{\lambda_B} \cdot \frac{n_1}{2n} \cdot N\lambda_B; \;\therefore\; \frac{n_1}{n} = \frac{2}{\pi}\left(\frac{\kappa L}{N}\right) = 2.55^{-3}$$

n(InP) = 2.27* $\qquad \therefore n_1 = 8.58 \times 10^{-3}$

*See C. M. Wolfe, Nick Holonyak, Jr., Greg Stillman,"Physical Properties of Semiconductors" Prentice–Hall, Englewood Cliffs, NJ 07632 (1989)

12.16

$a_{12} = b_{21}e^{-j\theta}$; $\qquad b_{22} = {}^2S_{12}\,a_{12} + {}^2S_{11}[a_{22}] = {}^2S_{12}a_{12} = [{}^2S_{12}\,e^{-j\theta}]\,b_{21}$

$\therefore \qquad b_{12} = {}^2S_{11}a_{12} + {}^2S_{12}[a_{22}{=}0] = {}^2S_{11}a_{12} = [{}^2S_{11}e^{-j\theta}]b_{21}$

$a_{21} = b_{12}e^{-j\theta} = [{}^2S_{11}e^{-j2\theta}]b_{21}$;

$b_{21} = {}^1S_{12}a_{11} + {}^1S_{11}a_{21} = {}^1S_{12}a_{11} + {}^1S_{11}{}^2S_{11}e^{-j2\theta}$

$$b_{21} = \frac{{}^1S_{12}a_{11}}{1 - [{}^1S_{11}][{}^2S_{11}]e^{-j2\theta}};$$

$$\therefore \quad \boxed{\frac{b_{22}}{a_{11}} \triangleq [S_{12}]_{net} = \frac{[{}^1S_{12}][{}^2S_{12}]\, e^{-j\theta}}{1 - [{}^1S_{11}][{}^2S_{11}]\, e^{-j2\theta}}}$$

$$b_{11} = {}^1S_{11}\, a_{11} + {}^1S_{12}[a_{21} = {}^2S_{11}e^{-j2\theta} b_{21}];$$

Use the above value for b_{21};

$$b_{11} = \frac{{}^1S_{11} - {}^2S_{11}e^{-j2\theta}[{}^1S_{11}\,{}^2S_{22} + {}^1S_{12}^2]}{1 - {}^1S_{22}\,{}^2S_{11}e^{-j2\theta}}\, a_{11};$$

the [ ] bracket in the above is equal to 1;

$$\therefore \quad \boxed{\frac{b_{11}}{a_{11}} \equiv \Gamma_{net} = \frac{{}^1S_{11} - {}^2S_{11}e^{-j2\theta}}{1 - {}^1S_{22}\,{}^2S_{11}e^{-j2\theta}}}$$

12.17

a) $I(r) = \dfrac{E_0^2}{2\eta_0}\{e^{-2(r/w_i)^2} - \Gamma_0^2\, e^{-2(r/w_r)^2}\};$

$$\frac{dI}{dr} = \frac{E_0^2}{2\eta_0}\left\{-\frac{4r}{(w_i)^2}\, e^{-2(r/w_i)^2} - \Gamma_0^2\left(\frac{-4r}{(w_r)^2}\right) e^{-2(r/w_r)^2}\right\}$$

$$\frac{d^2I}{dr^2} = \left\{\frac{E_0^2}{2\eta_0} + \left[\frac{8r^2}{w_i^4} - \frac{4}{w_i^2}\right] e^{-2(r/w_i)^2} - \Gamma_0^2\left[\frac{8r^2}{w_r^2} - \frac{4}{w_r^2}\right] e^{-2(r/w_r)^2}\right\}$$

d^2I/dr^2 represents the curvature of the intensity with respect to r.

$$\left.\frac{d^2I}{dr^2}\right|_{r=0} = -4\left[\Gamma_0^2\frac{1}{w_r^2} - \frac{1}{w_i^2}\right] \qquad \text{Note } \frac{1}{w_r^2} > \frac{1}{w_i^2}$$

If $\Gamma_0^2 > (w_r/w_i)^2$, then d^2I/dr^2 is positive, indicating a local minimum. If $\Gamma_0^2 < (w_r/w_i)^2$, then d^2I/dr^2 is negative, indicating a local maximum. At equality, we have a maximally flat case.

(b) We must use Eqs. 3.3.10 and 3.3.11 for the reflected beam

$$z_{2r} = \frac{\pi w_r^2}{\lambda} = \frac{(z_0^2 + z^2)}{z_0} = 1{,}115.1 \text{ cm} \qquad (1)$$

$$R_{2r} = \frac{(z^2 + z_0^2)}{z} = 527.21 \text{ cm} \qquad (2)$$

both $z_0 = \pi w_0^2/\lambda$ and z = distance from the hypothetical plane where $R = \infty$ are to be determined. Dividing (1) by (2):

$$\frac{z_1}{R_r} = \frac{z}{z_0} = 2.1151 \text{ and substitute back into (1) to obtain}$$

$$z_{2r} = z_0\left[1 + \left(\frac{z}{z_0}\right)^2\right] = 1{,}1151 \text{ cm} = z_0\,(5.4736)$$

or $\quad z_0 = 203.72 \text{ cm} = \dfrac{\pi w_0^2}{\lambda_0}$

$\therefore \quad w_0^2 = 6.8737\times10^{-2}$ cm² and $w_0 = 0.26218$ cm and $z = z_0\cdot 2.1151 = 430.89$ cm

Thus, the imaginary plane from which the reflected beam emerges is located 430.89 cm to the right of the mirror M_2. Thus we have the following sketch:

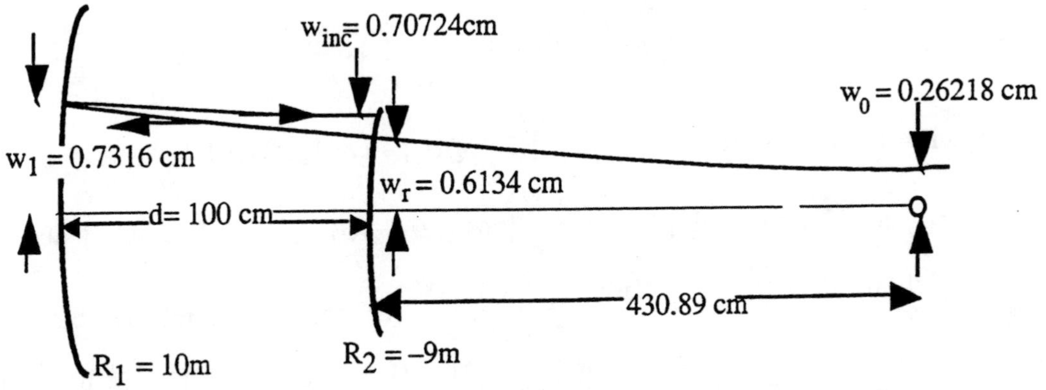

At M_1, the distance from the plane $z = 0$ is 530.89 cm

$\therefore \quad z_1 = \pi w_1^2/\lambda_0 = z_0\,(1 + (530.89/203.72)^2) = 7.7910\,z_0 = 15.872$ m

and thus $\quad w_1 = 0.7316$ cm

The radius of curvature of the wavefront incident on M_1 is:

$$R = \frac{(530.89)^2+(203.72)^2}{530.89} = 609.07\text{cm}$$

and for that reflected by M_1: $\dfrac{1}{R_{1r}} = \dfrac{1}{609.07} - \dfrac{1}{500} \Rightarrow R_{1r} = -35.814$ m

Note: $\dfrac{w_1}{w_r} = \dfrac{1.033}{0.8994} = 1.1931 > M$

If one had not neglected X with respect to M and worked from Eq. 12.9.9 directly, the values of the beam parameters would be: $R_{inc} = -30.36$ meters and $w_{inc} = 0.7518$ cm.

(e) One follows the same calculations as given in the text with the following results:

$R_{inc} = \infty$, $X = 1/22.5$, $a = 0.6161$; $w_{inc} = 0.6161$; $w_{ref} = 0.50305$;

$\Gamma_2^2(\text{eff}) = 0.6667\Gamma_0^2$ and $\Gamma_2^2(\text{max. flat}) = 0.444$; $\gamma_0 = 0.416\%/\text{cm}$

12.18

$$E(x_1) = \cos^2\frac{\pi x_1}{2w} \qquad |x_1| \le w;$$

Change variables to $u = \dfrac{x\sqrt{C}}{a}$ where $C = 2\pi N$; $N = \dfrac{\pi}{2}$;

$\therefore C = \pi^2$ and thus $\sqrt{C} = \pi$ leading to $u = \dfrac{\pi x}{a}$;

$$E(x_1) = \cos^2\frac{\pi x_1}{2w} = \cos^2\frac{\pi x_1}{a}\cdot\left(\frac{a}{2w}\right) = \cos^2 U_1 \text{ for } a = 2w.$$

$\therefore E(U_1) = \cos^2 U_1 = \dfrac{1}{2}(1+\cos 2U_1) \qquad -w < x_1 < w;$

$\therefore \quad -\pi/2 < U_1 < \pi/2$ for the limits on U_1

Disregarding the phase factor, the field on M_1 is given by:

$$E(U_2) = \frac{1}{\sqrt{2\pi}} \int_{-\pi/2}^{\pi/2} \frac{1}{2}(1+\cos 2U_1)e^{jU_1U_2}\, dU_1 = \frac{1}{\sqrt{2\pi}} \int_0^{\pi/2} (1+\cos 2U_1)\cos(U_2U_1)\, dU_1$$

since the sin (U_1U_2) is odd with respect to U_1 and thus its integral vanishes

$$\text{Now } I_1 = \int_0^{\pi/2} \cos(U_2U_1)\, dU_1 = \frac{\sin(U_1U_2)}{U_2}\Bigg|_{U_1=0}^{\pi/2} = \left(\frac{\pi}{2}\right)\cdot\frac{\sin\theta_2}{\theta_2} \quad \text{where } \theta_2 = \frac{\pi U_2}{2}$$

Expand: $\cos 2U_1 \cos(U_2U_1) = \frac{1}{2}\{\cos[(2-U_2)U_1] + \cos[(2+U_2)U_1]\}$

$$\therefore I_2 = \int_0^{\pi/2} \cos 2U_1 \cos(U_2U_1)\, dU_1 = \frac{1}{2}\int_0^{\pi/2} \{\cos[(2-U_2)U_1] + \cos[(2+U_2)U_1]\}\, dU_1$$

$$= \frac{1}{2}\left\{\frac{\sin(2-U_2)U_1}{(2-U_2)} + \frac{\sin(2+U_2)U_1}{(2+U_2)}\right\}_0^{\pi/2} \quad \text{only the upper limit contributes.}$$

$$= \frac{1}{2}\left\{\frac{2[\sin b(2-U_2) + \sin b(2+U_2)] + U_2[\sin b(2-U_2) - \sin b(2+U_2)]}{4-U_2^2}\right\}$$

Use: $\sin(\Psi-\theta) \pm \sin(\Psi+\theta) = 2\sin\Psi\cos\theta$ or $-2\cos\Psi\sin\theta$;

$b = \pi/2;\ \Psi = 2b = \pi;\ \theta = \frac{\pi}{2}U_2$

$$\therefore I_2 = \frac{1}{2}\left\{\frac{4\sin\Psi\cos\theta_2 - 2U_2\cos\Psi\cdot\sin\theta}{4-U_2^2}\right\}_{\Psi=\pi} = \frac{U_2\sin\pi U_2/2}{4-U_2^2}$$

$$= \frac{2}{\pi}\cdot\frac{\frac{\pi U_2}{2}\sin\pi U_2/2}{4/\pi^2(\pi^2-(\pi U_2/2))^2} = \frac{\pi}{2}\frac{\theta_2\sin\theta_2}{\pi^2-\theta_2^2}$$

$$\therefore \quad E(\theta_2) = \frac{\pi/2}{\sqrt{2\pi}}\cdot\left\{\frac{\sin\theta_2}{\theta_2} + \frac{\theta_2\sin\theta_2}{\pi^2-\theta_2^2}\right\} = \frac{1}{2}\sqrt{\frac{\pi}{2}}\left\{\frac{\sin\theta_2}{\theta_2}\left[1 + \frac{\theta_2^2}{\pi^2-\theta_2^2}\right]\right\}$$

$$\text{(a)}\quad E(\theta_2) = \frac{1}{2}\sqrt{\frac{\pi}{2}}\left\{\frac{\sin\theta_2}{\theta_2}\cdot\frac{\pi^2}{\pi^2-\theta_2^2}\right\} = \frac{1}{2}\sqrt{\frac{\pi}{2}}\left\{\frac{\pi^2}{\theta_2(\pi+\theta_2)}\cdot\frac{\sin\theta_2}{\pi-\theta_2}\right\}$$

where $\theta_2 = \frac{\pi U_2}{2}$; $U_2 = \frac{x_2\sqrt{c}}{a} = \frac{\pi x_2}{a}$; $\therefore \theta_2 = \frac{\pi^2 x_2}{2a}$

Note: The field does not blow up at $\theta_2=\pi$; indeed the limit of $\sin\theta_2/(\pi-\theta_2) \to 1$ at $x_2 = a$; $\theta_2 = \pi^2/a$; $E_2(x_2=a) = 0.1369$ of the peak value of 0.6266 or 0.084407. Hence the field plot for x>a is multiplied by 10 to show that small valuc.

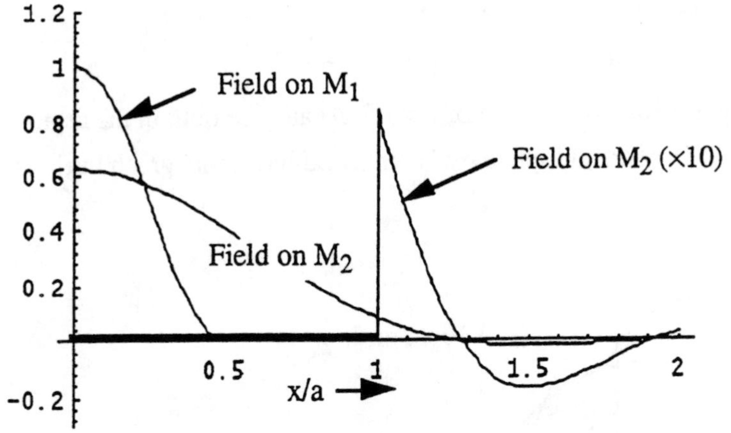

Now we change our specificatons and let a = 2 mw

$$E(x_1) = \cos^2\frac{\pi x_1}{2w} = \cos^2[\frac{\pi x_1}{a}\cdot\frac{a}{2w}] = \cos^2 mU_1 = \frac{1}{2}(1 + \cos 2mU_1)$$

The limits on x_1 are: $-w < x_1 < w$ and $U_1 = \frac{\pi x_1}{a}$; $\frac{a}{2w} = m$;

$\therefore$ the limits on U_1 are: $\quad -\pi/2m < U_1 < \pi/2m$

$$\therefore E(x_2) = \frac{1}{\sqrt{2\pi}}\int_0^{+\pi/2m}(1 + \cos 2mU1)\cos(U_2U_1)\,dU_1$$

where the integral involving the sin (U_2U_1) is again equal to zero.

$$I_1 = \int_0^{\pi/2m}\cos U_2U_1dU_1 = \frac{\sin U_2U_1}{U_2}\Bigg|_0^{\pi/2m} = \frac{\sin \pi U_2/2m}{U_2} = \frac{\pi}{2m}\cdot\frac{\sin\theta_2}{\theta_2};\ \theta_2 = \frac{\pi U_2}{2m}$$

$$I_2 = \int_0^{\pi/2m}\cos 2mU_1\cos(U_2U_1)dU_1 = \int_0^{\pi/2m}\frac{1}{2}[\cos(2m - U_2)U_1 + \cos(2m + U_2)U_1]dU_1$$

$$= \frac{1}{2}\left\{\frac{\sin(2m - U_2)U_1}{(2m - U_2)} + \frac{\sin(2m + U_2)}{(2m+U_2)}\right\}\Bigg|_0^{\pi/2m}$$

again, only the upper limit contributes

$$I_2 = \frac{1}{2}\,\frac{2m[\sin a(2m-U_2)+\sin a(2m+U_2)]+U_2[\sin a(2m-U_2)-\sin a(2m+U_2)]}{4m^2-U_2^2}$$

use the $\sin(\Psi - \theta) \pm \sin(\Psi + \theta) = 2\sin\Psi\cos\theta$ or $-2\cos\Psi\sin\theta$

$b = \frac{\pi}{2m}$; $\Psi = 2ma = \pi$; $\theta = \pi U_2/2m$ (almost as before)

$$\therefore I_2 = \frac{1}{2}\left\{\frac{4m\sin\Psi\cos\theta - 2U_2\cos\Psi\sin\theta}{4m^2 - U_2^2}\right\}_{\Psi=\pi} = \frac{U_2\sin\theta}{4m^2 - U_2^2}$$

$$= \frac{2m}{\pi}\cdot\frac{\pi U_2/2m\sin\theta_2}{\left(\frac{4m^2}{\pi^2}\right)(\pi^2 - (\pi U_2/2m)^2)} = \frac{\pi}{2m}\frac{\theta_2\sin\theta_2}{\pi^2 - \theta_2^2}$$

$$\therefore\ E(\theta_2) = \frac{\pi/2m}{\sqrt{2\pi}}\left\{\frac{\sin\theta_2}{\theta_2} + \frac{\theta_2\sin\theta_2}{\pi^2-\theta_2^2}\right\} = \frac{1}{2m}\sqrt{\frac{\pi}{2}}\left\{\frac{\sin\theta_2}{\theta_2}\cdot\frac{\pi^2}{\pi^2-\theta_2^2}\right\}$$

This is plotted below for the case of m=0.5. Again, the field in the region beyond the edge of the mirror has been multiplied by 10 to avoid having its graph buried in the linewidth of the axis.

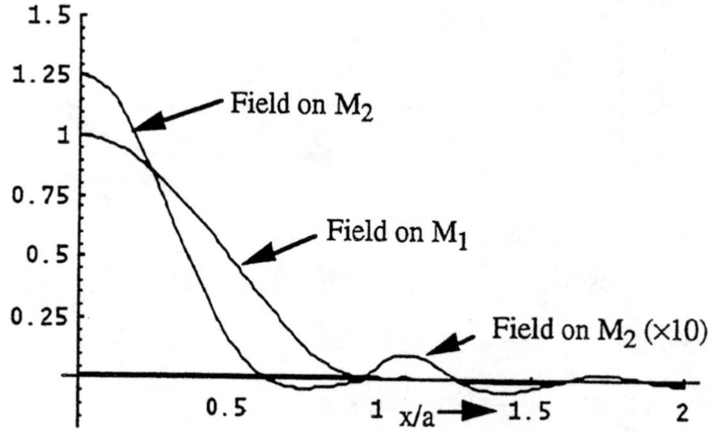

at $\theta_2 = 0$, $E_2(0) = \frac{1}{2m}\sqrt{\frac{\pi}{2}}$;

at $\theta_1 = 0$, $E_1(0) = 1$; at $\theta_2 = \pi$, $E_2(\theta_2 = \pi) = \frac{1}{2}E(0)$, $E_1\left(\theta_1 = \frac{\pi}{4}\right) = \frac{1}{2}E(0)$

$$\therefore\ \theta_2 = \frac{\pi U_2}{2m} = \frac{\pi^2 x'_2}{2ma} = \pi;\ \theta_1 = \frac{m\pi x'_1}{a} = \frac{\pi}{4};\ x'_2 = \frac{2ma}{\pi};\ x'_1 = \frac{a}{4m}$$

Making FWHM on each mirror equal, we find:

$$m^2 = \frac{\pi}{8} \text{ or } m = \frac{1}{2}\sqrt{\frac{\pi}{2}} = 0.627$$

$$\therefore\qquad E_2(\theta_2) = \left\{\frac{\sin\theta_2}{\theta_2}\frac{\pi^2}{\pi^2-\theta_2^2}\right\};$$

where $\theta_2 = \frac{\pi^2}{\sqrt{\pi/2}}\left(\frac{x_2}{a}\right) = 7.875\left(\frac{x_2}{a}\right)$;

$$E_1(x_1) = \cos^2 m\pi\left(\frac{x_1}{a}\right)$$

The two fields are plotted below and show that there is almost no difference between the two for most of the aperture of the mirror. The field for x> the first zero on M_2 has been multiplied by 10 to show the small deviation.

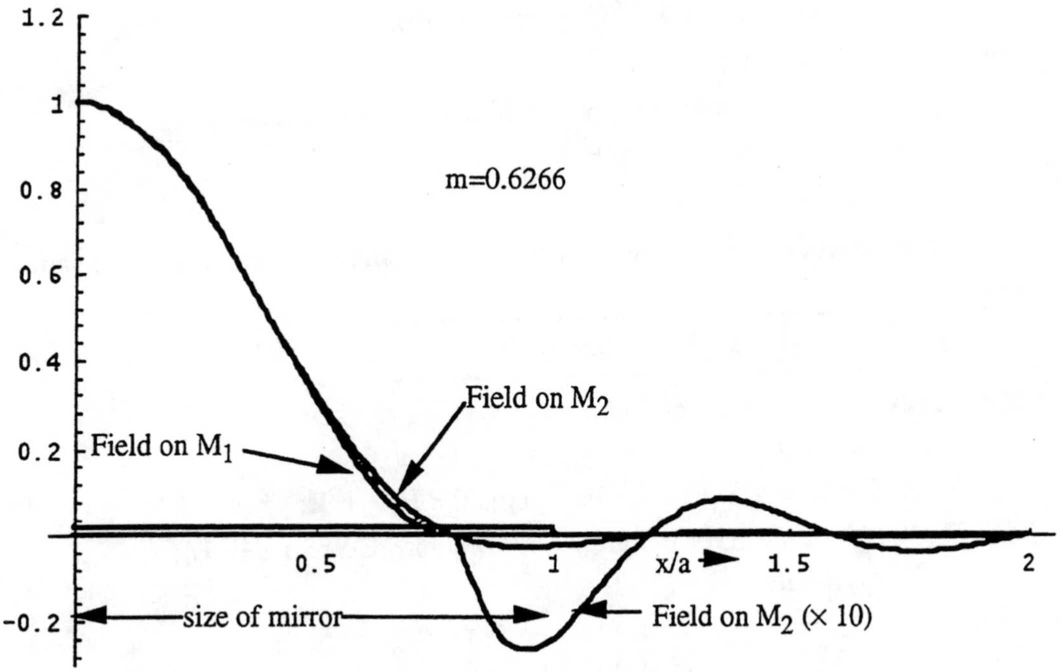

12.19

$\nabla\times\mathbf{A} = (\nabla_t - \gamma\mathbf{a}_z)\times(A_t\mathbf{a}_t + A_z\mathbf{a}_z) = \nabla_t\times(A_t\mathbf{a}_t) - \gamma\mathbf{a}_z\times\mathbf{a}_t A_t$

The first term is in the z direction whereas the last two lie in the transverse plane

$\nabla_t\times(A_z\mathbf{a}_z) = -\mathbf{a}_z\times\nabla_t A_z$

Equating transverse parts of Maxwell's Equations

$$-\mathbf{a}_z\times[\nabla_t H_z + \gamma(H_t\mathbf{a}_t)] = j\omega\varepsilon_0 n^2(E_t\mathbf{a}_t) \quad (1)$$

$$-\mathbf{a}_z\times[\nabla_t E_z + \gamma(E_t\mathbf{a}_t)] = -j\omega\mu_0(H_t\mathbf{a}_t) \quad (2)$$

or

$$j\omega\varepsilon_0 n^2(E_t\mathbf{a}_t) + \gamma[\mathbf{a}_z\times(H_t\mathbf{a}_t)] = -\mathbf{a}_z\times\nabla_t H_z \quad (3)$$

$$\gamma\mathbf{a}_z\times(E_t\mathbf{a}_t) - j\omega\mu_0(H_t\mathbf{a}_t) = -\mathbf{a}_z\times\nabla_t E_z \quad (4)$$

Form the following sum: $\gamma\mathbf{a}_z\times(3) + j\omega\varepsilon_0 n^2\,(4)$ and solve for $H_t\mathbf{a}_t$.

$$H_t\mathbf{a}_t = \frac{1}{\gamma^2 + (\omega n/c)^2}\{-\gamma\nabla_t H_z - j\omega\varepsilon_0 n^2\mathbf{a}_z\times\nabla_t E_z\} \quad (5)$$

Do the same to solve for $E_t\mathbf{a}_t$

$$E_t\mathbf{a}_t = \frac{1}{\gamma^2 + (\omega n/c)^2}\{-j\omega\mu\mathbf{a}_z\times\nabla_t H_z + \gamma\nabla_t E_z\} \quad (6)$$

which has no restrictions. However, the Helmholtz equation becomes quite complicated.

One might as well work with the vector form of Maxwell's equations and take the z component later.

$$\nabla\times\mathbf{H} = j\omega\varepsilon_0 n^2\mathbf{E} \quad (7)$$

$$\nabla \times \nabla \times \mathbf{H}) = \nabla(\nabla\cdot\mathbf{H}) - \nabla^2\mathbf{H} = j\omega\varepsilon_0 \nabla \times (n^2\mathbf{E})$$

Now $\nabla \times (n^2\mathbf{E}) = (\nabla n^2) \times \mathbf{E} + n^2(\nabla \times \mathrm{E})$

$$= \nabla \times (n^2\mathbf{E}) - j\omega\mu_0 n^2\mathbf{H};\quad \nabla\cdot\mathbf{H} \equiv 0;\quad k^2 = (\omega n/c)^2$$

$$-\nabla^2\mathbf{H} = j\omega\varepsilon_0(\nabla n^2) \times \mathbf{E} + k^2\mathbf{H}$$

or $\nabla^2\mathbf{H} + k^2\mathbf{H} = j\omega\varepsilon_0\mathbf{E} \times \nabla n^2$

Take the scalar product with $\mathbf{a}_z$, assume $e^{-\gamma z}$ variation, and allow only transverse variation of n^2.

$$\boxed{\nabla_t^2 H_z + [\gamma^2 + k^2]H_z = j\omega\varepsilon_0 \mathbf{a}_z\cdot(\mathbf{E} \times \nabla_t n^2)} \qquad (8)$$

Start with the other Maxwell equation,

$$\nabla \times \mathbf{E} = -\,j\omega\mu_0\mathbf{H}$$

$$\nabla \times (\nabla \times \mathbf{E}) = \nabla(\nabla\cdot\mathbf{E}) - \nabla^2\mathbf{E} = -\,j\omega\mu_0(\nabla \times \mathbf{H}) = k^2\mathbf{E}; \qquad (9)$$

Form $\nabla\cdot(7)$: $\quad \nabla\cdot(\nabla\times\mathbf{H}) \equiv 0 = j\omega\varepsilon_0(\nabla\cdot n^2\mathbf{E}) = j\omega\varepsilon_0[\mathbf{E}\cdot\nabla n^2 + n^2\nabla\cdot\mathbf{E}];$

$$\therefore \quad \nabla\cdot\mathbf{E} = -\frac{\mathbf{E}\cdot\nabla n^2}{n^2}$$

Therefore (9) becomes: $\quad -\nabla\left[\dfrac{\mathbf{E}\cdot\nabla n^2}{n^2}\right] - \nabla^2\mathbf{E} = \left(\dfrac{\omega n}{c}\right)^2\mathbf{E}$

Form the scalar product with $\mathbf{a}_z$, assume $e^{-\gamma z}$, and allow only transverse variation in n^2.

$$\nabla_t^2 E_z + [\gamma^2+k^2]E_z = \mathbf{a}_z\cdot\nabla\left[\frac{\mathbf{E}\cdot\nabla_t n^2}{n^2}\right] \qquad (10)$$

Please note that there are two symbols ∇_t and ∇. The one without a subscript includes the derivative with respect to z, $\partial/\partial z = -\,\gamma\mathbf{a}_z$.

$$\boxed{\nabla_t^2 E_z + [\gamma^2 + k^2]E_z = -\,\gamma\,\frac{\mathbf{a}_z\cdot\mathbf{E}_t\cdot\nabla_t n^2}{n^2}} \qquad (10)$$

One could use (5) and (6) to evaluate the RHS of (8) and (10), but the mess is rather formidable. The major mathematical problems are that E_z and H_z are coupled and thus do not separate into pure TE or TM modes unless certain circumstances exist:

If $\mathbf{E}\cdot\nabla_t n^2 = 0$, then pure TE modes are possible.

If $\mathbf{E} \times \nabla_t n^2 = 0$, then pure TM modes are possible.

Those are mutually exclusive unless $\nabla_t n^2 = 0$. (5)–(6)

$$\mathbf{H}_t = \frac{1}{\gamma^2 + (\omega n)^2/c^2}[-\,\gamma\nabla_t H_z - j\omega\varepsilon_0 n^2\mathbf{a}_z \times \nabla_t E_z]$$

which is the same as Eq. 12.1.4(b). A similar manipulation leads to Eq. 12.1.4(c). Note that n^2 may only be a function of the transverse coordinates.

12.20

(a) Using the quarter–wave transformer approach from transmission line theory:

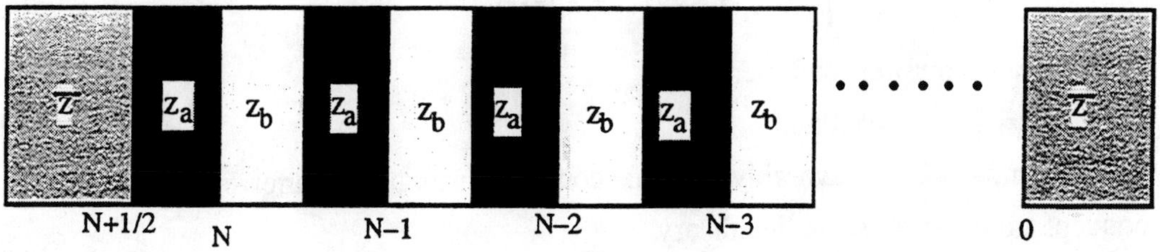

where $\bar{z}$ is the wave impedance at the input.

$$\therefore \quad z_N = \frac{z_b^{2N}\,\bar{z}}{z_a^{2N}}; \quad z_{N+1/2} = \frac{z_a^2}{z_b^{2N}\,\bar{z}/z_a^{2N}} = \frac{z_a^{2N+1}}{z_b^{2N}\,\bar{z}}; \; z_a^2 = \frac{\mu_0}{\varepsilon_0 n_a^2} = \frac{\eta_0^2}{n_a^2};$$

$$S_{11} = \Gamma = \frac{\bar{z} - z_{N+1/2}}{\bar{z} + z_{N+1/2}} = \frac{1 - z_a^{2N+1}/[z_b^{2N}\bar{z}^2]}{1 + z^{2(N+1)}/[z_b^{2N}\bar{z}^2]};$$

$$\therefore \quad \Gamma = \frac{1 - (n_a/n_b)^{2N}(n_a/\bar{n})^2}{1 + (n_a/n_b)^{2N}(n_a/\bar{n})^2}.$$

For $x = 0.2$, $n_a = \bar{n} + \Delta n = 3.42$;

for $x = 0.8$, $n_b = \bar{n} - \Delta n = 3.08$;

$\bar{n} = 3.25$ (x=0.5); $\Delta n = 0.17$; $N = 20$; $(n_a/n_b)^{40} = 65.92$; $(n_a/\bar{n})^2 = 1.107$

$\therefore \quad (n_a/n_b)^{2N}\,(n_a/\bar{n})^2 = 73.00$ and thus $\Gamma = -\,0.9730$;

$\Gamma^2 = 0.9467$ and $T = 0.0533$.

If $n_a = 3.08$; $n_b = 3.42$; $(n_a/n_b)^{40} = 0.01517$; $(n_a/n_b)^2 = 0.8981$

$(n_a/n_b)^{2N}\,(n_a/\bar{n})^2 = 0.01362$. $\Gamma = 0.9731$;

$\Gamma^2 = 0.9470$ and $T = 1 - \Gamma^2 = 0.0530$

(b) If one uses the theory for a DBR, the wave equation becomes:

$$\frac{\partial^2 E}{\partial z^2} + \left\{\left[\frac{\omega}{c}\right]^2\left[n_0 + 4(\Delta n/\pi)\sum_{(m,odd)}(1/m)\cos 2m\beta_m z\right]^2 + j(\omega n_0/c)\gamma_0\right\}E = 0.$$

For Δn small:

$$\frac{\partial^2 E}{\partial z^2} + \left\{\left[\frac{\omega}{c}\right]^2\left[n_0 + \frac{8\Delta n}{\pi n_0}\cos 2\beta_m z\right] + j(\omega n_0/c)\gamma_0\right\}E = 0;$$

$$\frac{\partial^2 E}{\partial z^2} + \{\beta_0^2 + j2\,g_0\beta_0 + 4\beta_0\left[(2/\pi)\Delta n(\omega/c)\right]\cos 2\beta_m z\}E = 0.$$

$$\therefore \quad \kappa = \frac{\omega}{c}\frac{2}{\pi}\Delta n = \frac{2\pi}{\lambda_B}\frac{2}{\pi}\Delta n = \frac{\omega}{c}\frac{4}{\pi}\Delta n\frac{1}{2}; \text{ and } n_1 = \frac{4}{\pi}\Delta n;$$

$$L = \frac{N\lambda_B}{4n_a} + \frac{N\lambda_B}{4n_b} + \frac{\lambda_B}{4n_a} = (N\lambda_B/4)\left[\frac{1}{n_a} + \frac{1}{n_b} + \frac{1}{Nn_a}\right] = \frac{N\lambda_B}{4}\frac{1}{1.583};$$

$$\kappa L = \frac{2\pi}{\lambda_B}\cdot\left[\frac{2}{\pi}\Delta n\right]\frac{N\lambda_B}{4}\cdot\frac{1}{1.583}] = 2.148;$$

Thus the transmission coefficient

$$T \approx 4e^{-2\kappa L} = 0.0545$$

which compares quite favorably with that computed using the quarter–wave transformer concept from transmission line theory.

Chapter 13

13.1

Let's supplement the classical force equation by adding one to account for radiation:

$$m\ddot{z} + kz = F_{rad}$$

where the characteristic frequency is given by: $\omega_0^2 = \frac{k}{m}$

Multiply by $\dot{z}$ $\qquad \frac{d}{dt}\left(\frac{m\dot{z}^2}{2} + \frac{kz^2}{2}\right) = F_{rad}\dot{z} = -P_{rad}$

Any book in electrodynamics shows that the power radiated by an oscillating charge is

$$P_{rad} = \frac{e^2}{6\pi\varepsilon_0 c^3}\ddot{z}^2$$

Now, $\frac{d}{dt}(\ddot{z}\dot{z}) = \ddot{z}^2 + \dot{z}\dddot{z}$

Average over a period T of oscillation and assume nearly periodic motion

$$<\frac{d}{dt}(\ddot{z}\dot{z})> = \int_0^T \frac{d}{dt}(\ddot{z}\dot{z})dt = \frac{1}{T}\left[(\ddot{z}\dot{z})\big|_T - (\ddot{z}\dot{z})\big|_0\right] = 0;$$

$\therefore \qquad \ddot{z}^2 \approx \dot{z}\dddot{z}$

Thus: $F_{rad}\cdot\dot{z} = \frac{1}{6\pi\varepsilon_0}\frac{e^2}{c^3}(\dddot{z})(\dot{z})$ or: $F_{rad} = \frac{1}{6\pi\varepsilon_0}\frac{e^2}{c^3}\dddot{z}$

Thus our equation of motion is modified and becomes:

$$\ddot{z} + \omega_0^2 z - \frac{1}{6\pi\varepsilon_0}\frac{e^2}{c^3}(\dddot{z}) = 0$$

Assume $z = Ae^{j\omega' t}$ where ω' = complex = (real part) − j (imaginary part)

$\therefore \qquad -(\omega')^2 + \omega_0^2 + j\frac{\gamma(\omega')^3}{\omega_0^2} = 0$ where $\gamma = \frac{e^2\omega_0^2}{6\pi\varepsilon_0 c^3}$

For $\omega' = \omega_1 - \varepsilon$; $\varepsilon << \omega_1$; $(\omega')^2 = \omega_1^2 - 2\omega_1\varepsilon$; $(\omega_1)^3 = \omega_1^3 - 3\omega_1^2\varepsilon$

$\therefore \qquad \omega_1^2 = \omega_0^2$ (as expected) and $-2\omega_1\varepsilon + j\gamma\omega_1^3 = 0$

$\therefore \qquad \varepsilon = j\frac{\gamma}{2}$

$$\omega' = \omega_0 - j\gamma/2 = \omega_0 - j\frac{1}{2\tau} \text{ where } \frac{1}{2\tau} = \frac{e^2\omega_0^2}{6\pi\varepsilon_0 c^3}$$

13.2

One can express the wave impedance as:

$$\eta_0 = \left[\frac{\mu_0}{\varepsilon_0}\right]^{1/2} = \frac{(\mu\varepsilon_0)^{1/2}}{\varepsilon_0} = \frac{1}{c\varepsilon_0}$$

$$P_{rad} = \frac{4\pi\omega^4}{2\pi c^5}\left[\frac{1}{4\pi\varepsilon_0}\right]m^2 = \frac{32\pi^4\nu^4}{c^5}\left(\frac{1}{4\pi\varepsilon_0}\right)m^2 = h\nu A_{mag}$$

Thus the classical expression for the magnetic A coefficient is:

Chapter 13

$$A_{mag} = \frac{32\pi^4 \nu^3}{c^5}\left[\frac{1}{4\pi\varepsilon_0}\right]\frac{m^2}{h};\ A_{elect} = \frac{16}{3}\frac{\pi^4\nu^3}{c^3}\left[\frac{1}{4\pi\varepsilon_0}\right]\frac{\mu^2}{h}$$

Ther are common factors between it and that for a electric dipole. The ratio:

$$\frac{A_m}{A_e} = \frac{6}{c^2}\frac{m^2}{\mu^2} = 6\left(\frac{\omega}{c}\right)^2 d^2 = 24\pi^2\left(\frac{d}{\lambda}\right)^2 \text{ since } m = Id^2 = \omega Q d^2;\ \mu = Qd$$

$\frac{A_m}{A_e} = 2.37 \times 10^{-7}$ for the numbers given

i.e., if $A_e = 10^8\ s^{-1}$ then $A_m = 23.7\ s^{-1}$ (very slow)

13.3

$\sigma = 1.27\times 10^{-20}\ cm^2$; $\Delta N\sigma = 0.05\ cm^{-1}$ $\therefore$ $\Delta N = 3.94\times 10^{+18}\ cm^{-3}$

$\Delta\overline{\nu} = 11.5\ cm^{-1}$; thus $\Delta\nu = 345$ GHz; $n = 1.77$

$$\omega^2 = \frac{\omega_e^2}{1 + \chi'/n^2} \text{ or using the binomial theorem: } \omega = \omega_e\left(1 - \frac{\chi'}{2n^2}\right)$$

$$\frac{\chi'}{2n^2} = -\frac{(\nu_0 - \nu)}{\Delta\nu}\frac{\gamma(\nu)}{k}\ ;\ k = \frac{2\pi n}{\lambda} = 1.61\times 10^{+5}\ cm^{-1};\ \frac{\chi'}{2n^2} = 9.5\times 10^{-10}\ ;$$

$\nu_e = 4.32\times 10^{+14}$ Hz; $(\nu - \nu_e) = \pm 0.391$ MHz (Not much but measurable)

13.4

$$\beta = \frac{\omega}{c}n\left(1 + \frac{\chi'(\omega)}{2n^2}\right) = k\left(1 + \frac{\chi'(\omega)}{2n^2}\right);$$

Now
$$\chi'(\nu) = \frac{\nu_0 - \nu}{\Delta\nu/2}\chi''(\nu)$$

and $\gamma(\nu) = -k\frac{\chi''(\nu)}{n^2}$ where $\chi''(\nu) = \frac{-n^2\gamma(\nu)}{k}$

$$\chi'(\nu) = -\frac{(\nu_0 - \nu)}{(\Delta\nu/2)}\cdot\frac{n^2}{k}\gamma(\nu) \text{ and } \frac{\chi'(\nu)}{2n^2} = -\frac{(\nu_0 - \nu)}{\Delta\nu}\frac{\gamma(\nu)}{k};\ \beta = k - \frac{(\omega_0 - \omega)}{\Delta\omega}\gamma(\omega)$$

$$\frac{d\beta}{d\omega} = \frac{1}{v_g} = \frac{dk}{d\omega} + \frac{\gamma(\omega)}{\Delta\omega} - \frac{(\omega_0 - \omega)}{\Delta\omega}\frac{d\gamma(\omega)}{d\omega};\ \text{At } \omega = \omega_0\text{: } \frac{d\gamma(\omega)}{d\omega} = 0 \text{ and } \frac{dk}{d\omega} = \frac{n}{c} \text{ and thus:}$$

$\therefore$

$$\boxed{v_g = \frac{c/n}{1 + \frac{\gamma(\omega)c}{n\Delta\omega}}}$$

13.5

(a) $\sigma = A_{21}\frac{\lambda_0^2}{8\pi}\left\{g(\nu_0) = \frac{2}{\pi\Delta\nu}\right\} = 2.78\times 10^{-11}\ cm^2$; $10\log_{10}\exp[\gamma_0 l_g] = 30$ for 1 m

(b) $\exp[\gamma_0 l_g] = 10^3$; $\gamma_0 l_g = 6.908$; $\gamma_0 = 6.9\times 10^{-2}\ cm^{-1}$

(c) $N_2 - \frac{g_1}{g_2} N = \frac{\gamma_0}{\sigma} = 2.58 \times 10^{+9}\ cm^{-3}$

(d) From Eq. 13.3.14: $\nu_q\left(\frac{2d}{c}\right) = q + \left(\frac{\nu_0-\nu_q}{\Delta\nu}\right)\frac{|\gamma(\omega_0)l_0|}{\pi}$; $\nu_q = \dfrac{q(c/2d)}{1 + \dfrac{\gamma_0(\nu_0)l_0 c}{\pi\Delta\nu\ 2d}}$

or $\nu_q - \nu_{q-1} = \dfrac{c/2d}{1 + \dfrac{\gamma_0(\nu_0)l_g}{\pi}\left(\dfrac{c/2d}{\Delta\nu}\right)} = 71.45$ MHz for d = 1 m and c/2d = 150 MHz

13.6

In terms of the complex frequency variable, s, the square bracket in Eq. 13.2.8 can be written as:

$$F(s) = \frac{1}{s^2 + s(1/\tau) + \omega_{21}^2}$$ with s=jω along the real frequency axis.

This function has no poles in the right-half plane and $F(j\omega) = F^*(-j\omega)$ as required.

Thus the Cauchy integral becomes $\oint \frac{F(s)}{s - j\omega_0}\, ds = 0.$

However, the path of integration goes straight through the poles at s= $j\omega_0$, and thus one obtains the principal value of the integral at that point or 1/2 of $2\pi \times$ residue at that point. This is, of course, the route used to develop the Kramers-Kronig relations given in Appendix III. Note that the approximate Lorentzian is accurate for positive frequencies but does not obey $F(j\omega) = F^*(-j\omega)$. The complete Lorentzian is good for both positive and negative frequencies and thus does satisfy the Kramers–Kronig relations. If there is gain, there are poles in χ in the right-half s plane and thus the Kramer-Kronig relations do not apply.

13.7

(a) Start with the definition of Slater modes with the boundary conditions $\mathbf{n}\times\mathbf{E}_m = 0 = \mathbf{n}\cdot\mathbf{H}_m$. The solution to the Helmholtz equation obeying those boundary conditions is:

$\mathbf{E}_m = \mathbf{A}_m \sin k_m z$ with $k_m d = m\pi$ 1.

$\mathbf{H}_m = \mathbf{a}_z \times \mathbf{A}_m \cos k_m z$ 2.

From the volume normalization condition: $\left[\frac{\pi a^2 d}{2}\right]^{1/2} |\mathbf{A}_m|^2 = 1$ 3.

Therefore, the Slater mode functions are:

$\mathbf{E}_m = \left[\frac{2}{\pi a^2 d}\right]^{1/2} \mathbf{a}_t \sin k_m z$ 4.

and $\quad \mathbf{H}_m = \left[\frac{2}{\pi a^2 d}\right]^{1/2} \mathbf{a}_z \times \mathbf{a}_t \cos k_m z$ 5.

(b) Use the standard expansion procedure

$$\mathbf{H} = \sum_m \frac{\omega_m}{\sqrt{\mu}} q_m(t)\, \mathbf{H}_m \qquad 6.$$

$$\mathbf{E} = -\sum_m \frac{1}{\sqrt{\varepsilon}} p_m(t)\, \mathbf{E}_m \qquad 7.$$

$$\sum_m \frac{\omega_m}{\sqrt{\mu}} q_m(t)\,[\omega_m \sqrt{(\mu\varepsilon)}\, \mathbf{E}_m] + \sigma \sum_m \frac{1}{\sqrt{\varepsilon}} p_m(t)\, \mathbf{E}_m + \varepsilon \sum_m \frac{1}{\sqrt{\varepsilon}} \frac{dp_m(t)}{dt} \mathbf{E}_m = \mathbf{J}_x + \frac{\partial \mathbf{P}_a}{\partial t} \qquad 8.$$

Multiply by $\mathbf{E}_m$, use the orthogonality, and divide by $\sqrt{\varepsilon}$.

$$\omega_m^2\, q(t) + \frac{\sigma}{\varepsilon} p_m(t) + \frac{dp_m(t)}{dt} = \frac{1}{\sqrt{\varepsilon}} \iiint \mathbf{J}_x \cdot \mathbf{E}_m dV + \frac{1}{\sqrt{\varepsilon}} \frac{\partial}{\partial t} \iiint \mathbf{P}_a \cdot \mathbf{E}_m dV \qquad 9.$$

Follow the same procedure for the other Maxwell Equation:

$$\frac{dq(t)}{dt} = p(t) - \frac{1}{\omega_m \sqrt{\mu}} \frac{\partial}{\partial t} \iiint \mathbf{M}_x \cdot \mathbf{H}_m dV \qquad 10.$$

Differentiate 4 with respect to time and substitute into 10:

$$\frac{d^2 p_m(t)}{dt^2} + \frac{\sigma}{\varepsilon} \frac{dp_m(t)}{dt} + \omega_m^2\, p_m(t) = \frac{1}{\sqrt{\varepsilon}} \frac{\partial^2}{\partial t^2} \iiint \mathbf{P}_a \cdot \mathbf{E}_m dV + \frac{\omega_m \partial}{\sqrt{\mu}\, \partial t} \iiint \mathbf{M}_x \cdot \mathbf{H}_m dV$$

13.8

One might as well work with the vector form of Maxwell's equations and take the z component later.

$$\nabla \times \mathbf{H} = j\omega\varepsilon_0 n^2 \mathbf{E};$$

take the curl: $\quad \nabla \times (\nabla \times \mathbf{H}) = \nabla(\nabla \cdot \mathbf{H}) - \nabla^2 \mathbf{H} = j\omega\varepsilon_0 \nabla \times (n^2 \mathbf{E})$ 1

Now $\quad \nabla \times (n^2 \mathbf{E}) = \nabla n^2 \times \mathbf{E} + n^2 (\nabla \times \mathbf{E}) = \nabla \times (n^2 \mathbf{E}) - j\omega\mu_0 n^2 \mathbf{H};$

$\nabla \cdot \mathbf{H} \equiv 0; \quad k^2 = (\omega n/c)^2$

$$-\nabla^2 \mathbf{H} = j\omega\varepsilon_0 (\nabla n^2) \times \mathbf{E} + k^2 \mathbf{H}$$

or $\quad \nabla^2 \mathbf{H} + k^2 \mathbf{H} = j\omega\varepsilon_0 \mathbf{E} \times \nabla n^2$

Take the scalar product with $\mathbf{a}_z$, assume $e^{-\gamma z}$ variation, and allow only transverse variation of n^2 (and k^2).

$$\boxed{\nabla_t^2 H_z + [\gamma^2 + k^2] H_z = j\omega\varepsilon_0 \mathbf{a}_z \cdot (\mathbf{E} \times \nabla_t n^2)} \qquad 2$$

Start with the other Maxwell equation,

$$\nabla \times \mathbf{E} = -j\omega\mu_0 \mathbf{H};$$

Take the curl; $\quad \nabla \times (\nabla \times \mathbf{E}) = \nabla(\nabla \cdot \mathbf{E}) - \nabla^2 \mathbf{E} = -j\omega\mu_0 (\nabla \times \mathbf{H}) = k^2 \mathbf{E};$ 3

From $\nabla \cdot (1)$: $\quad \nabla \cdot (\nabla \times \mathbf{H}) \equiv 0 = j\omega\varepsilon_0 (\nabla \cdot n^2 \mathbf{E}) = j\omega\varepsilon_0 [\mathbf{E} \cdot \nabla n^2 + n^2 \nabla \cdot \mathbf{E}];$

$$\therefore \qquad \nabla\cdot\mathbf{E} = -\frac{\mathbf{E}\cdot\nabla n^2}{n^2};$$

Therefore (3) becomes: $\quad -\nabla\left[\frac{\mathbf{E}\cdot\nabla n^2}{n^2}\right] - \nabla^2\mathbf{E} = \left(\frac{\omega n}{c}\right)^2\mathbf{E}$

Again, form the scalar product with $\mathbf{a}_z$, assume $e^{-\gamma z}$, and allow only transverse variation in n^2.

$$\nabla_t^2 E_z + [\gamma^2 + k^2]E_z = \mathbf{a}_z\cdot\nabla\left[\frac{\mathbf{E}\cdot\nabla_t n^2}{n^2}\right] \qquad 4$$

Please note that there are two symbols ∇_t and ∇. The one without a subscript includes the derivative with respect to z, $\partial/\partial z = -\gamma\mathbf{a}_z$.

$$\boxed{\nabla_t^2 E_z + [\gamma^2 + k^2]E_z = -\gamma\,\frac{\mathbf{a}_z\cdot\mathbf{E}_t\cdot\nabla_t n^2}{n^2}} \qquad 5$$

Note that E_z and H_z are coupled and thus do not separate into pure TE or TM modes unless certain circumstances exist.

If $\mathbf{E}\cdot\nabla_t n^2 = 0$, then pure TM modes are possible.

If $\mathbf{E}\times\nabla_t n^2 = 0$, then pure TM modes are possible.

Those are mutually exclusive unless $\nabla_t n^2 = 0$.

13.9

With external excitation, Eq. 13.6.16 becomes:

$$\left\{2j\omega\left[1 + \frac{f\chi_a'}{n^2}\right] + \left[\frac{1}{\tau_p} + 2\omega\,\frac{f\chi_a''}{n^2}\right]\right\}\dot{E}$$

$$+\left\{\omega_m^2 - \omega^2\left[1 + \frac{f\chi_a'}{n^2}\right] + j\omega\left[\frac{1}{\tau_p} + \omega\,\frac{f\chi_a''}{n^2}\right]\right\}E = \kappa E_x$$

Assumptions:

(1) $2j\omega[1 + f\chi_a'/n^2] \simeq 2j\omega >> [1/\tau_p + 2\omega f\chi_a''/n^2]$.

(2) $|2j\omega| >> [1/\tau_p + 2\omega f\chi_a''/n^2]$.

(3) $\omega_m^2 - \omega^2(1 + f\chi_a'/n^2) = [\omega_m - \omega(1 + f\chi_a'/n^2)^{1/2}]\,[\omega_m + \omega(1+ f\chi_a'/n^2)^{1/2}]$

$\omega_m^2 - \omega^2(1 + f\chi_a'/n^2) \simeq 2\omega[\omega_m - \omega(1+ f\chi_a'/2n^2)$.

Use $\quad \dfrac{\chi_a'}{\chi_a''} = 2\,\dfrac{\omega_{21}-\omega}{\Delta\omega}$ (Eq. 13.2.10); $\quad \dfrac{\chi_a''}{n^2} = -\dfrac{\gamma}{k} = -\dfrac{c\gamma}{\omega n}$ (Eq. 13.3.5);

$$\therefore \qquad \frac{\chi_a'}{2n^2} = \frac{2(\omega_{21}-\omega)}{\Delta\omega}\,\frac{\chi_a''}{2n^2} = -\frac{(\omega_{21}-\omega)}{\Delta\omega}\,\frac{\gamma c}{\omega n}.$$

Use assumptions 1, 2, and 3 to obtain:

$$2j\omega\dot{E}_m + \{j\omega[1/\tau_p + \omega f\chi_a''/n^2] + 2\omega[\omega_m - \omega(1 + f\chi_a'/2n^2] \}E = \kappa E_x$$

Divide by $2j\omega$, and substitute for $\chi_a''/2n^2$, $\chi_a'/2n^2$.

$$\dot{E}_m + \left\{\left(\frac{1}{2\tau_p} - \frac{fc\gamma}{n}\right) - j\left([\omega_m - \omega] + \frac{fc\gamma}{n}\cdot\frac{(\omega_{21}-\omega)}{\Delta\omega}\right)\right\}E_m = \kappa E_x.$$

Now $\left[\omega_m + \frac{fc\gamma}{n}\frac{\omega_{21}}{\Delta\omega}\right] - \omega\left[1 + \frac{fc\gamma}{n}\frac{1}{\Delta\omega}\right] \approx (\omega_m - \omega)\left[1 + \frac{fc\gamma}{n}\frac{1}{\Delta\omega}\right]$

$$2\dot{E}_m + \left\{\left[1 - \frac{fc\gamma}{n}(2\tau_p)\right] - 2j(\omega_m - \omega)\left[1 + \frac{fc\gamma}{n}\frac{1}{\Delta\omega}\right]\right\}E_m = 2\kappa E_x$$

Since $\Delta\omega = 1/\tau$ and $\tau << \tau_p$, the saturation in the imaginary term is a small effect. Making the usual substitutions:

$\Delta\omega_c = 1/\tau_p$; $Q = \omega/\Delta\omega_c = \omega\tau_p$ and dividing by 2 leads to:

$$\dot{E}_m + \frac{1}{2\tau_p}\left\{\left(1 - 2\frac{fc\gamma}{n}\frac{1}{\Delta\omega_c}\right) - j2\delta Q\left[1 + \frac{fc\gamma}{n}\frac{1}{\Delta\omega_a}\right]\right\}E_m = \kappa E_x$$

13.10

$$\nabla \times \mathbf{H} = \mathbf{i} + \frac{\partial}{\partial t}(\varepsilon_0\mathbf{E} + \mathbf{P}) \qquad 1$$

$$\nabla \times \mathbf{E} = -\frac{\partial}{\partial t}\mu_0(\mathbf{H} + \mathbf{M}) \qquad 2$$

Form the following difference between scalar products: $\mathbf{E}\cdot(1) - \mathbf{H}\cdot(2)$, and apply the well-known and easily forgotten vector identity: $\nabla\cdot\mathbf{A}\times\mathbf{B} = \mathbf{B}\cdot\nabla\times\mathbf{A} - \mathbf{A}\cdot\nabla\times\mathbf{B}$.

$$-\nabla\cdot(\mathbf{E}\times\mathbf{H}) = \mathbf{E}\cdot\mathbf{i} + \frac{\partial}{\partial t}\left[\frac{(\varepsilon_0\mathbf{E}\cdot\mathbf{E} + \mu_0\mathbf{H}\cdot\mathbf{H})}{2}\right] + \mathbf{E}\cdot\frac{\partial\mathbf{P}}{\partial t} + \mathbf{H}\cdot\frac{\partial\mathbf{M}}{\partial t} \qquad 3.$$

Multiply by the element of volume and use the divergence theorem to convert the volume integral on the left to a surface integral.

$$-\int \mathbf{E}\times\mathbf{H}\cdot\mathbf{n}\, dA = \int \mathbf{E}\cdot\mathbf{i}\, dV$$

$$+ \int \frac{\partial}{\partial t}\left[\frac{(\varepsilon_0\mathbf{E}\cdot\mathbf{E} + \mu_0\mathbf{H}\cdot\mathbf{H})}{2}\right]dV + \int \mathbf{E}\cdot\frac{\partial\mathbf{P}}{\partial t}dV + \int \mathbf{H}\cdot\frac{\partial\mathbf{M}}{\partial t}dV$$

13.11

(a) In order to have bi-stability one requires two values of x (or y) such that $dx/dy=0$.

$2\kappa\tau_p = y\left[\frac{(1+a) + y^2}{1+y^2}\right]$; $a = f\alpha_0(c/n)\tau_p$

$2\kappa\tau_p\frac{dx}{dy} = \frac{y^4 + (2-a)y^2 + (1+a)}{(1 + y^2)^2}$; $\frac{dx}{dy} = 0$ at $y^2 = \frac{-(2-a) \pm [a(a-8)]^{1/2}}{2}$;

$\therefore$ $a > 8$ to have a real value for y where $dx/dy=0$

(b) For a=9, the two values of y are

$y_{Low} = \sqrt{2} = 1.414$ for $2\kappa\tau_p x_L = 5.6569$

$y_{High} = \sqrt{5} = 2.2361$ for $2\kappa\tau_p x_H = 5.5902$

∴ Bias level = $2\kappa\tau_p(x_L+x_H)/2 = 5.6235 = b_0$

Switching margin: $2\kappa\tau_p\Delta x = 6.6684\text{x}10^{-2} = \Delta b$

∴ switching command (for part c) = 0.13337 = $2\Delta b$

The values for "0" and "1" can be found from a solution to:

$$\frac{y[(1+a) + y^2]}{(1+y^2)} = b_0 \text{ or } y^3 - b_0y^2 + (1+a)y - b_0 = 0$$

$y_0 = y(\text{"0"}) = 1.1921$; $y_1 = y(\text{"1"}) = 2.6539$

$y_{unstable} = 1.7775$

(c) The external change must drive the cavity beyond the y_L or y_H states for switching to take place. One can solve the differential equation directly using a computer or use a bit of physical reasoning.

$$\frac{dy}{d\tau} = \left\{\kappa_1\tau_p x(t) - \frac{1}{2}\frac{[(1+a) + y]\, y}{1+y^2}\right\}$$

In order for $\frac{dy}{d\tau} > 0$ $\quad \kappa_1\tau_p x(t) > \frac{1}{2}\frac{[(1+a) + y]\, y}{1+y^2}$

Thus $2\kappa_1\tau_p(x_b+\Delta x)$ must be maintained for a long enough time to make the second factor less than $\kappa\tau_p(x_b)$. Thus one must let y increase from y(0) to $y_{u.s.}$ before the inertia will take over and send the response to y(1).

(d) This operation is legimate, but $E_{int}\cdot E_{ext}$ is not I_x and thus the equation does not apply in spite of the intuitive appeal.

13.12

Use Prob. 13.9, set $\gamma=0$; $\omega_m = \frac{2\pi c}{2d(n_0 + n_s|E_m|^2)} = \frac{\omega_{m0}}{1 + (n_2/n_0)|E_m|^2}$

where ω_{m0} = resonant frequency in the absence of any nonlinearity.

$$\dot{E}_m + \frac{1}{2\tau_p}\left\{1 - j\left[\frac{\omega_{m0}}{1 + (n_2/n_0)|E_m|^2} - \omega\right]2\tau_p\right\}E_m = \kappa E_x.$$

Define $E_s^2 = n_0/n_2$; $E_m/E_s = y$, $u = 2\kappa\tau_p E_x/E_s$, $\tau = t/\tau_p$.

$$\dot{y} + \frac{1}{2}\left\{1 - j\left[\frac{\omega_{m0} - \omega|y|^2}{1 + |y|^2}\right]2\tau_p\right\}y = \frac{x}{2};\ \dot{y} + \frac{1}{2}\left\{1 - j\, 2\omega\tau_p\left[\frac{(\omega_{m0}/\omega - 1) - |y|^2}{1 + |y|^2}\right]\right\}y = \frac{x}{2};$$

Now $\omega\tau_p \triangleq Q$; $\frac{\omega_{m0}}{\omega} - 1 \triangleq \delta$; $\boxed{\dot{y} + \frac{1}{2}\left\{1 - j\, 2Q\left[\frac{\delta - |y|^2}{1 + |y|^2}\right]\right\}y = \frac{x}{2}.}$ 1.

Set $\dot{y} = 0$ and multiply by complex conjugate:

$$\left[1 + Q^2 \frac{(\delta - |y|^2)^2}{(1 + |y|^2)^2}\right] |y|^2 = |x|^2.$$

Let $z = |y|^2$; then $|x|^2 = \dfrac{(1 + z)^2 + Q^2(\delta - z)^2}{(1 + z)^2} z$ 2

Only if δ is positive will the presence of the internal field reduce the braces{ } in Eq. 1 (since z is always positive) to minimize the value of the external field x^2 required.

$$\frac{d|x|^2}{dz} = 0 \text{ or}$$

$$(1 + z)\{(1 + z)^2 + Q^2(\delta - z)^2 + 2z(1 + z) - 2Q^2z(\delta - z)\} - [2z(1 + z)^2 + 2zQ^2(\delta - z)^2] = 0;$$

or: $(1+z)^3 + (1 - z)Q^2(\delta - z)^2 + 2z(1+z)^2 - 2zQ^2(\delta - z)(1+z) = 0$

Combine terms:

$$(1+\delta^2Q^2) - (Q^2(2+2\delta+\delta^2)-3)z + 3(Q^2+1)z^2 + (Q^2+1)z^3 = 0;$$

By Descartes rule of signs, there are 2 positive solutions if:

$$\boxed{Q^2(2+2\delta+\delta^2)>3.}$$

If we assume δ small, then $Q > \sqrt{3/2}$. The following graph used δ=0.3 and Q =10.

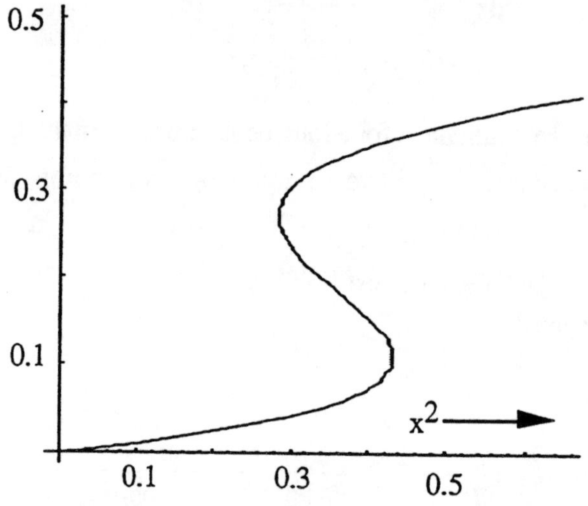

13.13

$$E_{m,p,q} = A_{m,p,q} \frac{w_0}{w(z)} H_m\left(\frac{\sqrt{2}u}{w}\right) H_p\left(\frac{\sqrt{2}x}{w}\right) \exp\left[-\left(\frac{x^2+y^2}{w^2}\right)\right] \exp -j \frac{kr^2}{2R(z)}$$

$$\times \sin\left[kz - (1+m+p) \tan^{-1}\frac{z}{z_0}\right]$$

where $kd - (1+m+p) \tan^{-1}\dfrac{d}{z_0} = q\pi = \theta_{m,p}(d)$

$$\int_{-\infty}^{+\infty} H_m \frac{\sqrt{2}x}{w} H_{m'} \frac{\sqrt{2}x}{w} e^{-2x^2/w^2} dx = \frac{w}{\sqrt{2}x} \int_{-\infty}^{+\infty} H_m(u) H_{m'}(u) e^{-u^2} du = I_x$$

where $u = \sqrt{2}x/w$; $u^2 = 2x^2/w$; $du = \sqrt{2}/w)$ dx

$I_x = \frac{w(z)}{\sqrt{2}} 2^m\, m!\sqrt{\pi}\, \delta_{m,m'}$

Do the same with y; notice that the $w^2(z)$ will cancel that term in $E_{m,p,q}$; to obtain:

$$I = A^2_{m,p,q} \cdot \left(\frac{\pi w_0^2}{2}\right) 2^{m+p}\, m!p![\delta_{m,m'}]\,[\delta_{p,p'}] \left\{\int_0^d \sin^2\theta_{mp}(z)\, dz \approx \int_0^d \sin^2 kz dz = \frac{d}{2}\right\}$$

$$\therefore \qquad I = A^2_{mpq} \frac{\pi w_0^2}{2} 2^{m+p}\, m!p! \frac{d}{2} = 1$$

$$A_{mpq} = \left\{\frac{1}{Vol.}\right\}^{1/2} \left\{\frac{1}{2^{m+p-1}} \frac{1}{m!} \frac{1}{p!}\right\}^{1/2} \text{ where } \frac{\pi w_0^2}{2} d/2 = \text{Volume of TEM}_{00q} \text{ mode.}$$

13.14

Make the abbreviations:

$y = E(t)/E_s$, $r = f\gamma_0(c/n)\tau_p = \gamma_0/\alpha$; E_s= saturation field; and $y_f = r - 1$, the final value of the laser field under steady state conditions. Eq. 13.6.18 becomes:

$$\frac{dy}{dt} = \frac{1}{2\tau_p}\left[\frac{y_f^2 - y^2}{1 + y^2}\right] y;$$

Use a partial fraction expansion:

$$\frac{1}{y_f^2}\left\{\frac{dy}{y} - \frac{(y_f^2+1)}{2}\left[\frac{dy}{y - y_f} + \frac{dy}{y + y_f}\right]\right\} = \frac{dt}{2\tau_p}$$

Integrate, collect terms, pick an initial value of the field to be $y_i = 10^{-6}$:

$$\boxed{\ln\left\{\frac{y^2}{y_f^2}\frac{y_f^2}{y_i^2}\left(\frac{1 - y_i^2/y_f^2}{1 - y^2/y_f^2}\right)^2\right\} = (r - 1)\frac{t}{\tau_p}}$$

(b) For $y/y_f = 0.9$, $r=3$, and $y_i = 10^{-6}$, $t/\tau_p = 10.2$

14.1 -

Since it is a 3p–2s transition, we know that 3p tells us n = 3, p $\rightarrow l = 1$ for the upper state and 2s indicates n = 2, $l = 0$ for the lower one. The normalized radial wavefunctions $R_{n,l}$ are: (See Merzbacker, page 196 or Eisberg, page 305):

$$R_{31} = \frac{4\sqrt{2}}{27\sqrt{3}}\left(\frac{1}{a_0}\right)^{3/2}\left(1 - \frac{r}{6a_0}\right)\left(\frac{r}{a_0}\right)\exp[-r/3a_0] \qquad (3p)$$

$$R_{20} = \frac{1}{\sqrt{2}}\left(\frac{1}{a_0}\right)^{3/2}\left(1 - \frac{r}{2a_0}\right)\exp[-r/2a_0] \qquad (2s)$$

where a_0= radius of the first Bohr orbit = 0.527×10^{-10} m

Now we compute the dipole moment between the two states and that is given by: (See Merzbacker p. 480 for details)

$$eR_{31}^{20} = e\int_0^\infty (R_{20}\, r\, R_{31})\, r^2\, dr = \frac{4}{27\sqrt{3}}\, ea_0\left[\int_0^\infty (1 - x/6)\,(1 - x/2)\, x^4\, e^{-5x/6}\, dx = I\right]$$

where $x = r/a_0$ and $I = \int_0^\infty [x^4 - (2/3)x^5 + (1/12)\, x^6]\, e^{-5x/6}\, dx$

$$I_n = \int_0^\infty x^n e^{-ax}\, dx = \Gamma(n+1)/a^{n+1} = \frac{n!}{a^{n+1}};\quad I = 35.832;$$

$eR_{31}^{20} = 2.5843 \times 10^{-29}$ c-m. = (7.83 Debye); $\lambda_0 = 6562.86$Å; $\nu = 4.5681 \times 10^{+14}$ Hz;

$$A_{21} = \frac{64\pi^4}{3}\left[\frac{1}{4\pi\varepsilon_0}\right]\left[\frac{\nu}{c}\right]^3 \frac{g_{2s}}{g_{3p}}\,\frac{|eR_{31}^{20}|^2}{h} = 2.24 \times 10^{+7}\ \text{sec}^{-1}$$

14.2

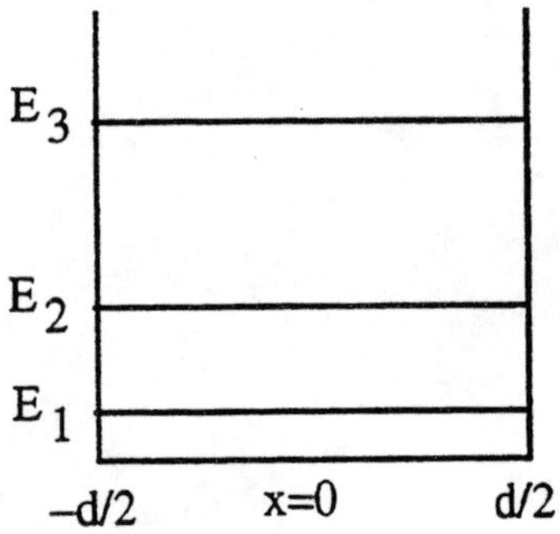

$$\frac{d^2\psi}{dx^2} + \frac{2m^*}{\hbar^2}\psi = 0$$

This leads to even and odd functions

$$\Psi_n(x) = \begin{cases} \sqrt{\frac{2}{d}}\cos\frac{n\pi x}{d} & (n = 1,3,5\ \text{(odd)}) \\ \sqrt{\frac{2}{d}}\sin\frac{n\pi x}{d} & (n = 2,4,6\ \text{(even)}) \end{cases}$$

(See Merzbacker p. 254 or solve it directly.)

$\mu_{m,n} = e\int_{-d/2}^{+d/2} \Psi_m\, x\, \Psi_n\, dx$ ($\neq 0$ only between states with opposite parity)

$$\mu_{2,1} = \frac{2e}{d}\int_{-d/2}^{+d/2} \sin\frac{2\pi x}{d}\, x \cos\frac{\pi x}{d}\, dx$$

$$\sin\frac{m\pi x}{d}\cos\frac{n\pi x}{d} = \frac{1}{2}\left[\sin(m+n)\frac{\pi x}{d} + \sin(m-n)\frac{\pi x}{d}\right]$$

$$\mu_{21} = \frac{ed}{\pi^2} \int_{-\pi/2}^{\pi/2} \theta \, (\sin 3\theta + \sin \theta) \, d\theta \; ; \; \theta = \frac{\pi x}{d}$$

$$\int \theta \sin a\theta = \frac{\sin a\theta}{a^2} - \frac{\theta \cos a\theta}{a}; \text{ Thus } \mu_{21} = \frac{16}{9\pi^2}(ed)$$

14.3

The gain coefficient is related to the imaginary part of the susceptibility by:

$$\gamma(\nu) = \frac{-k\chi''}{n^2} = \frac{2\pi\nu}{n^2 x} \cdot \frac{\mu_{21}^2 T_2}{3\varepsilon_0 \hbar} \frac{N_2 - N_1}{1 + (\omega_{21} - \omega)^2 \, T_2^2 + 4\Omega^2 T_2 \tau} \tag{1}$$

Convert to frequency units and get rid of $\hbar$

$$\gamma(\nu) = \frac{2\pi\nu}{n^2 c} \cdot \frac{4\pi}{4\pi\varepsilon_0} \frac{\mu_{21}^2 T_2}{\frac{h}{2\pi}} \frac{N_2 - N_1}{1 + (\nu_{21} - \nu)^2 4\pi^2 T_2^2 + 4\Omega^2 T_2 \tau}$$

Re-arrange some of the terms:

$$\gamma(\nu) = \frac{16\pi^3 \nu}{n^2 3c} \left(\frac{1}{4\pi\varepsilon_0}\right) \frac{\mu_{21}^2}{h} \frac{T_2}{4\pi^2 T_2^2} \frac{N_2 - N_1}{(\nu_{21} - \nu)^2 + \left(\frac{1}{2\pi T_2}\right)^2 + \frac{\Omega^2 \tau}{\pi^2 T_2}}$$

and indentify $\Delta\nu_h = \left(\frac{1}{\pi T_2}\right)$ which is the answer to part (a). The gain coefficient becomes:

$$\gamma(\nu) = \frac{8\pi^3 \nu}{n^2 3c} \left(\frac{1}{4\pi\varepsilon_0}\right) \frac{\mu_{21}^2}{h} (N_2 - N_1) \frac{\Delta\nu_h = \left(\frac{1}{\pi T_2}\right)}{\left\{2\pi \left[(\nu_{21} - \nu)^2 + \left(\frac{\Delta\nu_h}{2}\right)^2 + \frac{\Omega^2 \tau}{\pi^2 T_2}\right]\right\}} \tag{2}$$

For a weak field $\Omega \rightarrow 0$ and the last factor in (2) becomes the Lorentzian lineshape:

$$g(\nu) = \frac{\Delta\nu_h}{2\pi \left[(\nu_{21} - \nu)^2 + \left(\frac{\Delta\nu_h}{2}\right)^2\right]} \tag{3}$$

The expression is: $$A_{21} = \frac{64\pi^4 \nu^3}{3c^3} \left[\frac{1}{4\pi\varepsilon_0}\right] \frac{\mu_{21}^2}{h} = \frac{8\pi\nu^2}{c^2} \left\{\frac{8\pi^3 \nu}{3c} \left[\frac{1}{4\pi\varepsilon_0}\right] \frac{\mu_{21}^2}{h}\right\} \tag{4}$$

The last brace is the pre-multiplier in (2). Hence, we express it in terms of the A coefficient

$$\therefore \quad \frac{8\pi^3 \nu}{3c} \left[\frac{1}{4\pi\varepsilon_0}\right] \frac{\mu_{21}^2}{h} = \frac{c^2}{8\pi\nu^2} A_{21} = A_{21} \frac{\lambda_0^2}{8\pi} \tag{5}$$

Thus (2) can be written in terms of the stimulated emission cross-section given by:

$$\therefore \quad \sigma(\nu_{21}) = A_{21} \frac{\lambda_0^2}{8\pi} \frac{2}{\pi\Delta\nu_n} = \frac{16\pi^3}{3} \left[\frac{1}{4\pi\varepsilon_0}\right] \frac{\mu_{21}^2}{h} T_2 \tag{7}$$

Thus, $\gamma(\nu)$ can be re-written as

$$\gamma(\nu) = A_{21}\frac{\lambda_0^2}{8\pi n^2}\cdot\frac{2}{\Delta\nu_h}\cdot\frac{\left(\frac{\Delta\nu_h}{2}\right)^2}{(\nu_{21}-\nu)^2+\left(\frac{\Delta\nu_h}{2}\right)^2+\frac{\Omega^2\tau}{\pi^2 T_2}} \tag{8}$$

Define a "hole width" = $\Delta\nu_H$ by:

$$\left(\frac{\Delta\nu_H}{2}\right)^2 = \left(\frac{\Delta\nu_h}{2}\right)^2 + \frac{\Omega^2\tau}{\pi_2 T_2} = \left(\frac{\Delta\nu_h}{2}\right)^2 + \frac{\Omega^2\tau\Delta\nu_h}{\pi} \tag{9}$$

$$\therefore \quad \Delta\nu_H^2 = \Delta\nu_h^2\left(1+\frac{4\Omega^2\tau}{\pi\Delta\nu_h}\right) \tag{10}$$

Expanding the last term in the parenthesis:

$$\frac{4\Omega^2\tau}{\pi\Delta\nu_h} = \frac{4\mu_{21x}^2 E_x^2}{4\hbar^2}\cdot\tau\cdot\frac{1}{\pi\Delta\nu_h} \tag{11}$$

Now $I = \frac{E_x^2}{2\eta_0}$ and hence $E_x^2 = \frac{2I}{c\varepsilon_0}$

$$\therefore \quad \frac{4\Omega^2\tau}{\pi\Delta\nu_h} = \left\{\frac{16\pi^3\nu}{3c}\left(\frac{1}{4\pi\varepsilon_0}\right)\frac{\mu_{21x}^2}{h}T_2\right\}\cdot\frac{2I\tau}{h\nu} \tag{12}$$

The quantity in the braces is σ, evaluated at line center:

$$\frac{4\Omega^2\tau}{\pi\Delta\nu_h} = \frac{2\tau\sigma}{h\nu}I = \frac{I}{I_s};\ I_s = \frac{h\nu}{\sigma\tau_2};\ \Delta\nu_H^2 = \Delta\nu_h^2\left(1+\frac{I}{I_s}\right) \tag{13}$$

Thus the density matrix approach yields precisely the same result as from Chapters 7 and 8.

14.4

The imaginary part of the susceptibility is given by:

$$\chi' = \left\{\frac{A_{21}\lambda_0^2}{16\pi^2 n^3}\left(\frac{g_2}{g_1}N_1 - N_2\right)\right\}\left\{\frac{\nu_0-\nu}{\pi\left[(\nu_0-\nu)^2+(\Delta\nu_h/2)^2\right]}\right\}$$

If we assume a "square" distribution of center frequencies due to a square velocity distribution, we can evaluate all integrals in terms of elementary functions:

Let: $p(f) = \frac{1}{\Delta\nu_s}$ for $\begin{array}{l} f > \nu_0 - \Delta\nu_s/2 = LL \\ f < \nu_0 + \Delta\nu_s/2 = UL \end{array}$ $=0$ otherwise

$$\therefore \quad \chi_D' = \left\{\frac{A_{21}\lambda_0^2}{16\pi^2 n^3}\left(\frac{g_2}{g_1}N_1 - N_2\right)\right\}\int_{LL}^{UL}\frac{(f-\nu)\,df}{\pi\left[(f-\nu)^2+(\Delta\nu_h/2)^2\right]}$$

$$= \left\{\frac{A_{21}\lambda_0^2}{16\pi^2 n^3}\left(\frac{g_2}{g_1}N_1 - N_2\right)\right\}\frac{1}{2\pi\Delta\nu_s}\int_{LL}^{UL}\frac{2u\,du}{u^2+a^2}$$

where $u = f - \nu$ and $a = \Delta\nu_h/2$

$$\therefore \chi_D' = \left\{\frac{A_{21}\lambda_0^2}{16\pi^2 n^3}\left(\frac{g_2}{g_1}N_1 - N_2\right)\right\}\frac{1}{2\pi\Delta\nu_s}\ \ln\left\{\frac{(\nu_0-\nu+\Delta\nu_s/2)^2+(\Delta\nu_h,2)^2}{(\nu_0-\nu-\Delta\nu_s/2)^2+(\Delta\nu_h/2)^2}\right\}$$

Note: If $\nu_0 - \nu = \Delta\nu_h/2;\ \chi_L' = \{\ \ \}\ \dfrac{1}{\pi\Delta\nu_n}$

If $\Delta\nu_s = \Delta\nu_h$ and $\nu_0 - \nu = (\Delta\nu_s/2);\ \dfrac{\chi_D'}{\chi_L'} = \dfrac{(\ln 5/2\pi\Delta\nu_s)}{(1/\pi\Delta\nu_n)} = \dfrac{\ln 5}{2} = 0.805$

14.5

(a) $\Delta\nu_n\ (\text{natural}) = \dfrac{1}{2\pi}(A_2 + A_1) = 10.1$ MHz

(b) 3 Torr $\Delta\nu_n = 366.6$ MHz $= 1/(\pi T_2)$; $\therefore T_2 = 0.868$ nsec

(c) $\Delta\nu_D \approx 1.6\times10^{+9}$ Hz $= (33.3 + 111.p) \times 10^6$; $\therefore$ p = 14.1 Torr

(d) Since $A_{21} = 6.56\times10^6\ s^{-1}$, then $\mu_{21} = 7.68^{-30}$ coulomb–meter

$\therefore\ \mu_{21} = 2.3D = e\Delta x;\ \Delta x = 0.478$Å

(e) $I = 100W/cm^2 = 10^6 W/m^2 = E^2/(2\eta_0)$; $E = 27.5$ kV/m

$\Omega/(2\pi) = \mu E/2h = 159.1$ MHz; flopping period $= 2\pi/\Omega = 6.28$ nsec

$T_2 << \tau$ (flopping), and hence the rate equation approach is valid.

14.6

a (1) The $^2S_{1/2}$ is the ground state: $\therefore J_1 = 1/2$ and thus $g_1 = 2$; $^2P_{3/2}$ is the upper state

$\therefore$ $J_2 = 3/2$ and $g_2 = 4$

$\lambda_0 = 5889.95$Å; $\therefore \bar{\nu} = 16{,}978.07\ cm^{-1}$; $\nu = 508.99$ THz: $\Delta\nu_h = 1$ GHz

a (2) $B_{12} = \dfrac{2}{3}\cdot\dfrac{\pi^2}{\varepsilon_r\cdot\varepsilon_0}\dfrac{\pi_{21}^2}{h^2}$; but $g_1B_{12} = g_2B_{21}$ and $B_{21} = \dfrac{g_1}{g_2}B_{12}$

$$B_{21} = \frac{g_1}{g_2}\left\{\frac{2}{3}\frac{\pi^2}{\varepsilon_r\cdot\varepsilon_0}\frac{\mu_{21}^2}{h^2}\right\} = \frac{(c/n)^2}{8\pi h\nu^3}A_{21};\ A_{21} = \frac{g_1}{g_2}\left\{\frac{64\pi^4}{\varepsilon_r\cdot\varepsilon_0}\left[\frac{1}{4\pi\varepsilon_0}\right]\frac{\nu^3}{(c/n)^2}\frac{\mu_{21}^2}{h^2}\right\}$$

For the numbers of this problem

$6.9\times10^{+64}\ \mu_{21}^2 = 6.3\times10^{+7}$; $\mu_{21}^2 = 9.1^{-58}(c\text{–}m)^2$; $\boxed{\mu_{21x} = 1.74\times10^{-29}\ (c\text{–}m)}$

a (3) $\sigma_{SE} = A_{21}\dfrac{\lambda^2}{8\pi}\left[g(\nu_0) = \dfrac{2}{\pi\Delta\nu_h}\right] = \boxed{5.53\times10^{-12}\ cm^2}$; $\sigma_{ab} = (g_2/g_1)\sigma_{SE}$

a (4) $\alpha_0 = 16.59$ nepers/cm $= 72.05$ dB/cm; $\boxed{T = e^{-\alpha l} = 6.238\times10^{-8} = G_0}$

Now let's return to Sec. 9.6; $\boxed{w_s = h\nu/\sigma(1+g_2/g_1) = h\nu/3\sigma = 20.3\ nJ/cm^2}$

b (1) $I\tau_p = w_s$; $I_s = 13.54\ w/cm^2$; $\boxed{E_{0x} = 101.0\ V/cm = 10.1\ kV/m}$

b (2) Assume $u_1 = 1$; $e^{u_2} - 1 = g_0(e^{u_1} - 1) = 1.072\times10^{-7}$

$u_2 = 1.07\times10^{-7}$, $w_2 = 2.17\ \text{fJ/cm}^2$; $\therefore$ $\boxed{T = u_2/u_1 = 1.07\times10^{-7} = 1.72 \times \text{part a(4)}}$

c (1) $\Omega = \dfrac{\mu_{21x}E_{0x}}{2\hbar}$; $\dfrac{\Omega}{2\pi} = \dfrac{\mu_{21x}E_{0x}}{2\hbar} = 132.6$ MHz

c (2) $\Omega\tau_p = \pi$; $\mu_{21x}E_{0x} = h/\tau_p$; $\boxed{E_{0x} = 25.4\ \text{kV/m}}$

c (3) $I = 85.5\ \text{W/cm}^2$ $\boxed{w_{pulse} = 0.128\ \mu\text{J/cm}^2}$

c(4) The total energy. = w_{pulse} + (Number of atoms) $\times$ [$|C_2(t)|^2$] must be conserved. But since $C_2(t=\tau_p) = 0 = C_2(t=0)$, there is no attenuation.

c(5)
$$\frac{\mu_{21x}}{\hbar}\int_{-\infty}^{\infty} E_0 \operatorname{sech}(t/\tau_p)\, dt = 2\pi = \frac{\mu_{21x}\tau_p E_0}{\hbar}\int_{-\infty}^{\infty} \operatorname{sech} x\, dx$$

$$\int_{-\infty}^{\infty} \operatorname{sech} x\, dx = 2\tan^{-1}[e^x]\Big|_{-\infty}^{\infty} = 2\pi;\ \text{or}\ \frac{\mu_{21x}\tau_p E_0}{\hbar}\cdot 2\pi = 2\pi$$

$\therefore$
$$\boxed{E_0 = \frac{\hbar}{\mu_{21x}\tau_p} = 4.04\ \text{kV/m}}$$

$$w = \int_{-\infty}^{\infty}\frac{E_{0x}^2}{2\eta_0}\tau_p \sec^2 x dx = \frac{E_{0x}^2}{2\eta_0}\tau_p\left\{\tanh x \Big|_{-\infty}^{+\infty} = 2\right\} = 0.649\ \mu\text{J/cm}^2$$

14.7

$$\frac{\partial(\rho_{21} + \rho_{21}^*)}{\partial t} + \left(\frac{1}{T_2}\right)(\rho_{21} + \rho_{21}^*) + j\omega_{21}(\rho_{21} - \rho_{21}^*) = 0 \qquad (1)$$

$$(\rho_{21} - \rho_{21}^*) = -\frac{1}{j\omega_{21}}\left\{\frac{\partial}{\partial t}(\rho_{21} + \rho_{21}^*) + \left(\frac{1}{T_2}\right)(\rho_{21} + \rho_{21}^*)\right\} \qquad (2)$$

$$\frac{\partial}{\partial t}(\rho_{21} - \rho_{21}^*) + \frac{1}{T_2}(\rho_{21} - \rho_{21}^*) + j\omega_{21}(\rho_{21} + \rho_{21}^*) = \frac{-2j\mu_{21x}E_x}{\hbar}(\rho_{22} - \rho_{11}) \qquad (3)$$

$$\frac{\partial^2}{\partial t^2}(\rho_{21} + \rho_{21}^*) + \left(\frac{1}{T_2}\right)\frac{\partial}{\partial t}(\rho_{21} + \rho_{21}^*) + j\omega_{21}\frac{\partial}{\partial t}(\rho_{21} - \rho_{21}^*) = 0 \qquad (4)$$

Substitute (3) into (4)

$$\frac{\partial^2}{\partial t^2}(\rho_{21} + \rho_{21}^*) + \left(\frac{1}{T_2}\right)\frac{\partial}{\partial t}(\rho_{21} + \rho_{21}^*)$$
$$+ j\omega_{21}\left[-\frac{1}{T_2}(\rho_{21} - \rho_{21}^*) - j\omega_{21}(\rho_{21} + \rho_2^*) - \frac{2j\mu_{21x}E_{0x}}{\hbar}(\rho_{22} - \rho_{11})\right] = 0$$

After re-writing and re-arranging, we have:

$$\frac{\partial^2}{\partial t^2}(\rho_{21} + \rho_{21}^*)\left(\frac{1}{T_2}\right)\frac{\partial}{\partial t}(\rho_{21} + \rho_{21}^*)$$
$$+ \omega_{21}^2(\rho_{21} + \rho_{21}^*) - j\frac{\omega_{21}}{T_2}(\rho_{21} - \rho_{21}^*) = -\omega_{21}\frac{2\mu_{21x}E_x}{\hbar}(\rho_{22} - \rho_{11}) \qquad (5)$$

Now use (2) into (5)

$$\frac{\partial^2(\rho_{21}+\rho_{21}^*)}{\partial t^2}+\left(\frac{2}{T_2}\right)\frac{\partial}{\partial t}(\rho_{21}+\rho_{21}^*)+\left[\left(\frac{1}{T_2}\right)^2+\omega_{21}^2\right](\rho_{21}+\rho_{21}^*)$$
$$=-2\omega_{21}\frac{\mu_{21x}E_x}{\hbar}(\rho_{22}-\rho_{11})$$

Multiply by $N\mu_{21x}$ and remember $P_{ax}=N\mu_{21x}(\rho_{21}+\rho_{21}^*)$ and $\Delta N(t)=N(\rho_{22}-\rho_{11})$ to obtain:

$$\boxed{\frac{\partial^2 P_{ax}}{\partial t^2}+\left(\frac{2}{T_2}\right)\frac{\partial P_{ax}}{\partial t}+\left[\left(\frac{1}{T_2}\right)^2+\omega_{21}^2\right]P_{ax}=-2\omega_{21}\frac{\mu_{21x}E_x}{\hbar}\Delta N(t)} \qquad (6)$$

Start with the equation for the diagonal elements:

$$\frac{\partial}{\partial t}[(\rho_{22}-\rho_{11})-(\rho_{22}^0-\rho_{11}^0)]+\frac{[(\rho_{22}-\rho_{11})-(\rho_{22}^0-\rho_{11}^0)]}{\tau}=-j\frac{2\mu_{21x}E_x}{\hbar}(\rho_{21}-\rho_{21}^*)$$

and use (2) for RHS: $\rho_{21}-\rho_{21}^*=\frac{-1}{j\omega_{21}}\left[\frac{\partial}{\partial t}(\rho_{21}+\rho_{21}^*)+\left(\frac{1}{T_2}\right)(\rho_{21}+\rho_{21}^*)\right]$

Multiply by N and identify as above:

$$\frac{\partial}{\partial t}(\Delta N-\Delta N^0)+\frac{\Delta N-\Delta N^0}{\tau}=-j2\frac{E_x}{\hbar}\left\{\frac{-1}{j\omega_{21}}\left[\frac{\partial}{\partial t}\left(N\mu_{21x}(\rho_{21}+\rho_{21}^*)\right)+\frac{1}{T_2}(N\mu_{21x}(\rho_{21}+\rho_{21}^*))\right]\right\}$$

$$\boxed{\frac{\partial}{\partial t}(\Delta N-\Delta N^0)+\frac{\Delta N-\Delta N^0}{\tau}=\frac{2\mathbf{E}(t)\cdot}{\hbar\omega_{21}}\left\{\frac{\partial \mathbf{P_a}}{\partial t}+\frac{1}{T_2}\mathbf{P_a}\right\}} \qquad (7)$$

Note $\mathbf{E}\cdot(\partial\mathbf{P_a}/\partial t+\mathbf{P_a}/T_2)<0$ for gain. The energy is either in the field or in the atoms, and to increase the field requires that ΔN decrease and thus the L.H.S. must be negative and hence so also goes the R.H.S. Now $\dot{P}_a\sim\omega P_a \gg (1/T_2)P_a$; ignore the last term in (7).

$$E_x=\frac{E_{0x}}{2}(e^{j\omega t}+e^{-j\omega t})$$

$$P_a=\frac{P_{0x}}{2}e^{j\omega t}+\frac{P_{0x}^*}{2}e^{-j\omega t};\ \dot{P}_a=j\omega\left(\frac{P_{0x}}{2}e^{j\omega t}-\frac{P_{0x}^*}{2}e^{-j\omega t}\right)$$

$$\Delta N=\Delta N_0+\frac{\Delta N_2}{2}e^{j2\omega t}+\frac{\Delta N_2}{2}e^{-j2\omega t}$$

$$\mathbf{E}\cdot\dot{\mathbf{P}}_a=j\omega\frac{E_{0x}}{4}(P_{0x}-P_{0x}^*)+j\omega\frac{E_{0x}P_{0x}}{4}e^{j2\omega t}-j\omega\frac{E_{0x}P_{0x}^*}{4}e^{-j2\omega t}$$

Evaluate the DC or ($\omega=0$ frequency) terms in Eq. 7 ($\partial/\partial t=0$)

$$\Delta N_0=\Delta N^0+\frac{2\tau}{\hbar\omega_{21}}[\langle E\cdot\dot{P}_{ax}\rangle]=\Delta N^0+j\frac{\omega\tau}{\hbar\omega_{21}}\frac{E_{0x}}{2}(P_{0x}-P_{0x}^*)$$

Terms varying at $2\omega \gg 1/\tau$ so drop the latter term.

$$j2\omega\frac{\Delta N_2}{2}=j\frac{2\omega}{\hbar\omega_{21}}\frac{E_{0x}P_{0x}}{4}$$

$$\therefore\ \Delta N_2=\frac{1}{\hbar\omega_{21}}\frac{E_{0x}P_{0x}}{2}\qquad \therefore\ \Delta N_2^*=\frac{E_{0x}P_{0x}^*}{2\hbar\omega_{21}}$$

Now expand the RHS of (6):

$$E\cdot\Delta N = \frac{E_{0x}}{2}\left(e^{j\omega t} + e^{-j\omega t}\right)\cdot\left(\Delta N_0 + \frac{\Delta N_2}{2} e^{j2\omega t} + \frac{\Delta N_2^*}{2} e^{-j2\omega t}\right)$$

and pick out terms varying as $e^{+j\omega t}$ so as to obtain a resonance for P_{0x}.

$$\text{RHS } (e^{j\omega t}) = \frac{E_{0x}}{2}\Delta N_0\, e^{j\omega t} + \frac{E_{0x}}{4}\Delta N_2\, e^{j\omega t}$$

Substitute for ΔN_0 and ΔN_2 from above:

$$E\cdot\Delta N = \frac{E_{0x}}{2}\left[\Delta N_0 = \Delta N^0 + \frac{j\omega\tau}{\hbar\omega_{21}}\frac{E_{0x}}{2}(P_{0x} - P_{0x}^*)\right] e^{+j\omega t} + \frac{E_{0x}}{4}\left[\Delta N_2 = \frac{1}{\hbar\omega_{21}}\frac{E_{0x}P_{0x}}{2}\right] e^{+j\omega t}$$

Collect terms:

$$\left\{\left[\omega_{21}^2 - \omega^2 + \left(\frac{1}{T_2}\right)^2 + \frac{2\omega_{21}}{\hbar\omega_{21}}\frac{\mu_{21}^2 E_{0x}^2}{8\hbar}\right] + \frac{2j\omega}{T_2}\right\} P_{0x} e^{j\omega t}$$

$$= -2\omega_{21}\frac{\mu_{21}^2 E_{0x}}{2\hbar}\left[\Delta N^0 + \frac{j\omega\tau}{\hbar\omega_{21}}\frac{E_{0x}}{2}(P_{0x} - P_{0x}^*)\right] e^{j\omega t}$$

Cancel the $e^{j\omega t}$ factor and collect terms:

$$\left\{\left[\omega_{21}^2 - \omega^2 + \left(\frac{1}{T_2}\right)^2 + \Omega^2\right] + j\,\frac{2\omega}{T_2}\right\} P_{0x} = 2\omega_{21}\frac{\mu_{21}^2 E_{0x}}{2}\Delta N^0 - j2\omega\tau\frac{\mu_{21}^2 E_{0x}}{4\hbar^2}(P_{0x} - P_{0x}^*)$$

$$\boxed{\left\{\left[\omega_{21}^2 - \omega^2 + \left(\frac{1}{T_2}\right)^2 + \Omega^2\right] + \frac{2j\omega}{T_2}\right\} P_{0x} + j2\omega\Omega^2(P_{0x} - P_{0x}^*) = \frac{2\omega_{21}\mu_{21}^2 E_{0x}\Delta N^0}{2\hbar}} \qquad (8)$$

Eq. 8 is close enough: Resonance is determined by real part on LHS vanishing.

$$\omega^2 = \omega_{21}^2 + \left(\frac{1}{T_2}\right)^2 + \Omega^2 = \omega_0^2 + \Omega^2 \qquad \boxed{\omega - \omega_0 = \frac{1}{2}\frac{\Omega^2}{\omega_0}} \qquad (9)$$

which indicates a small $(\text{field})^2$ shift in the resonant frequency. For the nit-pickers, the following establishes that result more rigorously.

Equation 8 is of the form:

$$(a + jb)\, P_{0x} + jc(P_{0x} - P_{0x}^*) = K \text{ (real)} \qquad (10a)$$

$$\therefore \quad (a - jb)\, P_{0x}^* - jc(P_{0x}^* - P_{0x}) = K\,; \qquad (10b)$$

where $a = \omega_{21}^2 - \omega^2 + \left(\frac{1}{T_2}\right)^2 + \Omega^2$; [b,c are positive; a may be negative]

Subtract:

$$a(P_{0x} - P_{0x}^*) + jb(P_{0x} + P_{0x}^*) = 0 \Rightarrow (a + jb)P_{0x} - (a - jb)P_{0x}^* = 0;$$

or

$$P_{0x}^* = \frac{(a+jb)}{(a-jb)} P_{0x} \quad \therefore P_{0x} - P_{0x}^* = \frac{-j2b}{a-jb} P_{0x} \text{ and Eq. 9 becomes}$$

$$\left\{(a+jb) + \frac{2bc}{a-jb}\right\} P_{0x} = K \text{ or } \left\{(a+jb) + \frac{2bc(a+jb)}{a^2+b^2}\right\} P_{0x} = K$$

$$\left\{a\left(1+\frac{2bc}{a^2+b^2}\right)+jb\left(1+\frac{2bc}{a^2+b^2}\right)\right\}P_{0x}=K$$

maximum value of P_{0x} is when

$$a=\omega_{21}^2-\omega^2+\left(\frac{1}{T_2}\right)^2+\Omega^2=0 \text{ which is the same as (9) above.}$$

14.8

$$\frac{dA(z)}{dz}=\frac{\alpha}{2}\sin A(z);$$

or $$I=\int_{A_0}^{A(z)}\frac{dA(z)}{\sin A(z)}=\int_0^z\frac{\alpha}{2}dz; \text{ make the substitutions suggested:}$$

$$I=\int_{A_0}^{A(z)}\frac{\sec^2[A(z)/2]\,d[A(z)]}{2\tan[A(z)]}=\int_{\tan A_0}^{\tan A(z)}\frac{du}{u}=\int_0^z\frac{\alpha}{2}dz;$$

$$I=\ln\left\{\frac{\tan[A(z)/2]}{\tan[A_0/2]}\right\}=\frac{\alpha z}{2} \text{ or}$$

$$\boxed{A(z)=2\tan^{-1}\left\{\tan[A_0/2]\,e^{\alpha z/2}\right\}}$$

If α is positive, then $\{\ \}\to\infty$, $\tan^{-1}\{\}\to(2q+1)\pi/2$, and thus $A(z)\to(2q+1)\pi$

If α is negative, then $\{\ \}\to 0$, $\tan^{-1}\{\}\to q\pi$, and $A(z)\to 2q\pi$

14.9

Rate equation approach (c.f. Chapter 8); Let $\phi = 1$

$$\frac{dN_2}{dt}=P_2-\frac{N_2}{\tau_2}-\frac{\sigma I}{h\nu}(N_2-N_1); \text{ and thus} \qquad N_2^0=P_2\tau_2$$

$$\frac{dN_1}{dt}=P_1-\frac{N_1}{\tau_1}+\frac{N_2}{\tau_2}+\frac{\sigma I}{h\nu}(N_2-N_1); \text{ and thus} \qquad N_1^0=(P_1+P_2)\tau_1$$

For steady state and $I \neq 0$

$$N_2=\frac{P_2\tau_2+\frac{\sigma I}{h\nu}[P_1+P_2]\tau_1}{\left[\frac{1}{\tau_2}+\frac{\sigma I}{h\nu}\right]\tau_2}=\frac{N_2^0+\frac{I}{I_s}N_1^0}{1+\frac{I}{I_s}} \text{ where } I_s=h\nu/\sigma\tau_2$$

$$N_2-N_2^0=-\frac{I}{I_s}\frac{N_2^0-N_1^0}{1+I/I_s}=N_2(0);\ N_1(0)=N_1^0$$

(Since it does not make any difference whether the population comes from above by spontaneous or by stimulated emission for $\phi = 1$)

When the intensity returns to zero and $I = 0$, the populations recover as:

$$\left.\frac{dN_2}{dt}\right|_{t=0}=P_2-N_2(0);\quad \left.\frac{dN_1}{dt}\right|_{t=0}=P_1-\frac{N_1(0)}{\tau_1}+\frac{N_2(0)}{\tau_2};$$

Now: $N_2(0) = -\frac{I}{I_s}\frac{N_2^0 - N_1^0}{1 + \frac{I}{I_s}}$

$$\frac{d[N_2(0) - N_1(0)]}{dt}\Big|_{t=0} = P_2 - P_1 - \frac{2}{\tau_2}N_2(0) + \frac{N_1}{\tau_1} = \frac{2}{\tau_2}\left\{\frac{\frac{I}{I_s}(N_2^0 - N_1^0)}{1 + \frac{I}{I_s}}\right\}$$

The brace is $\Delta N(0)$ and hence the time constant for recovery $\boxed{\tau = (\tau_2/2)}$

For $\phi = 0$; $N_2^0 = P_2\tau_2$; $N_1^0 = P_1\tau_1$; $I_s = \frac{h\nu}{\sigma(\tau_1+\tau_2)}$

$$N_2 - N_2^0 = -\frac{(I/I_s)}{1 + (I/I_s)}\left[\frac{\tau_2}{\tau_1+\tau_2}\right](N_2^0 - N_1^0) = \Delta N_2(0)$$

$$N_1 - N_1^0 = +\frac{(I/I_s)}{1 + (I/I_s)}\left[\frac{\tau_2}{\tau_1+\tau_2}\right](N_2^0 - N_1^0) = \Delta N_1(0)$$

Using these relations, the recovery rate is $(\tau_1 + \tau_2)/2$. But since τ_1 is usually much less than τ_2, one obtains the same answer as above.

Chapter 15

15.1 and 15.2

Answers in text.

15.3

Rare gases have a closed shell. Hence, J = 0 for all in ground state. Now the metastable levels will also have J = 0 or J = 2, and since $\Delta J \neq 2$ and $J = 0 \leftarrow\!\!\!|\!\!\!\rightarrow J = 0$ (and triplet $\leftarrow\!\!\!|\!\!\!\rightarrow$ singlet for helium).

15.4

Gas	Name	E(cm^{-1})	E(eV)
He	2^3S (J=1)	159,850.318	19.82
	2^1S (J=0)	166,271.70	20.6
Ne	$^2P_{3/2}$ (J=2)	134,043.79	16.62
	$^2P_{1/2}$ (J=0)	134,820.59	16.72
Ar	$^2P_{3/2}$ (J=2)	93,143.8	11.55
	$^2P_{1/2}$ (J=0	94,553.71	11.72
Kr	$^2P_{3/2}$ (J=2)	79,972.54	9.91
	$^2P_{1/2}$ (J=0)	85,192.41	10.56
Xe	$^2P_{3/2}$ (J=2)	67,068.05	8.31
	$^2P_{1/2}$ (J=0)	76,197.29	9.45

15.5

The numbers are slightly off compared to those values given in the handbook of lasers.

15.6

See Section 15.3: The gain varies as $\dfrac{\gamma(\nu)}{N_{v'}\sigma(\nu)} = \dfrac{hcB}{kT_r}(2J+1)$ {other terms}. Hence, the gain coefficient varies inversely with rotational temperature which is closely coupled to the translational one.

15.7

According to Herzberg, the HF data is: $\omega_e = 4138.52$ cm^{-1}; $\omega_e x_e = 90.069$ cm^{-1}; $\omega_e y_e = 0.980$ cm^{-1}; $B_e = 20.939$ cm^{-1}; $\alpha_e = 0.770$. The rest is arithmetic:
$G(3) - G(2) = \overline{\nu}(3 \rightarrow 2)$

15.8

See Problem 10.17 for the calculation of σ: $\sigma(P) = 2.85 \times 10^{-17}$ cm^2; $\gamma = 0.05 = \Delta N\sigma$;

$$\therefore \quad (2J_u+1)\frac{hcB}{kT}\left\{N_{v'}\exp\left[-\frac{hcB}{kT_r}J_e(J_e+1)\right] - N_{v''}\exp\left[-\frac{hcB}{kT_r}J_e(J_e+1)\right]\right\} = \Delta N$$

$(2J_u+1)\frac{hcB}{kT} = 0.0478 \therefore\ \Delta N = 1.75\times10^{+15}$ cm^{-3};

$\{N_{v'}\, e^{-0.514} - N_{v''}\, e^{-0.563}\} = \frac{1.75^{+15}}{0.0478} = 3.65\times10^{+16}$ cm^3; $J_u = 21$, $J_L = 22$;

$\frac{hcB}{kT} J_u(J_u+1) = 0.514$; $\frac{hcB}{kT} J_e(J_e+1) = 0.514$;

$(0.598\, N_{v'} - 0.569\, N_{v''}) = 3.65\times10^{+16}$ cm^{-3}. Need another boundary, say
$N_{v'} + N_{v''} = 10^{17}$cm^{-3}; $\therefore$ $1.598\, N_{v'} = 1.365\times10^{+17}$ cm^{-3}; $N_{v'} = 8.54\times10^{+16}$ cm^{-3};
$1.569\, N_{v''} = 0.635^{+17}$ cm^{-3}; $N_{v''} = 4.04\times10^{+16}$ cm^{-3}. Ratio = 2.11

15.9

$E_1 = 0, J = 3/2$, Desig. = $5p^5\ {}^2P^0$; $E_2 = 7603.15$ cm^{-1}, $J = 1/2$, Desig.= $5p^5\ {}^2P^0$)}
Note: This is a $\Delta L = 0$ or a "forbidden" transition by electric dipole rules but allowed by the magnetic dipole route;

$\overline{\nu} = 7603.15$; $\quad\lambda = 1.3152\ \mu$m

15.10

See Sec. 15.3.6

$$\left\{\exp\left[\frac{-hcBJ(J+1)}{kT_r}\right] - \frac{N_{v''}}{N_{v'}}\exp\left[\frac{-hcB}{kT_r}(J+1)\,(J+2)\right]\right\} > 0;$$

where $N_{v''}/N_{v'} = \exp[\Delta G/kT_v]$

If $\quad T_v > 0$, $\quad \frac{N_{v''}}{N_{v'}} > 1 \rightarrow$ partial inversion

$\quad T_v < 0$, $\quad \frac{N_{v''}}{N_{v'}} < 1 \rightarrow$ total inversion

Solve the above for J to obtain Polanyi's result given in the text.

15.11

See reference cited. Let's compute the Doppler width of Hg(202); $\nu_0 = 1.183 \times 10^{+15}$ Hz;

$$\frac{\Delta\nu_D}{\nu_0} = \left[\frac{8kT\ \ln 2}{Mc^2}\right]^{1/2} = 9.9 \times 10^{-7};\ \therefore\ \Delta\nu_0 = 1.17 \times 10^{+9}\ \text{GHz};\ \Delta\bar{\nu}_D = 0.0391\ \text{cm}^{-1}.$$

Therefore, one should group transitions which fall within that width. Thus, the effective "stick heights" and effective distributions are:

Isotope	Relative abundance	Shift
204 + 199A + 201(a)	I = 19.2	$\Delta\bar{\nu} = -0.5$ cm^{-1}
202	I = 29.27	$\Delta\bar{\nu} = -0.337$
200 + 199B	I ≈ 34.7	$\Delta\bar{\nu} = -0.15$
198 + 201(b)	I = 14.6	$\Delta\bar{\nu} = 0$
196	I = 0.1	$\Delta\bar{\nu} = +0.137$
201(c)	I = 2.28	$\Delta\bar{\nu} = +0.229$

The composite lineshape is given below:

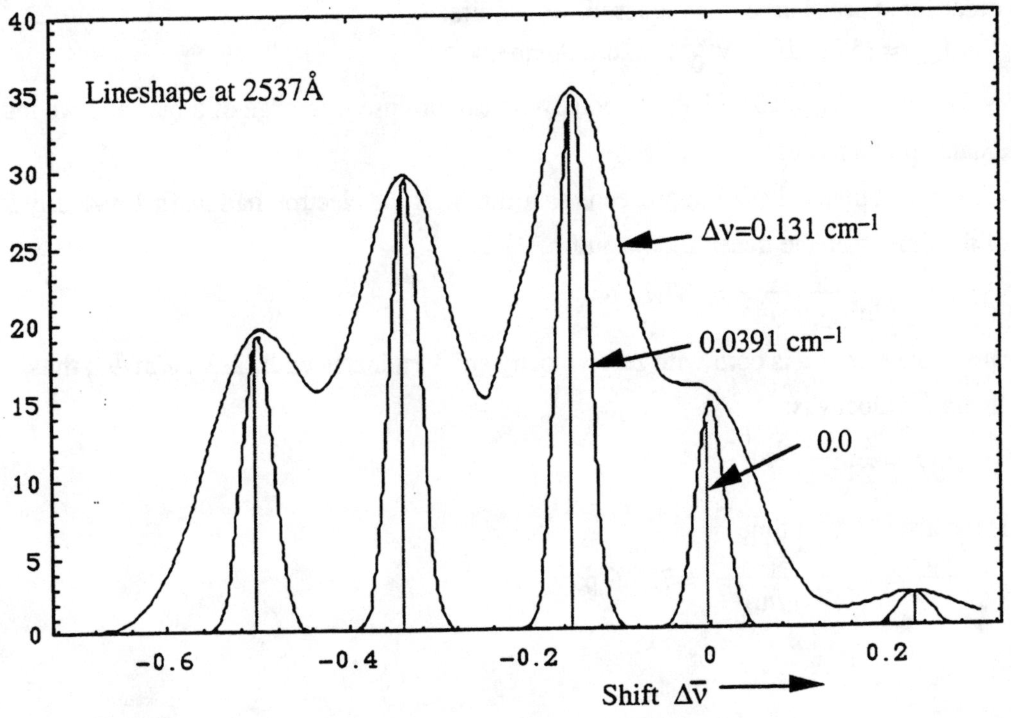

16.1

$$J = \eta \frac{P/A}{h\nu/e} = \frac{0.2 \times 10^3 \text{ w/cm}^2}{1.55} = 128.8 \text{ Amps/cm}^2 \text{ which is a lot!}$$

$$\nu = c/\lambda; \ \therefore \ J = 128.8 \left(\frac{\lambda(\text{Å})}{8000}\right)$$

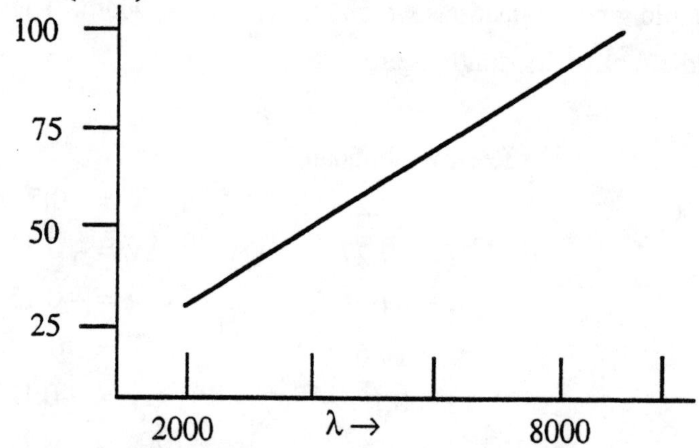

$$J_{CL.} = \frac{4}{9}\varepsilon_0 \left(\frac{2e}{m}\right)^{1/2} \frac{V_0^{3/2}}{d^2} = 2.33 \times 10^{-6} \frac{V_0^{3/2}}{d^2} \text{ A/cm}^2$$ (if d is in cm). For d = 2mm = 0.2cm

In order for space charge to be ignored, we require:

$$J_{CL.} = (5.82 \times 10^{-5}) V_0^{3/2} > 128.8 \text{ A/cm}^2,$$

Thus we require $V_0 > 16.95$ kV. Obviously we can not use this large of a bias and we must attenuate optical power.

The transit time calculation proceeds as follows. If the electron had its final velocity for all of the time, then the transit time woulf be:

$$\Delta t = \frac{d}{(2eV_{AK}/m)^{1/2}} = 37.73 \text{ ps}$$

However the electron is born with zero velocity and terminates with $(2eV_{AK}/m)^{1/2}$; thus, the average velocity is:

$$<v> = \frac{1}{2}\left(\frac{2eV_{AK}}{m}\right)^{1/2}$$

Thus the actual transit time is

$$\frac{d}{<v>} = \frac{2d}{(2eV_{AK}/m)^{1/2}} = 75.46 \text{ ps}$$

16.2

From part d of Problem 16.1: $\Delta t = 0.0755$ nsec which is the duration of the current spike carried by a single electron. Hence, its frequency spectrum extends to

$$\Delta\omega \approx \frac{1}{\Delta t} \text{ or } \Delta\nu = \frac{1}{2\pi\Delta t} = 2.1 \text{ GHz}$$

16.3

Consider the Gaussian pill-box shown around the sheet of charge shown on the diagram below:

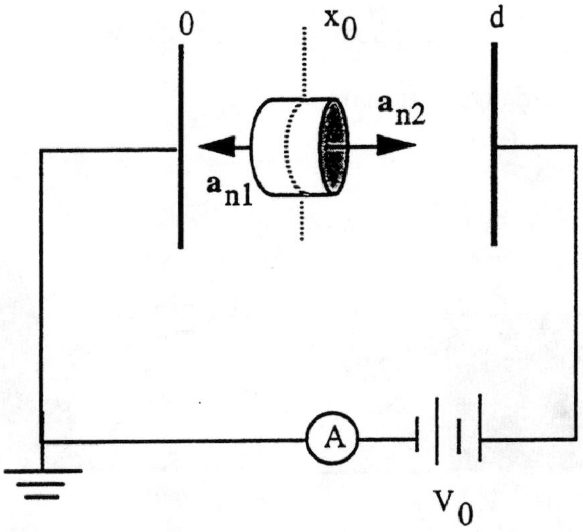

We start with Poisson's equation: $\nabla \cdot \mathbf{E} = \dfrac{\rho_s}{\varepsilon_0}\delta(x - x_0)$;

∴ $\quad \mathbf{E}_1 = A_1\mathbf{a}_x;\ x < x_0$ and $\mathbf{E}_2 = A_2\mathbf{a}_x;\ x > x_0$.

Boundary condition come from Gauss's law:

$\mathbf{E}_2\cdot\mathbf{a}_{n2} + \mathbf{E}_1\cdot\mathbf{a}_{n1} = (\rho_s/\varepsilon_0);\ \therefore\ A_2 - A_1 = -\rho_s/\varepsilon_0.$

The potential function for each region is the integral of the field and the two solutions must match at $x=x_0$:

$V(x < x_0) = -(A_1x + B_1)$; At $x = 0$, $V(0) = 0$; ∴ $B_1 = 0$;

$V(x > x_0) = -(A_2x + B_2)$; At $x = x_0$, $V(x = x_0^-) = V(x = x_0^+)$

∴ $\quad A_1x_0 = A_2x_0 + B_2$;

at $x = d$, $\quad V(x) = V_0 = -(A_2d + B_2)$;

$B_2 = -V_0 - A_2d;\ A_1x_0 = -A_2(d - x_0) - V_0$

and $\quad A_2 = -A_1 - (\rho_s/\varepsilon_0)$

∴ $\quad A_1d = -V_0 + (\rho_s/\varepsilon_0)(d-x_0)$ and $A_2 = \dfrac{-V_0}{d} - (\rho_s/\varepsilon_0)\cdot(x_0/d)$

$$\mathbf{E}_1 = -\frac{V_0}{d}\mathbf{a}_x + \frac{\rho_s}{\varepsilon_0}\left[1 - \frac{x_0}{d}\right]\mathbf{a}_x;$$

$$\mathbf{E}_2 = -\frac{V_0}{d}\mathbf{a}_x - \frac{\rho_s}{\varepsilon_0}\left[\frac{x_0}{d}\right]\mathbf{a}_x$$

The first term is that for a vacuum field whereas the second is the correction for space charge.

The total current, which must be a constant throughout the circuit, is given by:

$$i = \varepsilon_0 \frac{dE_2}{dt} = \varepsilon_0 \left\{ \frac{-\rho_s}{\varepsilon_0} \cdot \frac{1}{d} \frac{dx_0}{dt} \right\} = \frac{-\rho_s v}{d} \quad \text{where } \mathbf{v} = dx_0/dt$$

In a semiconductor, $\mathbf{v} = \mu\mathbf{E}$ = constant; hence, the current is also a constant while the carriers are in transit. In a vacuum photodiode, the velocity, $v = \frac{e}{m} \frac{V_0 t}{d}$, and thus, the current is changing in a triangular fashion.

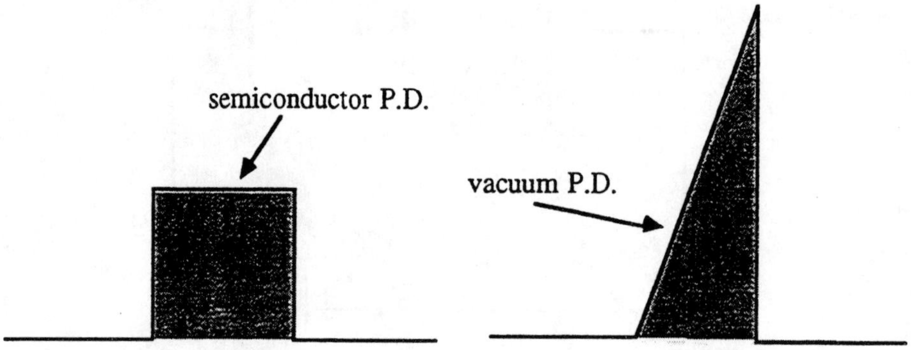

16.4

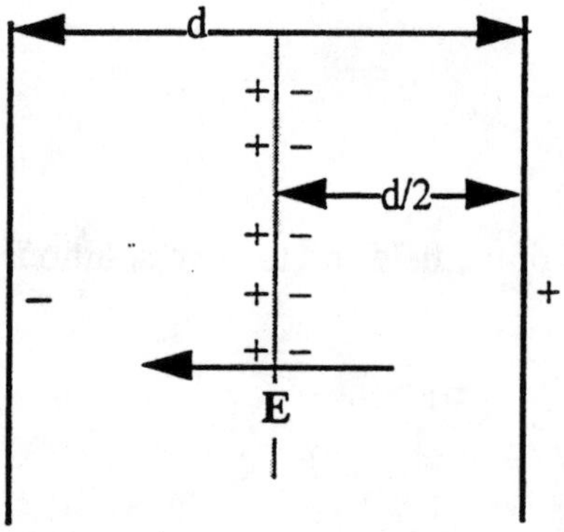

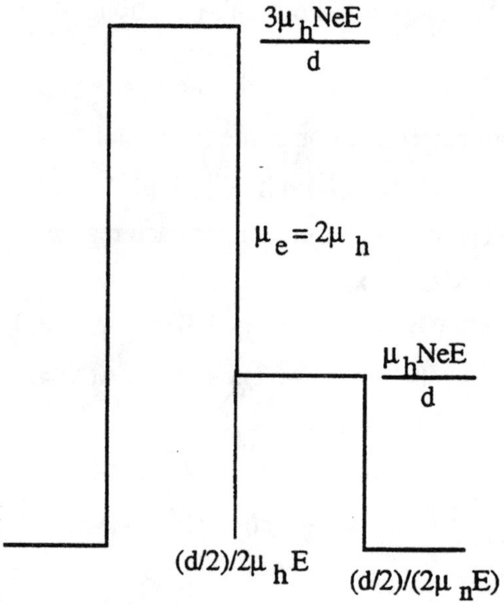

Assuming no space charge modification of m.c. field

$v_e = -\mu_e E$, $v_h = \mu_h E$, and

$$J = \rho \frac{v}{d} = \frac{Ne}{d} \{\mu_e E + \mu_h E\}$$

Total charge collected (per unit of area) Q/A:

$$Q/A = \int J \cdot dt = \frac{3\mu_n NeE}{d} \cdot \frac{d}{9\mu_h E} + \frac{\mu_n NeE}{d} \frac{d}{9\mu_n E} = Ne \text{ (as it should)}$$

16.5

Spectral Distribution of the power is as follows:

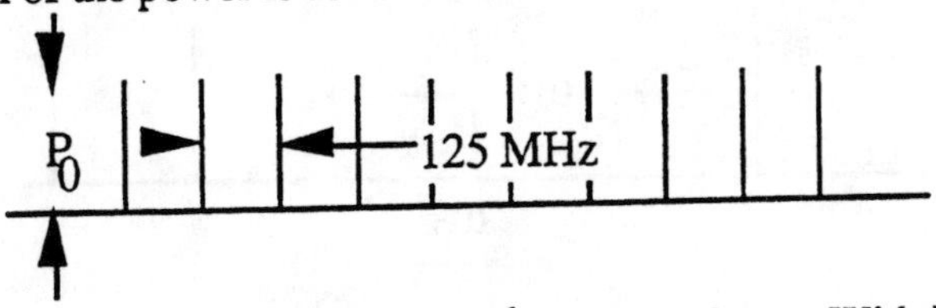

$P_{total} = 27$ mW; $\therefore$ $P_0 = 3$mW; $(c/2d) = 125^{+6}$ $\therefore$ d = 120 cm. With RC = $10^3 \times 10^{-8}$ = 10^{-5} sec = 10 μs, the output will be the average current.

$$i = \eta \frac{P}{h\nu/e} = \frac{0.15 \times 27^{-3}}{1.96} = 2.06 \text{ mAmp} \therefore V_{out} = 2.06^{-3} \times 1^{+3} = 2.06\text{V}$$

- For RC = $50 \times 10 \times 10^{-12} = 500 \times 10^{-12} = 0.5^{-9}$ sec. We have a chance of seeing mode–locked pulses. $\Delta t = (2d/c) \div N = 0.889$ns; $P_p = N\langle P\rangle = 9 \times 27 \times 10^{-3} = 0.24$ watts; $i_p = 18.54$ mA; $V_{peak} = 0.927$ volts

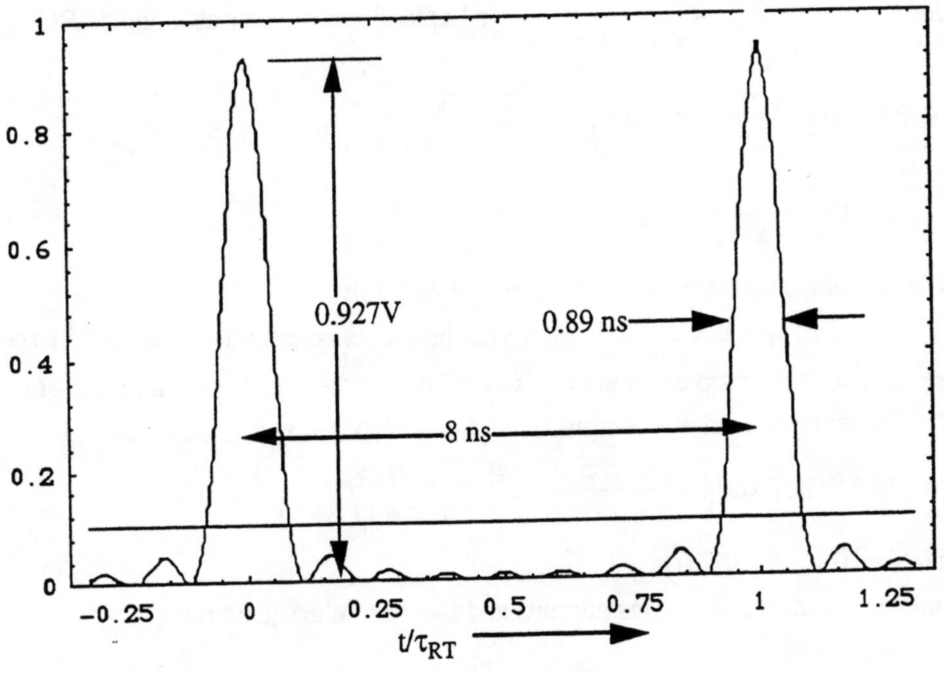

16.6

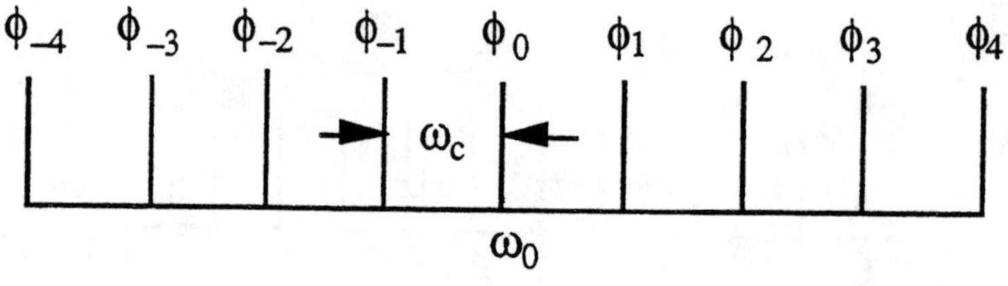

$$i = \frac{\eta_{qe}}{(h\nu/e)}\frac{E\cdot E^*}{\eta_0};\ E = E_0\,\{\cos[(\omega_0-4\omega_c)t+\phi_{-4}]\ \ldots\ \cos[(\omega_0+4\omega_c)t+\phi_4]\};$$

$$E\cdot E^*\Big|_{\omega_c} = \frac{2E_0^2}{2}\{\cos[(\omega_c t+(\phi_{-4}-\phi_{-3})]+\ldots\ \cos[\omega_c t+(\phi_3-\phi_4)]\}.$$

If mode-locked all the phases $\phi = 0$

$\therefore \qquad E\cdot E^* = 9E_0^2;$

Let's approximate the photocurrent by a delta function:

$$i(t) \approx \frac{\eta_{qe}}{(h\nu/e)}\frac{9E_0^2}{\eta_0}\tau_p\,\delta(t)\ \text{(ideal circuitry)};$$

For non-ideal circuitry, $Z(s) = \dfrac{R}{\tau}\dfrac{1}{s+1/\tau}$; s= the Laplace tranform variable and τ= RC

Thus $V_{out}(s) = I(s)\,Z(s)$ where $I(s) = \left[I_0\tau_p = \dfrac{\eta_{qe}}{(h\nu/e)}\dfrac{9E_0^2}{\eta_0}\tau_p\right]$;

$$V(s) = I_0R\,\tau_p\frac{1/\tau}{s+1/\tau};\ \text{or:}\ \ v(t) = I_0R\,\frac{\tau_p}{\tau}e^{-t/\tau}$$

where I_0R is the peak output with ideal circuitry = 0.927 Volts.

Now τ =RC = 1 ns τ_p = 0.89ns; and τ_{RT} = 8 ns; hence the output voltage would charge during the pulse, and then drop exponentially as $e^{-t/\tau}$ during the time between pulses. In terms of the frequency domain, we compute the relative response at ω_c, $2\omega_c$, etc.

At $s = j\omega_c = j7.85^{+8}$Hz; $|T(\omega_c)| = \left|\dfrac{1/\tau}{s+1/\tau}\right| = \left|\dfrac{10^{+9}}{10^{+9}+j7.85^{+8}}\right| = 0.787$

and at s= $j2\omega_c$ = $|T(2\omega_c)|$ = 0.537

For ϕ = random, one must add the rms currents and then take \the square root:

$$\therefore \qquad i = \frac{\eta_{qe}}{(h\nu/e)}\frac{3E_0^2}{2\eta_0}T(\omega)$$

16.7

For parts a → c, assume limited extent uniform plane waves. $\mathbf{e}_s = E_s\cos(\omega_s t - k_s z)$;

$\mathbf{e}_L = E_L\cos(\omega_L t - k_L\cos\theta z - k_L\sin\theta x)$;

$\mathbf{e}_s\cdot\mathbf{e}_L\Big|_{if} = 2E_sE_L\cos\{\Delta\omega t - (k_s - k_L\cos\theta)z + k_L\sin\theta x\}.$

For $z = \text{cnst}$, $(k_s - k_L\cos\theta)z = \phi$, ignore this difference;

$$I_{if} = \frac{\eta e}{h\nu}\cdot\frac{2E_sE_L}{2\eta_0}\cos(\Delta\omega t - k_L\sin\theta x);\ \theta \text{ is small};\ \therefore\ \sin\theta \approx \theta;$$

$$I_{if} = \frac{\eta e}{h\nu}\frac{2E_sE_L}{2\eta_0}w\int_{+w/2}^{-w/2}\cos(\Delta\omega t - k_L\theta x)dx = \left\{\frac{\eta e}{h\nu}\frac{2E_sE_L}{2\eta_0}w^2\cos\Delta\omega t\right\}\left\{\frac{\sin(k\theta w/2)}{(k\theta w/2)}\right\}$$

where the first brace represents the output with perfect alignment and the second is the degradation. The dc current and hence the shot–noise depends on each signal separately.

$$\therefore\quad \frac{S}{N} = \left(\frac{S}{N}\right)_0\left[\frac{\sin(k\theta w/2)}{(k\theta w/2)}\right]^2$$

(b) If the beams are aligned but detector is tilted, the local current density is the product of local fields. The tilt introduces a phase on both waves. Just as long as size of the detector is small compared to IF wavelength, the difference in phase is ≈ 0.

(c) If beams are different in size but aligned: $I_{if} = \frac{\eta e}{h\nu}\cdot\frac{2E_sE_L}{2\eta_0}w_1^2\cos\Delta\omega t$;

where w_1 = the smaller (say, local osc.);

$$I_{if} = \frac{\eta e}{h\nu}\left[\frac{E_s^2w_1^2}{2\eta_0}\right]^{1/2}\left[\frac{E_L^2w_2^2}{2\eta_0}\right]^{1/2}\frac{2w_1}{w_2} \text{ and } I_{DC} = \frac{\eta e}{h\nu}\cdot\frac{E_2^2}{2\eta_0}\cdot w_1^2 \text{ (for } P_L >> P_s)$$

$$\therefore\quad \frac{S}{N} = \frac{I_{if}^2/2}{I_{DC}} = \frac{\eta e}{h\nu}2P_s\left(\frac{w_1}{w_2}\right)^2$$

(d) Curvature also introduces a spatial phase shift which degrades S/N.

16.8

For equal probabilities, one needs to follow only one charge carrier. Start with η_{int} (eh pair) from a photon. These generate $\eta_{int}P$ secondaries which generate $\eta_{int}P^2$ tertiaries, etc.

$$\therefore\ \eta = \eta_{int}\,(1+P+P^2+P^3+\ldots) = \frac{\eta_{int}}{1-P};\ \therefore\ M = \frac{1}{1-P}$$

16.9

The power in each mode = 1 mW = P_0;

$$\therefore\quad \langle P\rangle = 9\text{mW};\ i = \frac{\eta P}{\hbar\nu/e} = 1.143 \text{ mA}$$

$$p(t) = P_0\left\{\frac{\sin(n\omega_c t/2)}{\sin\omega_c t/2}\right\}^2;$$

$\therefore\quad I_{peak} = 10.3$ mA

The current would have the following time dependence:

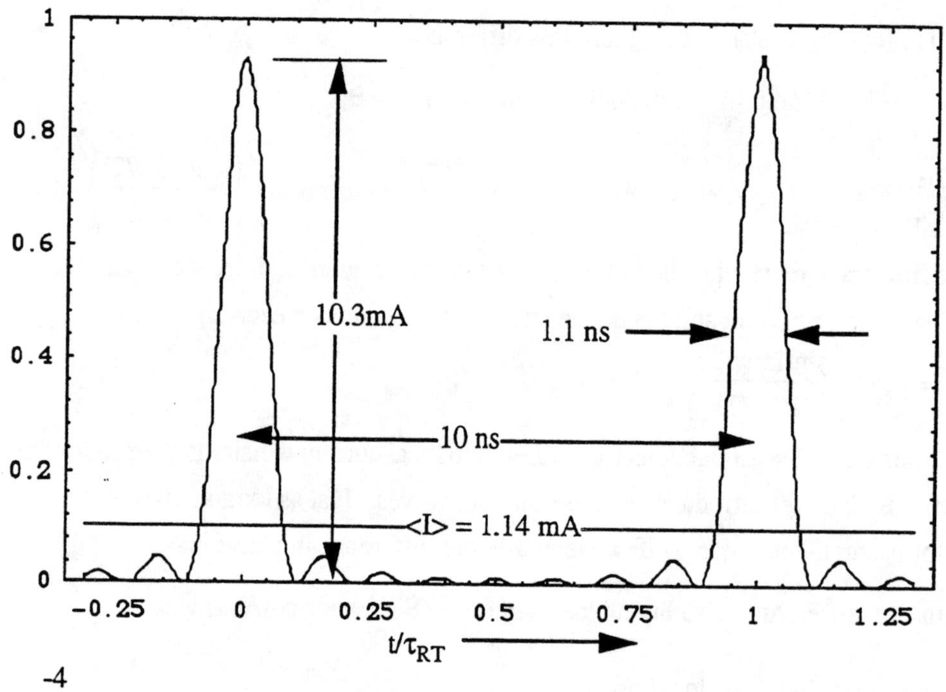

$$E_T = \sum_{-4}^{-4} E_n \cos[(\omega_0 + n\omega_c)t + \phi_n]$$

Form $E_T \cdot E_T^*$, identify the DC and c/2d beats; ignore the other terms.

$$E_T^2 = \sum_{-4}^{+4} \frac{E_n^2}{2} + \sum_{-4}^{+3} 2\left(\frac{E_n^2}{2}\right)^{1/2}\left(\frac{E_{n+1}^2}{2}\right)^{1/2} \cos[\omega_c t + (\phi_{n+1} - \phi_n)]$$

$\therefore\ I(if) = \dfrac{2\eta/e}{h\nu} \sum_{-4}^{+3} P_n^{1/2} P_{n+1}^{1/2} \cos[\omega_c t + (\phi_{n+1} - \phi_n)]$. If mode locked such that all $\phi_n = 0$

$I(if) = \dfrac{16\eta e}{h\nu} P_0 \cos \omega_c t = 2.04 \cos \omega_c t$, where 2.04 mA is the amplitude of the c/2d beat.

For phase distribution as given:

						Real	Imag.
ϕ_{-3}	$-\phi_{-4}$	=	$0.5 \times 2\pi$ =	180°		−1	0
ϕ_{-2}	$-\phi_{-3}$	=	$0.2 \times 2\pi$ =	72°		0.309	0.951
ϕ_{-1}	$-\phi_{-2}$	=	$-0.9 \times 2\pi$ =	36°		0.809	0.588
ϕ_0	$-\phi_{-1}$	=	$0.2 \times 2\pi$ =	72°		0.309	0.951
ϕ_1	$-\phi_0$	=	$0.7 \times 2\pi$ =	−108°		−0.309	-0.951
ϕ_2	$-\phi_1$	=	$-0.4 \times 2\pi$ =	−144°		-0.809	−0.588
ϕ_3	$-\phi_2$	=	$-0.2 \times 2\pi$ =	−72°		0.309	−0.951
ϕ_4	$-\phi_3$	=	$0.3 \times 2\pi$ =	108°		−0.309	0.951

Σ = −0.691 + j0.951

= 1.18 ∠ 126° (rather than 8 ∠ 0°)

$\therefore \quad i = \frac{\eta \cdot P_0}{h\nu/c} \cdot 2\langle 1.18) = 0.299\times10^{-3}\cos(\omega_c t + 126^\circ).$

In the limit of large N and random phases $\quad i\,(\text{Beat note}) = \frac{\eta e P_0}{h\nu} 2\sqrt{N}$

16.10

$\tau_{RT} = 5\text{ ns} = 2d/c$; thus d = 75 cm.

$$\langle P\rangle = P_{peak}\frac{1}{\tau_{RT}}\int_{-\infty}^{\infty} e^{-(t/\tau_p)^2}dt = P_{peak}\sqrt{\pi}\,\frac{\tau_p}{\tau_{RT}}$$

Thus $P_{peak} = \frac{\tau_{RT}}{\tau_p\sqrt{\pi}} = 1.128$ W

$i = \eta\frac{P_{peak}}{h\nu/e} = 93.6$ mA for the peak; $V_{peak} = 9.36$ V

RC< 0.25 ns; hence C< 2.5 pF

Chapter 17

17.1

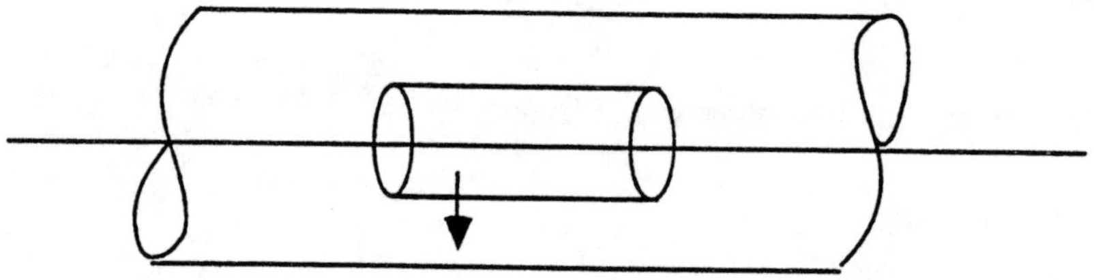

Use Gauss' Law: $\pi r D_r = \rho_v \pi r^2$; $\rho_v = Ne$; $D_r = \frac{\rho_v r}{2}$; $\mathbf{E} = \frac{\rho_v r}{2\varepsilon_0}\mathbf{a}_r$;

$V(0) = -\int_a^0 \frac{\rho_v r}{2\varepsilon_0}\mathbf{a}_r \cdot dr\,\mathbf{a}_r = \frac{\rho_v a^2}{4\varepsilon_0}$; $\rho_v = 10^{19} m^{-3} \times 1.6\times10^{-19} = 1.6$ coulombs/m^3;

$V(0) = 4.52$ MV clearly, this can't happen!

17.2

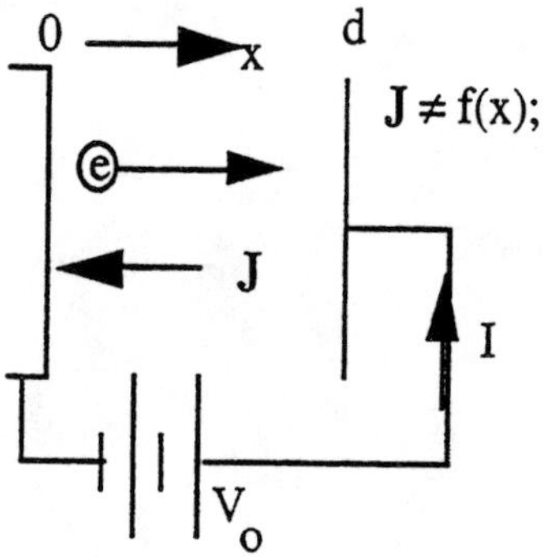

The velocity is given by:
$\mathbf{v}(x) = (2eV(x)/m)^{1/2}\,\mathbf{a}_x$
The current density is given by:
$\mathbf{J} = -J\,\mathbf{a}_x = \rho(x)\,\mathbf{v}(x) \neq f(x)$
where the last notes that the current must be continuous.
$\mathbf{J} = -\rho(x)\,(2eV(x)/m)^{1/2}\mathbf{a}_x$

$$\frac{d^2V}{dx^2} = -\frac{\rho}{\varepsilon_0} = \frac{J}{\varepsilon_0(2eV(x)/m)^{1/2}}.$$

Multiply by $2\frac{dV}{dx}$ and use the indefinite integral:

$$\left[\frac{dV}{dx}\right]^2 = \frac{4J}{\varepsilon_0(2e/m)^{1/2}}V^{1/2}(x) + K_1;$$

At x = 0, the boundary conditions are:

$V(x) = 0$ and $dV/dx = 0$ with the latter indicating that there is no field on the electron at $x = 0$ and thus this boundary condition is called the space charge limited one. If the elctron is emitted with a volcity, then a potential depression can appear in front of the cathode and this boundary condition becomes more complicated.

∴ $K_1 = 0$;

$$\int\frac{dV}{V^{1/4}} = \left[\frac{4J}{\varepsilon_0(2e/m)^{1/2}}\right]^{1/2}\int dx;\ \frac{4}{3}V^{3/4} = \left[\frac{4J}{\varepsilon_0(2e/m)^{1/2}}\right]^{1/2}x + K_2;$$

at $x = 0$, $V(x) = 0$; $K_2 = 0$; at $x = d$, $V(x) = V_0$. Solve for J:

$$J = \frac{4}{9}\varepsilon_0 \left(\frac{2e}{m}\right)^{1/2} \frac{V_0^{3/2}}{d^2} \text{ (Child-Langmuir Law)}$$

The effect on the potential variation is: $V(x) = V_0\left[\frac{x}{d}\right]^{4/3}$ and is shown below:

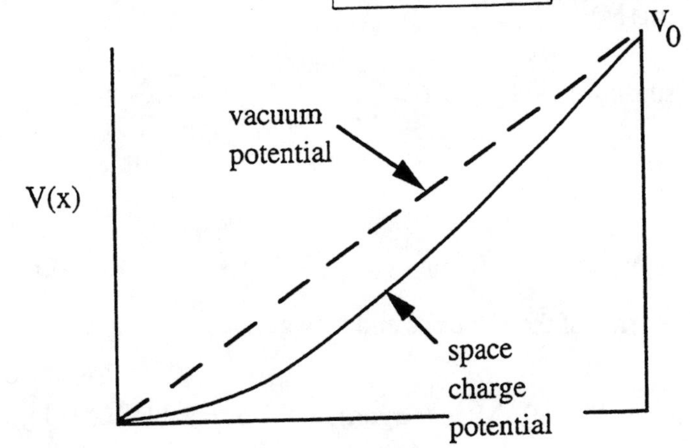

Figure for Problem 17.2

17.3

Consider the collision event shown below:

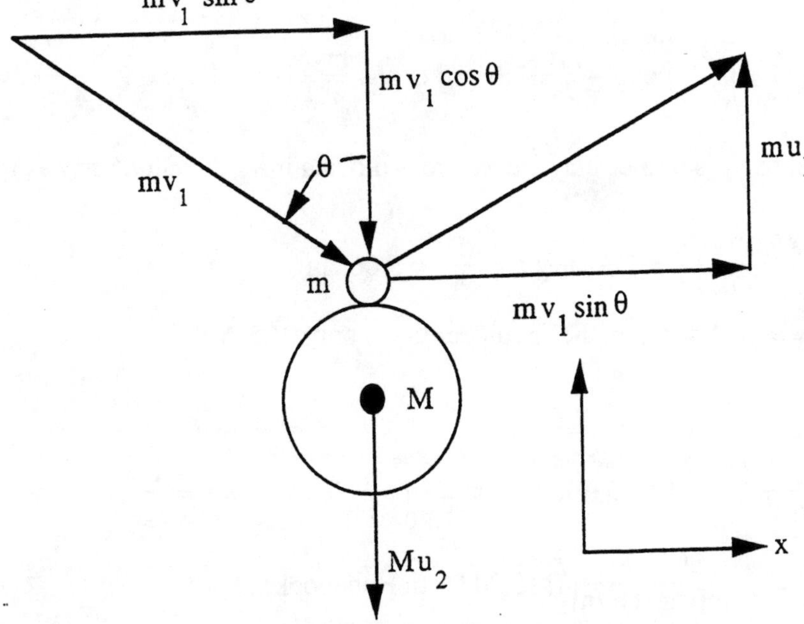

We must conserve momentum (x component is OK by construction):

$$mv_1\cos\theta = mu_1 + Mu_2.$$

and conserve energy:

$$\frac{1}{2}mv_1^2 = \frac{1}{2}m(u_1^2+v_1^2\sin^2\theta)+\frac{1}{2}Mu_2^2.$$

Eliminate the variable u_1: $mv_1^2\cos^2\theta = \frac{m}{M^2}(mv_1\cos\theta - Mu_2)^2 + Mu_2^2$.

Fraction of energy transferred to M:

$$\delta(\theta) = \frac{\frac{1}{2}Mu_2^2}{\frac{1}{2}mv_1^2} = \frac{4mM}{(m+M)^2}\cos^2\theta.$$

Averaging over θ and assuming $m+M \approx M$: $\delta = \frac{2m}{M}$

17.4

$$\frac{d\varepsilon_e}{dt} = \frac{d(\varepsilon_e - \varepsilon_g)}{dt} = -\delta\nu(\varepsilon_e - \varepsilon_g);$$

where ε_e = characteristic energy of the electrons and ε_g = gas;

∴ $\varepsilon_e - \varepsilon_g = (\varepsilon_e - \varepsilon_g)_0\, e^{-t/\tau}$;

$\tau = (1/\delta\nu)$; $\delta = (2m/M)$; $M = 40$AMUu (Argon); $m = 9.11\times10^{-31}$ kg;

$\nu \sim 1.2\times10^{+9}$ sec^{-1} (see Table 11.2); $\delta = 2.72\times10^{-5}$; ∴ $\tau = 30.6$ μsec.

Allow for three time constants to make $\varepsilon_e - \varepsilon_g$ essentially zero. $3\tau = 91.9$ μs ≈ 0.1 ms

17.5

$$J_r = N_e \exp\left[\left(\frac{m}{2\pi kT}\right)^{3/2}\right] \int_{-\infty}^{+\infty} \exp\left[-\frac{mv_x^2}{2kT}\right] dv_x \int_{-\infty}^{+\infty} \exp\left[-\frac{mv_y^2}{2kT}\right] dv_y \int_0^{\infty} v_z \exp\left[-\frac{mv_z^2}{kT}\right] dv_z \text{ i.e.,}$$

where the limit on v_z is 0 since only the electrons moving in +z direction carry a circuit current

$$J_r = \frac{Ne}{4}\left(\frac{8kTe}{\pi m}\right)^{1/2} = 3 \text{ A/cm}^2;\ a = \frac{\pi D^2}{4} = 5.06 \text{ cm}^2;$$

∴ $I_{random} = 16$ A whereas the circuit current is only 0.25 A.

17.6

$$f_0 = \frac{A}{1 + (v/v_0)^N};\ 1 = \int_0^{\infty} 4\pi v^2 f_0(v)dv = 4\pi v_0^3 A \int_0^{\infty} \frac{x^2 dx}{1+x^N} \quad \text{where } x = \frac{v}{v_0}.$$

$$\text{Now} \int_0^{\infty} \frac{x^m dx}{a+x^n} = \frac{\pi a^{m+1-n}}{n\sin[(m+1)\pi/n]} \text{ (\#15.20 Math Handbook)}$$

$a = 1$, $m = 2$, $n = N$; $(m+1) < N$;

∴ $A\cdot 4\pi v_0^3 \cdot \frac{\pi}{N\sin(3\pi/N)} = 1$; $A = \frac{N}{4\pi^2 v_0^3}\sin(3\pi/N)$ with $N > 3$;

$\int 4\pi v^2 f_0(v)dv = \int F(\varepsilon)\, d\varepsilon \qquad F(\varepsilon) \approx \frac{(\varepsilon/\varepsilon_0)^{1/2}}{1 + (\varepsilon/\varepsilon_0)^{N/2}}$

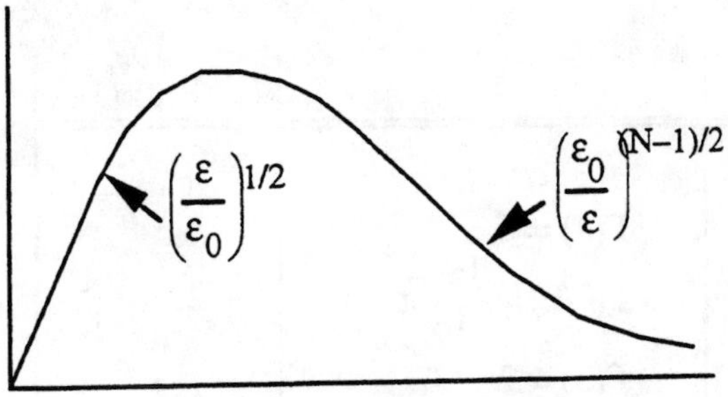

17.7

$$J = -\frac{4\pi Ne^2}{3m} E \int_0^\infty \frac{v^3}{v_c} \frac{\partial f_0}{\partial v} dv = \frac{-4\pi ne^2}{3mv_c} E \int_0^\infty v^3 \frac{\partial f_0}{\partial v} dv.$$ Integrate by parts: $u = v^3$; $dv = \frac{\partial f_0}{\partial v}$ dv; $du = 3v^2dv$; $v = f_0$; $\therefore$ $$J = \frac{ne^2}{mv_c} E \int_0^\infty 4\pi v^2 f_0 dv = \sigma E$$

17.8

$$J_z = New_d;\ \therefore\ w_d = -\frac{4\pi eE}{3m} \int_0^\infty \frac{v^3}{v_0\left(\frac{v}{v_0}\right)^p} \frac{\partial f_0}{\partial v} dv = \frac{eE}{mv_0}\left[-\frac{4\pi}{3} v_0^p \int_0^\infty v^{(3-p)} \frac{\partial f_0}{\partial v} dv\right]$$

for $f_0 = \left(\frac{m}{2\pi kT}\right)^{3/2} \exp\left[-\frac{mv^2}{2kT}\right]$; $\qquad \frac{\partial f_0}{\partial v} = \frac{m}{2\pi kT}^{3/2} \frac{2mv}{2kT} \exp\left[-\frac{mv^2}{2kT}\right]$;

$$\frac{w_d}{(eE/mv_0)} = \frac{8\pi}{3}\left(\frac{m}{2\pi kT}\right)^{3/2} v_0^p \int_0^\infty \frac{m}{2\pi kT} v^{(4-p)} \exp\left[-\frac{mv^2}{2kT}\right] dv$$

$$\frac{w_d}{(eE/mv_0)} = \frac{8}{3\sqrt{\pi}}\left(\frac{mv_0^2}{2kT}\right)^{p/2} \int_0^\infty x^{(4-p)} e^{-x^2} dx;$$

Now $\int_0^\infty x^m e^{-x^2} dx = \frac{\Gamma[(m+1)/2]}{2}$

See #15.77 Math Handbook and identify $m = 4 - p$

$$\frac{w_d}{(eE/mv_0)} = \frac{4}{3\sqrt{\pi}}\left(\frac{mv_0^2}{2kT}\right)^{p/2} \Gamma\left[\frac{5-p}{2}\right];$$ Assume $\frac{mv_0^2}{2kT} = 1$

The ratio is evaluated in the table below

p	Γ	Ratio
–3	$\Gamma(4) = 6$	4.5
–2	$\Gamma(7/2) = \frac{15}{8}\sqrt{\pi}$	2.5
–1	$\Gamma(3) = 2$	1.5
0	$\Gamma(5/2) = 3\sqrt{\pi}/4$	1
1	$\Gamma(2) = 1$	0.75
2	$\Gamma(3/2) = \sqrt{\pi}/2$	0.667
3	$\Gamma(1) = 1$	0.75

17.9

Elastic cross–section always extends down to zero energy whereas inelastic ones have a threshold > 0. Thus all electrons undergo elastic collision whereas only a fraction are capable of an inelastic one.

17.10

$$\mathbf{v} \cdot \nabla_r f(v) + \nu_c(f - f_0) = 0;$$

$$\therefore \quad f = f_0 - \frac{\mathbf{v}}{\nu_c} \cdot \nabla_r f(v) \approx f_0 - \frac{\mathbf{v}}{\nu_c} \cdot \nabla_r f_0;$$

since $v_z = v\cos\theta$ and $f = f_0 + f_1$ with $f_1 << f_0$

$$\Gamma_z = n\langle v_z \rangle = n \int 4\pi v^2\, v \cos\theta\, f\, dv = \int 4\pi v^2 f_0\, v \cos\theta\, dv$$

$$\Gamma_z = -\int 4\pi v^2 \frac{v \cos\theta \supseteq v}{\nu_c} \cdot \nabla_r f_0\, dv = -\nabla_r n \int_0^\infty \frac{4\pi v^4}{3\nu_c} f_0 dv \triangleq \nabla(Dn);$$

$$\therefore \quad \boxed{D = \int_0^\infty \frac{v^2}{3\nu_c} f_0 \cdot 4\pi v^2\, dv}$$

17.11

Use Fig.17.1 and plot the equation: $V_{discharge} = V_{power\ supply} - I(20k\Omega)$;

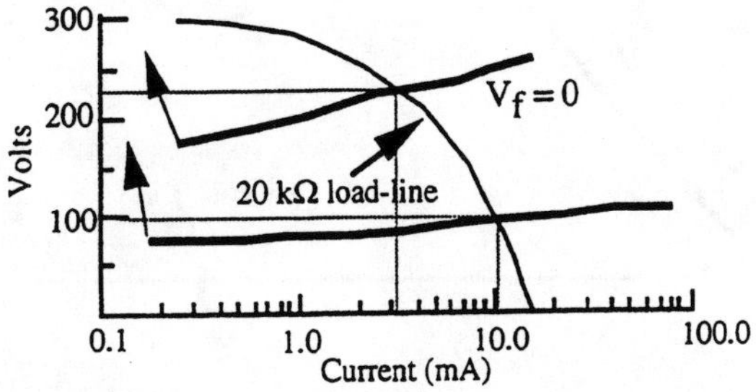

The intersection points are:

Hot Cathode $I \approx 10$ mA $\qquad V_d \approx 100^V$

Cold Cathode $I \approx 3.5$ mA $\qquad V_d = 230^V$

17.12

E/N (V-cm²)	$\frac{D_T}{\mu} = \varepsilon_K$ (Volts)	w_d (in 10^5 cm/s)	$\frac{1}{2}\frac{mw_d^2}{e}$ (Volts)	Drift Charac
1^{-18}	0.025	0.78	1.73^{-6}	6.8^{-5}
3^{-18}	0.0282	2.50	1.78^{-5}	6.3^{-4}
1^{-17}	0.0382	7.63	1.65^{-4}	4.3^{-3}
3^{-17}	0.081	19.4	1.07^{-3}	1.3^{-2}
6^{-17}	0.205	30.9	2.72^{-3}	1.3^{-2}
1^{-16}	0.473	37.2	3.94^{-3}	8.3^{-3}
2^{-16}	0.860	51.0	7.4^{-3}	8.6^{-3}
3^{-16}	1.08	65.0	1.2^{-2}	1.1^{-2}
5^{-16}	1.60	89.0	2.25^{-2}	1.4^{-2}
7^{-16}	2.17	112.0	3.57^{-2}	1.6^{-2}
1^{-15}	2.94	144	5.9^{-2}	2^{-2}
3^{-15}	6.96	308	0.27	3.8^{-2}

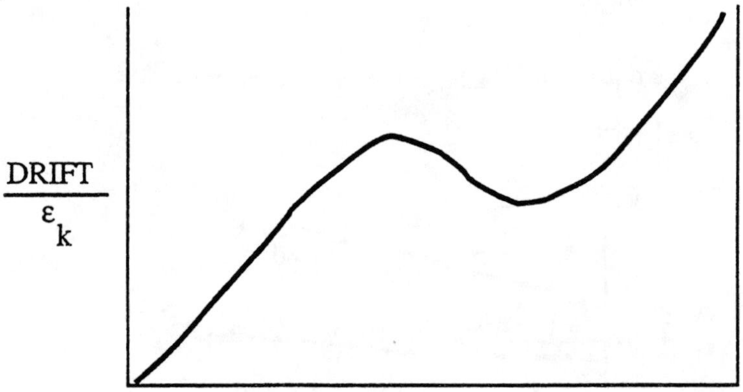

Figure for Problem 17.12

17.13 and 17.14

These problems follow directly from the example given in the text.

17.15

The flux of ions: $\Gamma_i = \frac{N_i e}{4}\left(\frac{8kT_i}{\pi M_i}\right)^{1/2}$.

The flux of electrons $= \frac{N_e e}{4}\left(\frac{8kT_i}{\pi M_i}\right)^{1/2} \exp\left[-\frac{eV_f}{kT}\right]$;

In order for the two fluxes to be equal

$$V_f = \frac{kT_e}{e} \ln\left(\frac{M_i}{m_e}\frac{T_e}{T_i}\right)^{1/2};$$

M(Hg) = 200.6 AMU = 3.26×10^{-25} kg; $V_f = 1.5 \ln\left(\frac{3.26\times10^{-25}}{9.11\times10^{-31}}\frac{1.5}{0.0259}\right)^{1/2} = 12.64$

volts.

The actual ion flux is given by the Bohm relation:

$$\Gamma_i = \frac{N_i e}{4}\left(\frac{8kT_e}{\pi M_i}\right)^{1/2} \text{ (Bohm flux)};$$

$$\therefore \quad V_f = \frac{kT_e}{e} \ln\left(\frac{M}{me}\right)^{1/2} = 9.59 \text{ volts}$$

17.16

(a) $\int_0^{v_0} 4\pi v^2 A\left(1 - \frac{u}{v_0}\right) dv = 1;\ \therefore A = \frac{4}{\pi v_0^3}$;

(b) $<\varepsilon> = \frac{4}{\pi v_0^3}\int_0^{v_0}\left(\frac{1}{2}mv^2\right)\cdot 4\pi v^2\left(1 - \frac{v}{v_0}\right) dv = \frac{8}{15}\left(\frac{1}{2}mv_0^2\right)$.

Because of the size of the elastic cross section,

$$J = \frac{-4\pi}{3}\frac{ne^2}{m} \times E \int_0^{v_0} \frac{v^3}{N\sigma v}\frac{\partial f_0}{\partial v}\,dv = \frac{16}{9}\frac{ne^2}{m\sigma v_0}\cdot\frac{E}{N} = new_d;$$

$$\therefore \qquad w_d = \frac{16}{9}\frac{e}{m(\sigma v_0)}\frac{E}{N};$$

$$\therefore \qquad \mu_e = \frac{16}{9}\frac{e}{m(\sigma v_0)}.$$

Caution: Be careful of units for w_d and μ_e. Note that v_0 is a function of (E/N).

$$D_e = \int_0^{v_0} \frac{v^2}{3v_c} f_0 4\pi v^2 dv \text{ (see Problem 12.10)} = \frac{8}{15}\frac{\left(\frac{1}{2}mv_0^2\right)}{m(N\sigma v_0)};$$

$$\therefore \qquad \boxed{\varepsilon_k = \frac{D_e}{\mu_e} = \frac{3}{10}\left(\frac{1}{2}\frac{mv_0^2}{e}\right)}.$$

If f_0 were a Maxwellian $\varepsilon_k = kT_e$ and $<\varepsilon> = (3/2)kT_e$ or $E_k = 2/3<\varepsilon>$. This is almost obeyed for our distribution function:

$$2/3<\varepsilon> = \frac{16}{45}\left(\frac{1}{2}mv_0^2\right) = 0.35\left(\frac{1}{2}mv_0^2\right) \Leftrightarrow 0.3\left(\frac{1}{2}mv_0^2\right)$$

Now let's use the energy balance equation:

$$0 = \frac{dWe}{dt} = J\cdot E - \delta n_e <v_1(\varepsilon-\varepsilon_1)> - n_e\varepsilon_2 <v_2>u(\varepsilon_0-\varepsilon_2) - n_e\varepsilon_3 <v_3>u(\varepsilon_0-\varepsilon_3)$$

where: $V_1 = \frac{\varepsilon_1}{e}$ = gas energy = 0.0259 eV; σ_1 = elastic = 10^{-16} cm^2;

$V_2 = \frac{\varepsilon_2}{e}$ = vibration = 5eV; σ_2 = vibration = 10^{-17} cm^2;

$V_3 = \frac{\varepsilon_3}{e}$ = ionization = 10 eV; σ_3 = ionization = 10^{-18} cm^2;

$V_0 = \frac{\varepsilon_0}{e} = \frac{1}{2}mv_0^2/e$ which must be greater than V_2, V_3 for those processes to contribute;

$$<v_1(\varepsilon-\varepsilon_1)> = \frac{4}{\pi v_0^3}\int_0^{v_0} N\sigma v\left[\frac{1}{2}mv^2 - \varepsilon_1\right]\left(1 - \frac{v}{v_0}\right)4\pi v^2 dv$$

$$= \frac{8}{21}(N\sigma_1 v_0)\left(\frac{1}{2}mv_0^2\right)\left[1 - \frac{21}{10}\frac{V_1}{V_0}\right].$$

(Note: Unless $V_0 > 2.1V_1$, the gas heats electrons)

$$<v_{2,3}> = \frac{4}{\pi v_0^3}\int_{v_{LL}}^{v_0} (N\sigma_{2,3}v)\left(1 - \frac{v}{v_0}\right)4\pi v^2 dv \text{ where } v_{LL} = \left[\frac{2e\varepsilon_{(2,3)}}{m}\right]^{1/2}$$

$$<v_{2,3}> = \frac{4}{5}(N\sigma_{2,3}v_0)\left[1 - 5\left(\frac{V_{(2,3)}}{V_0}\right) + 4\left(\frac{V_{(2,3)}}{V_0}\right)^{5/2}\right].$$

One must solve for v_0 in terms of E/N but it is easier to solve for E/N in terms of v_0.

The energy equation:

$$0 = \frac{16}{9}\frac{ne^2}{m(N\sigma v_0)}E^2 - \frac{8}{21}\delta\,(N\sigma_1 v_0)\left[1 - \frac{2\,1}{10}\frac{V_1}{V_0}\right]$$
$$-\frac{4}{5}(N\sigma_2 v_0)\,E_2\left[1 - 5\left(\frac{V_2}{V_0}\right)^2 + 4\left(\frac{V_2}{V_0}\right)^{5/2}\right]u(V_2 - V_0)$$
$$-\frac{4}{5}(N\sigma_3 v_0)\times E_3\left[1 - 5\left(\frac{V_3}{V_0}\right)^2 + 4\left(\frac{V_3}{V_0}\right)^{5/2}\right]u(V_3 - V_0)$$

or $\left(\frac{E}{N}\right)^2 = \frac{3}{14}\delta\sigma_1^2 V_0^2\left[1 - \frac{2\,1}{10}\frac{V_1}{V_0}\right]$ ①

$+\ \frac{9}{20}\sigma_1\sigma_2 V_0 V_2\left[1 - 5\left(\frac{V_2}{V_0}\right)^2 + 4\left(\frac{V_2}{V_0}\right)^{5/2}\right]u(V_0 - V_2)$ ②

$+\frac{9}{20}\sigma_1\sigma_3 V_0 V_3 \times\left[1 - 5\left(\frac{V_2}{V_0}\right)^2 + 4\left(\frac{V_2}{V_0}\right)^{5/2}\right]u(V_0 - V_3).$ ③

Recall that $\varepsilon_k = \frac{3}{10}\left(\frac{1}{2}mv_0^2\right) = \frac{3}{10}V_0 w_0 = \frac{16}{9}\frac{e}{m(\sigma v_0)}\frac{E}{N}$ ($\times\ 10^2$ if cm are used).

∴ Pick V_0; solve for ε_k; E/N; v_0 and w_0

The ratios: ①/Σ = R_1 (the fraction into elastic heating); ②/Σ = R_2 (fraction into vibration); ③/Σ = R_3 (fraction into ionization)

The tabular values are given in the table below

V_0	ε_k	E/N	w_d	R_1	R_2	R_3
0.1	0.03	3.1−20	5.21+2	1.0	0	0
0.2	0.06	7.9−20	9.31+2	1.0	0	0
0.5	0.15	2.19−19	1.63+3	1.0	0	0
1.0	0.3	4.5−19	2.37+3	1.0	0	0
2.0	0.6	9.1−19	3.4+3	1.0	0	0
5.0	1.5	2.3−18	5.4+3	1.0	0	0
5.1	1.55	4.05−18	9.46+3	0.34	0.66	0
5.05	1.51	2.86−18	6.7+3	0.66	0.34	0
5.2	1.56	6.9−18	1.6+4	0.12	0.88	0
5.5	1.65	1.58−17	3.5+4	2.6−2	0.97	0
6.0	1.8	2.9−17	6.3+4	8.8−3	0.99	0
8.0	2.4	7.1−17	1.3+5	2.7−3	0.99	0
10.0	3.0	1−16	1.7+5	2.1−3	0.99	0
10.5	3.15	1.08−16	1.76+5	2−3	0.996	2.2−3
11.0	3.3	1.1−16	1.82+5	1.97−3	0.991	7.4−3
15.0	4.5	1.9−16	2.87+5	8.8−2	0.76	0.15

The following is a graph of the previous data.

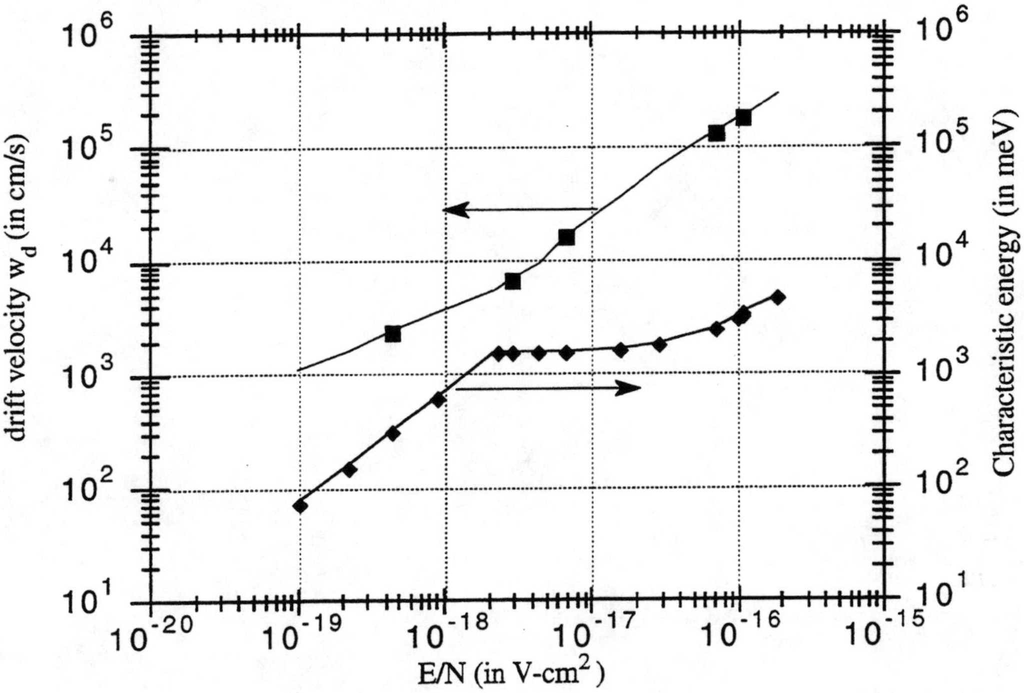

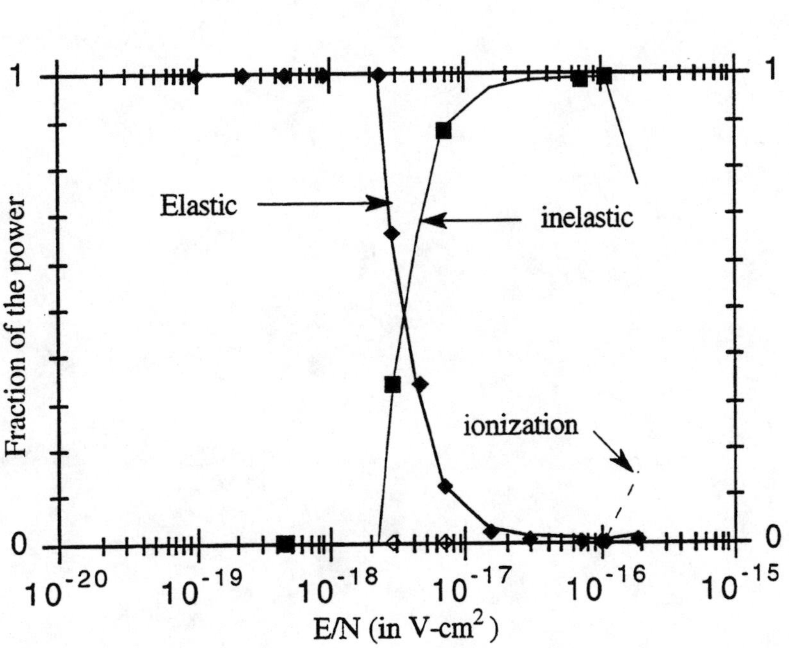